THE CAMBRIDGE COMPANION TO

CIVIL DISOBEDIENCE

The theory and practice of civil disobedience has once again taken on import, given recent events. Considering widespread dissatisfaction with normal political mechanisms, even in well-established liberal democracies, civil disobedience remains hugely important, as a growing number of individuals and groups pursue political action. "Digital disobedients," Black Lives Matter protestors, Extinction Rebellion climate change activists, Hong Kong activists resisting the PRC's authoritarian clampdown... all have practiced civil disobedience. In this *Companion*, an interdisciplinary group of scholars reconsiders civil disobedience from many perspectives. Whether or not civil disobedience works, and what is at stake when protestors describe their acts as civil disobedience, is systematically examined, as are the legacies and impact of Henry Thoreau, Mahatma Gandhi, and Martin Luther King.

WILLIAM E. SCHEUERMAN is James H. Rudy Professor of Political Science at Indiana University.

OTHER VOLUMES IN THE SERIES OF CAMBRIDGE
COMPANIONS

Continued at the back of the book

The Cambridge Companion to
CIVIL DISOBEDIENCE

Edited by
William E. Scheuerman
Indiana University

CAMBRIDGE
UNIVERSITY PRESS

CAMBRIDGE
UNIVERSITY PRESS

University Printing House, Cambridge CB2 8BS, United Kingdom

One Liberty Plaza, 20th Floor, New York, NY 10006, USA

477 Williamstown Road, Port Melbourne, VIC 3207, Australia

314–321, 3rd Floor, Plot 3, Splendor Forum, Jasola District Centre, New Delhi – 110025, India

79 Anson Road, #06–04/06, Singapore 079906

Cambridge University Press is part of the University of Cambridge.

It furthers the University's mission by disseminating knowledge in the pursuit of education, learning, and research at the highest international levels of excellence.

www.cambridge.org
Information on this title: www.cambridge.org/9781108478045
DOI: 10.1017/9781108775748

First published 2021

A catalogue record for this publication is available from the British Library.

ISBN 978-1-108-47804-5 Hardback
ISBN 978-1-108-74546-8 Paperback

Contents

Contributors

Christopher Bennett is Head of the Department of Philosophy at the University of Sheffield. His areas of research include the theory of punishment and its alternatives; forgiveness; moral emotions and expressive action; and political authority.

Kimberley Brownlee is the Canada Research Chair in Ethics and Political & Social Philosophy at the University of British Columbia. She is the author of *Being Sure of Each Other* (Oxford University Press, 2020) and *Conscience and Conviction: The Case for Civil Disobedience* (Oxford University Press, 2012).

Luis Cabrera is Associate Professor of Political Science at Griffith University in Brisbane, Australia. He has published widely in international political theory, with emphasis on global citizenship, individual rights, migration, and international organizations. His most recent monograph is *The Humble Cosmopolitan: Rights, Diversity and Trans-State Democracy* (Oxford University Press, 2020). It draws on the political thought of Indian constitutional architect B.R. Ambedkar to address some longstanding diversity issues around human rights and political institutions beyond the state.

Robin Celikates is Professor of Social Philosophy at the Free University in Berlin and Deputy Director of the Center for Humanities and Social Change. Before moving to the FU in 2019, he taught at the University of Amsterdam and was a Member at the Institute for Advanced Study in Princeton. He is Commissioning Editor of the journal *Critical Times: Interventions in Global Critical Theory* (Duke University Press) and publishes widely on critical theory, democracy, and social movements.

Maeve Cooke is a member of the Royal Irish Academy and is Full Professor in the School of Philosophy, University College Dublin. Her interests are in the area of critical social and political theory, with a focus on law, religion, autonomy, ideology, and power. She is the author of *Language and Reason* (MIT Press, 1994), *Re-Presenting the Good Society* (MIT, 2006), and many articles in major journals.

Candice Delmas is Associate Professor of Philosophy and Political Science at Northeastern University, and the Associate Director of the Politics, Philosophy, and Economics Program. Her work in moral, social, political, and legal philosophy has appeared in many academic venues. She is the author of *A Duty to Resist: When Disobedience Should Be Uncivil* (Oxford University Press, 2018).

Russell L. Hanson is Professor Emeritus of Political Science at Indiana University (Bloomington), where he has taught courses on urban politics, state politics, and the history of American political thought before retiring in 2017. During his long career at Indiana, he served as Executive Associate Dean and also Interim Dean of the College of Arts and Sciences, and later Department Chair. His principal publications are: *The Democratic Imagination: Conversations with Our Past* (Princeton University Press, 1985); *Political Innovation and Conceptual Change* (Cambridge University Press, 1989), coedited with Terence Ball and James Farr; *Governing Partners: State and Local Relations in the United States* (Routledge, 1989); and *Politics in the American States* (Congressional Quarterly Press, 4th ed., 2010), coedited with Virginia Gray.

James D. Ingram teaches political theory at McMaster University. He is the author of *Radical Cosmopolitics: The Ethics and Politics of Democratic Universalism* (Columbia University Press) and coeditor of *Political Uses of Utopia: New Marxist, Anarchist, and Radical Democratic Perspectives* (Columbia University Press).

Alexander Kaufman is Professor of Political Theory at the University of Georgia. His research explores the relation of central values of the democratic political tradition to issues and controversies in contemporary politics including the justification of the welfare state; the nature of egalitarian justice; and the basis of democratic legitimacy. Kaufman's most recent book, *Rawls's Egalitarianism* (Cambridge, 2018) provides a new interpretation and analysis of John Rawls's theory of distributive justice.

David Lefkowitz is Professor of Philosophy and founding Coordinator of the Philosophy, Politics, Economics, and Law (PPEL) program at the University of Richmond. His research interests span three overlapping areas: the morality of obedience and disobedience to law; analytical and normative issues in international law; and the moral conduct of international affairs. Lefkowitz is the author of *Philosophy and International Law: A Critical Introduction* (Cambridge University Press, 2020), as well as a number of essays on civil disobedience published in journals including *Ethics*, *Criminal Law and Philosophy*, and *Res Publica*.

Alexander Livingston is Associate Professor in the Department of Government at Cornell University. His interests include democratic theory, social movements, political violence and nonviolence, and religion and politics. He is the author of *Damn Great Empires! William James and the Politics of Pragmatism* (Oxford University Press, 2016) and editor of James Tully: To Think and Act Differently (Routledge, forthcoming)

Erin R. Pineda is the author of *Seeing Like an Activist: Civil Disobedience and the Civil Rights Movement* (Oxford University Press, 2021). Her work has appeared in *History of the Present*, *Contemporary Political Theory*, and *European Journal of Political Theory*, as well as the *Boston Review*. She is Assistant Professor of Government at Smith College.

Andrew Sabl is Professor of Political Science at the University of Toronto. His research interests lie in democratic and liberal theory, political realism, and the history of political thought (especially David Hume and the Scottish Enlightenment). His most important publications include: *Ruling Passions: Political Offices and Democratic Ethics* (Princeton University Press, 2002); *Hume's Politics: Coordination and Crisis in the History of England* (Princeton University Press, 2012); and *Realism in Political Theory* (Routledge, 2018), coedited with Rahul Sagar. In addition, he has authored numerous articles and book chapters on subjects including realist political theory, toleration, political ethics, democratic theory, civil disobedience, and David Hume's political thought.

William E. Scheuerman is James H. Rudy Professor of Political Science at Indiana University (Bloomington), where he has taught political theory since 2005. His most recent book is *Civil Disobedience* (Polity Press, 2018), which has also appeared in Spanish and Japanese translations. He is also the author of *Between the Norm and the Exception: The Frankfurt School and the Rule of Law* (MIT, 1994), which won two prestigious awards, as well as *Carl Schmitt: The End of Law* (Rowman & Littlefield, 1999; 2nd ed. 2019), *Liberal Democracy and the Social Acceleration of Time* (Johns Hopkins, 2004), *Frankfurt School Perspectives on Globalization, Democracy, and the Law* (Routledge 2008), *Hans J. Morgenthau: Realism and Beyond* (Polity Press, 2009), and *The Realist Case for Global Reform* (Polity Press, 2011). He has edited *The Rule of Law Under Siege* (California, 1996), *From Liberal Democracy to Fascism: Legal and Political Thought in the Weimar Republic* (Humanities Press, 2000) (with Peter Caldwell), and *High-Speed Society: Social Acceleration, Power, and Modernity* (Penn State, 2009) (with Hartmut Rosa).

Kurt Schock is Professor of Sociology, Rutgers University, Newark. He is the author of *Unarmed Insurrections: People Power*

Movements in Nondemocracies (University of Minnesota Press, 2005), which was awarded Best Book of the Year by the Comparative Democratization section of the American Political Science Association.

William Smith is Associate Professor in Government and Public Administration at the Chinese University of Hong Kong. He works in the field of contemporary political theory, with a particular focus on civil disobedience, direct action, policing, deliberative democracy, and international political thought. He is author of *Civil Disobedience and Deliberative Democracy* (Routledge, 2013) and has published in a wide range of international journals.

Theresa Züger is currently leading the AI & Society Lab at the Alexander von Humboldt Institute for Internet and Society in Berlin. Her research is focused on the question of how AI contributes to the public interest. Her dissertation was dedicated to bridging the analytic gap between activist practices of digital disobedience and political theories of civil disobedience. Previously, she oversaw the Third Engagement Report, a report on civic engagement for the German Federal Government that evaluated the role of digital transformation in civic engagement in Germany.

Introduction: Why, Once Again, Civil Disobedience?

William E. Scheuerman

Why another volume devoted to civil disobedience? Libraries are filled with thick tomes devoted to the topic. Henry David Thoreau, Mahatma Gandhi, and Dr. Martin Luther King, Jr., canonical figures in the history of civil disobedience, not only inspired countless familiar and not-so-familiar movements but also ignited extensive political and scholarly debate.[1] From the late 1960s to the early 1980s, civil disobedience became a fashionable subject for discussion among lawyers, philosophers, political scientists, and many others. Prominent intellectuals, including Hannah Arendt, Ronald Dworkin, Jürgen Habermas, John Rawls, and Bertrand Russell, produced significant theoretical statements about it. What possibly remains to be said about something that fascinated so many of the most innovative and influential political thinkers in the last century?

Ongoing political trends underscore the necessity of revisiting the theory and practice of civil disobedience. This volume aims to do so in a suitably systematic fashion.

Most significantly, we are witnessing a proliferation of (sometimes novel) politically motivated illegalities, with grassroots activists frequently viewing their actions as examples of *civil disobedience*. Given widespread dissatisfaction with normal political mechanisms even in well-established liberal democracies, in conjunction with the startling worldwide rise of authoritarian populism, the trend seems likely to continue, as a growing number of individuals and groups pursue controversial, unconventional, and oftentimes illegal political action. Black Lives Matter protestors targeting racialized policing, so-called "digital disobedients" (e.g., Chelsea Manning, Edward Snowden), Extinction Rebellion climate change activists, sexual harassment victims who fought unsuccessfully to derail Brett

1

Kavanaugh's US Supreme Court appointment, Hong Kong activists resisting the People's Republic of China's authoritarian clampdown: all have claimed that some of their activities constitute civil disobedience, even when their endeavors might have surprised Gandhi or King. Snowden, for example, has characterized his now famous US surveillance whistleblowing as civil disobedience. Yet he is widely interpreted as refusing to accept any legal repercussions, a decision that on the surface conflicts with standard views of it.[2]

Even more recently, critics of both Black Lives Matter and Hong Kong democracy activists fault them for allegedly jettisoning the requisite commitments to civility and nonviolence, widely viewed as essential to civil disobedience.[3] In Hong Kong, militants threw rocks and Molotov cocktails, and sometimes used heat-resistant gloves to throw tear gas canisters back at security personnel.[4] The massive and perhaps – for the US – unprecedented summer 2020 protests that followed the police killings of Ahmaud Arbery, George Floyd, and Breonna Taylor remained, for the most part, nonviolent. Yet property destruction and physical attacks on police officers and others, though usually undertaken in the name of self-defense, also occurred.[5]

In part because the term *civil disobedience* is sometimes employed loosely by activists and others, it seems imperative to clarify what it in fact entails. In part also because some activists and political writers are now unabashedly defending *uncivil disobedience*, its rowdy but arguably closely related cousin, clarifying civil disobedience's multifaceted, unavoidably controversial features seems timely as well. Even those movements now universally regarded as canonical practitioners of civil disobedience were once criticized for their (allegedly) uncivil elements.[6] Can we draw meaningful distinctions between the two phenomena?[7] How, more generally, might civil disobedience be usefully demarcated from other types of politically motivated lawbreaking? And why does it matter?

Since Gandhi and King, civil disobedience has appealed to those hoping to bring about constructive – and prospectively far-reaching –

political and social change. Civil disobedience has long represented a singularly influential approach to morally conscientious, civil, non-violent, politically motivated lawbreaking. In many political contexts, it possesses a moral and political stature that alternative terms (e.g., "leaking," "resistance," "rioting") lack, with one result being that prosecutors, judges, and juries will sometimes treat those grouped under its rubric with a measure of leniency. Writing in 1983, Dworkin noted that "we can say something now we could not have said three decades ago: that Americans accept that civil disobedience has a legitimate if informal place in the political culture of their community."[8] Dworkin's observation that civil disobedience had gained a measure of political legitimacy in the USA now surely could be interpreted as applying to many other countries and political settings as well. In this way, as in many others, civil disobedience has become a genuinely global practice. Even when condemned and its practitioners excoriated, it possesses a relatively privileged political and discursive status.

As Dworkin and others in his impressive generational cohort of commentators on civil disobedience correctly grasped, responsible political action benefits from conceptual clarity and theoretical coherence. We require analyses of civil disobedience that can help us distinguish it from related phenomena (e.g., whistleblowing, revolution), even if messy political and social realities unavoidably undermine the quest to formulate clear distinctions. We would do well, at any rate, to reconsider the main competing theoretical accounts of civil disobedience, reexamine their core components, and carefully reappraise how and why they demand special types of lawbreaking. The appearance of novel types of activism and protest politics enjoins us to determine not only what remains valuable in competing accounts, but also what is now perhaps obsolete or untenable about them.

Not surprisingly given recent political trends, we are also seeing a revival of sustained research dedicated to civil disobedience. Many scholars are again exploring the topic, with a number of creative and wide-ranging debates now underway.⁹ As in previous theoretical exchanges, political thinkers are reassessing civil disobedience as a way not only of connecting philosophical and theoretical reflections to real-life politics, but also in order to investigate fundamental questions about law and politics: what obligations are owed by citizens to their governments, especially in more-or-less liberal democratic contexts? What limits to the citizen's obligation to the state can be identified, and where do they lie? How should law be properly conceived, and when – if at all – is punishment for lawbreaking appropriate? To what extent should civil disobedience be viewed, at its core, as a moral, political, or legal type of activity?

As a result of such debates, we can quickly identify a variety of roughly overlapping, yet ultimately rival, visions of civil disobedience. Alongside influential religious and spiritual (e.g., Gandhi, King) and also liberal (e.g., Rawls, Dworkin) theoretical accounts, deliberative democrats, political realists, radical democrats, and also anarchists (both on the left and right) have been energetically weighing in with their own contributions. Some theorists even go so far as to question whether civil disobedience, in its most influential contemporary versions, has much if anything to do with Thoreau, the historical figure usually, albeit somewhat misleadingly, credited with introducing the term into political discourse.¹⁰ As this volume's readers will quickly observe, many of its contributions militate against the still commonplace assertion that there is some single "orthodox" view of civil disobedience. Not coincidentally, much recent debate seems inspired by deep skepticism about an (allegedly) erstwhile hegemonic liberal model of civil disobedience, and especially the influential account provided by Rawls in his classic *Theory of Justice* (1971). The underlying premise of a great deal of contemporary exchange is that only by transcending that liberal model of civil disobedience can we properly accommodate contemporary realities while preserving a sufficiently supple understanding of civil disobedience. Not surprisingly, liberals have responded to critics and creatively reformulated their ideas, claiming that their opponents rely on simplified interpretations of liberalism's contributions.

CIVIL DISOBEDIENCE AS AN ESSENTIALLY CONTESTED CONCEPT

Such disagreements should not surprise us: *civil disobedience* has always represented an "essentially contested concept" along the lines sketched by the Scottish philosopher W.B. Gallie in a now-classic essay.[11] A main premise of this volume is that only by taking its necessarily contestable character seriously will fruitful intellectual and political exchange about it be possible.

According to Gallie, contested concepts possess seven core features. First, a contested concept is one that is necessarily "appraisive" or evaluative. Second, it is internally complex, in the sense that it consists of a variety of different elements, each of which is usually interpreted as making up some part of the concept "as a whole."[12] Third, "there is nothing absurd or contradictory in any one of a number of [possible] rival descriptions" of contested concepts or their component parts.[13] Contestable concepts are relatively open-ended, and claims about them (especially when first introduced, or "prior to experimentation") will likely diverge in far-reaching ways.[14] Fourth, both the concept and its component pieces may undergo "considerable modification in the light of changing circumstances."[15]

We can readily apply these four initial conditions to civil disobedience and longstanding debates about it. First, civil disobedience is an unavoidably appraisive or evaluative concept. In this vein, Candice Delmas has correctly noted that "to call a disobedient civil" is already "to begin the work of ... justification."[16] The idea of a normatively neutral or morally indifferent rendition of civil disobedience seems odd and probably nonsensical. Indeed, the fact that the term is not just evaluative but also always operates within a *political* force field further complicates matters. As Judith Butler has accurately pointed out in a recent discussion of *nonviolence*, it and closely related terms are "subject to instrumental definitions that serve political interests."[17] One immediate consequence is that "we cannot race to the phenomenon itself without passing through the conceptual schemes that dispose the use of the term in various directions," always keeping in mind that such competing ideational schemes necessarily have far-reaching political and strategic implications.[18]

Second, the concept is typically defined with reference to a number of complex component parts, e.g., *civility, conscientiousness, nonviolence,* and a *willingness to accept legal sanctions.* Competing theoretical accounts of civil disobedience usually reference such elements, even as they provide competing and sometimes sharply opposed interpretations. Third, a great deal of theoretical debate can be interpreted as stemming from understandable differences about how best to make sense of and also weigh its various elements. Most writers have viewed nonviolence as a *sine qua non* of civil disobedience, for example, while disagreeing about what precisely it entails. Nonviolence meant something quite different for spiritually minded activists such as Gandhi or King than, for example, a modern liberal such as Rawls or the radical democratic Habermas.[19] Writers on civil disobedience have almost universally interpreted nonviolence as precluding physical and extreme psychological harm to other persons. However, there has been decidedly more controversy about "violent" acts that damage property, for example, or when motivated by physical self-defense.[20] Similarly, those deploying the term civil disobedience often highlight its *public* contours, though disagreeing about precisely when and where they seem most apposite. Should civil disobedients be expected, for example, to reveal their identities, or does it suffice for them to provide some public statement about their actions?

Fourth, "changing circumstances" have regularly shaped debates about civil disobedience. Think, for example, of the substantial attention paid to questions of the following type: can eco-sabotage, for example, or digital whistleblowing be plausibly characterized as civil disobedience?[21] What about politically motivated lawbreaking by transnational movements targeting supranational institutions (e.g., the World Trade Organization (WTO) or International Monetary Fund (IMF)), rather than specific nation-states or specific national laws? As altered political and social conditions generate novel forms of protest and lawbreaking, civil disobedience's changing political and social contexts take on a pivotal role in conversations about it.

Gallie's final conditions are more complex but potentially illuminating as well. The fifth implies that those deploying a contested concept recognize that their usage is not only likely to be challenged, but that it often remains sensible for them to continue defending their reading against those of rivals. Why? Opposing views may fail to highlight one or more key features. Each party to such a dispute, Gallie commented, nonetheless "must have at least some appreciation of the different criteria in the light of which the other parties claim to be applying the concept."[22] Sixth, those using a contested concept are not in fact trying to address basically different issues or simply "talking past one another." Instead, they at least implicitly aspire to capture an exemplary or perhaps idealized version of the *same* concept, even as they disagree about what weight its various components possess, or how they best fit together. In Gallie's own example of athletic competitors seeking to figure out who deserves to be called a "champion" absent any quantitative rankings system, rival teams plausibly view quite different individual and team traits as essential to gaining "championship" status. Despite their disagreements, the idea of championship relies on some account of exemplary or ideal play.[23] Athletes remain engaged in a common quest, and those evaluating them recognize it as such, even as they interpret its demands in variegated and sometimes opposing ways.

These conditions provide additional directives that help identify how ongoing discussions of civil disobedience might progress. While fiercely defending their own positions, those engaged in debates about it typically recognize, of course, the existence of competing interpretations. Even so, it is by no means clear that they sufficiently appreciate how their disagreements can potentially illuminate different faces of an irrepressibly contestable concept. Despite sometimes significant divides, most theorists (and activists) deploy a shared language when discussing civil disobedience, even as they sometimes remain inadequately self-aware about doing so. A great deal of controversy, as noted, has always been preoccupied with alternative ways of interpreting and then weighing its common elements (e.g., *civility*, *conscientiousness*, *nonviolence*, and *legal non-evasiveness*).[24] Even as different writers speak that language in ways that sometimes render it difficult to decipher even for other users, theirs nonetheless typically remains a *shared* conceptual and theoretical endeavor. Its plural and contested conceptual versions notwithstanding, discussions of civil disobedience rest on some familiar underlying aspirations, and even perhaps a latent quest to identify its exemplary or "best possible" types. Liberals and radical democrats who otherwise disagree heatedly about many features of civil disobedience, for example, are not simply "talking past one another" about unrelated practices. Instead, they implicitly hope to place what they picture as related activities in some overlapping – and perhaps: best possible – conceptual light.

Gallie also claimed that, seventh, competition between and among rival usages is potentially productive insofar as it allows for the concept "to be sustained and/or developed in optimum fashion."[25] Competing usages not only bring to light previously neglected elements, but also prepare the way for updated conceptual versions that can plausibly be described as "fuller" or more developed than their predecessors.[26] Gallie denied the existence of any clear-cut general principles or standards that would allow us to negotiate between and among rival versions; many concepts are contested in the first place partly because the requisite general standards are missing or unclear. Nonetheless, something along the lines of conceptual learning remains possible: over time, hitherto neglected elements of a concept can be brought to light, or perhaps understood more richly, opening the door to "more or less intellectually respectable conversions."[27] Those who previously endorsed one view may quite sensibly opt to embrace a new and arguably superior rendition, something Gallie rightly envisioned as resting on identifiably cognitive grounds and not reducible to human psychology or sociology.

Unfortunately, far too many participants in debates about civil disobedience continue to interpret its conceptual contestability as a weakness rather than potential strength. They view discord as a sign of theoretical immaturity, an unfortunate scenario to be overcome when we (finally) get the concept (and single correct theory) of civil disobedience "right." But this aspiration, Gallie presciently warned, rests on an inflated view of philosophy "as a kind of 'engine' of thought, that can be laid on to eliminate conceptual confusions wherever they may arise."[28] As he also provocatively inferred, taking conceptual contestability seriously does not in fact entail normative or cognitive relativism: battles about how best to make sense of a contestable concept can in fact generate some modest conceptual (and normative) gains and perhaps even something such as theoretical progress.[29] Discussing nonviolence and its politically contestable contours, Butler makes a similar observation: "The point is not to accept a general relativism."[30]

PLURAL VOICES, RIVAL FRAMEWORKS

The present volume represents a sustained effort to tap Gallie's fertile insights. Accordingly, Part I interrogates civil disobedience from the perspective of a broad range of competing political and theoretical orientations. The idea of civil disobedience has been articulated in diverse and indeed conflicting ways: its definitional contours, normative presuppositions, and political aspirations are best grasped when placed in the context of rival approaches. Accordingly, political thinking about civil disobedience can be helpfully viewed as consisting of a series of contrasting, yet frequently overlapping, models, each resting on relatively distinct assumptions.

Digging into neglected archival sources, Russell L. Hanson (Chapter 1) offers a revisionist rejoinder to the still commonplace reading of Thoreau as having introduced *civil disobedience* into political discourse. Thoreau, in fact, never used the term. The misleading attribution to him of a general injunction to disobey unjust laws nonviolently only emerged as a result of a series of tendentious political appropriations, undertaken in part by Arthur Fifield, a now forgotten London publisher. As Hanson documents, it was Fifield's substantially reworked version of Thoreau, heavily edited in accordance with Fifield's Tolstoy-inflected version of Christian pacifism, that Gandhi first encountered. Fifield's Thoreau, and not the original, played a role in shaping not only Gandhi's but also then, indirectly, King's influential ideas about civil disobedience, ideas that ultimately had little in common with Thoreau's original intent and meaning. The rest, as they say, is history: Thoreau's defense of (potentially violent) *resistance*, by means of *voluntary individual withdrawal* of support for unjust laws that directly conflict with *moral conscience*, became *civil disobedience*, interpreted as a *universal duty* to participate in *civil, conscientious, nonviolent, politically motivated* lawbreaking.

Erin R. Pineda (Chapter 2) provides a strikingly parallel narrative about King's complex political legacy and its selective, oftentimes misleading appropriation by liberal and radical democratic philosophers and political theorists. By reading King not as a radical intellectual and political militant focused chiefly on destroying the deeply rooted US system of racial domination, but instead as a fellow-traveling normative theorist principally concerned with legitimate lawbreaking and its moral presuppositions, thinkers have occluded his most striking political insights. According to Pineda, King's perspective should be interpreted less as a theory of civil disobedience than as a radical political practice of *disobedient civility*. Disobedient civility, she tells us, conceives of *"disobedience* not to law so much as to the norms of comportment inculcated by relations of domination, and through which we forge the new *civil* bonds necessary for a radically restructured multiracial democracy."

Subsequent chapters turn to consider the most important competing (liberal, deliberative democratic, radical democratic, political realist, and anarchist) approaches to civil disobedience, many of which emerged more-or-less directly as attempts to make sense of the canonical figures of Thoreau, Gandhi, and King. Alexander Kaufman (Chapter 3) carefully surveys Rawls's and Dworkin's influential liberal theories about civil disobedience, both of which highlighted its constructive role in correcting unjust majoritarian political decisions within basically liberal democratic contexts. Firmly resisting what he views as a tendency to misconstrue and then discard the liberal view, Kaufman argues that critics neglect its subtleties. Nonetheless, Kaufman expresses skepticism about Dworkin's attempt, in the context of criticizing cases of anti-nuclear civil disobedience during the early 1980s, to limit its legitimate forms to lawbreaking based on fundamental principles but not matters of public policy, a skepticism shared by other authors in the volume decidedly more hostile to liberalism.[31]

William Smith (Chapter 4) describes how recent deliberative democrats – most prominently: Habermas – have both tried to build on while improving previous liberal approaches. On the deliberative democratic account, by encouraging "public deliberation across a broad range of problems, issues, and agenda," civil disobedience "can be legitimate even in the absence of clear rights-violations" along the lines emphasized by Rawls and Dworkin. Though endorsing this more expansive, democracy-enhancing deliberative rendition of civil disobedience, Smith acknowledges the possible bite of some major criticisms, and particularly the worry that a deliberative framework cannot do justice to aesthetic-expressive and coercive-oppositional modes of political protest. Nonetheless, Smith ultimately insists that his preferred deliberative democratic framework can hold its own against critics.

Of course, for radical democrats (Chapter 5) and political realists (Chapter 6), both Kaufman's attempt to salvage liberalism and Smith's rescue of deliberative democracy constitute little more than rearguard actions destined to fail. Robin Celikates, defending a radical democratic position, targets what he views as the narrow, overly stringent account of civil disobedience advanced by Rawls as well as deliberative democrats such as Habermas, whom he faults for having failed to break decisively with Rawlsian liberalism. For Celikates, radical democratic civil disobedience represents not an episodic correction to liberal democracy's occasional failings, but instead a contestatory and participatory practice of collective self-determination essential to democracy, envisioned as a more-or-less constant, ongoing struggle to challenge the existing order and hegemonic consensus on which it rests. The political agency actualized in practices of civil disobedience can be understood in terms of a popular or democratic *constituent power*, never reducible to or identifiable with the institutions of the liberal (or perhaps any) state or system of law.

From a political realist perspective, Andrew Sabl similarly pushes back against (typically neo-Kantian) liberal and deliberative democratic views, censuring them for favoring excessively rationalistic modes of moral analysis over hard-headed political-theoretical analysis. A properly realist version of civil disobedience stresses the permanence of political conflict, centrality of power, irrelevance of rational debate to political life, and the fact that political action is rarely if ever ruled by abstract moral principles. On the realist view, mainstream normative approaches to civil disobedience have not only been answering the wrong questions about civil disobedience, but also too often have posed the wrong questions from the outset. Laying the groundwork for an identifiably realist theory, Sabl offers a complex reading of the nexus between political order and justice. Against neo-Kantian liberals and others who prioritize justice over political order, and also against crude realists who subordinate justice to order, he argues for interpreting political order as "imbricated with justice and equality rather than as a radical competitor." For Sabl, civil disobedience represents "an *inherently* political enterprise: one which seeks to effect change less by raising philosophical questions than by raising recalcitrant opponents' costs." Civil disobedience can potentially take on a crucial role in making sure that the political order instantiates the requisite dose of justice and equality.

In Part I's concluding chapter, James D. Ingram (Chapter 7) revisits Thoreau and Gandhi in order to reconstruct two main overarching anarchist approaches. Those – including many contemporary philosophical anarchists – inspired by Thoreau pursue a "negative and individualist" account of political disobedience, whereas others operating in Gandhi's shadows sketch a rival social, community-centered model. Ingram corroborates the suspicion, voiced also by Hanson and Pineda, that civil disobedience's canonical political figures have been misappropriated by mainstream (e.g., liberal democratic) accounts of civil disobedience. On Ingram's view, the best way to do justice to the complex legacies of both Thoreau and Gandhi is by means of an appreciative engagement with anarchism and its radical vision of disobedience and politics "beyond law and the state." In both its individualistic and communitarian modes, anarchists powerfully provincialize dominant ideas about civil disobedience by raising radical questions, neglected by other approaches, about state and law.

DIFFERENT ELEMENTS, COMPETING INTERPRETATIONS

Part II focuses on recurring theoretical issues raised by competing discussions of civil disobedience and its component parts. Though conceiving of it in a variety of ways, civil disobedience's practitioners and theorists have usually spoken, as noted, a more-or-less common conceptual language: they regularly describe civil disobedience as politically oriented lawbreaking that is *civil, conscientious, nonviolent,* and rests on some notion of *fidelity to law,* typically interpreted as requiring the *acceptance of legal penalties.* As forcefully suggested by contributors to Part II, there not only are legitimate disagreements about that shared framework's components; there may also be pressing reasons for rethinking conventional interpretations of them. Some contributors go so far as to propose discarding certain familiar elements of civil disobedience's joint language, or perhaps reinventing that language altogether.

Candice Delmas (Chapter 8) first traces the etymology of the term "civility," before proceeding to argue that philosophers have generally followed two different paths in discussions of principled lawbreaking. The first path, pursued by Rawls and many liberals, relies on a stringent concept of civil disobedience and correspondingly strict view of civility. Not surprisingly, this path leads to the conclusion that *uncivil* disobedience is unjustifiable in nearly just (liberal democratic) political contexts. The second path offers a more inclusive interpretation of civil disobedience and also a more relaxed idea of civility, but only at the risk of broadening both to include phenomena usually viewed as different and arguably opposed (e.g., the decorum and strict nonviolence practiced by US Civil Rights protestors, in contrast to Black Lives Matter's more militant protests). Insisting that it seems more "useful to conceptualize and justify the resort to incivility in disobedience" even in basically liberal political settings, Delmas favors a third path. Without discounting civil disobedience and its widely recognized virtues, Delmas worries that existing theoretical defenses fail to provide sufficient normative and political space for controversial modes of *uncivil* disobedience that can, in fact, be principally justified. Theories of legitimate lawbreaking in sum need to make room for covert, legally evasive, morally offensive, and potentially destructive actions. Only by doing so can a satisfactory normative justification be provided for recent Hong Kong protests, militant lawbreaking by Black Lives Matter, and other similarly uncivil acts.

Maeve Cooke (Chapter 9) also worries about a certain narrowness that plagues discussions of conscientiousness among civil disobedience's most influential theoreticians. Liberals and even most radical democrats neglect its deeply *ethical* contours, with ethical referring for Cooke to "the idea and conduct of a good human life in association with other entities, human and non-human." Existing models of civil disobedience reduce its decisive ethical connotations either to "an obligation to obey certain moral and/or legal principles or ... an appeal to individual conscience," with Rawls, Arendt, and their disciples usually relying on pallid, unsatisfactory ideas about moral conscience. In sharp contrast to such accounts, civil disobedience is better interpreted as resting on "a concern for the realization of a good life for humans in their associations with others – a kind of good life that may be obstructed by the established socio-political structures together with the prevailing, deeply rooted, individual and collective ethical self-understandings." Only this richer view of civil disobedience as a distinctly *ethical practice*, Cooke insists, can help make sense of King's view of civil disobedience as a path to "ethical self-transformation, most evidently on the side of the subjugated but also on the side of the societally dominant groups."

Usually seen as essential to civil disobedience, the idea of nonviolence has never been uncontroversial. Hoping to transcend the usual binary divide between (morally grounded) nonviolence vs. (politically oriented) violence, Alexander Livingston (Chapter 10) taps the "coercive turn" among recent political theorists to constructively reorient contemporary debates. Rejecting traditional ideas about nonviolence that Livingston views as both morally overloaded and conceptually overextended, and in agreement with some insights from political realism, he insists on the irrepressibility of both coercion and power. By doing so, we can then usefully reinterpret nonviolence "not [as] a spiritual force cleansed of coercion but a different way of wielding coercion to bind communication with confrontation." Only then, Livingston argues, can we get a proper handle on civil disobedience's messy, politically disruptive contours, many of which conflict with more conventional ideas about nonviolence. Nonviolence, he suggests, represents a distinctive way of mobilizing power and coercion. For inspiration, Livingston suggests that we learn from feminist notions of "nonviolent agonism," according to which "coercively exerting *power over* an adversary is bound to a transformative project of creating the conditions for sharing *power with* them as well."

At least since King's eloquent claim that civil disobedience rests on the "highest respect for law," both theorists and practitioners have commonly argued that respect for – or *fidelity to* – law is best evinced by civil disobedients' acceptance of legal penalties for their lawbreaking.[32] Others, including some who marched alongside King in the US Civil Rights Movement, have resisted this view.[33] Tackling the heated matter of whether disobedients can or should face punishment, Christopher Bennett and Kimberley Brownlee (Chapter 11) outline two main philosophical approaches for justifying civil disobedience, a *Limits of State Authority* and rival *Communicative Value of Civil Disobedience* strategy. Each contains far-reaching implications for the question of legal punishment. Though ultimately more persuaded by the *Communicative Values* than *Limits of State Authority* justification, the authors argue that neither strategy provides sufficient principled grounds for insisting on punishing civil disobedients, at least when their actions can be plausibly interpreted as having met certain basic preconditions. One consequence of this view is that state officials will need to distinguish lawbreakers whom it can legitimately punish from civil disobedients whom it should *not* punish. Does not such a call for differential legal treatment, however, threaten the ideal of the rule of law and its demand for consistency, predictability, and regularity within the law? Bennett and Brownlee think that rule of law values can still be properly maintained by a legal system that provides "layers of oversight of decision-making and the possibility of appeal by affected parties."

CHANGING CIRCUMSTANCES, POLITICAL CONSEQUENCES

Part III addresses critical questions about whether civil disobedience, in light of what Gallie dubbed "changing circumstances," can or should continue to connote what it meant even in the relatively recent past. Many inherited views about civil disobedience, for example, rest on implicitly national-statist, yet increasingly anachronistic, institutional and political premises. When Rawls, for example, demanded of civil disobedients that they act openly and address a general public, for example, the "public" he had in mind was the *national* public of (existing) liberal constitutional democracies. Protestors sought redress from errant majorities that had come to dominate policy making over a state apparatus described by Rawls as exercising "final and coercive authority over a certain [national] territory."[34] Fidelity to the law meant fidelity to the legal order of the existing nearly just (nation-state) constitutional democracies in which lawbreaking transpired.

How then might the messy, multi-pronged social processes typically associated with globalization challenge and perhaps undermine conventional views of civil disobedience?[35] What consequences should follow for our thinking about civil disobedience? Does it make any sense to conceive of civil disobedience as a cross-border phenomenon?[36] If so, whom should it target and try to address, if not national publics or domestic political institutions?

Against skeptics who question its merits when extended beyond the nation-state, Luis Cabrera (Chapter 12) argues that, with some minor adjustments, civil disobedience provides an appropriate political and theoretical framework for comprehending permissible legal violations by non-state actors, including migrants and asylum seekers, as well as non-governmental organizations (NGOs) and other supranational organizational players. Cabrera distinguishes *trans-state* from *global* civil disobedience, with the former "involving non-nationals of a state deliberately violating its laws to challenge a law or policy that may be misaligned with the commitments to human moral equality and individual rights," as already embedded within human rights law. The latter, in contrast, refers to violations challenging, either implicitly or explicitly, "structural principles of sovereignty" that are badly "misaligned with ... foundational moral principles" of our developing cosmopolitan order. New types of suprastate disobedience no longer necessarily represent critical responses to politically *recalcitrant* power holders, where lawbreakers are on an equal legal footing yet power holders have ignored their views or interests. Instead, they are best understood as responding to politically *arrogant* power holders who reject other political actors' "formally equal standing to give input or lodge formal challenges." Their lawbreaking, in sum, represents a form of political resistance that taps the normative potential of an emerging cosmopolitan political order, as already partly embedded within international law and binding human rights agreements. It does so in order to push back against those who would prefer to deny political standing to nascent global citizens.

David Lefkowitz (Chapter 13) addresses the question of whether it makes sense to view *states* as practicing civil disobedience. While standard accounts of civil disobedience envision grassroots activists and social movements as its primary agents, with their illegal acts directed *at* governments whose policies they aim to change, we can witness surprising calls for *state civil disobedience*. In Europe, for example, leftist critics of EU austerity measures have openly advocated civil disobedience by "cities, regions, and nation-states."[37] Others have tapped ideas about civil disobedience to countenance lawbreaking by developing countries (e.g., Argentina, Bolivia, Brazil, India, and South Africa) that have violated intellectual property laws, international investment rules, IMF rules on national debt, and other global economic legal regulations they consider rigged in favor of rich and powerful states. When doing so, countries have often acted publicly, respected norms of nonviolence, and justified their acts as part of a broader demand for global reform. So why not characterize them as state civil disobedience?[38] Although acknowledging some possible dangers, Lefkowitz answers the question in the affirmative, even as he concedes that there may not yet be any real-life cases that can be plausibly classified as proper exemplars of state civil disobedience, at least when interpreted in some minimally acceptable normative fashion. State civil disobedience nonetheless remains, in principle, a potentially legitimate update to its more conventional, civil society-centered variants.

What about challenges posed to existing ideas of civil disobedience by digitalization, arguably a social trend no less far-reaching and transformational than globalization? It remains unclear, for example, whether concepts designed with physical or "on-the-street" law-breaking in mind can be seamlessly assigned to new types of digital lawbreaking or "hacktivism." What is gained – and what is lost – by using the concept of civil disobedience to analyze them? Does it make sense to view politically motivated, digitally based whistleblowing as the "new civil disobedience," as some commentators have argued?[39]

Like other contributors to Part III, Theresa Züger (Chapter 14) remains convinced that the idea of civil disobedience, when properly interpreted in an inclusive fashion that pays attention to real-life political practices, still provides a strong basis for interpreting novel digital lawbreaking. Relying on a radical democratic interpretation of civil disobedience, she provides, some qualifications notwithstanding, a relatively optimistic assessment of the ways in which hacktivists and other digital activists have creatively deployed new informational technologies to oppose anti-democratic social and political developments. Some of their actions, she argues, can be placed under the rubric of legitimate civil disobedience. In a similar spirit, William E. Scheuerman (Chapter 15) opposes the tendency among recent writers to interpret whistleblowing, digital or otherwise, as categorically distinct from civil disobedience. To be sure, there are good reasons for distinguishing one from the other. Yet, civil disobedience and politically based whistleblowing remain parallel and occasionally overlapping practices; for both conceptual and political reasons, we should not exaggerate differences between them. Whistleblowers continue to describe their acts as types of civil disobedience not only because of political and legal advantages that accrue to them by doing so, but also because they intuit, more clearly perhaps than contemporary theorists, how they indeed are following in the footsteps of Thoreau, Gandhi, King, and others.

Unfortunately, most literature on civil disobedience has focused on its history, specific political tactics, and normative justifications, with too little attention given to empirical questions about its effectiveness.[40] When does civil disobedience "work"? Under what conditions, if any, is it likely to prove ineffective or even counterproductive? Conceding the need for more systematic empirical research, Kurt Schock (Chapter 16) lays out a framework for how social scientists and others might begin systematically to explore the impact of civil disobedience on individuals, politics, and culture. Though the empirical evidence is messy, Schock is unconvinced by critics who view civil disobedience as a recipe for lawlessness and anarchy. Preliminary evidence suggests, to the contrary, that "rather than undermining or subverting democracy or the democratic process, civil disobedience preserves and extends rights, restores a balance of power in government, and serves as a corrective to the manipulation of the democratic process."

CONCLUDING REMARKS

In Gallie's shadows, this volume presupposes a skeptical assessment of any attempt to view its scholarly reflections about civil disobedience as "as a kind of 'engine' ... that can be laid on to eliminate conceptual confusions wherever they may arise."[41] As attested by the volume's rich, multisided, oftentimes conflicting intellectual contributions, civil disobedience is destined to remain a matter of intense political and theoretical controversy. Those who practice and interpret it from a religious-spiritual standpoint, for example, will inevitably find themselves disagreeing with secular-minded liberals and radical democrats; such differences are unlikely to vanish in our pluralistic moral universe. By taking such contestability seriously, we need not succumb, however, to intellectual relativism or crude historicism. A reexamination of civil disobedience in its competing versions provides a glimpse of how progress *has been* made – and perhaps *still can be made*, if those arguing about civil disobedience see their efforts as constructive contributions to a still-incomplete intellectual and political story.

To be sure, the present volume's contributors typically posit that their own approaches, not surprisingly, are more "complete" and satisfactory than their rivals', even as they disagree about the sources and precise contours of theoretical progress. Because civil disobedience remains both an essentially contested concept and controversial political practice, any claims about its developmental path, either as a matter of theory or practice, are destined to remain objects of dispute. Nonetheless, contributors to this volume all endorse the cautious conviction that those willing to take such disagreement seriously are not only most likely to benefit intellectually, but also that their efforts should yield, if only modestly and perhaps indirectly, positive political dividends.

NOTES

1. For an illuminating, albeit US-centered, history, see Lewis Perry, *Civil Disobedience: An American Tradition* (New Haven, CT: Yale University Press, 2013). Hugo Adam Bedau (1926–2012) played a decisive role in bringing the topic into philosophical debates, not only by means of his own contributions but also his widely used "reader" that initiated generations of college students (Bedau, ed. *Civil Disobedience: Theory and Practice* [Indianapolis, IN: Bobbs-Merrill, 1969, 1st ed.]). Many prominent intellectual figures participated in Anglophone debates during the 1960s and 1970s, such as Christian Bay, Carl Cohen, Marshall Cohen, Kent Greenawalt, Sidney Hook, Jeffrie Murphy, Joseph Raz, Mulford Q. Sibley, Peter Singer, Michael Walzer, Richard Wasserstrom, and Howard Zinn. Of course, there have been impressive recent debates about civil disobedience, too complex to recount here, in non-Anglophone settings as well.
2. Melissa Chan, "Edward Snowden Invokes Martin Luther King to Defend Whistleblowing," *Time*, May 12, 2016, https://time.com/4327930/edward-snowden-martin-luther-king-whistleblowing/. On Snowden's whistleblowing, see Chapters 14 and 15.
3. On Black Lives Matter, the sympathetic critique from Randall Kennedy, "Lifting as We Climb: A Progressive Defense of Respectability Politics," *Harper's Magazine* (October 24, 2015): 26–34.

4. On Hong Kong and the apparent shift from civil to uncivil disobedience, Anthony Dapiron, "The End of Hong Kong as We Know It," *The Atlantic*, September 10, 2019, www.theatlantic.com/international/archive/2019/09/hong-kongs-protest-movement-getting-darker/597649/; also, Joayang Fang, "The Act of Protest: Struggling Against Beijing, Hong Kong Tries to Define Itself," *New Yorker* (December 16, 2019): 38–49. In defense of the Hong Kong movement's deployment of uncivil tactics: Candice Delmas, "Uncivil Disobedience in Hong Kong," *Boston Review*, January 13, 2020, http://bostonreview.net/global-justice/candice-delmas-uncivil-disobedience-hong-kong.

5. Some of the most controversial protests happened in Portland (Oregon), but the torching of a police station and destruction of many small businesses also occurred in Minneapolis and Saint Paul (Minnesota) in the immediate aftermath of Floyd's death. For an early attempt to make sense of the violence, see William E. Scheuerman, "Their Violence and Ours," *Public Seminar*, July 7, 2020, https://publicseminar.org/essays/their-violence-and-ours/.

6. On the ex post facto idealization of the US Civil Rights Movement, see Jeanne Theoharis, *A More Beautiful and Terrible History: The Uses and Misuses of Civil Rights History* (Boston, MA: Beacon Press, 2018).

7. See, in particular, Candice Delmas, Chapter 8; Jennet Kirkpatrick, *Uncivil Disobedience: Studies in Violence and Democratic Politics* (Princeton, NJ: Princeton University Press, 2008). Recent research on political riots is relevant here as well: Ferdinand Sutterlüty, "The Hidden Morale of the 2005 French and 2011 English Riots," *Thesis Eleven* 121, no. 1 (2014): 38–56; Avia Pasternak, "Political Rioting: A Moral Assessment," *Philosophy and Public Affairs*, 46, no. 4 (2018): 384–418. For a critical survey of the emerging defense of uncivil disobedience, see William E. Scheuerman, "Why Not Uncivil Disobedience?" *Critical Review of International Social and Political Philosophy* (forthcoming). Of course, the present volume cannot offer a systematic analysis of all forms of politically motivated lawbreaking. Yet by carefully examining civil disobedience (arguably its most important type), it can make an essential scholarly contribution toward the broader study of political protest, in general, and political lawbreaking, in particular.

8. Ronald Dworkin, "Civil Disobedience and Nuclear Protest" [1983], in Dworkin, *A Matter of Principle* (Cambridge, MA: Harvard University Press, 1985), 105.

9. Among the most important recent monographs: Kimberley Brownlee, *Conscience and Conviction: The Case for Civil Disobedience* (New York: Oxford University Press, 2012); David Lyons, *Confronting Injustice: Moral History and Political Theory* (New York: Oxford University Press, 2013); Tony Milligan, *Civil Disobedience: Protest, Justification, and the Law* (London: Bloomsbury, 2013); Piero Moraro, *Civil Disobedience: A Philosophical Overview* (Lanham, MD: Rowman & Littlefield, 2019); William Smith, *Civil Disobedience and Deliberative Democracy* (New York: Routledge, 2012).

10. See especially Chapter 1.

11. W.B. Gallie, "Essentially Contested Concepts," *Proceedings of the Aristotelian Society*, 56, no. 1 (1956): 167–98

12. Gallie, "Essentially Contested," 172.

13. Gallie, "Essentially Contested," 172.

14. Gallie, "Essentially Contested," 172.

15. Gallie, "Essentially Contested," 172.

16. Candice Delmas, *A Duty to Resist: When Disobedience Should Be Uncivil* (New York: Oxford University Press, 2018), 22.

17. Judith Butler, *The Force of Non-Violence* (New York: Verso, 2020), 7.

18. Butler, *The Force of Non-Violence*, 6. More generally on the political dynamics of conceptual change, see James Farr, "Understanding Conceptual Change Politically," in *Political Innovation and Conceptual Change*, eds. Terence Ball, James Farr, and Russell L. Hanson (Cambridge: Cambridge University Press, 1989), 24–49.

19. William E. Scheuerman, *Civil Disobedience* (Cambridge: Polity Press, 2018), 43–8, 77. See also Chapter 10 in this volume.

20. Unlike Gandhi, King, for example, sometimes condoned the former and on occasion advocated the latter. See King, "Nonviolence and Social Change" [1968], in *The Radical King*, ed. Cornel West (Boston, MA: Beacon Press, 2016), 147–54. On King's nonviolence, Karuna Mantena, "Showdown for Nonviolence: The Theory and Practice of Nonviolent Politics," in *To Shape a New World: Essays on the Political Philosophy of Martin Luther King, Jr.*, ed. Tommie Shelby and Brandon M. Terry (Cambridge, MA: Harvard University Press, 2018), 78–104. More recently, N.P. Adams, "Uncivil Disobedience: Political Commitment and Violence," *Res Publica*, 24 (2018): 475–91.

21. See, for example, Jennifer Welchman, "Is Ecosabotage Civil Disobedience?" *Philosophy & Geography*, 4, no. 1 (2001): 97–107.
22. Gallie, "Essentially Contested," 172.
23. Gallie, "Essentially Contested," 176–77.
24. Scheuerman, *Civil Disobedience*, 5–8.
25. Gallie, "Essentially Contested," 180.
26. Gallie, "Essentially Contested," 191.
27. Gallie, "Essentially Contested," 190.
28. Gallie, "Essentially Contested," 168.
29. Unfortunately, this is missed by those who incorrectly interpret Gallie as embracing a "subjectivist outlook" and "ethical relativism" (e.g., Vittorio Bufacchi, *Violence and Social Change* [New York: Palgrave, 2007], 29).
30. Butler, *The Force of Non-Violence*, 139.
31. See, for example, Robin Celikates's comments in Chapter 5.
32. Martin Luther King, "Letter from Birmingham City Jail," in *Civil Disobedience in Focus*, 74.
33. Howard Zinn, *Disobedience and Democracy: Nine Fallacies on Law and Order* (Cambridge, MA: South End Press, 2002 [1968]), 29.
34. John Rawls, *Theory of Justice* (Cambridge, MA: Harvard University Press, 1971), 222. For a discussion, see Scheuerman, *Civil Disobedience*, 101–21.
35. For a useful discussion, Manfred Steger, *Globalization: A Very Short Introduction* (New York: Oxford University Press, 2019, 2nd ed.).
36. For important discussions, see the special issue of *Journal of International Political Theory* (15, no. 1 [2019]), on "Resistance, Disobedience, or Constituent Power? Emerging Narratives of Transnational Protest," edited by Peter Niesen.
37. Yanis Varoufakis, "Europe's Left After Brexit," *Jacobin*, accessed July 30, 2018, www.jacobinmag.com/2016/09/european-union-strategy-democracy-yanis-varoufakis-diem25.
38. Nancy Kokaz, "Theorizing International Fairness," *Metaphilosophy*, 36, nos. 1–2 (2005): 68–92.
39. Dannah Boyd, "Whistleblowing Is the New Civil Disobedience," *Medium*, July 18, 2013, https://medium.com/@zephoria/whistleblowing-is-the-new-civil-disobedience-9a53415933a9.

40. However, see Erica Chenoweth and Maria J. Stephen, *Why Civil Resistance Works: The Strategic Logic of Nonviolent Conflict* (New York: Columbia University Press, 2011); Kurt Schock, *Unarmed Insurrections: People Power Movements in Nondemocracies* (Minneapolis, MN: University of Minnesota Press, 2005).
41. Gallie, "Essentially Contested," 168.

PART I **Plural Voices, Rival Frameworks**

I The Domestication of Henry David Thoreau

Russell L. Hanson

Henry David Thoreau's essay on civil disobedience is said to have influenced Mohandas K. Gandhi's nonviolent campaign for Indian rights in South Africa, and subsequent drive for Indian independence, which in turn is thought to have inspired Martin Luther King, Jr.'s direction of the American Civil Rights Movement. In this chapter I reverse that genealogy, showing that King construed elements of satyagraha in ways that served the political agenda of the Civil Rights Movement in the United States, while playing down aspects of satyagraha that did not fit the American case or even clashed with Judeo-Christian themes that were important within the American movement.

Of course, Gandhi did the same thing with Thoreau's concept of civil disobedience, which he borrowed selectively in making satyagraha the defining feature for protest movements in South Africa and Indian independence. What was left out, and indeed what had to be excluded, was Thoreau's famous skepticism regarding reform movements and his equivocations on nonviolence.

As it happens, Gandhi first encountered Thoreau's reflections on civil disobedience in a 1905 edition published in London by Arthur C. Fifield, whose Simple Life Press specialized in issuing inexpensive paperbacks for mass consumption. Fifield edited Thoreau's essay with a very heavy hand, and gave it a new title, "On the Duty of Civil Disobedience," which suited his own pacifist views.

Nor was that all; Fifield was working from the 1866 reprint of Thoreau's 1849 essay, which appeared posthumously under a new title, "Civil Disobedience," and without certain passages from the original essay that clashed with its nonviolent connotations. The changes were made by Thoreau's executors and publisher, and there is scant evidence they reflected Thoreau's wishes. The title he gave the essay when it was first published in 1849 was "Resistance to Civil Government." The word "resistance" in this title belies an unequivocal commitment to nonviolence, as Thoreau made clear in his 1854 speech on "Slavery in Massachusetts" and his staunch defense of John Brown's bloody raid on Harpers Ferry.

Thus, Thoreau's work as it is widely interpreted today – as a general injunction to disobey unjust laws by nonviolent means – is the result of a series of political appropriations, each building on the other, all of them leading toward a conclusion different from the author's intent and meaning.

RESISTANCE TO CIVIL GOVERNMENT

"Resistance to Civil Government, A Lecture Delivered in 1847" expressed Thoreau's opposition to the war with Mexico. He began from the proposition that "The only obligation which I have a right to assume is to do at any time what I think right."[1] The same is true of every other person. Each is a sovereign moral agent, free to act as he or she thinks best, based on a deliberate assessment of the options before them. Even if all agreed on what was right, they still might differ on how best to achieve it, or at what cost to themselves in view of other priorities.

Some might protest or even disobey an unjust law, but Thoreau denied they were morally obliged to do so.

> It is not a man's duty, as a matter of course, to devote himself to the eradication of any, even the most enormous, wrong; he may still properly have other concerns to engage him; but it is his duty, at least, to wash his hands of it, and, if he gives it no thought longer, not to give it practically his support. If I devote myself to other pursuits and contemplations, I must first see, at least, that I do not pursue them sitting upon another man's shoulders.[2]

It is important to emphasize the difference between opposing an unjust law and withdrawing "practical support" for institutions, practices, and deeds sanctioned by law. In such cases the duty is owed, not to the State, but to the victims of injustice, i.e. those whose self-sovereignty has been invaded or repressed. Those who claim the right to choose for themselves, in defiance of the State if necessary, must acknowledge the same right for all others. To deny self-sovereignty to others is to invite others to deny one's own sovereignty, and to forfeit any right to resist the State.

Thus, abolitionists and non-abolitionists alike were duty bound to withdraw support for institutions that made them agents of injustice to others. "This people must cease to hold slaves, and to make war on Mexico, though it cost them their existence as a people."[3] The withdrawal of practical support from slavery might take different forms. For some, it was benefitting the victims of slavery, spiriting them to Canada aboard the Underground Railroad, or interfering with slave catchers from the South. Others wore homespun clothing, boycotting cotton picked by slaves, hoping to depress the profits of owners – and ultimately the viability of slavery itself, in comparison to "free labor."

Thoreau asserted that

> if one thousand, if one hundred, if ten men whom I could name – if ten honest men only – ay, if one HONEST man, in this State of Massachusetts, ceasing to hold slaves, were actually to withdraw from this copartnership, and be locked up in the county jail therefore, it would be the abolition of slavery in America. For it matters not how small the beginning may seem to be: what is once well done is done forever. But we love better to talk about it: that we say is our mission.[4]

Yet Thoreau opened the door to more violent forms of resistance, suggesting that even in the absence of physical violence, the test of conscience involved the shedding – or letting – of blood.

> If the tax-gatherer, or any other public officer, asks me, as one has done, "But what shall I do?" my answer is, "If you really wish to do

anything, resign your office." When the subject has refused allegiance, and the officer has resigned his office, then the revolution is accomplished. But even suppose blood should flow. Is there not a sort of blood shed when the conscience is wounded? Through this wound a man's real manhood and immortality flow out, and he bleeds to an everlasting death. I see this blood flowing now.[5]

If the blood of those whose conscience is wounded by the institution of slavery is already flowing, are they not entitled to defend themselves? Yes, indeed.

All men recognize the right of revolution; that is, the right to refuse allegiance to, and to resist, the government, when its tyranny or its inefficiency are great and unendurable. But almost all say that such is not the case now. But such was the case, they think, in the Revolution of '75. If one were to tell me that this was a bad government because it taxed certain foreign commodities brought to its ports, it is most probable that I should not make an ado about it, for I can do without them. All machines have their friction; and possibly this does enough good to counterbalance the evil. At any rate, it is a great evil to make a stir about it. But when the friction comes to have its machine, and oppression and robbery are organized, I say, let us not have such a machine any longer. In other words, when a sixth of the population of a nation which has undertaken to be the refuge of liberty are slaves, and a whole country is unjustly overrun and conquered by a foreign army, and subjected to military law, I think that it is not too soon for honest men to rebel and revolutionize. What makes this duty the more urgent is that fact that the country so overrun is not our own, but ours is the invading army.[6]

Any questions about Thoreau's meaning of resisting civil government were answered in his reaction to passage of the Fugitive

Slave Act of 1850 and the subsequent rendition of Anthony Burns from Boston in 1854.

"The majority of the men of the North, and of the South and East and West, are not men of principle," he said. Instead of confronting the enormity of slavery, they submit to unjust laws, even those that might harm their own families. Effectively they say,

> Do what you will, O Government, with my wife and children, my
> mother and brother, my father and sister, I will obey your
> commands to the letter. It will indeed grieve me if you hurt them, if
> you deliver them to overseers to be hunted by hounds or to be
> whipped to death; but, nevertheless, I will peaceably pursue my
> chosen calling on this fair earth, until perchance, one day,
> when I have put on mourning for the dead, I shall have persuaded
> you to relent.[7]

Blind obedience to the law was wrong, said Thoreau; it was a form of self-enslavement for which he had no patience.

> Such is the attitude, such are the words of Massachusetts. Rather
> than do thus, I need not say what match I would touch, what
> system endeavor to blow up; but as I love my life, I would side with
> the light, and let the dark earth roll from under me, calling my
> mother and my brother to follow .... My thoughts are murder to the
> State, and involuntarily go plotting against her.[8]

Thoreau was even more explicit in an essay published during John Brown's trial for seizing control of the Federal arsenal and Hall Rifle Works at Harpers Ferry in 1859, with the intention of arming slaves. The raid failed, and in the midst of Brown's trial for treason against the Commonwealth of Virginia, Thoreau issued his "Plea for Captain John Brown." It was Brown's

> peculiar doctrine that a man has a perfect right to interfere by force
> with the slaveholder, in order to rescue the slave. I agree with
> him ... I shall not be forward to think him mistaken in his method

> who quickest succeeds to liberate the slave. I speak for the slave
> when I say that I prefer the philanthropy of Captain Brown to that
> philanthropy which neither shoots me nor liberates me.[9]

Driving the point home, Thoreau later admitted that

> I do not wish to kill nor to be killed, but I can foresee circumstances
> in which both these things would be by me unavoidable . . . . I know
> that the mass of my countrymen think that the only righteous use
> that can be made of Sharps rifles and revolvers is to fight duels with
> them, when we are insulted by other nations, or to hunt Indians, or
> shoot fugitive slaves with them, or the like. I think that for once the
> Sharps rifles and the revolvers were employed in a righteous cause.
> The tools were in the hands of one who could use them.[10]

This is not merely an acceptance of violence as being necessary;
it avers that violence is sometimes virtuous. He reiterated the point in
"The Last Days of John Brown," who demonstrated "a more intelli-
gent and generous spirit than that which actuated our forefathers" and
raised "the possibility, in the course of ages, of a revolution in behalf
of another and an oppressed people."[11] Toward that end, Thoreau
even exhorted his fellows to honor the martyred Brown "by our
admiration, rather than by short-lived praises, and, if nature aid us,
by our emulation of [him]."[12]

CIVIL DISOBEDIENCE

The process of selective appropriation began soon after Thoreau died
of consumption in 1862. In October 1866, Ticknor and Fields issued
A Yankee in Canada, with Anti-Slavery and Reform Papers. No
editor was listed for the volume, and no explanation was offered for
juxtaposing a travel essay with "reform papers" covering a range of
political issues addressed by Thoreau at different moments in his life.
The anti-slavery papers included "Slavery in Massachusetts" and "A
Plea for John Brown," as well as an essay entitled "Civil
Disobedience." There was no indication that "Civil Disobedience"

was published previously under a different title, or that certain elements of the original essay had been excised and new material of undeclared origin incorporated.

A full catalogue of the differences between the 1866 essay called "Civil Disobedience" and the 1849 "Resistance to Civil Government" is found here.[13] From a marketing standpoint, Ticknor and Fields might have preferred the non-rebellious-sounding "Civil Disobedience" as more palatable in the wake of civil war. Remembering critics' reaction to the 1849 essay, Thoreau's friend and sister might have agreed, so as to present Thoreau in a gentler light out of concern for his reputation.

But Henry did not subscribe to nonresistance. As early as January 27, 1841, he and his brother John debated Bronson Alcott in the Concord Lyceum on the question, "Is it ever proper to offer forcible resistance?"[14] The Thoreau brothers argued in the affirmative. This was no mere formality. In his 1844 "Herald of Freedom" salute to Nathaniel P. Rogers, Thoreau commended the editor for insisting that slavery is "an evil to be abolished by other means than sorrow and bitterness of complaint."[15] Moral suasion was insufficient, as disunion would have left slavery undisturbed in the South.

This was the theme of Thoreau's lecture to the Concord Lyceum on January 26, 1848. It was entitled "The Relation of the Individual to the State," and repeated, probably in revised form, three weeks later as "The Rights and Duties of the Individual in relation to Government." A year later Elizabeth Peabody, a Transcendental enthusiast, solicited the essay and published it under the title of "Resistance to Civil Government" in the first and only issue of *Aesthetic Papers*.

Lawrence Rosenwald attributes the change in title to Thoreau's growing appreciation for the 1845 *Narrative of the Life of Frederick Douglass, An American Slave, Written by Himself*.[16] In his *Narrative* Douglass recalled a day on which Edward Covey, a slave-breaker, attempted to beat him, as Covey had done many times before. For the first time, Douglass resisted, drawing blood,

and putting an end to the whippings. The incident was transformative, in a way that Thoreau himself could appreciate, even to the
point of setting aside strictures against meeting violence with
violence.

Moreover, Thoreau may have concluded that a more militant
title was required. In the two months between his second lecture and
the publication of *Aesthetic Papers*, a "Treaty of Peace, Friendship,
Limits and Settlement between the United States of America and the
Mexican Republic" went into effect. It did not include a proviso
banning slavery in the newly acquired territory; a significant westward expansion of slavery was imminent, and a stronger response was
necessary.

Ironically, the 1866 substitution of "Civil Disobedience" for
"Resistance to Civil Government" placed Thoreau's argument
squarely within a context of nonviolence. Before Thoreau's death
in 1862 the term "civil disobedience" had acquired a specific
meaning, thanks to a bevy of sermons protesting the Fugitive
Slave Law and its enforcement. The earliest was Nathaniel
P. Hall's sermon, *The Limits of Civil Obedience: A Sermon
Preached in the First Church, Dorchester, January 12, 1851.*
Running a close second was Charles Beecher's *Duty of
Disobedience to Wicked Laws: A Sermon on the Fugitive Slave
Law*, published later in 1851. In 1853 Samuel Colcord Bartlett
published *The Duty and Limitations of Civil Obedience:
A Discourse Preached at Manchester, N.H. on the Day of Public
Thanksgiving, November 24, 1853.*

As Hall put it, the institution of government is a blessing from
God. Hence "obedience to civil government is a sacred obligation,"
but only insofar as "its requirements are not in conflict with the law
of God" as "made known in our souls and in his Word," for "we are
bound by an authority higher ... to do, in all cases and always, what is
therein proclaimed to us as right."[17] However, any resistance to
unjust laws "is not the forcible resistance which is rebellion, but
that which consists in disobedience, with a passive submission to

whatever penalty may be thereto attached. The authority is acknowledged which enacts the law, and enforces the penalty."[18]

The proposition that citizens have a standing obligation to obey
the law, or at least to recognize the rightful authority of the law to
punish disobedience, is antithetical to Thoreau's argument in
"Resistance to Civil Government." There he presents a robust
defense of every individual's continuing right to self-determination.
Only the deliberate, moment-by-moment consent of individuals
makes compliance obligatory for Thoreau.[19] Anything short of that
leaves individuals free to resist, disobey, or ignore directives of the
State, which is why those who serve the State with their consciences
"and so necessarily resist it for the most part" are "commonly treated
by it as enemies."[20]

Because nonviolent "civil disobedience" was in the Northern
air of this time, it seems improbable that Thoreau would have substi-
tuted that term for "Resistance to Civil Authority," which truly
captures his sense of the life-long struggle to act in accordance with
one's conscience. Whoever suggested the new title, and for whatever
reason, badly served the rugged moralism of Thoreau's objection to
slavery as a fundamental threat to self-determination.

ON THE DUTY OF CIVIL DISOBEDIENCE

The 1866 essay entitled "Civil Disobedience" became the standard
source for American editions of Thoreau's essays. It was also the
source for late nineteenth-century editions published in London,
where Victorian reformers embraced the simple life advocated by
Thoreau in *Walden*, and practiced civil disobedience in protest of
Britain's second war on the Boers of South Africa.

One of the earliest popularizers of Thoreau in Britain was Henry
S. Salt, who published an insightful and sympathetic biography of
Thoreau in 1890. In that same year he selected and edited *Anti-
Slavery and Reform Papers by Henry D. Thoreau*, which was pub-
lished by Swan Sonnenschein & Co. in London. British interest in
Thoreau was sufficiently high that Walter Scott Limited also

published *Essays and Other Writings of Henry David Thoreau, Edited, with a Prefatory Note*, by Will H. Dircks in 1891. It was reissued in 1895. Both editions included "Civil Disobedience" and "A Plea for Captain John Brown."

There was even a Russian translation of "Civil Disobedience" produced in 1898 by a publisher in Essex who was acting upon the recommendation of Count Leo Tolstoy, who read "Civil Disobedience" around 1894 and commended it to his followers.[21] The Russian publisher was Vladimir Tchertkoff, an associate of Tolstoy's and a passionate defender of the Christian Dukhobors, a pacifist sect that refused to perform military service for the Tsar. Tchertkoff was banished to the Baltic provinces for condemning the authorities' persecution of Dukhobors, but was permitted to become a permanent exile in England instead.[22]

In England Tchertkoff began publishing Tolstoy's writings in Russian for the benefit of other exiles and emigres, and for clandestine circulation in Russia, where many of Tolstoy's works were banned. But Tchertkoff also wanted to make Tolstoy's writings available in inexpensive English editions, as did Tolstoy himself. Toward that end Tchertkoff established the Free Age Press, with typesetting, printing, and binding facilities in Tuckton, a small village near Christchurch in Hampshire.

To manage the press Tchertkoff engaged Arthur C. Fifield, a former editor at the James Bowden publishing house in London. Under Fifield's direction, the Free Age Press issued 43 Tolstoyan publications, for a combined total of 2,024 pages, with a circulation of 209,000.[23] After three years Fifield resigned from the Free Age Press to establish his own publishing company, the Simple Life Press, which stressed self-reliance and peaceful cooperation with others as an alternative to capitalism.

The Simple Life Press published inexpensive, and more or less abridged, versions of Thoreau's *Walden*, *Life Without Principle*, and *Walking*, along with Ralph Waldo Emerson's *Man the Reformer* and various essays on Tolstoy. These were pocket-sized editions sold at railway stations, as well as booksellers. Reviewers praised them for being well-printed, neatly bound, and inexpensive (6d or 3d, depending on length).

The first number in the Simple Life Series was "Tolstoy and His Message," a brief exposition of Tolstoy's Christian pacifism, by Ernest Crosby. Number 4 in the Simple Life Series was a version of "Civil Disobedience," sold by Fifield under the misleading title "On the Duty of Civil Disobedience." It was "A handy little pamphlet containing Thoreau's great essay against the Mexican War and slave-owning. Examines the relation between individual conscience and submission to a majority," according to the *London Daily News*.[24]

"On the Duty of Civil Disobedience" was first issued in 1903, and reprinted in 1905. The later rendition of Thoreau reached Gandhi in South Africa, who recommended the Simple Life version to his English readers in the October 26, 1907, edition of *Indian Opinion*. Had Gandhi received Thoreau's essay in the form it was presented under the title "Civil Disobedience" alongside "A Plea for Captain John Brown," he might not have been so quick to recommend Fifield's "On the Duty of Civil Disobedience," which altered key sections of the already domesticated "Civil Disobedience."

Fifield's selective appropriation of the 1866 essay entitled "Civil Disobedience" was breathtakingly bold. It departed from the 1866 edition in several important respects. Taken together they have the effect of further pacifying Thoreau's original argument. Indeed, the result is an essay that Nathaniel Hall and Samuel Bartlett, two American ministers of the Gospel who expounded on civil disobedience in the 1850s, might well have applauded.

The differences included unacknowledged changes to the 1866 version, some of which were stylistic, such as substituting "gaol" for "jail" and conforming punctuation to the publisher's style sheet. Others were more substantial, including a new title, "On the Duty of Disobedience," which implies there is a general obligation to disobey unjust laws. The implication is reinforced by dividing most of

Thoreau's long paragraphs in a way that emphasize duties and exaggerates the efficacy of disobedience.

There were excisions, too. The Fifield version deleted the entire discussion of Thoreau's imprisonment and his reflections on the imbecility of the State.[25] Fifield also deleted criticism of Daniel Webster in "Civil Disobedience," which was added to the published essay "Resistance to Civil Government"; the overall effect is to place the State in implacable opposition to individual conscience, making disobedience a duty.

Taken together, Fifield's alterations obscure Thoreau's willingness to consider violent forms of resistance to unjust laws. That process was begun in 1866, but Fifield carried it much further, taking passages in the essay out of context and ignoring the relevance of Thoreau's defense of John Brown to the issues raised in "Civil Disobedience." That defense was impossible to square with a Tolstoyan message of nonresistance, so Fifield led readers to assume that "Civil Disobedience" was Thoreau's last word.

SATYAGRAHA IN SOUTH AFRICA AND INDIA

Gandhi received a form of Thoreau's essay that lent itself to his purposes: overturning the Black Law in South Africa and then achieving independence for India. The cause was the same – resistance to unjust laws – but the mode of protest was different. Gandhi favored collective action; Thoreau condemned associations, societies, and other forms of collective action in favor of individual acts that might resonate with others, but which stood on their own, morally speaking, as expressions of conscience. Fifield's appropriation of Thoreau, or to be more precise, his appropriation of Thoreau's literary executors' appropriation of Thoreau, was inflected by the publisher's Christian anarchism and his opposition to the second Boer War, from October 1899 through May 1902. Simple Life Series No. 4, "On the Duty of Civil Disobedience," came into Gandhi's hands around 1907.[26] By then Gandhi was organizing mass protests against the Asiatic Law Amendment Act in the Transvaal, which required all persons of Indian or Chinese descent over the age of eight to register with the colonial authorities. A certificate of registration was issued to anyone who provided identifying information (name, age, residence, and caste), along with a set of fingerprints. The certificate was to be carried at all times, and was required in order to conduct business in the Transvaal. Anyone stopped by the authorities who could not produce a certificate was liable to be fined, jailed, or even deported.

1903/05

Under a government which imprisons unjustly, the true place for a just man is also a prison. The proper place to-day, the only place which Massachusetts has provided for her freer and less despondent spirits, is in her prisons, to be put out and locked out of the State by her own act, as they have already put themselves out by their principles. It is there that the fugitive slave, and the Mexican prisoner on parole, and the Indian come to plead the wrongs of his race, should find them; on that separate but more free and honorable ground, where the State places those who are not with her but against her, – the only house in a slave-state in which a free man can abide with honor.

If any think that their influence would be lost there, and their voices no longer afflict the ear of the State, that they would not be as an enemy within its walls, they do not know by how much truth is stronger than error, nor how much more eloquently and effectively he can combat injustice who has experienced a little in his own person.

Cast your whole vote, not a strip of paper merely, but your whole influence. A minority is powerless while it conforms to the majority; it is not even a minority then; but it is irresistible when it clogs by its whole weight.

If the alternative is to keep all just men in prison, or give up war and slavery, the State will not hesitate which to choose. If a thousand men were not to pay their tax bills this year, that would not be a violent and bloody measure, as it would be to pay them, and enable the State to commit violence and shed innocent blood.

(cont.)

This is, in fact, the definition of a peaceable revolution, if any such is possible. If the tax-gatherer, or any other public officer, asks me, as one has done, "But what shall I do?" my answer is, "If you really wish to do any thing, resign your office." When the subject has refused allegiance, and the officer has resigned his office, then the revolution is accomplished.

But even suppose blood should flow. Is there not a sort of blood shed when the conscience is wounded? Through this wound a man's real manhood and immortality flow out, and he bleeds to an everlasting death. I see this blood flowing now ….

1866

Under a government which imprisons unjustly, the true place for a just man is also a prison. The proper place to-day, the only place which Massachusetts has provided for her freer and less despondent spirits, is in her prisons, to be put out and locked out of the State by her own act, as they have already put themselves out by their principles. It is there that the fugitive slave, and the Mexican prisoner on parole, and the Indian come to plead the wrongs of his race, should find them; on that separate but more free and honorable ground, where the State places those who are not with her but against her, – the only house in a slave-state in which a free man can abide with honor. If any think that their influence would be lost there, and their voices no longer afflict the ear of the State, that they would not be as an enemy within its walls, they do not know by how much truth is stronger than error, nor how much more eloquently and effectively he can combat injustice who has experienced a little in his own person. Cast your whole vote, not a strip of paper merely, but your whole influence. A minority is powerless while it conforms to the majority; it is not even a minority then; but it is irresistible when it clogs by its whole weight. If the alternative is to keep all just men in prison, or give up war and slavery, the State will not hesitate which to choose. If a thousand men were not to pay their tax bills this year, that would not be a violent and bloody measure, as it

> **(cont.)**
>
> would be to pay them, and enable the State to commit violence and
> shed innocent blood. This is, in fact, the definition of a peaceable
> revolution, if any such is possible. If the tax-gatherer, or any other
> public officer, asks me, as one has done, "But what shall I do?" my
> answer is, "If you really wish to do any thing, resign your office."
> When the subject has refused allegiance, and the officer has resigned
> his office, then the revolution is accomplished. But even suppose blood
> should flow. Is there not a sort of blood shed when the conscience is
> wounded? Through this wound a man's real manhood and
> immortality flow out, and he bleeds to an everlasting death. I see this
> blood flowing now . . ..

Gandhi led opposition to the certificates, at first under the banner of "passive resistance," evoking the example of British Non-Conformists' opposition to the Education Act of 1902, which mandated teaching tenets of the Church of England in publicly supported schools. But he soon concluded that "passive resistance" was misleading for a movement opposed to South African pass laws. Passive resistance was considered a "weapon of the weak," but Gandhi wanted to project an image of strength emanating from the united resolve of Indians in the Transvaal. He also worried that passive resistance was only a tactical concession to the majorities' strength; the doctrine itself implied an openness to more aggressive, even violent, forms of resistance, should the opportunity arise or the balance of power shift.

Because Gandhi was irrevocably committed to nonviolence, he needed "to invent a new term clearly to denote the movement of the Indians in the Transvaal to prevent its being confused with passive resistance generally so-called."[27] He settled on the Gujarati word, "satyagraha," "the Force which is born of Truth and Love or non-violence," to characterize the campaign in the Transvaal.

Satyagraha was well underway in South Africa before Gandhi became aware of Thoreau's essay.[28] Gandhi himself later denied influence of that sort.[29] But Thoreau was useful to Gandhi in two important respects. First, the term "civil disobedience" was a fair English approximation for the Gujarati satyagraha, an important consideration since Gandhi's newspaper, *Indian Opinion*, was distributed in both languages. Gandhi was probably unaware that Thoreau never used "civil disobedience" himself, but that was immaterial, since Thoreau's name was indissolubly linked to civil disobedience by his literary executors in 1866.

Thoreau's ardent opposition to slavery made him particularly valuable to Gandhi in a campaign against racial injustice in South Africa. It also required Gandhi to present Thoreau as a champion of nonviolent protest, though in 1921 Gandhi admitted that "Thoreau was not perhaps an out-and-out champion of nonviolence. Probably, also, Thoreau limited his breach of statutory laws to the revenue law, i.e. payment of taxes, whereas 'civil disobedience' as practiced in 1919 covered a breach of any statutory and unmoral law."[30] Gandhi admitted no such limitations in 1907, however. He adopted the English term "civil disobedience" to describe a wide range of protest activities, all of them nonviolent, and all obligatory for those suffering from injustice.

Readers of the English edition of *Indian Opinion* first learned of Gandhi's discovery of Thoreau on September 7, 1907. In a column entitled "On the Duty of Civil Disobedience," Gandhi, citing Thoreau by name, insisted "there is no obligation imposed upon us by our conscience to give blind submission to any law, no matter what force or majority backs it." Gandhi noted that "British Indians have not only a law which has some evil in it, that is to say, using Thoreau's words, a machine with friction in it, but it is evil legalized, or it represents friction with machinery provided for it. Resistance to such an evil is a divine duty which no human being can with impunity disregard."[31]

The September 7, 1907, edition of *Indian Opinion* for English readers included a second column with the heading "Duty of

Disobeying Laws," which, according to Gandhi, "conveys the general sense of the English title" of Thoreau's book. A brief extract was offered in evidence, though it was silently amended by Gandhi: "I do not ask for no government at once, but at once for a better government. *This is the duty of every citizen.*"[32]

Gandhi was generating the impression that Thoreau believed there was a general obligation to disobey unjust laws. That reading was certainly useful for someone building a protest movement. Toward that end Gandhi grossly exaggerated Thoreau's success in order to bolster the case for widespread civil disobedience. His note on Thoreau reported that unnamed "[h]istorians say that the chief cause of the abolition of slavery in America was Thoreau's imprisonment and the publication by him of the above-mentioned book after his release. Both his example and writings are at present exactly applicable to the Indians in the Transvaal."[33]

Linck Johnson avers that

> Gandhi almost certainly knew that Thoreau's actions and essay
> had done nothing to end slavery in the United States, but he needed
> to establish the impact of Thoreau's protest in order to promote its
> applicability to Indians in South Africa . . . . By asserting that
> Thoreau had single-handedly brought about momentous change,
> Gandhi sought to inspire those whose resistance to pass laws was
> calculated to provoke their arrest and incarceration in the "Fort,"
> the infamous prison in Johannesburg.[34]

Ramachandra Guha concurs with this explanation for Gandhi's hyperbolic language, and his selective appropriation of Thoreau's reputation and terminology.[35]

The lesson on civil disobedience continued a week later. The September 14, 1907, edition of *Indian Opinion* offered a crude synopsis of Thoreau's argument for Gujarati readers, again presented under the heading "Duty of Disobeying Laws." The synopsis consisted of three silently amended passages from Thoreau, presented as if he were addressing readers directly:

I do not say that it is a man's duty, as a matter of course, to eradicate a wrong wherever he finds it; but it is his duty, at least, not to give it practically his support. *How can a man be satisfied to entertain an opinion merely, and enjoy it!*

I meet the American government directly and face to face once a year in the person of its tax-gatherer. *At that time, I must definitely refuse to pay the tax.*

I think it is disgraceful to submit to a tyrannical State. *It is easy and good to oppose it.* I have paid no poll-tax for six years. I was put into gaol once on this account for one night. As I stood considering the walls of the prison and its iron gates, I could not help being struck with the foolishness of the State.[36]

All three amendments reinforced Gandhi's claim that disobedience was a duty or obligation.

There was a third installment on October 26, 1907, when *Indian Opinion* offered guidance "For Passive Resisters." It opened with a quotation attributed to Tolstoy that underscored the religious nature of the duty to disobey: "The principle of State necessity can bind only those men to disobey God's law who, for the sake of worldly advantages, try to reconcile the irreconcilable; but a Christian, who sincerely believes that the fulfilment of Jesus's teaching shall bring him salvation, cannot attach any importance to this principle."[37]

This was followed by Gandhi's characterization of Thoreau, and recommendation of Fifield's "On the Duty of Civil Disobedience" to those who wanted to explore further:

[Henry] David Thoreau was a great writer, philosopher, poet, and withal a most practical man, that is, he taught nothing he was not prepared to practise in himself. He was one of the greatest and most moral men America has produced. At the time of the abolition of slavery movement, he wrote his famous essay "On the Duty of Civil Disobedience". He went to gaol for the sake of his principles and suffering humanity. His essay has, therefore, been sanctified by suffering. Moreover, it is written for all time. Its incisive logic is unanswerable. During the last week of October – a month of sore temptation to Asiatic passive resisters, whose silent suffering has now reached the whole civilised world – we present the following extracts from Thoreau's essay. The original occupies a little over thirty pages of a pocket book and has been published by Mr. Arthur C. Fifield of 44 Fleet Street, London, in his beautiful "Simple Life" series, at 3d.[38]

All of this suggests that Gandhi's estimate of what was required for satyagraha to succeed in South Africa was at odds with Thoreau's vision of civil disobedience in the United States, where, he boldly asserted, only one honest man might trigger reform. Noting with approval the ease of drawing 2,000 people to attend protest meetings, Gandhi proudly noted that such gatherings would be considered large and satisfactory in any part of the world. "A movement of mass Satyagraha is impossible on any other condition," he said. "Where the struggle is wholly dependent upon internal strength, it cannot go on at all without mass discipline."[39]

NONVIOLENT RESISTANCE

In the summer of 1947 India and Pakistan gained independence from Britain, and also from each other. Gandhi had resisted any partition of Indians along religious lines, as he preferred to stress their common civilization. Some Hindus felt betrayed by Gandhi's acceptance of Muslims, and on January 30, 1948, one knelt before Gandhi as he was being led to a prayer meeting at Birla House in New Delhi. The obeisant drew a pistol, shot, and killed the world's foremost advocate of nonviolence.

On that same day Martin Luther King, Jr. was halfway through his senior year at Morehouse College in Atlanta, Georgia. In his autobiographical *Stride Toward Freedom* (1958) King recollected that "During my student days at Morehouse I read Thoreau's Essay on Civil Disobedience for the first time. Fascinated by the idea of refusing to cooperate with an evil system, I was so deeply moved that

I reread the work several times. This was my first intellectual contact with the theory of nonviolent resistance."[40]

King certainly knew of Gandhi and his success in leading a successful campaign to achieve independence by nonviolent means. Benjamin Mays, the president of Morehouse, was familiar with satyagraha, and surely conveyed its essence to those who attended his weekly chapel meeting with students – which King attended religiously, as attendance records show.[41] Moredecai Johnson and Bayard Rustin later deepened King's appreciation for satyagraha and its relevance to the American Civil Rights Movement.

Ultimately, King preferred Gandhi's version of nonviolent resistance to Thoreau's more robust concept. The change became evident in 1954, when King became pastor of the Dexter Avenue Baptist Church in Montgomery, Alabama. As King later recalled,

> The Negro people of Montgomery came to see that it was ultimately more honorable to walk the streets in dignity than to ride the buses in humiliation. At the beginning of the protest the people called on me to serve as their spokesman. In accepting this responsibility my mind, consciously or unconsciously, was driven back to the Sermon on the Mount and the Gandhian method of nonviolent resistance. This principle became the guiding light of our movement. Christ furnished the spirit and motivation while Gandhi furnished the method.[42]

King's 1957 essay on "Nonviolence and Racial Justice" explained the ethos of nonviolent resistance to laws that were not merely unjust, but genuinely evil, when viewed through a religious lens. Nonviolent opposition to these laws exhibits five qualities or characteristics of agape:

First, and foremost, nonviolent resistance is a form of resistance. Second, "nonviolent resistance does not seek to defeat or humiliate the opponent, but to win his friendship and understanding." Third, nonviolent resistance "is directed against forces of evil rather than against persons who are caught in those forces." Fourth, nonviolent resistance "avoids not only external physical violence but also internal violence of spirit. At the center of nonviolence stands the principle of love ... the love of God working in the lives of men." Fifth, "the method of nonviolence is based on the conviction that the universe is on the side of justice. It is this deep faith in the future that causes the nonviolent resister to accept suffering without retaliation. He knows that in his struggle for justice he has cosmic companionship. This belief that God is on the side of truth and justice comes down to us from the long tradition of our Christian faith."[43]

Obviously, King's admiration for Thoreau was filtered through Gandhi's reading of him in South Africa. In his autobiography, King wrote

> I became convinced that noncooperation with evil is as much
> a moral obligation as is cooperation with good. No other person has
> been more eloquent and passionate in getting this idea across than
> Henry David Thoreau. As a result of his writings and personal
> witness, we are the heirs of a legacy of creative protest. The
> teachings of Thoreau came alive in our civil rights movement;
> indeed, they are more alive than ever before. Whether expressed in
> a sit-in at lunch counters, a freedom ride into Mississippi,
> a peaceful protest in Albany, Georgia, a bus boycott in
> Montgomery, Alabama, these are the outgrowths of Thoreau's
> insistence that evil must be resisted and that no moral man can
> patiently adjust to injustice.[44]

The Christian basis for King's commitment to nonviolence set him apart from Thoreau in other ways, too.[45] But the most significant difference was that Thoreau was committed to individual action, while King followed Gandhi's example and promoted collective action of the most disciplined sort. King, a Baptist preacher, had a genuine appreciation for the dramaturgy of nonviolent protest, particularly in the age of television, when a whole nation witnessed legal authorities' brutal treatment of peaceful protesters who were claiming their due under the law of the land as interpreted by the Supreme Court in a nation supposedly committed to liberty and justice for all.

Consider the skillful dramaturgy of King's April 16, 1963, "Letter from a Birmingham Jail."[46] The letter was ostensibly a reply to local clergymen's call for compromise, but the intended audience for King's letter was much larger than that.[47] Everyone in the nation needed to understand that "justice too long delayed is justice denied," and that "injustice anywhere is a threat to justice everywhere." In other words, the race problem is not just a Southern issue, it is a national challenge – and even an international one.

With this letter, King invited the nation and its federal government to intervene on behalf of protesters who acknowledged the authority of the State, even as they resisted its unjust laws.

> In no sense do I advocate evading or defying the law, as would the rabid segregationist. That would lead to anarchy. One who breaks an unjust law must do so openly, lovingly, and with a willingness to accept the penalty. I submit that an individual who breaks a law that conscience tells him is unjust and who willingly accepts the penalty of imprisonment in order to arouse the conscience of the community over its injustice, is in reality expressing the highest respect for law.[48]

King appealed to whites, as well as blacks, in the name of religious values.

> One day the South will know that when these disinherited children of God sat down at lunch counters, they were in reality standing up for what is best in the American dream and the most sacred values in our Judeo-Christian heritage, and thusly, bringing our nation back to those great wells of democracy which were dug deep by the

founding fathers in their formulation of the Constitution and the Declaration of Independence.[49]

Of this King was supremely confident:

I have no fear about the outcome of our struggle in Birmingham, even if our motives are presently misunderstood. We will reach the goal of freedom in Birmingham and all over the nation, because the goal of America is freedom. Abused and scorned though we may be, our destiny is tied up with the destiny of America . . .. If the inexpressible cruelties of slavery could not stop us, the opposition we now face will surely fail. We will win our freedom because the sacred heritage of our nation and the eternal will of God are embodied in our echoing demands.[50]

CONCLUSION

King always claimed to be indebted to Thoreau's "Essay on Civil Disobedience," and in one sense he was. Northern intervention was what Thoreau represented, and what King needed for nonviolent resistance to succeed in the South. Some very selective appropriation was necessary for King to claim Thoreau as his forebear though, and even then it was necessary for King to impute his own ideas to Thoreau in order for the claim to seem plausible. Witness his expansive assertion that "Whether expressed in a sit-in at lunch counters, a freedom ride into Mississippi, a peaceful protest in Albany, Georgia, a bus boycott in Montgomery, Alabama, these are the outgrowths of Thoreau's insistence that evil must be resisted and that no moral man can patiently adjust to injustice."[51]

Of this list, only a sit-in at segregated lunch counters might conform to Thoreau's injunction that no one was obliged to resist even enormous wrongs, as long as he or she lent no support of any kind to laws treating others unjustly. The same could be true of someone, for example, Bayard Rustin, who refused to sit in the back of a segregated bus, but that is well short of an organized bus boycott that all are obliged to join.

King's appropriation of Thoreau's name, reputation, and (after the First World War) iconic status as *the* American philosopher of self-reliance was strikingly similar to Gandhi's use of Thoreau in 1907, when he, too, needed an example of successful civil disobedience. To Indians in South Africa, Gandhi presented Thoreau as a courageous individual who was wholeheartedly committed to nonviolence, and whose reliance on that method actually brought an end to slavery in the US. It was not the message of Thoreau that Gandhi appropriated, for he had already settled on satyagraha as his philosophy and political strategy. What Gandhi needed was an inspiring example, one that proved the efficacy of satyagraha as a means of challenging racial injustice. Suitably presented to an audience that was not familiar with Thoreau, and no more conversant in American history than Gandhi in 1907, the appropriation delivered the expected political dividend for King, too.

NOTES

1. Henry D. Thoreau, *Reform Papers*, ed. Wendell Glick (Princeton, NJ: Princeton University Press, 1973).
2. Thoreau, *Reform Papers*, 71.
3. Thoreau, *Reform Papers*, 68.
4. Thoreau, *Reform Papers*, 75.
5. Thoreau, *Reform Papers*, 76–77.
6. Thoreau, "Resistance to Civil Government," Thoreau, *Political Writings*, ed. Nancy L. Rosenblum (Cambridge: Cambridge University Press, 1996), 4.
7. Thoreau, *Reform Papers*, 102.
8. Thoreau, *Reform Papers*, 102, 108.
9. Thoreau, *Reform Papers*, 133.
10. Thoreau, *Reform Papers*, 133.
11. Thoreau, *Reform Papers*, 147.
12. Thoreau, *Reform Papers*, 142.
13. Thoreau, *Reform Papers*, 313–29.
14. Raymond R. Borst, *The Thoreau Log: A Documentary Life of Henry David Thoreau, 1817–1862* (New York: G.K. Hall, 1992), 62.

15. Thoreau, *Reform Papers*, 50.

16. Lawrence Rosenwald, "The Theory, Practice and Influence of Thoreau's Civil Disobedience," in *The Oxford Historical Companion to Thoreau*, ed. William Cain (Oxford: Oxford University Press, 2000), 153–79.

17. Nathaniel P. Hall, *The Limits of Civil Obedience: A Sermon Preached in the First Church, Dorchester, January 12, 1851*, at 12, 17.

18. Hall, *The Limits of Civil Obedience*, 19.

19. "Must the citizen ever for a moment, or in the least degree, resign his conscience to the legislator? Why has every man a conscience, then? I think we should be men first, and subjects afterward" (Thoreau, *Reform Papers*, 65).

20. Thoreau, *Reform Papers*, 66.

21. The Russian edition was very faithful to the 1866 "Civil Disobedience." It was commissioned by Tolstoy himself. Cf. Tolstoy's March 25, 1897, letter to Eugen Heinrich Schmitt.

22. Michael J. De K. Holman, "Translating Tolstoy for the Free Age Press: Vladimir Tchertkov and His English Manager Arthur Fifield," *The Slavonic and East European Review*, 66, 2 (April, 1988): 184–97.

23. Holman, "Translating Tolstoy," 196.

24. April 29, 1903, 8.

25. Fifield did append a more familiar example to English readers in place of the deleted paragraphs on Thoreau's night in jail. He included William L. Hare's report in the Tolstoyan *Candlestick*, from Derby, 1902, on "The Cost of Disobedience by One Who Has Tried It."

26. Gandhi to Henry S. Salt, October 12, 1929: "My first introduction to Thoreau's writings was I think in 1907 or later when I was in the thick of passive resistance struggle. A friend sent me Thoreau's essay on civil disobedience. It left a deep impression on me. I translated a portion of that essay for the readers of *Indian Opinion* in South Africa which I was then editing and I made copious extracts from that essay for that paper."

27. Mohandas K. Gandhi, *Satyagraha in South Africa* (hereafter *SISA*), trans. Valji Govindji Desai (Triplican, Madras: S. Ganesan, 1928), 177.

28. Thomas Weber, *Gandhi as Disciple and Mentor* (Cambridge: Cambridge University Press, 2004).

29. Gandhi to P. Kodanda Rao in 1935 in the *Collected Works of Mohandas Gandhi*, hereafter *CWMG*, vol. 61: 401, no. 577; cf. www .gandhiashramsevagram.org/gandhi-literature/collected-works-of-mahatma-gandhi-volume-1-to-98.php.
30. Gandhi, *CWMG* 19: 466–67, no. 238.
31. Gandhi, *CWMG* 7: 211–12, no. 169.
32. Gandhi, *CWMG* 7: 217–18, no. 176.
33. Gandhi, *CWMG* 7: 217–18, no. 176.
34. Linck Johnson, "The Life and Legacy of 'Civil Disobedience'," in *The Oxford Handbook of Transcendentalism*, ed. Joel Myerson, Sandra Harbert Petrulionis, and Laura Dassow Walls (Oxford: Oxford University Press, 2010), 634.
35. Ramachandra Guha, *Gandhi Before India* (New York: Alfred A. Knopf, 2013).
36. Gandhi, *CWMG* 7: 228–30, no. 185.
37. Gandhi, *CWMG* 7: 304–05, no. 243.
38. Gandhi, *CWMG* 7: 279, no. 221.
39. Gandhi, *SISA*, 204.
40. Martin Luther King, *Stride Toward Freedom: The Montgomery Story* (Boston, MA: Beacon Press, 1958).
41. Rufus Burrow, Jr. *Extremist for Love: Martin Luther King Jr., Man of Ideas and Nonviolent Social Action* (Minneapolis, MN: Fortress Press, 2014).
42. Martin Luther King, "Pilgrimage to Nonviolence" [1960], in *A Testament of Hope: The Essential Writings of Martin Luther King, Jr.*, ed. James M. Washington (New York: Harper Collins, 1986), 38.
43. Martin Luther King, "Nonviolence and Racial Justice," in *Christian Century*, February 6, 1957.
44. Martin Luther King, *The Autobiography of Martin Luther King, Jr.*, chapter 2, https://swap.stanford.edu/20141218230026/http://mlk-kp p01.stanford.edu/kingweb/publications/autobiography/chp_2.htm, 14.
45. George E. Carter, "Martin Luther King: Incipient Transcendentalist," *Phylon*, 40, 4 (4th Qtr., 1979): 318–24.
46. The original letter was written by hand and smuggled out of jail, whereupon it was revised more than once. An early revision is here: http://okra .stanford.edu/en/permalink/document630416-011. The following

quotations are from this version of King's letter, which was never sent to the clergymen.

47. S. Jonathan Bass, *Blessed Are the Peacemakers: Martin Luther King, Jr., Eight White Religious Leaders, and the "Letter from Birmingham Jail"* (Baton Rouge, LA: Louisiana State University Press, 2001).

48. King, "Letter from Birmingham Jail," 9–10.

49. King, "Letter from Birmingham Jail," 20.

50. King, "Letter from Birmingham Jail," 19–20.

51. King, *Autobiography*, 14.

2   Martin Luther King, Jr. and the Politics of Disobedient Civility

Erin R. Pineda

In the popular imagination of civil disobedience, few figures loom as large as Martin Luther King, Jr. His "Letter from a Birmingham Jail" is considered essential reading for any student of civil disobedience; it regularly features on high school and college syllabi covering the topic. Whenever new civil disobedience erupts, particularly in the United States, journalists and political commentators routinely reach for King and the familiar refrains contained within the "Letter" in order to interpret (and sometimes scold) rising movements and their tactics.[1] Yet, much like the broader reception of King within political philosophy, his centrality to civil disobedience obscures the fact that, until quite recently, his political thought was strikingly marginal to academic philosophizing about civil disobedience. Scholarly debates too often have rested on a combination of what Brandon Terry and Tommie Shelby call "ritual celebration" and "intellectual marginalization" that served to diminish King's contributions as "derivative of long-standing American ideals."[2] To be sure, King and the "Letter" make regular appearances in theories of civil disobedience from the 1960s onward, as they do in popular discourse. But in these texts, King operates less as a theorist, offering a novel account of civil disobedience, and more as a proving ground for the political purchase of liberal and deliberative theories or a testament to their limits.[3]

Theories of civil disobedience that emerged out of the 1960s and 1970s were, in some ways, responsive to King and the Civil Rights Movement more broadly. Writing, by and large, in the midst of two decades of intense social, political, and cultural upheaval, liberal political and legal theorists such as John Rawls were intent on defending the civil disobedience of the Civil Rights and Anti-War

Movements against the charge that lawbreaking, no matter how conscientious, was directly tied to a general degradation of state authority that would lead to violence, criminality, and anarchy. The Civil Rights Movement, and the arguments King makes in his "Letter," seemed to Rawls and others exemplary of transformative political action that was appropriately self-limiting, conscientious, nonviolent, persuasive, and constitutionally bound: while remaining within the confines of "fidelity to the law" and the norms of public reason, properly *civil* disobedience could successfully challenge Jim Crow.[4]

More recently, amid what Guy Aitchison has called the "new civil disobedience debate," theorists have returned to the example of King in order to clear space for more radical, democratic interpretations of civil disobedience.[5] Echoing David Lyons's insightful analysis of the ways that liberal theory systematically mischaracterizes the historical claims of its most celebrated practitioner-theorists – King, but also Henry David Thoreau and M.K. Gandhi – Robin Celikates, for example, turns back to King in order to undermine the definitional and justificatory underpinnings of the mid-century liberal theories, by wielding precisely the example that someone such as Rawls seems best equipped to theorize.[6] In contrast, others deploy King and the Civil Rights example to fix intuitions about what a classic case of civil disobedience presumably looks like. Here, the emphasis is on showing how King's ideas or the activities of the movement are, in fact, broadly cognizable in liberal or Rawlsian terms, thereby clearing the way for an analysis of movements and actions that the standard conception cannot so easily contain.[7]

King's movement both within and between these accounts is revealing on two fronts. First, for all the virtues of these liberal, democratic, and radical engagements with civil disobedience, the reliance on King as exemplar or object lesson rather than as theorist avoids serious engagement with King's own purposes in thinking about civil disobedience in the first place, eliding the question of whether he shares a common interpretive framework with contemporary theorists who rely on his example. Second, the shuttling of

King, as an exemplary figure who seems to provide crucial evidence for multiple sides of a debate, back and forth between liberal-normative and radical-democratic interpretations illuminates important fault lines that run through King's political thought, that is, King as a moralist, a moderate, and a radical democrat.

This chapter takes up both prongs. I argue that the necessary context for understanding King's account of civil disobedience is his investigation of the ways in which the ethics and politics of nonviolent direct action respond to and also transform the habits, relationships, and structures that define racial domination as he saw them. Thus, King is not principally concerned with legitimate lawbreaking per se, nor even with the political value of purposeful lawbreaking as a unique protest activity. Instead, he offers a detailed diagnosis of the problem posed by an "evil system" of racial oppression, including the habituated condition of "adjustment" that it cultivates among Black and white citizens. He offers nonviolent direct action as a practice of "creative maladjustment" uniquely suited to transforming it. In formulating these arguments, King navigates the terrain between moral commitments and political entailments, a moderate's insistence on the value of civic ties with white Americans, and a militant's understanding of the radical transformation required to build them.[8] In the end, I present King's perspective less as a theory of civil disobedience than a practice of *disobedient civility*. By this I mean *disobedience* not to law so much as to the norms of comportment inculcated by relations of domination, and through which we forge the new *civil* bonds necessary for a radically restructured multiracial democracy. In closing, I briefly consider what King's account suggests for the present moment in the United States, amid renewed mass protests for racial justice under the banner of "Black Lives Matter."

INJUSTICE IN AND BEYOND THE LAW

In distinction to most liberal and democratic theorists of civil disobedience, King did not cleanly separate civil disobedience from other forms of nonviolent activism. King's interest in civil disobedience neither began nor ended with the problem that purposeful lawbreaking poses for political obligation or the maintenance of democratic norms and institutions. He was not primarily motivated by the justificatory puzzles that have animated academic philosophers and political theories on this topic, nor was he fixated by the dynamic effects of purposeful lawbreaking per se. Of course, King was not wholly unconcerned with the task of justifying disobedience to law. Faced with the problem of segregationist backlash against court-ordered desegregation (a counterexample frequently raised by King's critics), he was acutely aware of the need to spell out the difference between civil rights disobedience and "massive resistance" to integration. Famously, in his "Letter from a Birmingham Jail," King took up precisely this problem. Yet the analysis he provided there is revealing for the way that it extends beyond the immediate issue of justifying disobedience to law, uncovering a different set of motivating questions that orient King's distinctive understanding of civil disobedience as but one avenue for nonviolent direct action.

Reworking and extending a distinction between just and unjust laws that he first articulated after his release from Reidsville Prison in 1960, in the "Letter" King famously argues that only just laws are morally binding, while unjust laws not only justify disobedience, but also require it.[9] There, he provides four definitions of unjust laws, spanning from the abstract to the concrete, and sounding themes from natural law to democratic legitimacy, liberal proceduralism, and constitutional law. His first explanation, and the one with the longest provenance in his thinking, defines an unjust law as one that is "out of harmony with the moral law," and that "degrades human personality."[10] Yet, acknowledging the need to make the distinction as concrete as possible, King provides three further examples: unjust laws are evident when the powerful exempt themselves from following laws imposed on the powerless; unjust laws are produced by undemocratic processes in which disenfranchised minorities are subject to laws that they had no role in making; finally, just or facially neutral laws become unjust when they are wielded in bad faith, as a means of imposing or maintaining relations of domination. Taken together, these four definitions provide a snapshot of the uses and abuses of law for racial hierarchy. They provide a defense of the civil disobedience of civil rights activists from multiple angles, at multiple levels. The case for breaking the law under Jim Crow is, as King explains to his audience of eight clergymen, overdetermined.

Familiar as these ideas have become, King's assessment of law-breaking (and its justification) forms but one part of his broader exploration of nonviolent resistance in the "Letter" and beyond. Such resistance is theorized not in narrow terms, as a limited exception to political obligation in the face of unjust laws, but in broad ones, as a uniquely transformative, thoroughgoing response to the problem of a society structured by racial domination. Indeed, the analysis of just and unjust laws did not feature at all in King's thought until late 1960. Archival evidence suggests that he came to his explanations somewhat slowly, through trial and, in at least one case, a very public error. In November of 1960, in a televised debate with James Kilpatrick, the segregationist editor of the *Richmond News Leader*, King fumbled repeatedly as he tried to defend the legitimacy of the sit-ins. Against Kilpatrick's insistence on the constitutional inviolability of private property and the relativism of appeals to morality, King offered only that an "unjust law is no law at all," and struggled to specify what the moral law entails, beyond what Kilpatrick insisted were just the vagaries of individual conscience. It was clear to many – the students of the Student Nonviolent Coordinating Committee, as well as King himself – that he had lost the debate, and with it, a chance to provide a strong, public defense of the movement's ethics and tactics against an articulate opponent versed in the statutory bases of segregation. Whereas King failed to demonstrate convincingly how segregation violated a version of natural law that is both concrete and binding on democratic citizens, Kilpatrick successfully privatized conscience, insisting that there is no legitimate way to arbitrate between different citizens' perceptions about what counts as unjust.[11] As members of a federal commission would put it nearly

a decade later, echoing the same logic, "if we allow individual consciences to guide obedience to the law, we must take all consciences.
The law cannot distinguish between the consciences of saints and
sinners."[12]

In a response to an editorial about the debate in *The Call*,
a Kansas City-based African American newspaper, a young political
science graduate student named John H. Herriford defended King's
insistence on the injustice of segregation statutes, while critiquing his
use of the moral law to make his point. The distinction between just
and unjust laws, Herriford argued, could be made more compellingly
in legal and democratic terms: a "tyrannous law" is imposed by
majorities who have no intention of following it themselves;
a tyrannous law is imposed on minorities without giving them
a voice in the process. While general laws that are the product of
fair, democratic processes are "sameness made legal," tyrannous
laws represent "differences made legal," and as such, do not deserve
our obedience. Herriford forwarded his letter to King, and after an
additional exchange of correspondences, gave permission for King to
use his arguments in his public and written defenses of the
movement.[13] For his part, King thanked Herriford – "you have done
more to clarify my thinking on this issue than anyone with whom
I have talked" – and incorporated Herriford's points, along with the
language of legalized "sameness" and "difference," in his
September 1961 article, "The Time for Freedom has Come," and in
statements and essays thereafter.[14]

Yet King never abandoned the insistence that an unjust law is
one that contradicts the moral law and degrades the "human personality." Instead, he consistently mobilized his two (and later, three)
legal-political examples, including those taken from Herriford and
more in keeping with liberal and democratic theories of civil disobedience, as *concrete illustrations* of this core idea.[15] Laws resulting from
minority disenfranchisement, laws designed for the domination of
some by others, laws deployed to reinforce racial hierarchy: they do
not simply violate the rule of law or democratic principles (though

they plainly do); they also run afoul of a deeper truth about who humans are, how they are connected, and what they owe to each other. King's stubborn insistence on segregation as a form of violence against the human personality – a violence manifested in law, but far exceeding it – alerts us to the fact that, for King, legalized segregation and political disenfranchisement were *symptomatic* of a more profound societal crisis for which nonviolent collective action was the solution. As I detail below, understanding King's ontological commitments to the equal worth of individuals and the interconnectedness of all humanity is crucial for interpreting his analysis of civil disobedience. That analysis was not primarily centered on specifying the conditions for legitimate lawbreaking, but rather on accounting for the ways that nonviolence can transform the distorted, damaging relations that result from (and also produce and maintain) racial domination.

ADJUSTING TO AN "EVIL SYSTEM"

To understand the way King viewed civil disobedience, we need to appreciate how he inhabited a particular "problem-space," or what David Scott describes as the "ensemble of questions and answers around which a horizon of identifiable stakes (conceptual as well as ideological-political stakes) hangs."[16] King's interpretation of civil disobedience and nonviolent direct action is directly linked to his characterization of racial injustice both within and beyond the law; it constructs the kind of answer he thought civil disobedience provided to that problem. What was the kind of moral violation and systemic problem, posed by segregation and racial domination? What does it mean to degrade the human personality?[17]

In terms both theological and political, King was committed to the equal worth of each individual, a principle he sometimes described in terms of a Kantian categorical imperative – humans are always to be treated as ends in themselves, and never instrumentalized as means or objectified as things – as well as in theological terms – as a recognition that humans are made in God's image.[18] In a 1962 speech delivered in Nashville, Tennessee, King expresses what he calls the "ethical demands of integration" by pointing to this bedrock notion of human equality: "Deeply rooted in our political and religious heritage is the conviction that every man is an heir to the legacy of equality and worth …. There is no graded scale of essential worth; there is no divine right of one race which differs from the divine right of another."[19] This idea, King argues there, espoused both by Christian theology and the history of democratic revolutions, commits us to treating each person as a free agent – someone with the capacity to "deliberate, decide, and respond."[20] To do otherwise was to objectify and debase what it means to be fully human.

King pairs this idea with a quasi-Hegelian insistence on the role of intersubjectivity, and thus mutual recognition, in individual human development: "the self cannot be self without other selves," and persons "cannot truly be persons unless we interact with other persons." For King, intersubjective relations are constitutive of individuality – there is no abstract, unattached individual self, no "I" without "thou." But King was not simply describing human psychological or social development here. His account of intersubjectivity carries significant normative and political weight. Because humans are inherently social, they are driven toward "the mutually cooperative and voluntary venture of man to assume a semblance of responsibility for his brother" – what he called the "solidarity of the human family," or the "inescapable network of mutuality." That is, it is because "all life is interrelated," that all persons, as individuals and groups, bear responsibility for the wellbeing of others, no matter how distant. In a myriad of complex, unseen, and untraceable ways, we are all implicated in the conditions of the lives of others, and therefore have a duty to fight against their domination and exploitation: "The universe is so structured that things do not quite work out rightly if men are not diligent in their concern for others"; or, as King famously put it, "injustice anywhere is a threat to justice everywhere."[21]

While King's path to this set of ideas was clearly, albeit ecumenically, theological, he consistently located the proof of human equality, freedom, and intersubjectivity in the history of both democratic institutions and religious principle. In King's view, human institutions can be arranged in ways that recognize human connectedness, and that enable us to appreciate the relational webs in which we are necessarily embedded. Alternately, they can be organized to promote separation, objectification, degradation, and disavowal. Reading the *Declaration of Independence* and the *US Constitution* through the lens of Black abolitionist thought, King saw real, but unfulfilled, affirmations of the principles of equal dignitary worth.[22] In the federal structure of the United States, King identified a kind of concrete demonstration of the principle of interdependence and mutuality. What we ought to learn from the fact that we are "united" across distinct "states," he suggested, is that we (as individuals) are dependent upon our relations to others, and we cannot ourselves escape responsibility for others. Equally, then, we cannot escape the consequences when we choose to abdicate this responsibility. The human condition situates us such that there are no innocent bystanders within systems of oppression. Racial justice, he argued, "is a problem that meets every man at his front door" – one that can only be solved "to the degree that every American considers himself personally confronted with it."[23] This made racial injustice a national rather than Southern problem, with consequences for collective democratic life as well as individual moral psychology.

Against this background, King understood segregation and racial domination as a particular form of evil or sin. Segregation was not merely a violation of another's rights or a betrayal of constitutional principle, but a more profound and systemic perversion of the very nature of human beings.[24] When King referred to "segregation" as an "evil system," he meant something more than the set of specific Jim Crow statutes. He was conceptualizing an entire order defined by racial hierarchy and its perverse effects on individuals, relations, and institutions. "Segregation" meant a system in which persons were treated as things, while property rights were held sacrosanct; it referred to the systematic degradation of Black Americans' equal moral worth and ethico-political status as free agents and democratic subjects; it designated a way of structuring society that fundamentally disavowed the condition of mutuality, by imagining that free, equal citizenship and material comfort for white Americans could be secured while violently imposing political subordination and economic exploitation on African Americans.[25]

More specifically, King depicted segregation – understood broadly as a particular formulation of racial domination – as a kind of vicious cycle: a regime built on violence, fear, and separation leads to the degradation of moral capacities and political judgment, ultimately reinforcing and exacerbating the forms of alienation that define a broken community. "Men often hate each other because they fear each other," King argued in *Stride Toward Freedom*, his 1958 "autobiography" of the Montgomery movement. "[T]hey fear each other because they do not know each other; they do not know each other because they cannot communicate; they cannot communicate because they are separated." Moreover, this separation is not for its own sake, but is designed to "oppress and exploit the segregated."[26] Consequently, both Black and white Americans become habituated into oppressive relations and are increasingly anesthetized to their effects: they learn to adjust to injustice.

In King's analysis, the long, tortured history from chattel slavery through the twentieth century's "slaveries other than the physical" gradually eroded the sense of self-worth and agency of African Americans, who are forced to acquiesce to being treated as "a thing to be used, not a person to be respected." The political, social, and economic conditions enforced by Jim Crow in its *de jure* and de facto varieties transformed physical slavery into a kind of "mental slavery," such that domination appeared to be an unchangeable, permanent status that may even be deserved.[27] Black Americans were confined to ghetto schools, substandard housing, menial jobs, and segregated neighborhoods cut off from political power and avenues of self-rule, placing them within concentric circles of political disenfranchisement, social isolation, and economic exploitation. At the same time, the mechanisms of racial violence served to stabilize a potentially explosive status quo, breeding fear and fatalism – a "stagnant passivity and deadening complacency" – among its victims, who learn to toe the line and keep quiet.[28] In the end, however, that acquiescence only provided "the oppressor" with "a convenient justification for his acts."[29]

On the other side of the imposed color line, King argued that the consequences of the "evil system" of segregation were no less profound. In racial animus and segregationist violence, King perceived a self-destructive denial of one's own humanity, a denial of the self in the form of the destruction of others; a hatred that degrades the human "personality" from the inside out. More subtle forms of white acceptance of the status quo also took their toll, creating their own series of distortions: an endemic blindness and "callous indifference" that hid the full costs of adjusting to evil, making them unseen and unfelt by most white people. It was a pain dulled by the enjoyment of privilege, and obscured by layers of rationalization.[30] This denial of mutuality had material as well as moral consequences; indeed, as King argued, for impoverished whites, the comforts of white supremacy were cold ones indeed. Echoing W.E.B. Du Bois's analysis of the "public and psychological wage," and presaging his own turn to organizing a multiracial Poor People's Campaign nearly a decade later, in 1958 King observed that in exchange for their "empty pride in a racial myth," poor whites "paid the crushing price of insecurity, hunger, ignorance, and hopelessness" across generations.[31]

The grave consequence, in King's view, was a collective abandonment of responsibility for each other, and for the community as a whole. The moral and political dimensions of this abandonment are inseparable; they are entirely entangled with each other. The central task of nonviolent direct action (including civil disobedience) was thus, in George Shulman's words, the "[reanimation of] *whites'* capacity to acknowledge the reality of their conduct and of those they dominate," along with an equivalent reanimation of Black Americans' capacities for creative, constructive, and emancipatory action.[32] Only through the confluence of both could social and political structures be transformed.

PRACTICING "CREATIVE MALADJUSTMENT"

In a 1967 speech before the American Psychological Association, King reiterated his commitment to "the militant middle between riots on the one hand and weak and timid supplication" to injustice on the other. "That middle ground," he argued, "is civil disobedience. It can be aggressive but nonviolent; it can dislocate but not destroy." In the midst of the wreckage of what he had earlier called the "malignant kinship" between racism and economic exploitation, in the face of violent white "backlash and frontlash," civil disobedience offered King a practice of "creative maladjustment," that is, a rejection of the habituated acquiescence to injustice that King diagnosed at the center of segregation, and a means of transforming structures that are both produced by and simultaneously reproduce a culture of adjustment to racism, poverty, militarism, and violence.[33] It was a way of disrupting the perverse forms of civility, along with the damaged civic relations and oppressive modes of comportment, required by "white democracy," while creatively enacting new habits and new relations required to build a multiracial democracy.[34]

Despite important changes in his thinking over time (particularly concerning racism, capitalism, and the depth of white investment in racial hierarchy), this core understanding of the dynamics of nonviolence remained consistent in King's work. In the first instance, nonviolent direct action enabled a recovery of agency by the oppressed, and hence their freedom to act collectively. Writing about the 1963 Birmingham campaign and the wave of protests in its aftermath, King remarked that the "old order ends, no matter what Bastilles remain, when the enslaved, within themselves, bury the psychology of servitude." This self-emancipation and collective transformation lay at the heart of King's account of the value of nonviolent action. Given a racial order upheld through fear and violence, and dependent for its maintenance on continued acquiescence, King consistently argued that, apart from the external effects of civil disobedience, the "full dimensions of victory can be found only by comprehending the change within the minds of millions of Negroes." Through the uptake of mass nonviolent action, "an impulse for liberty burst through." In short, "the Negroes of America wrote an emancipation proclamation to themselves. They shook off three hundred years of psychological slavery and said: 'We can make ourselves free.'"[35] This inward moral dimension of nonviolence had important political implications: it was a refusal to let the "timetable for freedom" be dictated by white citizens or white state officials. It raised the idea that participation in civil disobedience was not only a means of *fighting for* freedom and dignity, but also a way of *enacting* freedom and dignity directly. It was, in sum, a way of being a full citizen, even as existing conditions denied Black Americans that very status.[36]

By revealing the deep wells of violence and hate on which the system was built, the performance of agency through mass nonviolent action had the profound effect, in King's view, of shattering the myth that segregation ensured racial peace. Paired with the inward-facing transformative work of nonviolent practice was the outward-facing transformative work of disclosing the realities of racial domination, and inviting white Americans to take responsibility. "Instead of submitting to surreptitious cruelty in thousands of dark jail cells and on countless shadowed street corners," to the violent conditions of the Jim Crow racial ordinary, engaging in nonviolent direct action "would force [the] oppressor to commit his brutality openly – in the light of day – with the rest of the world looking on."[37] This entailed much more than just the shrewd use of the media to gain publicity for a cause: it was a dramatic, public work of provocation and disclosure that Brandon Terry aptly characterizes as the movement's "civic pedagogy."[38] Given that, on King's account, white citizens adjust to racial domination by indulging and cultivating forms of moral blindness and political abdication, the dramatic clash of nonviolent protestors with violence (whether wielded by agents of the state or by citizens) would force white Americans to confront realities they had learned to ignore – and also to choose whether they wished to actively identify themselves with them. As Karuna Mantena contends, the white public that King imagined, "spoke to, named, and upbraided" in his analysis of nonviolence was thus "a figure of *identification* and *aspiration*," not a description of a preexisting constituency of "white moderates." Nonviolent direct action presented white citizens with the invitation to take active responsibility for racial justice, and to reconsider how they wished to conceive of themselves and the democracy that they claimed as their own. That is, King "described how people *ought to think and act if they want to see themselves* as being on the side of justice."[39]

One of the mechanisms for this transformative reflexivity, both at the level of the event and more systemically, was the power of nonviolence to disrupt and delegitimize the logic of violent response or retaliation. Within the embodied, intimate dynamics of a single protest, resolute, militant nonviolence would prompt a crisis over how to respond, throwing adversaries off balance and creating an opening to question the system more broadly. In "cities across the map," King suggested, a commitment to nonviolence had removed the justification for quashing rebellion with force, "paralyz[ing] and confus[ing] the power structures against which" nonviolence was directed, sowing "confusion, uncertainty, and disunity."[40] This was never a purely symbolic or straightforwardly persuasive affair. King was always clear that nonviolence needed the power of disruption, pressure, and coercion in order to create the kind of "crisis" or "tension" necessary to force systemic change. Moreover, violence and recalcitrance was to be expected: even when confronted nonviolently, "the privileged first react with bitterness and resistance" when "the underprivileged demand freedom."[41] Faced with a persistent, iterative, and ongoing campaign of nonviolence, however, King imagined that these dynamics of "creative maladjustment" could profoundly unsettle the stability of racial domination as a way of ordering institutions and relations, and in the rupture, empower citizens – white as well as Black – to reimagine what American democracy might entail.

The ultimate value of nonviolent direct action, then, was not desegregation but *integration*, understood as the reconstitution of a broken community on fundamentally new terms. King consistently differentiated "desegregation" from "integration," identifying the latter with "genuine intergroup, interpersonal doing" that could only be the product of the kind of dialectical, creative transformation of self and structure made possible through nonviolence.[42] Integration, in other words, was the worldly, political realization of King's ontological commitments: a multiracial democracy produced through the free, creative agency of individuals, fully alive to their equal moral worth and their constitutive dependence on and responsibility for each other.

FROM CIVIL DISOBEDIENCE TO DISOBEDIENT CIVILITY

King provides less a theory of *civil disobedience* than an expansive politics of *disobedient civility*. The questions raised by theories of civil disobedience about the justification and nature of lawbreaking do not mesh seamlessly with King's questions: he does not differentiate between civil disobedience and other forms of nonviolent direct action, either to specify a legitimate threshold for breaking the law or to analyze the specific political value of purposefully breaking the law. Even his characterization of the distinction between just and unjust laws serves not to spell out the conditions under which democratic citizens justifiably practice civil disobedience but instead to characterize the profound violation represented by racial domination as precisely the kind of problem that demanded nonviolent direct action. As we have seen, King envisioned the use of nonviolence as "creative maladjustment," a set of practices that could radically remake civic relations and reconstitute society anew.

The disobedience that King calls for is broad. It militates against what passes for civility under conditions of racial domination – for example, forms of passivity, complacency, moral blindness, and disavowal that secure the existing order and signal its oppressive nature but that individuals might mistake for decorum and citizenly comportment, given their habituation and adjustment to injustice. King views this injustice as both expansive and deep: it is an "evil system" that structured economic, political, and social relations, as well as individuals' moral judgments about self and others. In this sense, King's account is radical: it is not oriented toward citizens and civic ties as they already exist, but toward the practices through which they might be remade. As such, the practices of "maladjustment" as King sees them require the most profound commitments to acting and thinking differently – to the risk entailed by placing oneself out of joint with the existing society – in order to build a democracy deserving of the name.

Even so, King maintains an investment in what we might still productively think of as *civility* insofar as he focuses on remaking the essential relations between individuals as fellow citizens, eschewing violence against and hatred for those who dominate, and insisting on the possibility of constructing new bonds between oppressed and oppressor – and forging new identities and relations not defined by domination. This, for King, is the only way of being truly, meaningfully civil within an inhuman order.

King explicitly recognized the risky proposition he was making. He knew that he had to press back against the assumption that nonviolence and civility of this type were weak and acquiescent, and the view that nonviolent action ignored the scale and violence of American white supremacy. He also knew that even when faced with disobedience of the most disciplined and nonviolent sort, white citizens would likely react, at least initially, on the basis of fear, resentment, and defensive privilege. Yet, as we have seen, King viewed the first argument as winnable and the second argument as a virtue disguised as a vice: the initial backlash of white citizens would reveal the latent, fearful violence constitutive of white supremacy, and – faced with steadfast, mass nonviolent activism –

whites would eventually be forced to confront the hypocrisy of their own violent refusal. Continued investment in or acceptance of white supremacist violence – whether at the hands of the state or its citizens – simply would not square with their own self-understandings. In Hannah Arendt's terms, the provocation of nonviolent direct action would "fill" white citizens "full of obstacles," prompting reconsideration of whether they would be able to live with themselves if they continued to reject their responsibilities for collective democratic life.[43]

There are reasons to view King's account skeptically: the practice of disobedient civility is demanding, as it requires oppressed citizens to place their bodies on the line without any guarantees that the privileged and the comfortable will take up the difficult, collaborative work of reconstituting the polity. Indeed, the capacities of white citizens for ongoing disavowal seem greater than even King recognized. As Juliet Hooker has recently argued, if the solidarities of white citizens do not extend across racial lines – if the enactment of disobedient civility lacks the transformative potential King saw in it – the price of "democratic repair" is simply too great. It is untenable to continue demanding still greater sacrifices from those who already bear the lion's share of the political losses in a fundamentally unreconstructed democracy, on the shaky premise that Black suffering will eventually spur white moral transformation.[44] From the vantage point of the present – amid the wreckage of mass incarceration, neoliberal abandonment, militarized policing, and a revitalized white nationalism empowered by President Trump – it may appear as though King's account is simply ill-equipped to meet contemporary demands for racial justice.

Yet in the summer of 2020, catalyzed by the gruesome footage of George Floyd's murder at the hands of Minneapolis police, a mass movement under the banner of "Black Lives Matter" reemerged in cities and towns across the United States, eventually spreading to countries around the globe. The movement is notable for its scale (the largest in US history), its demographics (Black-led, but strikingly multiracial), and its demands (to defund and abolish the police). Though the movement's critics have fixated on isolated incidents of property destruction, looting, or interpersonal violence, to condemn the protests as illegitimate and out of step with the tradition of the Civil Rights Movement, in fact they have been both sustained and overwhelmingly – but militantly – nonviolent.[45]

Indeed, far from breaking with the tradition of the Civil Rights Movement, Black Lives Matter mobilizations reveal the continuing relevance of King's insights. At its core, the call to abolish policing – and the systems of oppression that underpin and surround it – is nothing short of a demand to reimagine and reconstitute new relations, forged in part through a commitment to collectively disobey the overlapping violences of the present order. It is an invitation to practice a new way of "[caring] for one another," and of recognizing responsibilities to one another.[46] Additionally, the active involvement of many white Americans in these protests – at a rate much higher than during the Civil Rights Movement – suggests that pessimism about the inevitability of white (re)investment in supremacy may be unwarranted.[47] As we have seen, King's insistence on the potential for transformation among oppressors as well as oppressed was not based on a naive belief that the necessary kinds of subjects and relations already existed, and thus simply needed to be activated. Rather, disobedient civility was premised on the risky but radical proposition that individuals could remake themselves – and the world around them – anew, through nonviolent collective action.

Even as new debates swirl around Black Lives Matter about the moral and political legitimacy of disruption – debates that tend to follow the narrower lines of civil disobedience, taking up when laws may be broken in protest, to what effect, and to what extent – King's thought remains as vital as ever, and urges an alternative starting point. In effect, the question King asked, and the question still in need of an answer, is how citizens habituated into a form of inhuman domination that we nevertheless call "democracy," can build democracy together, and for the first time.

NOTES

1. On this latter point, see Erin R. Pineda, "Civil Disobedience and Punishment: (Mis)reading Justification and Strategy from SNCC to Snowden," *History of the Present*, 5, no. 1 (Spring 2015): 1–30; Candice Delmas, *A Duty to Resist: When Disobedience Should Be Uncivil* (New York: Oxford University Press, 2018), chapter 1.

2. Brandon Terry and Tommie Shelby, "Martin Luther King, Jr. and Political Philosophy," in *To Shape a New World: Essays on the Political Philosophy of Martin Luther King, Jr.*, ed. Tommie Shelby and Brandon Terry (Cambridge, MA and London: Belknap Press, 2018), 2–3.

3. For notable recent exceptions, see the essays in Shelby and Terry, *To Shape a New World*. Particularly on civil disobedience, see: Bernard Boxill, "The Roots of Civil Disobedience in Republicanism and Slavery," 58–77; Karuna Mantena, "Showdown for Nonviolence: The Theory and Practice of Nonviolent Politics," 78–101; Michele Moody-Adams, "The Path of Conscientious Citizenship," 269–89. See also James M. Patterson, "A Covenant of the Heart: Martin Luther King Jr., Civil Disobedience, and the Beloved Community," *American Political Thought*, 7, no. 1 (Winter 2018): 124–51; William Scheuerman, *Civil Disobedience* (Cambridge: Polity, 2018); Alexander Livingston, "'Tough Love': The Political Theology of Civil Disobedience," *Perspectives on Politics*, 18, no. 3 (September 2020): 851–66; Scheuerman, "Recent Theories of Civil Disobedience: An Anti-Legal Turn?" *The Journal of Political Philosophy*, 23, no. 4 (December 2015): 427–49; Barbara Allen, "Martin Luther King's Civil Disobedience and the American Covenant Tradition," *The Journal of Federalism*, 30, no. 4 (Fall 2000): 71–113.

4. John Rawls, *A Theory of Justice* (Cambridge, MA: Harvard University Press, 1971), 364. On the context of these theories, see Erin R. Pineda, *Seeing Like an Activist: Civil Disobedience and the Civil Rights Movement* (Oxford University Press, 2021), chapter 1.

5. Guy Aitchison, "(Un)civil Disobedience," *Raisons politiques*, 1, no. 69 (2018): 7.

6. David Lyons, "Moral Judgment, Historical Reality, and Civil Disobedience," *Philosophy & Public Affairs*, 27, no. 1 (1998): 31–49; Robin Celikates, "Rethinking Civil Disobedience as a Practice of Contestation – Beyond the Liberal Paradigm," *Constellations*, 23, no. 1 (2016): 37–45.

7. See, for example, Daniel Markovits, "Democratic Disobedience," *Yale Law Journal*, 114 (2005): 1897–952; Bernard Harcourt, "Political Disobedience," in *Occupy: Three Inquiries in Disobedience*, ed. W.J. T. Mitchell, Harcourt, and M. Taussig (Chicago, IL: University of Chicago Press, 2013), 45–92; Delmas, *Duty to Resist*.

8. The language of the "militant" and the "moderate" comes from Martin Luther King, Jr., *Stride Toward Freedom: The Montgomery Story* (Boston, MA: Beacon Press, 2010), 48.

9. King was arrested during a sit-in campaign, and was sent to prison to serve a yearlong sentence on charges that he had violated the terms of a prior suspended sentence for driving without a license. Upon his release in October 1960, he gave an interview in which he first articulated the distinction between just and unjust laws – a distinction he would continue to sharpen and develop, eventually reworking it for his 1963 "Letter from a Birmingham Jail." While King had elaborated the first three explanations given in this latter text several years earlier, as he defended the sit-in movement through 1960–61, the last one – the just law wielded unjustly – was devised to speak specifically to the conditions that landed King in jail in Birmingham; it appeared for the first time in the "Letter." See "Interview after Release from Georgia State Prison at Reidsville," in *The Papers of Martin Luther King, Jr. Volume V: Threshold of a New Decade, January 1959– December 1960*, ed. Clayborne Carson (Berkeley and Los Angeles, CA: University of California Press, 2005), 535–36.

10. King, *Why We Can't Wait* (New York and Toronto: New American Library, 1964), 82.

11. Debate with James J. Kilpatrick on "The Nation's Future," in *King Papers V*, 556–64.

12. Milton Eisenhower et al., *To Establish Justice, To Insure Domestic Tranquility: The Final Report of the National Commission on the Causes and Prevention of Violence* (Washington, D.C.: United States Government Printing Office, 1969), 99.

13. A detailed account of this exchange is provided in Allen, "Covenant Tradition."

14. King, Letter to John H. Herriford, in *The Papers of Martin Luther King, Jr. Volume VII: To Save the Soul of America, January 1961–August 1962* (Berkeley and Los Angeles, CA: University of California Press, 2014),

190–91; King, "The Time for Freedom Has Come," in *King Papers VII*, 275–76.

15. When King explains the difference between just and unjust laws, he always begins with a moral law principle, then goes on to specify additional ways of making the matter more "concrete" or practical. My interpretation of this differs slightly from Scheuerman, who reads King as "implicitly" recognizing the insufficiency of natural law arguments about "the fundaments of the human personality" in "a pluralistic society with radically diverging moral and religious views." In contrast, I find it meaningful that King continued to insist on the *centrality* of the problem in terms of the "human personality," rendering his other explanations of unjust laws as concrete examples of this core problem. Nevertheless, I share with Scheuerman the view that King's thinking here cannot be reduced to the purely moral, but is also constitutively political. See Scheuerman, "Anti-Legal Turn," 430. For a complementary account to my one, but one which situates King's insistence on the human personality within his theology, see Livingston, "Tough Love."

16. David Scott, *Conscripts of Modernity: The Tragedy of Colonial Enlightenment* (Durham and London: Duke University Press, 2004), 4.

17. The account that follows in this section and the next is adapted from Pineda, "The Awful Roar: Civil Disobedience, the Civil Rights Movement, and the Politics of Creative Disorder" (PhD thesis, Yale University, 2015), chapter 4. It also largely comports with Mantena, "Showdown for Nonviolence," and Livingston, "Tough Love."

18. On the role of the theology of personalism in King's thought, see Allen, "Covenant Tradition"; Livingston, "Tough Love"; and Patterson, "A Covenant of the Heart."

19. King, "The Ethical Demands of Integration," in *A Testament of Hope: The Essential Writings and Speeches of Martin Luther King Jr.*, ed. James M. Washington (New York: Harper, 1986), 118–19.

20. King, "Ethical Demands," 120.

21. King, "Ethical Demands," 121–22; King, *Why We Can't Wait*, 77.

22. King, "Ethical Demands," 119; King, *Why We Can't Wait*, 93, 119–20. Beyond the particular documents of the American founding, King identifies the principle of democracy as centered on this conception of equality and mutuality. See, e.g., King, "The Negro and the American Dream," in *King Papers VII*, 113.

23. King, *Stride Toward Freedom*, 193.

24. To recognize this is not, I think, to render King's thought purely moral and religious, rather than political and democratic. Rather, as Alexander Livingston has compellingly argued, for King, the two are interdependent. See Livingston, "Tough Love." In contrast, see Patterson, "Covenant of the Heart."

25. Within this framework, segregation was not the only evil or sin of this kind that King identified in the world; rather, segregation shared this essential "sinful" status with colonialism, militarism, poverty, and all forms of racial domination (what he called "racialism"). King's ontology tied these structures together as related systems of oppression; furthermore, for King the stakes of nonviolent struggle in the US increasingly took on world-historical importance, as the struggle to transform the mid-century American state sat at the nexus of all of them. See, e.g., King, "Nonviolence: The Only Road," in *Testament of Hope*, 61; King, *Where Do We Go from Here: Chaos or Community?* (Boston, MA: Beacon Press, 2010).

26. King, *Stride Toward Freedom*, 20, 101.

27. King, "Facing the Challenge of a New Age," in *Testament of Hope*, 137.

28. King, "The Case Against Tokenism," in *Testament of Hope*, 108.

29. King, *Stride Toward Freedom*, 39.

30. King, *Why We Can't Wait*, 127.

31. King, *Stride Toward Freedom*, 70, 198; W.E.B. Du Bois, *Black Reconstruction in America, 1860–1880* (New York: Free Press, 1992), 700–01.

32. George Shulman, *American Prophecy: Race and Redemption in American Political Culture* (Minneapolis, MN: University of Minnesota Press, 2008), 111.

33. King, "The Role of the Behavioral Scientist in the Civil Rights Movement," *Journal of Social Issues*, 24, no. 1 (January 1968): 218, 220, 222. The term "malignant kinship" comes from King, *Why We Can't Wait*, 24.

34. Here, I use the term "white democracy" in the sense of Joel Olson, *The Abolition of White Democracy* (Minneapolis, MN: University of Minnesota Press, 2004).

35. King, *Why We Can't Wait*, 111–12. This idea places King in the tradition of theorizing "comparative freedom" within the tradition of Black political thought. See Boxill, "Roots of Civil Disobedience."

36. King was well aware (particularly by the late 1960s) that the gains of this renewed sense of political efficacy were fragile ones if they consistently failed to produce tangible, meaningful external gains – or if nonviolence was repeatedly met with violent white recalcitrance. See Moody-Adams, "Conscientious Citizenship."

37. King, *Why We Can't Wait*, 37.

38. Terry, "After Ferguson," *The Point* (June 2015), https://thepointmag.com /politics/after-ferguson/.

39. Mantena, "Showdown for Nonviolence," 99. Emphasis added.

40. King, *Why We Can't Wait*, 34–35.

41. King, *Stride Toward Freedom*, 214.

42. King, "Ethical Demands"; Grace Lee Boggs, "The Beloved Community of Martin Luther King, Jr.," *Yes! Magazine*, May 20, 2004.

43. Hannah Arendt, "Civil Disobedience," in *Crises of the Republic* (New York: Harcourt Brace 1972), 67. Unlike Arendt's suggestion, however, that these obstacles are purely individual and internal, King relies on the dynamic dialectic between self and others, rendering the work of nonviolent direct action collective and political as well as individual and moral.

44. Juliet Hooker, "Black Lives Matter and the Paradoxes of U.S. Black Politics: From Democratic Sacrifice to Democratic Repair," *Political Theory*, 44, no. 4 (2016): 448–69.

45. See, for example, Harmeet Kaur, "About 93% of racial justice protests in the US have been peaceful, a new report finds," CNN.com, September 4, 2020, www.cnn.com/2020/09/04/us/blm-protests-peaceful-report-trnd/index.html; Janie Haseman et al., "Tracking protests across the USA in the wake of George Floyd's death," *USA Today*, June 18, 2020, www.usatoday.com/in-depth/graphics/2020/06/03/map-protests-wake-george-floyds-death/5310149002/; Kim Parker, Juliana Menasce Horowitz, and Monica Anderson, "Amid Protests, Majorities Across Racial and Ethnic Groups Express Support for the Black Lives Matter Movement," *Pew Research Center*, June 12, 2020, www .pewsocialtrends.org/2020/06/12/amid-protests-majorities-across-racial -and-ethnic-groups-express-support-for-the-black-lives-matter-movement/.

46. Robin D.G. Kelley, "How Today's Abolitionist Movement Can Fundamentally Change the Country," interview by Jeremy Scahill,

Intercepted, June 27, 2020, transcript, https://theintercept.com/2020/06/27/robin-dg-kelley-intercepted/.

47. To be clear, given the reality – and durability – of white supremacy in the United States, neither is there cause for unmitigated optimism. Rather, I want to suggest that – learning from King – disobedient civility requires a radical belief in the power of action to create new subjects and relations, *not* a simplistic faith in a white moral psychology already primed to respond meaningfully to Black collective action. On the theological underpinnings of this "faith," see Livingston, "Tough Love," 861.

3   Liberalism: John Rawls and Ronald Dworkin

Alexander Kaufman

A liberal theory of civil disobedience aims to address the following question: if social institutions are for the most part just, what should a citizen with a sense of justice do when confronted with an unjust law? Liberal theory responds to this question by arguing that moderately unjust legislation remains legitimate – and the duty of citizens to comply with the law remains effective – only as long as the legislation could be accepted by rational persons reflecting under fair conditions on the justice of their institutions. A liberal theory must therefore offer an account of the conditions under which the duty to comply with laws enacted by the legislature of a nearly just democratic ceases to be binding and the forms of lawbreaking or resistance that may be employed once legislation passes this point. More particularly, a liberal theory of disobedience must address two issues. First, it must set out the grounds that justify disobedience and the conditions under which such action is justified. Second, it must provide an account of justifiable noncompliance that explains the role of civil disobedience in a nearly just constitutional system and specify the kind of dissent that distinguishes civil disobedience from other forms of opposition to political authority.

The work of John Rawls and Ronald Dworkin dominates contemporary liberal civil disobedience theory. Rawls provides a comprehensive discussion that addresses both the justification and the nature of justifiable noncompliance with the law, while Dworkin addresses objections to civil disobedience relating to issues of fairness and legal validity. This chapter will provide a relatively expansive account of Rawls's and Dworkin's treatment of these issues.

LEGITIMATE POLITICAL POWER AND ITS LIMITS

An account of civil disobedience, Rawls argues, must begin with an account of why a person has any duty at all to obey an unjust law. Such an account must then determine the point at which the enactments of the majority must be viewed as so unjust that the duty to support just institutions is no longer binding – such an account, that is, must determine "the grounds and limits of political duty and obligation" (TJ 172).[1]

Rawls thus develops his account of civil disobedience from an analysis of the grounds and limits of the concepts of duty and obligation. Rawls's argument works from the assumption that if citizens have a duty to obey institutions or an obligation to respect the authority of the rules of those institutions, then the institutions possess legitimate political authority. This section will examine Rawls's accounts of duty and obligation as they relate to political authority and its limits. In particular, the section will discuss Rawls's accounts of (1) the duties and obligation of citizens; (2) the duty to obey unjust laws; and (3) the nature of a legitimate constitutional regime.

Duty and Obligation

Rawls begins his analysis by distinguishing between natural duties and social obligations. Social obligation (TJ 96) is the condition of being required to obey the rules of an institution or practice, and a social obligation applies if two requirements are met: (1) the institution or practice is just or fair; and (2) the person has voluntarily accepted benefits provided by the institution. All obligations, Rawls argues, arise from the principle of fairness which holds that a person is obligated to "do his part" under the rules of a just or fair institution if he or she "has voluntarily accepted the benefits of the scheme or has taken advantage of the opportunities it offers to advance his interests" (TJ 301). Obligations, Rawls notes, have three characteristic features: they arise from our voluntary acts; the content of the obligation is defined by the rules of the institution or practice; and the obligations generated are to specific persons, in particular, the other persons cooperating within the institution or practice.

If the authority of political institutions derived solely from a principle of obligation, however, then citizens would only be bound to respect the authority of a just constitution if they had voluntarily accepted and intend to continue to accept the social benefits that the constitution produces. Yet citizens who are born into and begin their lives under a constitution could reasonably question the degree to which their acceptance of benefits should be viewed as voluntary. Rawls therefore concludes that a complementary principle – the principle of natural duty – provides a better foundation for an account of political authority than a principle of obligation.

Natural duties apply to persons irrespective of their voluntary acts and do not have any necessary relation to the rules of institutions or practices. A person may be subject to a duty even if she has not acted in a way that might justify claims against her by others. Natural duties are not owed to definite individuals – they are owed to all others "as equal moral persons" (TJ 99). Examples of natural duties include the duty to help others in need, the duty not to harm others, and the duty not to cause unnecessary suffering. Our most reliable considered judgments, Rawls suggests, confirm that a person need not commit a voluntary act in order to become subject to such duties. In fact, as Rawls notes, "a promise not to be cruel is normally ludicrously redundant" (TJ 98). Natural duties, rather than deriving from acts or practices, reflect the requirements of the principles for social behavior that rational persons would accept in the original position.

The most fundamental natural duties include a duty to support just institutions that exist and to further just arrangements when they are absent. Since persons have a duty to support just institutions, those institutions may be properly viewed as possessing legitimate political authority. The foundation of political authority is thus the natural duty to support just institutions. This duty is not limited to institutions that are perfectly just – rather, citizens may have a natural duty to support and maintain a regime that is moderately unjust. Unless citizens have a duty to obey the moderately unjust legislation of a normally just regime, Rawls appears to assume, the stable maintenance of a just constitution may not be feasible. Rather, if institutions and laws *could* have been generated through a just process and do not invade fundamental liberty interests, they satisfy the minimum criterion of legitimacy: "if the law actually voted is, so far as one can ascertain, within the range of those that could reasonably be favored by rational legislators conscientiously trying to follow the principles of justice, then the decision of the majority is practically authoritative, though not definitive" (TJ 318).

In *Political Liberalism*, Rawls further develops this criterion: "our exercise of political power is proper and hence justifiable only when it is exercised in accordance with a constitution the essentials of which all citizens may reasonably be expected to endorse in light of principles and ideals acceptable to them as reasonable and rational" (PL 217).[2] This criterion of legitimacy, Samuel Freeman emphasizes, does not simply constitute an interpretation of the *formal* notion of legitimacy. Rather than requiring merely that authority must be conferred in accordance with recognized procedures, Rawls's criterion of legitimacy provides a "moral/political standard" specifying the minimum moral requirements that must be met before an institution, official, or law may be viewed as possessing legitimate authority.[3] In particular, laws and institutions must satisfy a specific substantive requirement: they must be consistent with the substance of a constitution that could reasonably be accepted by democratic citizens.

Sebastiano Maffetone neglects precisely this aspect of Rawls's principle of legitimacy when he argues that "Rawls' concept of legitimacy in [*Political Liberalism*] oscillates ambiguously between two notions."[4] One of these notions, he claims, corresponds to the formal notion of legitimacy deriving from the Weberian tradition; while the second notion imposes specific substantive requirements that must be satisfied before a regime may be viewed as legitimate. To establish that Rawls sometimes employs a purely formal Weberian notion of legitimacy, Maffetone cites language from Rawls's "Reply to Habermas": "we may think 'legitimate' and 'just' the same. A little reflection shows that they are not. A legitimate king or queen may rule by just and effective government, but then they may not .... Their being legitimate says something about their pedigree: *how they came to their office.*"[5] In stating that legitimacy is a weaker requirement than justice and one that focuses on pedigree, Maffetone asserts, this passage in Rawls must refer to a purely formal notion of legitimacy. Thus, Maffetone concludes, Rawls in some cases employs a purely formal notion of legitimacy.

Maffetone, however, misunderstands the passage that he cites, because he incorrectly assigns a purely formal meaning to the phrase "how they came to office." As discussed above, Rawls argues that a law or institution is legitimate if it falls "within the range of those that could reasonably be favored by rational legislators conscientiously trying to follow the principles of justice" (TJ 318). Rawls's account of legitimacy therefore requires not merely that a regime came to power in a manner consistent with recognized procedures, but rather that the regime could have come to power through a process in which reasonable and rational persons conscientiously trying to follow the principles of justice consented to those institutions. Far from describing a purely formal notion of legitimacy, then, the language that Maffetone cites sets out a normative account of legitimacy. Maffetone thus fails to provide evidence that Rawls employs a purely formal Weberian notion of legitimacy. Maffetone's argument that Rawls's concept of legitimacy in *Political Liberalism* oscillates ambiguously between two notions of legitimacy therefore fails.[6]

The Duty to Obey Unjust Law

In his account of political authority, Rawls first focuses on a problematic implication of the duty to support just institutions – if just institutions enact unjust legislation, the duty to support just institutions would appear to require obedience to those unjust laws. If social institutions are for the most part just, Rawls asks, what should a citizen with a sense of justice do when confronted with an unjust law? Rawls immediately reframes the issue as a question to be examined from the perspective of the second (constitutional) stage of the original position: could a rational person in an initial position of equality consent to a constitutional rule that would require obedience to unjust laws? In particular, how could a free rational person consent to institutions that would bind him to accept as authoritative laws that give effect to opinions that he views as unjust?

Once the question is restated in this form, Rawls argues, "the answer is clear enough" (TJ 311). Among the limited number of feasible political institutions that we could adopt, none would always produce legislation that each individual views as just. The choosers know the standard of justice that they aim to realize – the standard defined by the two principles of justice as fairness. No form of constitution, however, could ensure that this standard will be fully realized. Political institutions under feasible constitutions are particularly prone to injustice, Rawls notes, because any acceptable form of constitution must respect the principle of majority rule by assigning legislative power to a democratically elected representative body. The first principle of justice, Rawls has argued in Chapter 4 of *Theory*, requires that each citizen possess as close as possible to equal opportunity to influence the resolution of questions of public justice and policy. But while justice requires democratic government, Rawls notes, "[t]here is nothing to the view ... that what the majority wills is right" (TJ 313). As Rawls notes, "none of the traditional conceptions of justice have held" such a view (TJ 313). Majorities of voters are bound to make mistakes of judgment due to lack of information, errors of judgment, and partial or self-interested views. Thus, while it is appropriate for the citizens of a well-ordered society to accept democratic decisions as authoritative, "they do not [and should not] submit their judgment to it" (TJ 314). The best feasible constitution, then, will predictably lead to the enactment of unjust legislation.

Nevertheless, the best feasible constitution provides the closest approximation of justice.

The choosers of a just constitution in the second stage of the original position deliberations know the standard that they wish to realize but must employ an imperfect procedure to realize that standard. Consent to a form of constitution by the choosers in the original position therefore constitutes an instance of imperfect procedural justice. While any feasible constitution will therefore realize justice imperfectly, Rawls argues that consent to one of these forms of constitution "is surely preferable to no agreement at all" (TJ 311). The choosers in the second stage of the original position would therefore consent both to the principle of majority rule and to accept the authority of legislation enacted under that principle that they view as unjust.

Certain conditions, however, limit this consent to the authority of unjust laws. First, the burdens produced by unjust legislation should be "more or less evenly" distributed over individuals and groups, and hardships produced by unjust policies "should not weigh too heavily in any particular case" (TJ 312). Second, no citizen should be required to accept invasions of his or her basic liberties. Generally, Rawls concludes, the duty to comply with unjust laws holds only as long as those laws "do not exceed certain bounds of injustice" (TJ 312). In order to apply this intuition, Rawls's theory requires a specific account of the nature of a just regime that defines the form and degree of injustice that justifies or requires civil disobedience.

A Just Constitutional Regime

Citizens have a duty to obey law and to respect the authority of existing institutions that are established by a (for the most part) just constitution. Such a just constitution must satisfy the requirements of equal liberty and must be the feasible just arrangement most likely to result in a just and effective system of legislation. A just constitutional regime, Rawls notes, consists of a number of basic elements. First, the authority to legislate is assigned to a representative legislature that is accountable to the electorate. Second, firm constitutional protections are provided for certain liberties, in particular freedom of speech and assembly, and the liberty to form political associations.

The principle of equal liberty, when applied to constitutional design, requires that all citizens must be assured "an equal right to take part in, and to determine the outcome of, the constitutional process that establishes the laws with which they are to comply" (TJ 194). Rawls refers to the liberty principle, as applied at the constitutional level, as the equal participation principle. This principle, Rawls states, transfers the notion of fair representation from the original position to the constitution.

Rawls emphasizes three requirements that the equal participation principle imposes on constitutional regimes. First, each vote should have approximately the same weight in determining the outcomes of elections. Interpreted strictly, this requirement would mandate that each member of the legislature should represent the same number of constituents and that legislative districts are drawn up under the guidance of standards designed to prevent gerrymandering. Rawls concedes, however, that it may be necessary to introduce some "random elements" in the process of designing districts since "the criteria for designing constituencies are no doubt to some extent arbitrary" (TJ 196). In addition, citizens must have equal access to public office – that is, each must be eligible to join political parties, to run for office, and to hold political offices.

Second, the principle of equal participation requires that significant political decisions must be decided by the bare majority rule, as long as those decisions do not involve issues on which the constitution limits the scope of majority power. Employment of the bare majority rule is intended to implement the requirement that all citizens must be assured an equal right to determine the outcome of the process that establishes the laws. The restriction on the scope of majority power simply acknowledges that equal political liberty is only one of the basic political liberties and that respect for the will of the majority cannot justify institutional arrangements that violate fundamental interests protected by the other basic liberties.

Third, the constitution must contain elements that secure the worth of political liberty. In particular, the constitution must underwrite fair opportunity for citizens to participate in the political process. Freedom of speech and assembly, and liberty of thought and conscience, which are protected under the first principle, are essential to ensuring the worth of political liberty. In addition, all citizens should have the means to be informed about political issues and should have a fair opportunity to affect the political agenda. Moreover, Rawls notes, liberties protected by the equal liberty principle will lose much of their value if those with greater private means are permitted to exploit their advantages to dominate public debate. A just arrangement must therefore take steps to preserve the equal value of political liberties. These steps may include the provision of funds to encourage free public discussion, public financing of political campaigns, and government efforts to avoid extreme concentration of wealth. In addition, just arrangements must secure the worth of liberty by ensuring that constraints such as poverty, ignorance, or lack of means generally do not deprive persons of their capacity to take advantage of their rights.

While a just constitutional order must satisfy the equal participation principle, however, Rawls notes that such a just social arrangement will nevertheless need to regulate or restrict certain aspects of political liberty. Following Kant, Rawls argues that a basic liberty may be limited "only for the sake of liberty itself" (TJ 179) – that is, only to ensure that that liberty or some other basic liberty is properly protected. The basic liberties, Rawls argues, are to be assessed as a whole – that is, as a single system (TJ 178). Each liberty is to be defined so that the central applications of each can be simultaneously secured.

Rawls notes that liberties may be limited in three ways: (1) the constitution may define freedom of participation more or less extensively; (2) the constitution may allow inequalities in political liberties; and (3) larger or smaller amounts of social resources may be devoted to insuring the worth of freedom. The *extent* of the principle of participation is determined by the extent to which the constitution restricts the application of the bare majority rule. A bill of rights generally removes certain liberties from majority regulation altogether, and separation of powers and judicial review also restrict the power of the legislature. These and other permissible restrictions on the extent of the principle of participation must bear equally on all persons. These restrictions are justified because they protect the other freedoms. Thus, restrictions on majority rule in a constitution are justified to the extent that the arrangements structured by the constitution further the ends of liberty, in particular, by mitigating the defects of the majority principle (TJ 201).

JUSTIFIABLE NONCOMPLIANCE

If social institutions are for the most part just, what should a citizen with a sense of justice do when confronted with an unjust law? While citizens have a general duty to obey unjust laws, Rawls discusses two forms of justifiable resistance: (1) civil disobedience; and (2) conscientious refusal. Since the contrast between these forms plays an important role in Rawls's specification of the qualities of civil disobedience, his discussion of conscientious refusal constitutes an essential component of his account of civil disobedience, and the two forms of noncompliance are therefore discussed together in this section.

Civil Disobedience

Rawls's account of civil disobedience is designed to extend his account of the principles of natural duty and obligation by determining the point at which the duty to comply with laws enacted by the legislature of a nearly just democracy ceases to be binding. A constitutional theory of disobedience, Rawls notes, has three parts. It must define civil disobedience by specifying the kind of dissent that distinguishes it from other forms of opposition to political authority; it must set out the grounds that justify disobedience and the conditions under which such action is justified; and it must explain the role of civil disobedience in a nearly just constitutional system.

Kind of Dissent

Rawls defines civil disobedience as a public, nonviolent political act contrary to law that is done with the aim of bringing about a change in law or policy. Civil disobedience specifically addresses the sense of justice of the majority and declares that the principles of justice that the majority accepts are not being respected. Civil disobedience, then, challenges the majority to live up to its own principles. Rawls immediately offers two qualifications of this definition. First, he notes that the civilly disobedient act need not violate the particular act that is being protested. There are, Rawls notes, often strong reasons for not violating a particular unjust law. For example, if the government enacts a vague or unacceptably harsh law against treason, civil disobedience in protest of that law need not – in fact, should not – take the form of committing treason. Rather, the protestor may present her case by violating traffic ordinances or laws of trespass. In other cases, such as laws affecting foreign affairs or another part of the country, there may be no way for an individual to violate the law directly. Second, Rawls notes that a civilly disobedient act must in fact be contrary to law, in the sense that the protestors are not merely raising a test case to be resolved in the courts. Rather, they must be prepared to continue violating the statute even if it is upheld and to accept the legal consequences.

A civilly disobedient act is essentially political in nature, both because it is addressed to the majority and because the act is "guided and justified by political principles" (TJ 321). That is, in civil disobedience, the protestor does not appeal to her personal moral or religious views or principles. Rather, she appeals only to a conception of justice that is commonly shared. The majority's deliberate and persistent violation of the principles of that conception, in particular the violation of basic liberties, invites submission but justifies resistance. Civil disobedience, Rawls notes, "forces the majority to consider whether it wishes to have its actions construed in this way" (TJ 321) or whether it wishes, instead, to conform to its own conception of justice. Civil disobedience, then, is designed to call attention to an inconsistency between the conception of justice that the majority affirms and its policies.

A related point, Rawls notes, is that civil disobedience is public. The protestor does not merely violate an unjust law; her action, rather, is the public expression of her case against the law. One may, Rawls suggests, compare it to public speech – it is a form of address, an expression of conscientious political conviction. It tries to avoid the use of violence, not because of personal or principled abhorrence of the use of violence, but because violent acts are likely to undermine the case that the protestor is attempting to present to the majority. Interference with the civil liberties of others, Rawls asserts, in fact "tends to obscure the civilly disobedient quality of one's act" (TJ 321).

The avoidance of violence is also appropriate for civilly disobedient resistance because civil disobedience has the curious quality of expressing disobedience to the law within the limits of fidelity to the law. Fidelity to the law is expressed by the public and nonviolent nature of the act, and by the actor's willingness to accept the legal consequences of her conduct. This quality, Rawls notes, distinguishes civil disobedience from militant resistance to the state. Militant resistance, Rawls notes, is much more profoundly opposed to the existing political arrangements. The militant does not view those arrangements as nearly just; rather, he views them as committed to a mistaken conception of justice or one that departs significantly from its fundamental principles. The militant, then, does not appeal to the majority's sense of justice; rather, he seeks to disrupt and replace what he views as an unacceptable public conception of justice. The contrast with militant resistance, then, illustrates the sense in which civil disobedience is informed by the quality of fidelity to the law. While militant resistance is profoundly opposed to the public's understanding of justice and existing political arrangements, civil disobedience is designed to restore the justice of law or policy within existing institutional arrangements.

Grounds Justifying Civil Disobedience

Civil disobedience is justified, Rawls argues, only under a limited number of circumstances. First, civil disobedience is justifiable as a response only to instances of substantial and clear injustice. Thus, Rawls suggests that there must be a presumption that civil disobedience is justified only in circumstances involving serious infringements of the first principle of justice or blatant denials of equal opportunity under the principle of fair equality of opportunity. When, for example, certain minorities are denied the right to participate in the process of democratic self-government or to own property, the infringement of basic rights is sufficiently serious to justify civil disobedience. In contrast, Rawls suggests, since it is generally more difficult to establish definitively that the difference principle has been violated, violations of that principle provide a less acceptable justification for civil disobedience. Second, civil disobedience is appropriate only after the normal forms of appeal to the political majority have been made and have failed – attempts to repeal the unjust laws have failed, and legal protests have had no success. Third, it must not be the case that the civil disobedience threatens to cause disorder so serious that the existing and generally just constitution could no longer be effective.

Each individual must judge for herself the precise point at which these conditions are satisfied and the prima facie duty to obey the law ceases to be binding. Whether existing circumstances justify civil disobedience is therefore a question that is likely to generate reasonable disagreement.

Role of Civil Disobedience

In engaging in civil disobedience, Rawls asserts, citizens serve notice on the majority that the conditions of fair cooperation are being violated. As long as society is understood as a scheme of cooperation among equals, civil disobedience can be understood to be a stabilizing (if illegal) device of a constitutional system. As long as it is employed with restraint, Rawls suggests, civil disobedience can be seen to operate in a manner similar to regular elections and judicial review – that is, as a device that helps to maintain the justice of institutions.

A number of commentators have raised objections to Rawls's account of civil disobedience. While some critics have argued that this account is too narrowly restrictive, others have argued that it is too broadly inclusive. Here I discuss both forms of criticism and focus on articles by Robin Celikates and Robert Jubb that develop these objections.

In an influential article, Robin Celikates argues that Rawls's account improperly requires that acts of civil disobedience must conducted within the limits of fidelity to existing law.[7] Such an account, Celikates argues, unjustifiably excludes from the category of civil disobedience acts that express the rejection of an existing political order. Many disobedients – including but not limited to Mahatma Gandhi and Martin Luther King, Jr. – expressly rejected any duty of obedience to law as it exists here and now. In contrast, Celikates concludes, Rawls defines civil disobedience in a way that inappropriately limits it to peaceful protests of rights-bearers – who acknowledge the legitimacy of existing political institutions – against acts of the majority that violate constitutionally guaranteed protections. Such an account, Celikates argues, obscures the transformative character of civil disobedience as a form of contestation that challenges state authority.

Celikates's argument, however, misunderstands Rawls's argument. Rawls's account of civil disobedience is "designed only for the special case of a nearly just society, one that is well-ordered for the most part but in which some serious violations of justice do nevertheless occur" (TJ 319). Rawls is examining a particular question: how, *in a nearly just society*, could citizens have a right or duty to violate laws properly generated by their (nearly) just institutions.

Rawls's account of civil disobedience does not, then, require acceptance of the authority of political institutions generally – Rawls simply examines the case in which institutions *are* sufficiently just to be accepted as legitimate. Indeed, since "Rawls' restrictive conditions for politically motivated law-breaking apply only in nearly just societies," Robert Jubb argues, "Rawls' theory of when illegal protest is justified is, if anything, too permissive rather than too restrictive."[8]

In Rawls's account, Jubb claims, "[p]olitical orders either are fully authoritative or lack all authority,"[9] and the necessary condition for political authority is (near) justice. Therefore, political institutions in "societies that are not [nearly] just have no political authority."[10] Societies fail to satisfy the *near justice* criterion, Jubb claims, if they fail to meet the requirements of Rawls's two principles or if they endorse different and inadequate principles of justice. Thus, Jubb concludes, Rawls's criteria of *near justice* are so demanding that they are satisfied by very few – if any – existing societies. According to Jubb's interpretation, then, Rawls's theory licenses any and all forms of disobedience or violent resistance against the governments of almost existing political societies.

While Jubb corrects one error in the interpretation of Rawls's argument, his interpretation is based upon an equally serious confusion. Rawls does not argue that political regimes are either fully authoritative (because *nearly just*) or lack all authority. Rather, as discussed above, Rawls argues that citizens have a duty to support and maintain a regime that is *moderately unjust*. As long as institutions and laws *could* have been generated through a just process and do not invade fundamental liberty interests, Rawls argues, they satisfy the minimum criterion of legitimacy: "if the law actually voted is, so far as one can ascertain, within the range of those that could reasonably be favored by rational legislators conscientiously trying to follow the principles of justice, then the decision of the majority is practically authoritative, though not definitive" (TJ 318). Since Rawls does not argue for a rigidly binary criterion of legitimacy (either nearly just or lacking authority) as

Jubb claims, Rawls's account of civil disobedience is not unduly permissive.

Celikates's critique of Rawls's account of civil disobedience argues that Rawls's account is too restrictive, while Jubb's critique suggests that Rawls's account is too permissive. Both critiques, however, fail. Celikates misunderstands Rawls's argument because he fails to recognize its limited scope. Jubb assumes that Rawls would determine whether political institutions possess legitimate authority by imposing a binary test, but Rawls explicitly rejects such a view.

Conscientious Refusal

Rawls contrasts civil disobedience with conscientious refusal in order to define the character of civil disobedience more precisely and to provide an account of justifiable nonpolitical resistance to unjust law in nearly just conditions. Like his theory of civil disobedience, Rawls's account of conscientious refusal has three parts. It specifies the kind of dissent that distinguishes conscientious refusal from other forms of opposition to political authority; it sets out the conditions under which conscientious refusal is justified; and it explains the role of civil disobedience in a nearly just constitutional system.

Kind of Dissent

Rawls defines conscientious refusal as noncompliance with a legal injunction or administrative order. The order is addressed to the dissenter, and the authorities are aware of her noncompliance. Rawls cites as examples the refusal of early Christians to participate in rites prescribed by pagan states, the refusal of pacifists to serve in the armed forces, and the refusal of a soldier to obey a manifestly unjust order.

Conscientious refusal is not political in nature, since acts of conscientious refusal are not designed to appeal to the majority's sense of justice. While such acts are not covert, they do not constitute efforts to address the majority. Rather, the dissenter simply refuses to obey a command or legal injunction. The dissenter does not, then, justify his act by appealing to the community's conception of justice or political principles. Thus, unlike civil disobedience, conscientious refusal – while not covert – is not public.

Grounds Justifying Conscientious Refusal

In his account of the grounds justifying conscientious refusal, Rawls extends the discussion beyond the range of domestic affairs to a consideration of the law of nations. Rawls's purpose in this discussion is to illustrate *the kind of moral reflection* that could generate judgments justifying conscientious refusal. In order to form reliable judgments relating to issues concerning the law of nations, Rawls suggests, a person must view those issues from a standpoint reflecting an extended interpretation of the original position. In this interpretation, the parties are viewed as representatives of different nations who must choose fundamental principles to regulate conflicting claims among states. The extended interpretation of the original position, Rawls argues, provides a basis for the judgment that representatives of free and equal nations would choose a set of principles including the principles of the equality of nations, the right to self-determination, the right to self-defense, and respect for treaties. As in the case of the domestic original position, this extended interpretation of the original position is designed to neutralize the influence of considerations that are arbitrary from the moral point of view – such as contingencies of history or endowment of natural resources – over the choice of principles.

Role of Conscientious Refusal

Rawls declines to provide an explicit account of the justifying conditions of conscientious refusal,[11] but his discussion of both the definition of and grounds justifying conscientious refusal offers some indication of his views regarding its role. In discussing pacifism as a justified form of conscientious refusal, for example, Rawls suggests that respect accorded to pacifism may alert citizens to the wrongs that may be committed by the state. Even if the views of the pacifist are not completely sound, Rawls asserts, the pacifist's warnings "may have the result that on balance the principles of justice are more rather than less secure" (TJ 325). Rawls's accounts of civil disobedience and conscientious refusal thus supplement his account of the principles of natural duty and obligation by determining the point at which the duty to comply with laws enacted by the legislature of a nearly just democracy ceases to be binding.

FAIRNESS

How, Dworkin asks, should the government treat persons who disobey the law on the basis of principled disagreement or conscience? Is it fair to treat such persons more leniently than persons who deliberately violate laws that they acknowledge to be valid? Dworkin's response to these questions focuses on the distinction between deliberately violating a valid law and testing the validity of legal standard.

Dissenting behavior designed to test the validity of a law or to express reasonable resistance to a particular interpretation of a law, Dworkin asserts, performs an important and protected function within America's legal system. Such behavior constitutes "the chief vehicle we have for challenging the law on moral grounds" (TRS 212).[12] A person engaging in dissenting behavior designed to challenge a law "does not behave unfairly so long as he proceeds on his own considered and reasonable view of what the law requires" (TRS 214).

But what, Dworkin asks, about persons who do not possess the expertise to question the law's validity and instead offer moral justifications for their behavior? Dworkin offers the examples of persons who objected to the draft laws during the Vietnam War on the grounds that the law (1) unfairly deferred or exempted only students from privileged backgrounds, and (2) exempted religious dissenters but not moral dissenters. These and similar moral objections, Dworkin notes, provide a persuasive basis for legal (in particular, constitutional) arguments against the validity of the law in question.

Discrimination in favor of privileged students arguably denied less privileged students equal protection under the law, while the draft law's failure to show the same respect for moral objections that it showed for religious objections was arguably arbitrary and unreasonable. The constitution, Dworkin concludes, "makes our conventional morality relevant to the question of validity; any statute that appears to compromise that morality raises constitutional questions" (TRS 208). Dissent grounded in a persuasive moral objection should, therefore, be viewed as equivalent to a legal argument questioning a law's validity.

When a plausible case can be made for an interpretation of law at variance with the view of established legal institutions, a citizen may – Dworkin asserts – fairly act on his or her own judgment. The practices and tradition of American law "permit and encourage him to follow his own judgment in such cases" (TRS 215). The government and the courts therefore have a responsibility to protect such citizens from the most severe legal consequences of such action when doing so will not do significant damage to other policies. The government cannot guarantee immunity from prosecution in all such cases, because such a position would interfere too seriously with the government's ability to carry out its policies. But if the case for prosecuting is relatively weak, the government should – Dworkin argues – err in favor of tolerance.

DISTINGUISHING THE GROUNDS OF DISOBEDIENCE: PRINCIPLE VS. POLICY

Dworkin distinguishes between civil disobedience grounded in (1) convictions of principle and (2) judgments of policy.[13] A person who refused to return an escaped slave under the Fugitive Slave Act because their consciences forbade them to obey such an unjust law, for example, acted based upon convictions of principle. Disobedience grounded in policy, in contrast, is motivated by the conviction that the law being violated constitutes dangerously bad policy.

Principle-Based Disobedience

Dworkin distinguishes between two forms of principle-based disobedience. In the case of *integrity-based* civil disobedience, a person refuses to do what her conscience absolutely forbids.[14] Such refusals to obey unjust laws, Dworkin argues, constitute the most clearly justifiable form of civil disobedience. While violence and terrorism cannot be justified based on this form of reasoning, integrity-based civil disobedience is not subject to conditions that might seem reasonable in other cases.

In the second form of principle-based civil disobedience – *justice-based disobedience* – people deliberately break the law in order to protest political programs that they cannot avoid viewing as unjust. While this form of behavior remains justified in many circumstances, Dworkin argues, its justification is subject to more stringent conditions. First, the protestor must have exhausted the normal appeals to the political process; second, the protestor must not break the law if the likely consequence of the disobedience will be to make the situation worse from the standpoint of justice.

An additional distinction – between *persuasive* and *nonpersuasive* strategies – becomes relevant in the case of justice-based disobedience. A persuasive strategy aims to force the majority to listen to arguments against their position. A nonpersuasive strategy aims to increase the costs of pursuing the unjust program that the majority favors. Nonpersuasive strategies, Dworkin notes, are in tension with the principle of majority rule, since their goal is to pressure the majority to change its position. Nonpersuasive strategies of justice-based civil disobedience are therefore justified only under limited conditions: if appeals to the political process offer no realistic chance of success; persuasive strategies offer no hope of success; nonviolent nonpersuasive strategies offer a reasonable chance of success; and if the use of a nonpersuasive strategy will not make matters worse.

Policy-Based Disobedience

In policy-based disobedience, those disobeying the law act on the conviction that the law or policy in question is dangerously unwise. Since the protestor does not claim that the policy is unjust in itself, the justification is weaker than in the case of principle-based disobedience, and the distinction between persuasive and nonpersuasive strategy becomes crucial. Since persuasive strategy merely aims to persuade the majority to change its mind, policy-based disobedience that engages in persuasive strategy is subject only to the two conditions (discussed above) that restrict justice-based disobedience.

Policy-based disobedience that employs nonpersuasive strategies is, however, in serious tension with the principle of majority rule. Dworkin argues that persons considering this form of disobedience must accept "the burden of showing how a working theory [of civil disobedience] could accept it."[15]

While Dworkin presents a plausible case that policy-based civil disobedience that employs *nonpersuasive strategy* is less well-motivated – and therefore deserves significantly less deference from state officials – than policy-based civil disobedience employing *persuasive strategy*, Dworkin's attempt to employ this distinction practically is unconvincing. Specifically, Dworkin argues that demonstrations against the deployment of nuclear missiles in western Europe in the 1980s were clearly designed to impose costs on society rather than to persuade the majority to change its mind.[16] This conclusion, Dworkin argues, justifies the judgment that the arguments that he develops for state deference for civil disobedience in most cases should not be given full weight in this case.

More particularly, Dworkin argues that the nuclear protestors must be presumed to be implementing a nonpersuasive strategy because they clearly had little prospect of changing the majority's mind. The policy questions involved – requiring complex judgments regarding the relative effectiveness of denuclearization and strategic defense systems in securing stability – were simply too complex and ambiguous for a persuasive strategy to be effective. To illustrate a contrasting case in which civil disobedience had a reasonably good probability of persuading the majority, Dworkin points to the Civil Rights demonstrations of the 1960s. The discriminatory policies protested were so shamefully unjust, Dworkin claims, that merely shedding light on them was sufficient to change minds.[17]

Dworkin's characterization of the prospects of successful persuasion in both cases, however, is misleading. His assessment of the Civil Rights Movement's persuasive potential relies unacceptably on hindsight. The Civil Rights protestors' activities did in fact eventually persuade the majority, but the majority's long-standing tolerance of racist law and policy – not merely in the South, but throughout the entire country – made the a priori probability of successful persuasion rather low.

On the other hand, Dworkin's dismissal of the persuasive potential of the nuclear protestors depends upon a misleadingly narrow characterization of their message. Dworkin claims that the protestors needed to persuade the majority to accept the complex claim that denuclearization was less likely to lead to instability than deterrence strategies based upon deployment of missiles.[18] It would be equally plausible, however, to argue that the nuclear protestors were trying to call attention to a simple and morally compelling issue – the unacceptability of deterrence strategies that rely on the credibility of threats to irradiate the planet with radioactive material. Viewed in that light, their probability of successful persuasion was much greater than Dworkin is willing to concede.

All of this suggests that, while Dworkin's distinction between forms of policy-based disobedience that rely upon persuasive and nonpersuasive strategies may be plausible, the attempt to distinguish between persuasive and nonpersuasive strategies in practice is highly complex, error-prone, and dependent upon contentious assumptions about probability of successful persuasion. Judges and legal practitioners should therefore exercise extreme caution in characterizing strategies of disobedience as nonpersuasive and in relying on that characterization to justify stringent penalties for civil disobedience.

GOVERNMENT RESPONSE

If Dworkin's more general argument is persuasive, he has established that the government has a responsibility to be lenient to dissenters who act upon reasonable judgments that a law is not valid. Dworkin summarizes the substance of this responsibility in a series of recommendations. First, prosecutors – in deciding whether to press charges – should carefully balance the responsibility to be lenient against policy considerations that favor prosecution. Second, in making her decision, the prosecutor should consider whether the law violated was designed to pursue a policy goal or to vindicate a right of individuals to be free of some harm (e.g. assault, fraud) and should assign less weight to the violation of laws that are not designed to vindicate a right. Third, persons who promote and encourage civil disobedience should not be prosecuted unless those persons promote violence or otherwise violate the rights of others. Finally, in deciding whether to prosecute the civilly disobedient, the prosecutor should reserve prosecution for cases in which failure to prosecute will *definitely* result in *serious* damage to *important* policy goals. If the impact on policy is uncertain, the prosecutor should defer prosecution until the impact is more clearly defined. In the case of draft avoiders during the Vietnam War, for example, the government should have prosecuted only when and if it had been clearly established that a failure to prosecute draft avoiders would have led to "wholesale refusals to serve" (TRS 219).

Dworkin concludes that his recommendations for leniency are consistent with fairness because a policy of strictly enforcing laws against those who reasonably question their validity would require forcing citizens to accept an unacceptable prescription for behavior. Such a policy instructs citizens to assume that their reasonable objections are wrong and to act on that assumption – it instructs the citizen, that is, to obey the authorities even when he judges that doing so is wrong. This model of behavior, Dworkin argues, is inconsistent with actual practice within our liberal tradition – a tradition that invites citizens to evaluate the arguments for various legal views and to act upon these judgments. In addition, Dworkin argues, by deterring effective challenges to statutes, such a policy would effectively give Congress, and not the courts, the final say on the constitutionality of statutes – thus violating the separation of powers.

CONCLUSION

A liberal account of civil disobedience must address two issues. First, it must set out the grounds that justify disobedience. Second, it must provide an account of justifiable noncompliance that explains the role of civil disobedience in a nearly just constitutional system. Rawls's theory offers the following accounts of these issues. Civil disobedience is justified because a just constitutional regime will require a democratic form of government, and democratically elected legislatures will predictably enact at least some unjust legislation. When the legislation enacted is sufficiently unjust – when it violates fundamental rights or liberties – the injustice outweighs the duty to obey unjust law that is usually effective under a (nearly) just constitution. Justifiable noncompliance under such conditions challenges the majority to live up to its own principles, thus strengthening both the justice and the stability of the political system. Dworkin argues, in addition, that the courts in such a system have a special responsibility to dissenters who act upon reasonable judgments that a law is not valid. In light of the important political and legal role that such dissenters perform, the courts have a responsibility to treat them as leniently as possible unless imperative policy concerns require a different decision.

NOTES

1. John Rawls, *A Theory of Justice* (Cambridge, Mass.: Harvard University Press, [1971] 1999). This work is cited in the text in parentheses and preceded by TJ.

2. John Rawls, *Political Liberalism* (New York: Columbia University Press, [1993] 1996). This work is cited in the text in parentheses and preceded by PL.
3. Samuel Freeman, *Rawls* (London: Routledge, 2007), 376.
4. Sebastiano Maffetone, *Rawls: An Introduction* (Cambridge: Polity, 2010), 225.
5. Maffetone, *Rawls: An Introduction*, 226, emphasis added.
6. Questions regarding the scope of Rawls's notion of legitimacy continue to stimulate controversy. Paul Weithman, for example, persuasively rebuts the suggestion, which he attributes to Charles Larmore, that Rawls views the liberal principle of legitimacy as imposing a necessary condition upon the choice of the principles of justice, themselves. See Paul Weithman, *Why Political Liberalism? On John Rawls's Political Turn* (Oxford: Oxford University Press, 2010), 350–52.
7. Robin Celikates, "Rethinking Civil Disobedience as a Practice of Contestation – Beyond the Liberal Paradigm," *Constellations* 23, no. 1 (2016): 37–45. On Celikates's radical democratic view of civil disobedience, see Chapter 5 in this volume.
8. Robert Jubb, "Disaggregating Political Authority: What's Wrong with Rawlsian Civil Disobedience?" *Political Studies* 67, no. 4 (2019): 955. More generally, on political realist ideas about civil disobedience, see Chapter 6.
9. Jubb, "Disaggregating Political Authority," 956.
10. Jubb, "Disaggregating Political Authority," 960.
11. "In a fuller account the same kind of explanation could presumably be given for the justifying conditions of conscientious refusal . . . . I shall not, however, discuss these conditions here" (TJ 337).
12. Ronald Dworkin, *Taking Rights Seriously* (Cambridge, Mass.: Harvard University Press, [1977] 1978). This work is cited in the text in parentheses and preceded by TRS.
13. Ronald Dworkin, *A Matter of Principle* (Cambridge, Mass.: Harvard University Press, 1985), 104–18.
14. As discussed above, Rawls would describe this form of behavior as conscientious refusal.
15. Dworkin, *A Matter of Principle*, 113.
16. Dworkin, *A Matter of Principle*, 112.
17. Dworkin, *A Matter of Principle*, 112.
18. Dworkin, *A Matter of Principle*, 112.

4 Deliberative Democratic Disobedience

William Smith

Democratic theory has undergone a much discussed "deliberative turn" in recent years, according to which "the essence of democracy itself is now widely taken to be deliberation, as opposed to voting, interest aggregation, constitutional rights, or even self-government."[1] Deliberative democrats place mutual respect, epistemic reason-giving, and inclusive dialogue at the center of public life.[2] The philosophical study of civil disobedience has simultaneously undergone a notable "communicative turn," such that theorists increasingly define this form of protest as "a way of engaging in dialogue."[3] The legitimacy of civil disobedience is related to its role as an unconventional but essentially respectful means of conveying oppositional arguments to publics and authorities.[4] There is, moreover, a notable overlap between these trends in democratic theory and civil disobedience theory. John Rawls and Jürgen Habermas, for instance, have made major contributions to both deliberative democracy and the communicative turn in theorizing civil disobedience.

The upshot of this convergence is that deliberative approaches to civil disobedience are an increasingly significant feature of the theoretical terrain, complementing but also competing with more established liberal and republican accounts. The liberal approach conceptualizes civil disobedience as a guardian of rights, holding that suitably conducted forms of lawbreaking can be a legitimate response to violations of our personal and political freedoms.[5] Deliberative accounts build upon this basic idea, but generally push for a more expansive account of the role of civil disobedience. Their claim is that civil disobedience can be legitimate even in the absence of clear rights-violations, thus stimulating public deliberation across a broader range of problems, issues, and agendas. The republican approach, by contrast, conceptualizes civil disobedience as a guardian of popular sovereignty, contesting failures of government to enact the sovereign will of the people.[6] Deliberative accounts accept the democratic intuition that civil disobedience is a bridge between state and society, but dispense with the republican idea of the people as a kind of "macro-subject." Civil disobedience is instead cast as a defender of "the subject-less forms of communication and discourse" within which popular sovereignty resides in decentered societies.[7]

This chapter maps the emerging overlap between the deliberative turn in democratic theory and the communicative turn in civil disobedience theory. Civil disobedience is defined here as a constrained, communicative protest, contrary to law, that people engage in to support a change in governmental or nongovernmental practices.[8] Communication is an intersubjective process in which agents share and convey meanings to each other via verbal and nonverbal utterances. Deliberation, by contrast, is a more specific kind of communicative action, involving the public use of reason to diagnose complex issues and resolve shared problems. Deliberative approaches can be regarded as a special subset among broadly communicative accounts of civil disobedience, which place a particular emphasis on its capacity to enhance the epistemic processes through which publics weigh up competing claims and perspectives. It might seem that, as a result of this emphasis, deliberative theorists treat civil disobedience as a rationalistic, polite, and peaceful mode of expression. This impression is understandable but, as we shall see, deliberative theorists have a far greater appreciation of the performative, confrontational, and disruptive nature of civil disobedience than their critics often suppose.

CIVIL DISOBEDIENCE AND PUBLIC REASON

Deliberative democracy is sometimes associated with ideas such as public discussion about the common good, accountability of government, and civic virtue among citizens. These ideas, though important, tend to be shared by most plausible conceptions of democracy and are not unique to deliberative conceptions. The deliberative paradigm is distinguished by its account of the reason-giving process that precedes decision-making and the way in which this process should be institutionalized. Samuel Freeman is quite right in his contention that "what makes a democracy *deliberative* is common *public reasoning* and argument by members of the body politic about ends of legislation and means needed to achieve them."[9] The philosophical literature on deliberative democracy devotes considerable attention to the content of public reasoning, whereas the more empirical debates focus on novel institutional forums or designs that can be utilized as a means of realizing public reasoning.

Civil disobedience, according to deliberative democrats, is intimately connected to the idea of public reasoning in two ways. First, the *justification* of civil disobedience is dependent upon political principles that underpin the legitimacy of the lawmaking process and lend content to public reasoning. Civil disobedience is thought to require a justification because it is an unlawful act that imposes burdens on others, including inconvenience, economic costs, and – in some contexts at least – significant political and societal upheaval. There must, therefore, be a compelling case for imposing these burdens, which would mean that the presumption against it is overridden by the good of communicating oppositional arguments through civil disobedience. As Habermas argues, civil disobedience is defensible only "under the proviso, of course, that the 'disobedient' citizen offer plausible reasons for their resistance by appealing to constitutional principles."[10]

Second, the *role* of civil disobedience is associated with the impetus it gives to public reasoning. Civil disobedience is not merely justified in light of public political principles but is also a means of protesting violations of those principles. As Rawls puts it, "by acting in this way one addresses the sense of justice of the majority of the community and declares that in one's considered opinion the principles of social cooperation among free and equal men are not being respected."[11] This communicative framework supports the various conduct-related constraints that should be observed by protesters, in the sense that tactics such as evasion, coercion, and violence are thought to be "incompatible with civil disobedience as a mode of address."[12] Civil disobedience is thus treated as an *input* to public reasoning, an appeal aimed at both elected office holders with the power to reverse decisions and to members of the general public with the power to offer or withdraw electoral support.[13]

There are different accounts of public reasoning among deliberative democrats, which coincide with somewhat different approaches to civil disobedience. The Rawlsian account, for instance, incorporates substantial restrictions on what can count as an authentic "public reason" in deliberative democracy. This reflects a particular view of the role of public reason, which is to identify a range of reasons that citizens with diverse conceptions of the good could accept as an appropriate basis for coercive political power. Rawls places citizens under a "duty of civility" to deliberate on the basis of a "family of political conceptions of justice" rather than their "religious and secular comprehensive doctrines," at least in relation to "constitutional essentials and matters of basic justice."[14]

These formulations are more-or-less identical to those that are utilized in his account of civil disobedience, which requires protesters to appeal to "the principles of justice which regulate the constitution" and not "principles of personal morality or to religious doctrines."[15] The duty of civility applies here because civil disobedience should be limited to protesting clear and serious infringements of basic liberties and fair equality of opportunity, paradigmatic examples of the "constitutional essentials and matters of basic justice" that Rawls sees as the main subject matter of public reason. Civil disobedience is an essentially *defensive* mechanism on this approach, safeguarding principles of justice that are already accepted in the community. Rawls goes so far as to say that "in a fragmented society as well as in one moved by group egoisms, the conditions for civil disobedience do not exist."[16] This is, as Jean Cohen and Andrew Arato point out, a rather restrictive account of civil disobedience, which prevents it from introducing novel perspectives on justice to the process of public reasoning or creating better channels of influence between public opinion and public authorities.[17]

The Habermasian account of public reason, by contrast, underpins a less restrictive approach to civil disobedience. Habermas's "two-track" model of democracy envisages a more-or-less unconstrained process of "opinion-formation" in the public sphere, geared toward "detecting and identifying new problem situations."[18] The public sphere acts as a bridge between the dispersed networks and associations of civil society and the institutionalized process of decision-making – or "will-formation" – that occurs in the legislative complex. The process of opinion-formation in civil society is thus open and free-flowing, though Habermas insists that institutionalized will-formation must observe the requirement that "all coercively enforceable political decisions must be formulated and be justifiable in a language that is equally intelligible to all citizens."[19]

Habermas follows Rawls in claiming that civil disobedience should be justified through appeal to "constitutional principles" rather than our personal convictions, but he interprets this requirement in a somewhat different way. Consider the following passage:

> the justification of civil disobedience relies on a *dynamic understanding* of the constitution as an unfinished project. From this long-term perspective, the constitutional state does not represent a finished structure but a delicate and sensitive – above all fallible and revisable – enterprise, whose purpose is to realize the system of rights *anew* in changing circumstances, that is, to interpret the system of rights better, to institutionalize it more appropriately, and to draw out its contents more radically.[20]

Civil disobedience is thus a *creative* mechanism, in the sense that its practitioners can mobilize around better or more radical interpretations of the system of rights. Environmental activism, for example, implicitly or explicitly compels publics to reconsider the meaning of justice and democracy in the "changing circumstances" of ecological threats and escalating climate change. Civil disobedience, for Habermas, does not require the extensive degree of societal agreement envisaged by Rawls, because his more dynamic account implies the possibility of conflicting interpretations of constitutional norms and divergent political judgments. Civil disobedience, according to this perspective, is not a particularly "stabilizing device," as Rawls puts it, but a potentially *de*stabilizing agent of change and innovation.[21] And this appears to be in keeping with Habermas's more dynamic and inclusive account of public reasoning.

The fact that Habermas treats civil disobedience as a communicative device should not detract from its disruptive impact on the public sphere. Habermas, arguably more so than Rawls, understands that civilly disobedient citizens do not rely solely on moral appeals but often adopt an adversarial stance to provoke a forceful reaction from public authorities. On this account, civil disobedience "manifests the self-consciousness of a civil society confident that at least in a crisis it can increase the pressure of a mobilized public on the political system to the point where the latter switches into conflict mode and neutralizes the unofficial circulation of power."[22] The emphasis on mobilizing public opinion as a means to increase pressure on public authorities does not signify an abandonment of the communicative frame, but rather recalls Habermas's insistence that "communicative power is exercised in the manner of a siege."[23] Civil disobedience should nonetheless remain nonviolent and symbolic, in order to retain its legitimating relationship to "valid constitutional principles."[24] William Scheuerman plausibly interprets Habermas as allowing for unruly forms of conduct, such as blockades, psychological pressure, and even property damage, but not campaigns that would "cripple [the] day-to-day operations" of formal institutions of will-formation.[25]

CIVIL DISOBEDIENCE AND THE PUBLIC SPHERE

The theory of civil disobedience put forward by Habermas incorporates what he describes as a "self-referential" dimension, according to which "independent of the current object of controversy, civil disobedience is also always an implicit appeal to connect organized will-formation with the communicative processes of the public sphere."[26] The thought appears to be that maintaining a close relationship between opinion-formation and will-formation is itself a formal or informal constitutional norm. Civil disobedience might be legitimate, then, if that relationship breaks down or if opinion-formation in the public sphere is compromised in some way. This is an intriguing suggestion, but Habermas does not offer much by way of an account of these breakdowns in the public sphere or an account of how civil disobedience functions as a remedial measure.[27] This section explores each of these issues in turn.

Civil Disobedience and Deliberative Breakdowns

Deliberative breakdowns are sometimes diagnosed in terms of the detrimental actions or attitudes of strategically well-placed groups or individuals, who act to constrain or prevent meaningful public reasoning. Archon Fung, for example, puts forward an ethics of "deliberative activism," recommending actors to abide by principles of fidelity, charity, exhaustion, and proportionality in their engagements with such adversaries. The deliberative activist should first employ lawful but nondeliberative forms of campaigning, and then "when these methods fail because resistance to deliberation runs deep and resulting injustices are substantial, he might resort to civil disobedience."[28] This type of approach, though important and insightful, is vulnerable to the charge that it arguably downplays the significance of *structural* constraints that limit prospects for deliberation, which may be difficult to relate to the conscious actions or revealed attitudes of specific agents in the deliberative process.[29]

The deliberative theory of civil disobedience that I develop identifies three process-related failings in the public sphere, which can be attributed to a variety of causes.[30] First, actors that have a clear stake in opinion-formation may be *excluded* from effective participation in the public sphere. This problem might derive from malicious attempts at exclusion, but also disagreement about the proper scope of societal inclusion, or negligence or ignorance on the part of relevant publics. Asylum seekers, migrants, and other nonnationals, for example, typically lack the standing necessary to articulate their interests in domestic public spheres despite the fact that domestic laws and policies have profound impacts upon their life prospects. Civil disobedience, either carried out by or on behalf of these groups, might function as a means of highlighting the failure of the public sphere to adequately include the interests and perspectives of excluded parties. The use of civil disobedience by organized groups of irregular migrant workers is an example of this dynamic. The *sans papiers* movement in France engaged in symbolic and high-profile occupations of churches, in order to cast light on legislative changes that made it harder for migrants to retain their status as authorized residents. These legislative changes pushed irregular migrants to the margins of French society, rendering them more-or-less invisible in the public sphere and exposing them to threats from state officials, unscrupulous employers, landlords, and criminal gangs.

Second, opinion-formation in the public sphere and its influence over will-formation may be distorted by structural inequalities in *social power*. The beneficiaries may be able to exercise considerable political influence through means such as donations, networking, lobbying, advertising, ownership of the mass media, or threat of economic sanctions. Those who lose out lack equivalent social and political capital, and may also suffer as a result of entrenched cultural stereotypes that make it harder to receive deliberative uptake for their views. Civil disobedience could thus function as a means of protesting the enhanced capacity of powerful actors to advance their interests in the public sphere and/or the relative incapacity of less powerful actors to do so. The use of civil disobedience against the power of economic corporations, for instance, often serves to contest a particular decision (such as the building of a dam or resort) while at the same time publicizing the power and capacity of such actors to sidestep the opposition of less well-endowed opponents (such as conservationists or residents). The strength of the case for civil disobedience, it should be noted, is not dependent upon the mere presence of some kind of alleged bias within opinion or will-formation, but instead rests on the distorting impact of enduring power relations that tend to enhance the influence of some and/or diminish the influence of others. Civil disobedience against legislation to regulate fox hunting in the United Kingdom, for instance, might be framed as a protest against class prejudice and cultural stereotypes about the upper class. But this frame would be compelling only if it could be shown that the upper class are victims of underlying power relations that compromise their capacity to receive deliberative uptake for their views.

Third, the cognitive function of the public sphere – its capacity to recognize new social problems and generate solutions – can be inhibited due to *deliberative inertia*. The problem of inertia arises because of the central role in opinion and will-formation of discourses, defined as the conceptual frameworks that are utilized in making sense of the world, identifying problems, and proposing solutions. Deliberative inertia occurs insofar as hegemonic discourses are so entrenched that competing and potentially superior discourses are marginalized in the public sphere. This phenomenon can have the effect of either preventing a discourse at the margins of the public sphere from influencing opinion-formation or preventing a discourse that has widespread support across the public sphere from influencing will-formation.

Civil disobedience is a means of contesting the inertial dead-weight of hegemonic discourses, while creating space for alternative frameworks that offer competing diagnoses of emergent societal problems. The use of civil disobedience in anti-globalization activism, for instance, contests inertia within national governments, regional bodies, and global economic organizations. This inertia, according to activists, is associated with the pervasive influence of neoliberalism, which prioritizes capital market liberalization, reduced spending on welfare, flexible labor markets, and privatization of state industries and services. The alternative discourses that protesters introduce to the public sphere focus on the impact of globalization on human rights and poverty, the inefficiency and instability of unregulated markets, and the absence of transparency and accountability in global governance. These alternative discourses were not prominent in opinion-formation until concerted disruptive protests raised their profile. Another example is the use of civil disobedience in environmental activism, which increasingly functions as a means of pressuring governments to take more effective action in combating problems such as global warming. The goal here is not so much to raise the profile of discourses that already command considerable support in the public sphere, but to disrupt the entrenched hold of competing discourses – such as those that foreground the imperative of economic growth – in institutionalized will-formation.

Civil Disobedience and Epistemic Reflection

Civil disobedience, according to Habermas, Fung, and myself, should be guided by the goal of ameliorating deliberative breakdowns and reinstating the values associated with deliberative democracy as far as possible. An important way in which this is achieved is through triggering processes of *epistemic reflection* across the public sphere. These processes should lead to the emergence of "preferences, opinions, and decisions that are appropriately informed by facts and logic and are the outcome of substantive and meaningful consideration of relevant reasons."[31] Civil disobedience instigates reflection through engaging the rational capacities of its audience and by making certain information or perspectives available to them. Protesters can relate their protest to a consciousness-raising campaign, using the opportunities created by their actions to expose their arguments to greater public scrutiny. There are, though, deeper communicative dynamics at work in civil disobedience, which can be exploited by activists to enhance the capacity of their protest to promote genuine reflection about – rather than mere consciousness of – a particular issue or agenda.

Civil disobedience is paradigmatically a *disruptive* form of protest, at least when carried out by large or small groups. This is significant because the disruption of routines and spaces unsettles audiences and pushes them out of their comfort zones, which accounts for the potential superiority of an unruly or unexpected protest over more conventional advocacy as a means of triggering reflection. The power of such acts is enhanced through staging performances or crafting spectacles that transmit multiple meanings.

Pollyanna Ruiz illustrates this with a protest carried out against Starbucks in Brighton (UK) by Save Omar, a civil liberties movement that campaigned for the release of a local resident imprisoned in Guantanamo Bay. Save Omar activists occupied two Starbucks cafes in Brighton, on the grounds that the company sold coffee to military personnel stationed in Guantanamo. Activists dressed in the orange overalls and black hoods of Guantanamo inmates, kneeling or standing in silence while fellow activists read statements that invited customers to reflect upon Starbucks's policy, the imprisonment of the Brighton resident, and general issues surrounding Guantanamo. This protest operates as a more-or-less straightforward means of communicating a thematically linked range of issues to customers and the anonymous publics that follow the action through online and local media. It also, as Ruiz argues, operates on a more sophisticated level by disrupting a space normally taken to be free from politics and teasing out unexpected associations between it and the treatment of terrorist suspects. The protest thus "jolts spectators out of their usual state of distraction and encourages them to re-evaluate the discourses which surround them."[32] These cognitive processes could be triggered through less confrontational methods, but a disruptive protest has the considerable advantage of both unsettling expectations and creating striking images for dissemination.

Civil disobedience also has a certain communicative power by virtue of its *illegality*. Kimberley Brownlee shows how this form of action expresses the weight that a particular issue holds for the actor, because their act is likely to have consequences – such as the risk of arrest and lawful punishment – that are more burdensome for him or her than lawful advocacy. It therefore functions better as a means of impressing upon an audience both the intensity of their beliefs and the urgency of their cause.[33]

This dynamic can be especially effective in cases where protesters are reaching out to an audience that includes persons who might already sympathize with their perspective. The use of unlawful tactics by activists associated with the environmental movement, for example, often has the effect of reaffirming the necessity and urgency of a green agenda in contexts where this agenda is already accepted as salient by significant numbers of persons. The message communicated is that the personal burdens of unlawful protest that are assumed by the activists are warranted due to the importance of their concerns. This can trigger the reflective capabilities of their audience through challenging us to decide whether we should follow protesters in according much more weight to these concerns in our deliberations than we might otherwise be inclined to do. It is also worth noting that civil disobedience can signal an implicit or explicit condemnation of conventional methods of political participation. Protesters are, in effect, saying that the failings of "politics as usual," blighted as it is by structural exclusions, power inequalities, or inertial dynamics, mean that the use of unlawful methods is their best hope of commanding attention in the public sphere. The layers of meaning added to a speech act if it is expressed through unlawful, rather than lawful, advocacy can thus be significant in terms of stimulating reflection on the part of an audience.

There are, of course, factors that inhibit the capacity of civil disobedience to instigate reflection, such as a documented tendency for traditional media organizations to frame protest in a way that both detracts from the issues at stake and casts protesters in a negative light. Neil Gavin, drawing on these findings, suggests that environmental activists should set aside disruptive forms of action in favor of "diligent lobbying, careful research, discriminating collaboration, public relations professionalism and the cultivation of the conventional media."[34]

This conclusion may, though, be premature. Protest movements tend to differ in their capacity to anticipate and influence the way in which their message will be disseminated through media outlets. Greenpeace, for instance, has refined the art of employing disruptive protest as a means of reaching out to public opinion. It utilizes a hierarchical structure that allows for tight control over protest planning and media strategy; it has intensive training in media relations for its activists; it cultivates relationships with sympathetic journalists; and it retains significant control over the flow of information through publications, press releases, and a sophisticated web platform. These characteristics may chafe against the notion that protest should be a less managerial business, but structural constraints erected by the media often necessitate a more professional approach on the part of activists. A further characteristic of Greenpeace is that it engages in disruptive forms of civil disobedience *and* institutionalized forms of advocacy and negotiation. The goal of prompting publics to think about a particular set of issues might, therefore, be best served not through choosing between civil disobedience and lawful advocacy, but through the selective use of disruptive protest alongside more conventional tactics of lobbying, collaboration, public relations, and the like.

CIVIL DISOBEDIENCE AND THE LIMITS OF DELIBERATION

Deliberative democracy has been the subject of intense scrutiny in democratic theory, with critics challenging the faith that it places on reason-giving as the essence of democratic politics. There is, perhaps unsurprisingly, considerable overlap between the themes explored in this critical literature and objections that have been levelled against the way in which deliberative theorists approach modes of protests such as civil disobedience. There is, for instance, criticism of the tendency to frame civil disobedience as both a response to deficiencies *in* public reasoning and as a contribution *to* public reasoning.

This section focuses in particular on the criticism that deliberative democrats overstate the reason-giving dimension of civil disobedience at the expense of both its *aesthetic-expressive* and *oppositional-coercive* dimensions.

Civil Disobedience as Aesthetic-Expressive

Deliberative democrats tend to treat civil disobedience as a means of communicating arguments about contentious laws, policies, or practices, thus locating it within ongoing processes of public reasoning. This strikes some critics as an approach that is far too rationalistic, in the sense that it focuses on the reason-giving dimension of civil disobedience at the expense of its emotional, performative, or aesthetic dimensions. The risk is that the deliberative perspective paints a picture of civil disobedience that is at best incomplete and at worst misleading, as it may drastically overstate the extent to which disruptive protest can be assimilated into a deliberative process.

This objection is elaborated by Stephen White and Evan Farr, in a sympathetic but critical reading of Habermas's theory of civil disobedience. The authors focus on what they describe as the "no saying" dimension of civilly disobedient acts, challenging the tendency of Habermas and other deliberative theorists to reduce such acts to "an embodied argument that makes a rational appeal to the government and public opinion."[35] No saying, they argue, has an "aesthetic-expressive" dimension that cannot be reduced to the search for consensus over the pros and cons of this or that law or policy. Civil disobedience is bound up with issues of identity, as agents often engage in such acts to express opposition to a dominant form of life and affirm an alternative. Civil disobedience is also bound up with the faculty of imagination, as protesters aim to make an injustice "real" to an audience through aesthetic-spectacle rather than moral argument. These rich communicative dynamics mean that civil disobedience "cannot be understood simply as an argument; rather it aims to engage the imagination in the virtual construction of a different form of life."[36]

Deliberative democrats could respond to this criticism by accepting, for the sake of argument, that the aesthetic-expressive dimension of civil disobedience cannot be incorporated into public reasoning. This concession is not fatal to their theories of civil disobedience, provided that the aesthetic-expressive and reason-giving dimensions are not played against each other. White and Farr do not argue that civil disobedience *lacks* a reason-giving dimension, but hold that civil disobedience typically includes a reason-giving *and* an aesthetic-expressive dimension. They argue that the "no saying" implicit in civil disobedience "seems more like a variable blend of an embodied appeal to a universal moral audience and a less articulate, existential taking-of-a-stand against the normative force of a dominant form of life." The authors thus present Rosa Parks's refusal to surrender her bus seat as "both a courageous, existentially rooted act against the normative terms of public transportation in the southern United States at that time, and a concomitant appeal to the moral sense of the rest of the country."[37] Even if this characterization is accurate, the "appeal" to the community's moral sense that is implicit in this act can still be treated as a valid input to an ongoing deliberative process. The aesthetic-expressive dimension is an important remainder, which contributes to the meaning of the act but escapes translation into the give-and-take of opinions about the issue at hand. This might be problematic if we thought that such an approach somehow diminishes the aesthetic-expressive dimension, but there seems no reason to think it would.

Deliberative theorists might, alternatively, contest the claim that aesthetic-expressive speech acts cannot be treated as inputs to reason-giving. White and Farr argue that "no saying" is incompatible with the search for consensus, as conflicts involving competing identities and forms of life are unlikely to culminate in a convergence of views.[38] The problem here is the assumption that the exchange of perspectives and arguments in the public sphere should necessarily be characterized as a search for rational consensus. There is scope for debate about whether Habermas holds such a view, but it is certainly a position that many deliberative theorists reject.[39] Public reasoning might require participants to present their arguments in terms that *could* be accepted by discursive interlocutors, but it is not necessary that such a process culminate in consensus. The deliberative credentials of speech acts can be ascertained not through their contribution to a rational consensus, but their role in the process through which perspectives are grasped, sifted, and tested in the public sphere. The trend within deliberative theory has, in fact, been toward ever more inclusive accounts of public reasoning, with apparently non-rationalistic modes of expression such as testimonies, narrative, humor, art, rhetoric, and protests increasingly treated as valid inputs to deliberation.[40] There is, on such accounts, no reason why an act of civil disobedience embodying an aesthetic-expressive dimension could not be fully incorporated into public deliberation.

Civil Disobedience as Oppositional-Coercive

Deliberative democrats tend to treat civil disobedience as a form of reasoned persuasion, which aims to achieve its goals through reaching out to and mobilizing public opinion. Rawls, for instance, characterizes civil disobedience as a moral appeal rather than a coercive threat, while Habermas, as discussed above, treats it as a disruptive but essentially symbolic means of dramatizing a conflict with authorities. This exemplifies the pronounced preference on the part of deliberative democrats for political conflicts to be resolved through reason and argument, rather than through coercion, manipulation, or other forms of treatment that fail to embody appropriate respect for autonomy. The problem is that, according to some critics, protesters often confront imbalances in power that necessitate the kind of coercive tactics that deliberative democrats appear to frown upon.

This objection has been articulated forcefully by John Medearis, in a probing analysis of the failure of deliberative democracy to take seriously the politics of social movements. His argument is that inequalities in power, defined as a capacity to act that is bestowed by social structures and relationships, often compel the disadvantaged to pursue their goals through coercion rather than persuasion. Deliberative attempts to present civil disobedience as a tactic of moral persuasion fail to acknowledge its coercive reality. Social movements have "engaged in disruptive civil disobedience that forced others to alter routines and to act differently, they have provoked crises that undermined some people's interests and challenged others' complacency, and they have staged actions that threatened governments with a loss of credibility."[41] Civil disobedience is not, on accounts such as this, motivated by the goal of stimulating epistemic reflection, but rather functions as a threat or sanction that is directed toward opponents to force their hand. The theory of "oppositional democracy" that Medearis proposes as an alternative to deliberative democracy evaluates all forms of political action, including civil disobedience, according to whether or not it is "reasonably orientated toward collectively managing the social world on egalitarian terms."[42]

Deliberative democrats might respond by casting doubt on whether the disruptive forms of protest that Medearis discusses should be regarded as coercive. Piero Moraro, for instance, argues that civil disobedience embodies an appropriate respect for agency to the extent that its addressees remain free to reach judgments about the matter at hand on the basis of a consideration of the relevant reasons. He develops this idea through noting that "some acts that interfere with the behaviour of others might temporarily impinge on their freedom, without affecting their status as autonomous participants in the democratic discourse."[43] He considers an unlawful protest carried out in 2008 by environmental activists at Stansted Airport (UK) against the building of a new runway, which grounded some morning flights and disrupted the plans of travelers. This protest, according to Moraro, caused temporary inconvenience to passengers, but "did not infringe upon [their] autonomy, for it did not aim to coerce others into opposing the planned expansion of the airport."[44]

Brownlee argues, in a similar vein, that civil disobedience carried out as an attempt to pressure an interlocutor into entering a dialogue is not necessarily incompatible with showing appropriate respect for their agency. This is so provided that the degree of force that is used does not overwhelm our interlocutor, such that he or she retains sufficient agency to either accept or reject the attempt to initiate a dialogue.[45] The mobilization of public opinion against public authorities is, as we have seen, an attempt to exert pressure, but it seems counterintuitive to characterize this as an attempt to curtail their agency. The modern state, after all, retains considerable scope to resist such pressure and to persuade the public of the merits of its current position. It may be the case that public authorities do not welcome the temporary disruption or negative publicity brought about by protest actions, but it is not clear that their rational agency has been compromised in such a situation. The categorization of civil disobedience as coercive or noncoercive is, at the very least, a complex matter, which must be sensitive to the nature and severity of its impact on opponents.[46] Rawls may be wrong to assume that it can be reduced to a moral appeal, but Medearis may also be too hasty in treating it as coercive.

Deliberative democrats might, alternatively, concede that civil disobedience is often a coercive mechanism, but hold that such a use of force is compatible with their broader normative commitments. The tension that Medearis identifies between social movement tactics and deliberative democracy arises, at least in part, because he treats a norm of noncoercion as the defining feature of deliberative democracy. As he puts it, "for the most part [deliberative democrats] have generally chosen to frame deliberative democracy around the norm that citizens should not coerce each other, rather than a critique of unequal power relations."[47] However, although it is a prominent feature of several accounts, the norm of noncoercion is arguably not as central to the deliberative paradigm as this characterization suggests.

The recent "deliberative systems" approach, for instance, recognizes a presumptive norm of noncoercion, but does not accord it special priority. Deliberative democracy is instead treated as a complex, dynamic, and multifaceted system, involving a diverse range of actors, behavior, and institutions related to each other across temporal and spatial dimensions. On this account, epistemic reflection, mutual respect, and democratic inclusion are treated as constitutive values for deliberative democracy that may come into conflict at any given time. This creates the possibilities for "trade-offs within the system."[48] So, for instance, coercive forms of conduct that are unlikely to advance the goals of epistemic reflection or mutual respect may nonetheless function as defensible means of promoting the value of greater democratic inclusion. Deliberative systems theorists thus recognize that "if [an] audience is unreceptive to reasons because it has already made up its mind or has decided not to think more about the question, civil disobedience will not advance public deliberation."[49] Civil disobedience, along with other forms of coercive or indeed noncoercive activism, might nonetheless be system-enhancing over time if it strengthens the capacity of oppressed actors to access the public sphere. This type of argument, if sound, appears to reduce the gap between deliberative accounts of civil disobedience and the "oppositional" approach favored by Medearis, at least in the sense that both allow for the possibility that civil disobedience can utilize coercion to enhance what are taken to be core democratic values.

CONCLUSION

This chapter has shown how deliberative theories defend civil disobedience as legitimate in light of their commitment to public reason. Their accounts treat civil disobedience as a mode of communicating arguments across the public sphere, but also recognize its disruptive dimensions. A challenge for deliberative democrats, in fact, is to consider just how far they are prepared to go in embracing disruption, particularly in light of recent arguments in favor of *uncivil* disobedience in conditions of manifest injustice. The "systemic turn," as we have seen, is prepared to countenance coercive protest as a means of advancing its core democratic values, despite its ambivalent relationship with deliberation as a normative ideal. One might wonder whether systems theorists could adopt a similarly permissive attitude toward other modes of action that appear incompatible with deliberation, such as covert attempts to sabotage will-formation or violent attempts to reorient opinion-formation.

Deliberative democracy is a heterogeneous paradigm, which means that there are a range of potential responses to this challenge. There is, in particular, a notable but often overlooked strand that treats deliberative democracy as an "emancipatory project," whose underlying values are explicitly associated with "leftist political concerns."[50] The emancipatory perspective may be highly receptive to, say, Candice Delmas's theory of resistance, which offers a nuanced defense of covert, offensive, and moderately violent tactics in support of progressive social causes.[51] It is, though, somewhat difficult for a consistent deliberative democrat to evaluate instances of civil or uncivil disobedience purely in terms of their *outcomes*, as one of their defining normative commitments is to public reasoning as a *process*. There should, in other words, be a constructive relationship between acts of disobedience and the communicative structures of democracy, even if there is a certain tension between such acts and the presumptive norms that underpin those structures. Moraro speaks to this intuition when he notes that "there comes a point where the 'nonpersuasiveness' of [an] act would lose any semblance of a commitment to the ideals of deliberative democracy – for example, the use of force aiming to injure or terrorise others could not be justified as an expression of deliberative values."[52] The difficult but pressing task is to determine when this point is reached.[53]

NOTES

1. John Dryzek, *Deliberative Democracy and Beyond: Liberals, Critics, Contestations* (Oxford: Oxford University Press, 2000), 1.

2. James Bohman and William Rehg, eds., *Deliberative Democracy: Essays on Reason and Politics* (Cambridge, Mass.: The MIT Press, 1997).

3. Tony Milligan, *Civil Disobedience: Protest, Justification, and the Law* (London: Bloomsbury, 2013), 18.

4. Kimberley Brownlee, *Conscience and Conviction: The Case for Civil Disobedience* (Oxford: Oxford University Press, 2012).

5. Ronald Dworkin, *A Matter of Principle* (Cambridge, Mass.: Harvard University Press, 1985), 104–16.

6. Daniel Markovits, "Democratic Disobedience," *The Yale Law Journal* 114, no. 8 (2005): 1897–952.

7. Jürgen Habermas, *Between Facts and Norms: Contributions to a Discourse Theory or Law and Democracy*, trans. William Rehg (Cambridge: Polity Press, 1997), 301.

8. William Smith and Kimberley Brownlee, "Civil Disobedience and Conscientious Objection," *Oxford Research Encyclopedia of Politics*, May 24, 2017, https://oxfordre.com/politics/view/10.1093/acrefore/978 0190228637.001.0001/acrefore-9780190228637-e-114.

9. Samuel Freeman, "Deliberative Democracy: A Sympathetic Comment," *Philosophy & Public Affairs* 29, no. 4 (2000): 378. Emphasis in original.

10. Jürgen Habermas, *Between Naturalism and Religion*, trans. Ciaran Cronin (Cambridge: Polity Press, 2008), 256.

11. John Rawls, *A Theory of Justice, revised ed.* (Oxford: Oxford University Press, 1999), 320.

12. Rawls, *A Theory of Justice*, 321.

13. Habermas, *Between Facts and Norms*, 383.

14. John Rawls, *The Law of Peoples with "The Idea of Public Reason Revisited"* (Cambridge, Mass.: Harvard University Press, 1999), 133–41.

15. Rawls, *A Theory of Justice*, 321.

16. Rawls, *A Theory of Justice*, 340.

17. Jean L. Cohen and Andrew Arato, *Civil Society and Political Theory* (Cambridge, Mass.: The MIT Press, 1994), 574–77.

18. Habermas, *Between Facts and Norms*, 381.

19. Habermas, *Between Naturalism and Religion*, 134.

20. Habermas, *Between Facts and Norms*, 384. Emphasis in original.

21. Rawls, *A Theory of Justice*, 336.

22. Habermas, *Between Facts and Norms*, 383–84.

23. Habermas, *Between Facts and Norms*, 486.

24. Habermas, *Between Facts and Norms*, 382–83.
25. William E. Scheuerman, *Civil Disobedience* (Cambridge: Polity, 2018), 78.
26. Habermas, *Between Facts and Norms*, 383.
27. William Smith, "Civil Disobedience and Social Power: Reflections on Habermas," *Contemporary Political Theory* 7, no. 1 (2008): 72–89.
28. Archon Fung, "Deliberation Before the Revolution: Toward an Ethics of Deliberative Democracy in an Unjust World," *Political Theory* 33, no. 2 (2005) 409.
29. Iris Marion Young, "Activist Challenges to Deliberative Democracy," *Political Theory* 29 no. 5 (2001): 670–90.
30. The following ideas are discussed at greater length in William Smith, *Civil Disobedience and Deliberative Democracy* (London: Routledge, 2013), chapters 2 and 3.
31. Jane Mansbridge, James Bohman, Simone Chambers, Thomas Christiano, Archon Fung, John Parkinson, Dennis F. Thompson, and Mark E. Warren, "A Systemic Approach to Deliberative Democracy," in *Deliberative Systems: Deliberative Democracy at the Large Scale*, eds. John Parkinson and Jane Mansbridge (Cambridge: Cambridge University Press, 2012), 11.
32. Pollyanna Ruiz, *Articulating Dissent: Protest and the Public Sphere* (London: Pluto Press, 2014), 136.
33. Brownlee, *Conscience and Conviction*, 37–42.
34. Neil T. Gavin, "Pressure Group Direct Action on Climate Change: The Role of the Media and the Web in Britain – A Case Study," *British Journal of Politics and International Relations* 12, no. 3 (2010): 459–75, at 471.
35. Stephen K. White and Evan Robert Farr , "'No Saying' in Habermas," *Political Theory* 40 vol. 1 (2012): 41.
36. White and Farr, "No Saying," 47.
37. White and Farr, "No Saying," 38.
38. White and Farr, "No Saying," 42.
39. Jürg Steiner, *The Foundations of Deliberative Democracy: Empirical Research and Normative Implications* (Cambridge: Cambridge University Press, 2012), 139–52.
40. Steiner, *The Foundations of Deliberative Democracy*, 57–87.
41. John Medearis, *Why Democracy Is Oppositional* (Cambridge, Mass.: Harvard University Press, 2015), 29.

42. Medearis, *Why Democracy is Oppositional*, 148. On coercion and non-violence, see also Chapter 10 in this volume. More generally, on political realism, Chapter 6.

43. Piero Moraro, "Respecting Autonomy Through the Use of Force: The Case of Civil Disobedience," *Journal of Applied Philosophy* 31, no. 1 (2014): 69.

44. Moraro, "Respecting Autonomy," 67.

45. Brownlee, *Conscience and Conviction*, 219.

46. Guy Aitchison, "Coercion, Resistance and the Radical Side of Non-Violent Action," *Raisons Politiques* 69, no. 1 (2018): 51.

47. Medearis, *Why Democracy Is Oppositional*, 28.

48. Mansbridge et al., "A Systemic Approach," 21.

49. Mansbridge et al., "A Systemic Approach," 24.

50. Michael A. Neblo, *Deliberative Democracy Between Theory and Practice* (Cambridge: Cambridge University Press, 2015), 36.

51. Candice Delmas, *A Duty to Resist: When Disobedience Should Be Uncivil* (Oxford: Oxford University Press, 2018).

52. Piero Moraro, *Civil Disobedience: A Philosophical Overview* (London: Rowman and Littlefield, 2019), 81.

53. For some tentative reflections, see William Smith, "Disruptive Democracy: The Ethics of Direct Action," *Raisons Politiques* 69, no. 1 (2018): 13–27.

5   Radical Democratic Disobedience

Robin Celikates

Civil disobedience is a practice of political contestation, of challenging established norms, practices, institutions, and self-understandings that involves deliberately breaking the law while typically stopping short of full-scale revolt in terms of both its ends and its repertoire of actions. It is usually situated between legal protest, on the one hand, and more radical – for example, revolutionary – forms of resistance, on the other. Where exactly the lines are drawn, and, as a result, how radical civil disobedience in fact turns out to be, depends on how the meaning, justification, and role of civil disobedience are understood. As this volume documents, different theoretical paradigms propose rival accounts, ranging from the rather restrictive proposals of mainstream liberal accounts to more expansive positions developed by theorists of radical democracy.[1]

While the theoretical discussion among and between competing paradigms has followed its own dynamics, the latter also has to be understood in relation, and partly as a reaction, to the practice of civil disobedience and its prospects under changing political circumstances. It is no surprise, then, that radical democrats propose different interpretations of historical and contemporary instances of disobedience, starting with the early paradigmatic cases of Henry David Thoreau and Mahatma Gandhi, followed by the US Civil Rights Movement and the social movements of the 1980s, to, more recently, Occupy and the Black Lives Matter response to police brutality and structural racism, and new forms of digital and transnational disobedience. In line with their overarching aim of reclaiming the radical potential of "civil disobedience" by giving it a decidedly political and radical meaning, radical democratic approaches claim to be better attuned to the complex political reality of disobedience.

While theories of radical democracy take a large variety of forms, the following set of claims seem to provide some shared ground:[2]

1. Democracy cannot be reduced to or identified with the institutions of the liberal state (e.g., elections, parliaments, referenda). Instead, democracy is actualized in practices that challenge the existing order and the hegemonic consensus it rests on, highlighting the essentially political and thus contestable character of all institutions and norms, and opening up the space for a radical reconstitution of this order.

2. The emancipatory potential of such a reconstitution is primarily defined negatively, by being directed against entrenched forms of unfreedom and inequality, rather than by realizing a substantial and positive normative ideal.

3. Lacking any secure foundations to stand on (such as legal or moral principles that would be immune from contestation), or a specified ideal to realize, radically transformative political practices aim at a democratization of democracy through struggles for freedom and equality; these struggles remain central in addressing democracy's need for continuous self-transformation as the latter cannot, or only very partially, be institutionalized.

4. The democratic agency that is actualized in these practices can be understood in terms of constituent power, which the radical democratic perspective extends beyond the process of constitution-making. In a lineage that stretches back to Niccolò Machiavelli, Karl Marx, and Hannah Arendt, radical democratic theory understands constituent power as the capacity of the demos to act, its capacity to overturn an old order and to establish a new one in a collective act of creativity and spontaneity.

5. The radical democratic notion of the demos, however, is not to be confused with the idealized, and ideological, vision of the united

and homogeneous people (or nation) that is presumably the subject of constitution-making and constitutes itself as the sovereign. Rather, it is a collective subject that is irreducibly plural, inherently conflictual, and thus incapable of being represented by one voice or of being fully articulated in a constituted system. In addition, the act or process of constitution is itself pluralized in the radical democratic tradition as it expands beyond the realm of the law and the state, and takes on a multiplicity of forms.[3]

From this perspective, democracy is not just a system of government among others. Rather, it is a political process and form in which the constituent power of the *demos* manifests and articulates itself in a necessarily open-ended and conflictual manner. To put it in Baruch Spinoza's influential terms: only democracy is able to recognize and make explicit the actual foundation of all legal and state power (*potestas*) in the power of the *demos* or the multitude (*potentia multitudinis*).[4] In the same vein, the young Marx claimed that democracy is "the solved riddle of all constitutions," as it is the only form of politically organizing society that gives institutional expression to the fact that the state, the constitution, and the law find their "actual basis" in the social and political practices of the actual *demos*.[5]

Although civil disobedience is just one among a number of bottom-up practices in which this collective agency of the *demos* – the *potestas in populo* – articulates itself,[6] one can argue that it occupies a special place within the repertoire of radical democratic contestation for two reasons. First, civil disobedience transcends, or at least promises to transcend, some of the central dichotomies structuring the realm of political action, such as legal vs. illegal, reform vs. revolution, and militant vs. peaceful. Second, it can be viewed as the result of a learning process among emancipatory movements in which confrontations with the authoritarian potential of classical models of revolutionary activism and democratic self-government spurred a recognition of the democratic need for self-reflexivity and some sort of self-limitation to which some of the classical authors of the radical democratic tradition (e.g., Jean Jacques Rousseau and Marx) were insufficiently attentive. In this way, thinking about insurrectionary politics in terms of civil disobedience can avoid some of the mythologies and idealizations to which radical democratic theory has not always been immune, such as the tendency to hypostatize the event, focus on the heroic and pure nature of politics, and idealize past revolutions. All of these tendencies involve an ahistorical and sociologically crude uncoupling of the event of the eruption of constituent power (in founding moments or great revolutions) from ongoing struggles and movements, and their dialectical relation to forms of constituted power that a radical democratic understanding of civil disobedience aims to avoid.[7]

In what follows, I sketch the contours of a radical democratic approach to civil disobedience by following the useful Rawlsian distinction between questions concerning its definition, justification, and role in a democratic society, respectively.[8] I build on the contributions of radical democratic theorists such as Arendt, Etienne Balibar, and James Tully, whose work contributes to a conception of civil disobedience that is more militant and radical in its transformative ambitions than that offered by the moderate and reformist liberal mainstream. Instead of seeing protest and dissent in general, and civil disobedience in particular, as a minor, at best exceptional, corrective to existing democratic institutions, this perspective allows us to locate the contestatory practice of civil disobedience at the very heart of democracy. By doing so, we can counter the still widespread public sentiment that disobedience represents an essentially antidemocratic form of political blackmail, which renounces the civic duty to obey the law in order to impose the views of a militant minority on the democratic majority.[9] We can also resist the ultimately antidemocratic and anti-political attempt to eliminate dissonance, resistance, conflict, or struggle from the realm of politics through juridical and administrative regulation.[10]

In this context, the radical democratic approach aims at "politicizing" or "democratizing" disobedience in a dual sense: first,

disobedience is an essential part of political struggles for democratization ("from below") and thus opens up one way to address the crisis of
representative democracies and their oligarchic tendencies without
falling back into the non- or antidemocratic dynamics of right-wing
populism. Second, theorizing disobedience in a critical vein has to be
democratized both methodologically and substantially, against the
depoliticizing frame employed by the liberal mainstream, in order to
adequately grasp the democratizing potential of disobedience.[11] Far
from being a purely theoretical exercise, radical democratic theory is
thereby squarely situated within political practice and understands
its own aim as tied to the aim of emancipation that guides the struggles it seeks to theorize.

AN ESSENTIALLY CONTESTED CONCEPT? RADICALIZING THE DEFINITION OF CIVIL DISOBEDIENCE

Civil disobedience is an essentially contested concept, not just in
theory[12] but also in practice. As a result, the struggles about how to
best conceptualize the contestatory practices in question are not
merely theoretical exercises. This is tied to the fact that the label
"civil disobedience" has a political cachet carrying a normative sur-
plus that gives rise to symbolic struggles, first and foremost, about the
label itself. The outcomes of these struggles have tangible political
and legal consequences: it matters whether dissent is successfully
framed as "civil disobedience," not just in terms of how the public
perceives it, but also in terms of who might be mobilized to join it,
which types of political dynamics it can trigger, and how the police,
prosecutors, and courts approach it. Participants in struggles, protests, and movements are not passive bystanders to these debates
but actively intervene in them by appropriating, resignifying, and
using established notions of both civility and disobedience for their
own purposes.[13] A radical democratic theory of civil disobedience
cannot stand apart from these struggles about terminology and framing that are so clearly part of any political struggle. Indeed, part of the
rationale of a radical democratic account of civil disobedience is to

resist hegemonic attempts to co-opt, normalize, and depoliticize this practice, or to delegitimize it by framing it as a riot, a disturbance of public order, or even terrorism, which happens increasingly when states, from the US and the EU to Turkey and Hong Kong, attempt to deflect critique and resistance by framing them as violent.[14]

A radical democratic approach to civil disobedience does not pretend to be uncoupled from these struggles, as if the theorist could take on a neutral position on the sidelines with the aim of legislating definitional and moral constraints for activist practice. Rather, in arguing for an alternative and more capacious understanding of the term "civil disobedience," radical democratic approaches both seek to do justice to and enable struggles for the democratization of democracy from below.

From this perspective, the influential definition put forth by John Rawls is highly problematic. To recall, Rawls understands civil disobedience as "a public, nonviolent and conscientious yet political act contrary to law usually done with the aim of bringing about a change in the law or policies of the government" and with which one appeals to the "sense of justice of the majority," all "within the limits of fidelity to law."[15] To begin with, the exercise of most well-established forms of civil disobedience (e.g., blocking an intersection or occupying a building) depends on *not* giving the authorities advance notice. Rawls, however, takes the public character of civil disobedience to preclude its clandestine preparation. The criterion of nonviolence is even more disputed given the (conceptual, but also political and legal) difficulty of establishing what counts as violence in the relevant sense. While serious violations of the physical integrity of others will be difficult to reconcile with any understanding of the "civil" in civil disobedience, including the radical democratic one, the same does not hold for violence against property, violence against oneself, or restrained violence in self-defense. Similarly, civil disobedience does not always involve an appeal to the sense of justice of the larger public. Not only does civil disobedience in many cases seem at odds with, and indeed directed against, the majority's moral sentiments, but in some cases civil disobedience aims not at convincing but at forcing the majority to confront an issue it would prefer to ignore, such as racial injustice and oppression. Another important element of the liberal definition, that civil disobedience takes place within the limits of fidelity to law, is supposed to distinguish it from more radical and revolutionary forms of protest and resistance that put into question the political or social system itself. The line between these different varieties of protest, however, apart from being politically contested in practice, is more difficult to draw in theory than the liberal definition suggests. It is more than doubtful, for example, that Martin Luther King, Jr. and the Civil Rights Movement were merely aiming at more or less local corrections within the existing system or that their disobedience was an expression of their recognition of the system's general legitimacy.[16]

Given that the questions raised here about the standard liberal definition show that its elements are far from unproblematic and uncontested, it seems appropriate to define civil disobedience in a way that is less normatively demanding and therefore less restrictive, as an intentionally unlawful and principled collective act of protest (in contrast to legal protest, "ordinary" criminal offenses, or "unmotivated" rioting), with which citizens – in the broad sense that goes beyond those recognized as citizens by a particular state – pursue the political aim of changing norms, practices, institutions, and self-understandings (in contrast to conscientious objection, which is protected in some states as a fundamental right and does not seek such change) in ways that should be seen as civil (as opposed to military).[17] Those who engage in civil and civic practices of disobedience and contestation continue to act as citizens: they exemplify what it means to be a citizen in reasserting their political agency against entrenched and often seemingly invisible forms of domination, exclusion, or marginalization.

In acting as citizens, they acknowledge some kind of civil bond with their adversaries, which goes hand in hand with certain forms of self-limitation and self-restraint that exclude military or quasi-military action aiming at the destruction of an enemy. These self-imposed limits are, however, more flexible and less constraining than the liberal emphasis on the nonviolent, symbolic, and law-abiding character of civil disobedience suggests. From a radical democratic perspective, contestation, as a form of political self-empowerment in the face of the disempowering logic of state institutions, does not have to be public, nonviolent, directed only at state institutions, limited in its goals, and restricted to transforming the system within its existing limits, to count as civil disobedience. Although civil disobedience has to be distinguished from legal opposition, revolutionary revolt, and other forms of resistance, these boundaries are politically contested in practice and probably cannot be drawn as easily as theory implies.[18]

In relation to both mainstream liberal theory and the dominant understanding of civil disobedience operative in public discussions, the radical democratic approach is revisionist in suggesting a more minimalist (less normative, but not nonnormative) definition and a significant reinterpretation of core elements of civil disobedience. On a radical democratic understanding, the "civil" in civil disobedience is not tied to conventional expectations regarding reasonable, nonviolent, and purely symbolic public claim-making by recognized members of the political community. These expectations reach beyond mainstream liberal political philosophy and clearly shape, or rather, distort, much public debate where contemporary protest movements, from Black Lives Matter and Extinction Rebellion to migrant activism, are measured against idealized instances of civil disobedience from the past (especially mythologized figures such as King), aiming to discredit and discipline those in the present.[19] However, both the history and the present of civil disobedience are significantly more complex: King's commitment to nonviolence was embedded in a broader set of radical ethical and political commitments, theoretical arguments, strategies, and "realistic" assessments of the field of struggles that address important questions about the meaning of both violence and nonviolence.[20] Liberals routinely sidestep these questions by stipulating that civil disobedience is and has to be nonviolent. In the absence of further elaboration, however, making nonviolence part of the definition of civil disobedience is theoretically and politically suspect, as it contributes to the silencing of dissent especially by often racialized minorities.[21]

In contrast, the radical democratic model embraces political contestation based on an understanding of practices of citizenship and the capacity of political actors (including those not recognized as citizens by the state) to act together *as* citizens that often results in acts perceived as violent, uncivil, and destructive of norms of public order. Accordingly, insofar as the "civil" in civil disobedience remains central for radical democratic approaches, civility needs to be contrasted not with the incivility of confrontational contestation, or demands that are deemed too radical and hence unreasonable, but the incivility of organized violence following a military logic or of exclusions based on race, gender, or class. And insofar as the "civil" in this genuinely political understanding is linked to citizenship, the latter is to be understood, not as a formal status assigned by the state, but as a practice, that is, in terms of political agents' capacity to act together as citizens, not only within but also outside and against formal institutions.[22] In this way, the radical democratic approach hopes to avoid both the danger of underinclusiveness afflicting the liberal model, as well as the inverse danger of conceptual overstretch preoccupying those who argue for sticking with the more restrictive definition by insisting on the law-abiding and nonviolent character of disobedience.[23]

The consequence of the radical democratic critique of identifying the "civil" in civil disobedience with a strict commitment to nonviolence cannot be an embrace of violence. As pointed out above, even on the minimalist view the "civil" in civil disobedience has some normative content and force that manifests itself in the self-limitation of disobedience with regard to its means and methods. While most liberal justifications for such self-limitation are based on moral arguments (often relying on ideas of human dignity or autonomy as a normative basis), there is a rich tradition of theorizing violence (and nonviolence) in a radical democratic register that has produced a whole set of not primarily normative arguments that caution against inferring the unproblematic character of violence from the critique of one-sided and state-centered notions of nonviolence.[24] Without being able to spell them out here, these can be divided into action-theoretic arguments against the fallacy of instrumentalism (emphasizing that in its inescapably irreversible and destructive dynamic, violence is not a mere instrument that leaves the agents and their aims and practices untouched),[25] and social or relational arguments from non-sovereignty and interdependent embodiment (emphasizing how violence relies on masculine illusions of self-sufficiency and invisibilizes social bonds and dependencies that are constitutive of life).[26] None of these arguments relies on a simplistic embrace of nonviolence, a blanket rejection of violence, or a reduction of civil disobedience to a merely symbolic appeal. Civility then appears not as incompatible with violence per se but as the expression of a militant commitment that is incompatible with an unreflective embrace of violent means that neglects how violence – in addition to (potentially) harming others – affects and transforms both the subjects and the aims as well as the context of political action. As Balibar argues, civility should then rather be seen as a capacity to act within conflicts and upon them, as a commitment to an open-ended struggle of transforming conflicts from excessively violent into not-that-violent ones, that is, into conflicts that allow for a genuinely political relation. Indeed, this is what study of the discourses and practices of civility within movements of civil disobedience that find themselves in a violent environment suggests.[27] Civility then can only be conceived beyond the dichotomy of nonviolence and counterviolence, and calls for a permanent negotiation of possibilities in the specific context in light of both the reality of violence and its many traps.[28]

COUNTERING DEMOCRATIC DEFICITS: RADICALIZING THE JUSTIFICATION OF CIVIL DISOBEDIENCE

From a radical democratic perspective, the philosophical debate about the justification of civil disobedience makes two problematic presuppositions. First, the mainstream discussion proceeds on the background assumption that there is a general (prima facie or pro tanto) moral duty to obey the law, and that disobedience is thus allowed (if not required) under exceptional circumstances only. However, were there no such general duty, as philosophical anarchists hold, there would be no moral presumption in favor of obedience to law, hence no special moral justification required for civil disobedience.[29] Second, it is standardly seen as the task of the philosopher to develop criteria for the justifiability of specific acts of disobedience. However, from a radical democratic perspective this misconstrues the task of the theorist as a legislative one. Instead of developing criteria based on an ideal theory of a just and/or democratic society that would allow us to judge individual cases, radical democratic theory aims at developing a general view of the legitimacy of civil disobedience under broadly liberal-democratic conditions and at reformulating claims arising in struggles for democratization, leaving context-dependent issues of justification open to discursive validation in the public arena – a validation that will, of course, itself be subject to contestation. For these reasons, radical democrats end up having more to say about the role of civil disobedience than its justification. Nevertheless, as we shall see, their position has some implications for discussions about justifiability.

On the liberal view exemplified by Rawls's approach, acts of civil disobedience need to be justified with regard to serious infringements of the basic principles of justice and, in particular, basic individual liberties.[30] Implicitly or explicitly, this view takes for granted that civil disobedience cannot be justified in the name of democracy as it provides a last recourse for countering the unjust outcomes of procedurally legitimate majoritarian decision-making. From the radical democratic perspective, this focus seems far too narrow: it excludes a variety of potential justifications for civil disobedience that figure prominently in practice and are democracy- rather than rights-based. Next to socioeconomic inequalities (excluded by Rawls as a legitimate justification for civil disobedience), radical democrats move procedural and institutional democratic deficits into focus.[31] These deficits may well leave basic individual liberties intact, at least formally, while restricting the effective participation of citizens – and subjects in general – in democratic self-government. The development of semi-oligarchic party structures, the problem of hegemonic agenda-setting, the predominance of the executive over the legislative (e.g., with regard to foreign policy decisions), the rise of technocratic elites, and top-down forms of corporate globalization, all come to mind here.[32] The social and political reality of protest and its normative grammar call for a more pluralistic understanding of possible justifications.

The main radical democratic claim is that civil disobedience is legitimate not as constraint on, but rather as an expression of, a democratic practice of collective self-determination. It opens up possibilities of contestation and participation for citizens and other subjects where and when regular institutional channels for articulating their claims are blocked or ineffective.[33] Even in liberal, representative democracies this is not the exception to the rule but instead a structural or "normal" feature of politics that regularly affects individuals and groups. While the liberal model assumes that the justification of civil disobedience proceeds in the name of principles and rights that impose substantial limits on democracy and popular sovereignty, on the radical democratic model it is guided by the aim of a more intensive and/or extensive form of democratic self-rule, that is, a democratization of democracy that makes self-determination more effective and extends it into more areas of social life.[34] To put it schematically: on the liberal understanding, civil disobedience seeks to prevent or implement specific policy options, which are either inconsistent with or mandated by the substantive norms and values of liberalism, that is, norms and values that have been established in and that can be applied by a form of moral reasoning that stands apart from political contestation. On the radical democratic understanding, civil disobedience instead seeks to initiate or resume political contestation, opening up rather than closing down the political process and the space of political possibilities.

If it assumed that "in a decent working democracy, like the United States, the democratic conditions set out in the Constitution are sufficiently met,"[35] then the only legitimate type of civil disobedience occurs in the name of individuals who claim that their rights and other morally justified and legally codified restrictions on the political process have been violated by a democratic majority. Ronald Dworkin's influential liberal view makes a strict distinction between "matters of principle" and "matters of policy," holding that civil disobedience should be restricted to the former. Accordingly, protesting against the infringement of civil liberties will count as justified civil disobedience (with the Civil Rights Movement as a paradigm case) while protesting against nuclear weapons or against the decision of one's government to go to war will not.[36] However, this distinction is itself politically contested in ways that Dworkin's ideal theory downplays. Surely those who disobeyed in protest of the stationing of US nuclear missiles in Europe in the 1980s or of the US-led wars in Iraq and elsewhere had good reason to think they were addressing "matters of principle" and not simply of "policy."

Within the standard liberal-constitutionalist vision of democracy, the rule of law, the separation of powers, and judicial review combine with relatively limited opportunities for the *demos* to participate beyond elections. Focused on the risks of the tyranny of the majority, such a view risks being insufficiently attentive to the dangers of a tyranny of an elite that tries to arrogate and monopolize the power of the *demos*.[37] Arguably, these oligarchic and authoritarian tendencies are exactly the challenges many contemporary protest movements try to address. Daniel Markovits, writing with the Global Justice Movement in mind (though his claim could easily be applied to Occupy and other more recent movements), argues that such movements cannot be reduced to liberal attempts to secure and defend basic rights against an overreaching government.[38] Obviously, justifications of civil disobedience still make prominent, albeit sometimes primarily strategic, reference to civil and human rights. Yet, claims about substantial injustices of an economic nature (as

neglected by Rawls), and concerning systemic constraints on democratic self-government, raised by disenfranchised minorities within
states, or by transnational protest constituencies who challenge
unaccountable forms of transnational political and economic power,
take on an increasingly important role. Beyond the defensive character of the liberal model, such types of civil disobedience are tied to
struggles for democratic (self-)empowerment that address the structural democratic deficits of the liberal (and not so liberal) regimes of
the present.

While the liberal conception has played an important role in
challenging the law-and-order mentality of what Jürgen Habermas
has called "authoritarian legalism,"[39] its one-sided focus on criteria
for the justification of lawbreaking in a democratic system with the
rule of law has led to a moralized and reformist account of the genuinely political practice of disobedience. As a result, the transformative
potential of disobedience is obscured and its reach is limited to seeking local changes within an overall system whose framework remains
unquestioned.[40]

In the context of existing political systems, political processes
of deliberation and decision-making are distorted by massive structural democratic deficits in the dimensions of representation, participation, and deliberation. This is sometimes due to asymmetrical
power differences in debate, hegemonic discourses, and ideological
self-conceptions. State institutions have a poor record of addressing
such democratic deficits from within; accordingly, activist challenges
to these institutions take on a crucial democratic role.[41] This fact
constitutes the starting point for the radical democratic account of
civil disobedience's legitimacy. Given the structural shortcomings of
institutionalized democracy, civil disobedience can be understood as
a form of democratic empowerment that aims for a more intensive
and/or extensive form of democratic self-determination. Rather than
being viewed as the actions of individual rights-bearers, civil disobedience represents an essentially collective and political practice of
contestation, in which the vertical form of state authority (or

constituted power) is confronted with the horizontal *constituting power* of the association of citizens or of those who are governed.[42] Since structural deficits, despite all promises of representation and participation, are unlikely to be addressed from within existing institutions, activist forms of political protest, such as civil disobedience, play a central role in a democracy. Although the motivations behind protest will often be substantive, their justification follows a procedural rather than a substantive logic, pointing to problems with the "input" and organization or process of democratic opinion- and will-formation rather than with the "output" or decisions these processes generate.[43] In such cases even disruptive and, on the face of it, nondeliberative forms of disobedience – not directly aiming at rational persuasion, and involving pressure or even coercion so as to risk undermining deliberative quality and deliberative respect – can potentially play a deliberation-enhancing role, and, in fact, can be characterized as deliberative in terms of their motivation, organization, and short- and long-term effects.

DEMOCRATIZING DISOBEDIENCE: RADICALIZING
THE TRANSFORMATIVE ROLE OF CIVIL DISOBEDIENCE

The third line of discussion in the contemporary debate about civil disobedience concerns its political and social role. Rawls, Habermas, and others who write in the liberal tradition tend to understand civil disobedience as a kind of warning signal to existing institutions that needs to be activated under extraordinary circumstances, pointing to potential trouble and allowing political leaders to react in ways that increase the overall stability of the existing order.[44] This, however, seems to underestimate the transformative effects civil disobedience can have as a specifically extra-institutional form of political practice whose democratizing potential has been stressed by radical democratic theorists from Arendt onward. From this latter perspective, the role of civil disobedience can be described in more general terms as dramatizing a tension within the very notion of democracy, namely: the tension between democracy as a system of institutions and democracy as a practice of citizenship that can also potentially take an insurrectional form.[45] While from a liberal perspective civil disobedience mainly appears as a form of protest by individual rights-bearers against governments and political majorities that transgress the limits established by constitutionally guaranteed moral principles and values, the radical democratic perspective does not view civil disobedience primarily in terms of limitations on popular sovereignty. Rather, it envisions civil disobedience as a possible expression of democratic citizenship and a dynamizing counterweight to the rigidifying tendencies of state institutions.[46]

This radical democratic potential of civil disobedience cannot be adequately understood, however, if civil disobedience is reduced to purely symbolic protest and framed as essentially nonviolent, thereby excluding a variety of more confrontational forms of action that are part of its repertoire. Against this background, it seems that civil disobedience can only function as symbolic protest if it involves moments of real confrontation, including practices (e.g., blockades and occupations) that sometimes contain elements of violence, at least if the destruction of private property and the blocking of roads and buildings – forms of action which clearly belong to the repertoire of civil disobedience – are regarded as violent. At the same time, civil disobedience can only function as a confrontational practice if its protagonists are aware of its irreducible symbolic dimension.[47]

Both in terms of means and in its ends, civil disobedience therefore can, and often needs to, take much more radical forms than the liberal model allows for. It can aim at systemic transformations, as arguably has been the case with the US Civil Rights, Occupy, and the Black Lives Matter Movements. Furthermore, it can pursue these aims in ways that will be regarded as uncivil because of their confrontational or even violent character, including massive disruption, the destruction of property, and the use of restrained force in self-defense.[48]

By inscribing the conflictual and unresolvable dialectic between constituent and constituted power into the existing order itself, civil disobedience turns constituent power into a moment of that order that nevertheless transcends its logic. The resulting tension is precisely what civil disobedience as a genuinely political and democratic practice of contestation – never reducible to an ethical or legal understanding either in terms of individual conscience or of fidelity to the rule of law – exploits: it dramatizes "the tension between the poles of positive law and existing democratic processes and institutions on the one hand, and the idea of democracy as self-government on the other, which is not exhausted by established law and the institutional status quo."[49] In other words, it keeps in motion the "indefinite oscillation ... between two obviously antinomical forms of 'politics': an insurrectional politics and a constitutional politics, ... a politics of permanent, uninterrupted revolution, and a politics of the state as institutional order."[50] Far from being a merely corrective or defensive reaction to transgressions of state power, civil disobedience then comes into view as a transformative, and potentially comprehensive, political practice aimed at reconstituting the political order. As an essentially collective and political practice of contestation, in which the vertical form of state authority or (constituted) power is confronted with the horizontal (constituting) power of the association of citizens or of those who are governed, it is a form of democratic empowerment that aims at a more intensive and/or more extensive form of democratic self-determination.[51]

CHALLENGES AND PERSPECTIVES

On a general level, there are two developments that can be seen as requiring a fundamental rethinking of the practice of civil disobedience in a radical democratic register. First, the globalization of political and economic power structures seems to challenge an understanding of civil disobedience as a form of protest citizens engage in within bounded political communities.[52] Second, the rise of the Internet both as a tool of political action and as a politically contested space seems to go hand in hand with the development of new digital forms of activism, including electronic disobedience, that are fundamentally different from more established "offline" forms of protest.[53] While further elaboration is necessary, the radical democratic approach seems to offer a promising starting point for addressing these developments. Its overarching project of politicizing and democratizing spaces that we do not necessarily consider political for structural reasons, thus allowing for unaccountable power structures to develop, applies to both transnational and digital spaces.[54]

More specifically, the radical democratic approach faces at least four challenges that will shape future discussions on its transformative potential.

The first concerns the prospects of developing a more sustainable perspective for radical democratic disobedience beyond merely episodic disruptions. Which forms of organization and which avenues of institutionalization, including those beyond the state, are open to an approach that is at risk of disregarding its own enabling conditions and the afterlife of its momentary actualization?[55] This is precisely the challenge Arendt addressed under the heading of the *constitutio libertatis*: how can the practice of self-determination and self-organization sustain itself without being replaced by rigid forms of institutional closure? Apart from developing and experimenting with inclusive and self-reflexive organizational structures that remain open to outside challenges, it is precisely practices such as civil disobedience that keep the "revolutionary spirit" of radical new beginnings alive within an institutionalized political order in a way that functions as a check against tendencies toward closure.[56]

Second, the relation between radical democratic disobedience and (non)violence will necessarily remain a challenge in a historical context marked by structural and state violence, and the hypocrisy of many one-sided critiques of insurrectionary violence. Beyond the question of whether disobedience can be effective against structural forms of domination that can block or distort the collective agency of the oppressed, the history of political transformation shows how contestation is often caught in a complex field shaped by commitments to nonviolence, violent alternatives, and the resort to forms of militancy and force that are experienced or framed as violent.

Third, the democratizing potential of civil disobedience seems under threat in increasingly non-liberal and openly repressive and authoritarian political settings in which political institutions become less and less responsive to public claims, a functioning public sphere cannot be presupposed, the political culture provides little space for contestatory claims by those who are excluded or marginalized, and civil forms of contestation often face aggressive countermovements.

Fourth, even an expanded radical democratic notion might be ill-suited to capture some of the most challenging radical struggles of today. For example, indigenous struggles for self-determination and against the colonial and imperial project of the modern nation-state to impose homogeneity and (territorial, cultural, political, legal) uniformity escape both the framework of protest and that of civility, even if they might appear as "constituent powers" and "civic powers" in the plural.[57]

The radical democratic theory and practice of civil disobedience will need to take these challenges seriously. If the project of democratization is to remain relevant, it will have to be interpreted as a complex one in which irreducibly plural dynamics, temporalities, subjects, and practices are entangled in such a way that open-endedness and plurality become features of this project itself – as they should on a radical democratic understanding.

NOTES

1. For an overview, see William E. Scheuerman, *Civil Disobedience* (Cambridge: Polity, 2018).
2. See, e.g., Aletta Norval, "Radical Democracy," in *Encyclopedia of Democratic Thought*, eds. Paul Clarke and Joe Foweraker (London: Routledge, 2001), 587–94; Dagmar Comtesse, Oliver Flügel-Martinsen, Franziska Martinsen, and Martin Nonhoff, eds., *Radikale Demokratietheorie. Ein Handbuch* (Berlin: Suhrkamp, 2019).
3. See, e.g., James Tully, *Public Philosophy in a New Key, vol. I: Democracy and Civic Freedom* (Cambridge: Cambridge University Press, 2009),

135–59; Judith Butler, *Notes Toward a Performative Theory of Assembly* (Cambridge, Mass.: Harvard University Press, 2015).

4. Spinoza, *Political Treatise* (Indianapolis, Ind.: Hackett, 2000), VII, 25, 26, 31.

5. Karl Marx, "Contribution to the Critique of Hegel's Philosophy of Right," in *The Marx-Engels Reader*, ed. Robert C. Tucker (New York: Norton, 1978), 21; see also Miguel Abensour, *Democracy Against the State* (Cambridge: Polity, 2011).

6. Hannah Arendt, *On Violence* (New York: Harcourt Brace & Co., 1970), 44; see also Josiah Ober, "The Original Meaning of 'Democracy'. Capacity to Do Things, Not Majority Rule," *Constellations* 15, no. 1 (2008): 3–9; Sheldon Wolin, "Democracy. Electoral and Athenian," *PS. Political Science & Politics* 26, no. 3 (1993): 475–77; Etienne Balibar, "Historical Dilemmas of Democracy and Their Contemporary Relevance for Citizenship," *Rethinking Marxism* 20, no. 4 (2008): 528; Jacques Rancière, *Hatred of Democracy* (London: Verso, 2014), 51–70.

7. Etienne Balibar, "'Rights of Man' and 'Rights of the Citizen': The Modern Dialectic of Equality and Freedom," in *Masses, Classes, Ideas* (London: Routledge, 1994), 39–60; Etienne Balibar, *Equaliberty* (Durham: Duke University Press, 2014); Robin Celikates, "Constituent Power Beyond Exceptionalism: Irregular Migration, Disobedience, and (Re-)Constitution," *Journal of International Political Theory* 15, no. 1 (2019): 67–81. For a critique of radical democratic theory along these lines, see Lois McNay, *The Misguided Search for the Political: Social Weightlessness in Radical Democratic Theory* (Cambridge: Polity, 2014).

8. John Rawls, *A Theory of Justice* (Cambridge, Mass.: Harvard University Press, 1971), 363–64.

9. See also the defense of the democratic potential of civil disobedience in Albert Ogien and Sandra Laugier, *Pourquoi désobéir en démocratie?* (Paris: La Découverte, 2010); Andrew Arato and Jean L. Cohen, *Civil Society and Political Theory* (Cambridge, Mass.: MIT Press, 1992), 564–604.

10. See Bonnie Honig, *Political Theory and the Displacement of Politics* (Ithaca, N.Y.: Cornell University Press, 1993), 2–5; Sheldon Wolin, "The Liberal/Democratic Divide," *Political Theory* 24, no. 1 (1996): 97–119.

11. Robin Celikates, "Democratizing Civil Disobedience," *Philosophy and Social Criticism* 42, no. 10 (2016): 982–94; Robin Celikates, "De-, Hyper-, or Pseudo-Politicization? Undoing and Remaking the Demos in the Age of Right-Wing Populism," in *The Critical Theory of Wendy Brown*, eds. Amy Allen and Eduardo Mendieta (University Park, Pa.: Penn State University Press, forthcoming).

12. See William E. Scheuerman's Introduction to this volume as well as the discussion in Çiğdem Çıdam, William E. Scheuerman, Candice Delmas, Erin R. Pineda, Robin Celikates, Alexander Livingston, "Theorizing the Politics of Protest: Contemporary Debates on Civil Disobedience," *Contemporary Political Theory* (2020), https://doi.org/10.1057/s41296-02 0-00392-7.

13. See, e.g., Ruth Braunstein, "Boundary-Work and the Demarcation of Civil from Uncivil Protest in the United States: Control, Legitimacy, and Political Inequality," *Theory and Society* 47, no. 5 (2018): 603–33.

14. See, e.g., Judith Butler, *The Force of Nonviolence* (London: Verso, 2020), 23–24, 144–45.

15. Rawls, *A Theory of Justice*, 364–66. For a more detailed discussion of what follows, see Robin Celikates, "Rethinking Civil Disobedience as a Practice of Contestation – Beyond the Liberal Paradigm," *Constellations* 23, no. 1 (2016): 37–45.

16. See, e.g., David Lyons, "Moral Judgment, Historical Reality, and Civil Disobedience," *Philosophy and Public Affairs* 27, no. 1 (1998): 31–49.

17. See Celikates, "Democratizing Civil Disobedience," 985–86.

18. For an early statement of this view, first published in 1968, see Howard Zinn, *Disobedience and Democracy* (Boston, Mass.: South End Press, 2002).

19. See, e.g., Jeanne Theoharis, *A More Beautiful and Terrible History: The Uses and Misuses of Civil Rights History* (Boston, Mass.: Beacon Press, 2018).

20. See, e.g., Erin R. Pineda, *Seeing Like an Activist: Civil Disobedience and the Civil Rights Movement* (New York: Oxford University Press, 2021), and her chapter in this volume.

21. See my contribution in Çıdam et al., "Theorizing the Politics of Protest."

22. See James Tully et al., *On Global Citizenship: James Tully in Dialogue* (London: Bloomsbury, 2014).

23. See, e.g., Scheuerman, *Civil Disobedience*, 1–10.

24. See, e.g., Todd May, *Nonviolent Resistance* (Cambridge: Polity, 2015); and Hourya Bentouhami, *Le dépôt des armes. Non-violence et désobéissance civile* (Paris: Presses universitaires de France, 2015).

25. Arendt, *On Violence*; Etienne Balibar, *Violence and Civility* (New York: Columbia University Press, 2015).

26. Butler, *The Force of Nonviolence*.

27. See, e.g., Robin Celikates, "Learning from the Streets: Civil Disobedience in Theory and Practice," in *Global Activism: Art and Conflict in the 21st Century*, ed. Peter Weibel (Cambridge, Mass.: MIT Press, 2015), 65–72.

28. Balibar, *Violence and Civility*, 19–24. See also Alexander Livingston's chapter in this volume.

29. See, e.g., the discussion in Christopher Wellman and A. John Simmons, *Is There a Duty to Obey the Law?* (Cambridge: Cambridge University Press, 2005) and James D. Ingram's contribution to this volume. An alternative critique of the standard view claims that the same grounds invoked for a duty to obey the law justify a duty to disobey (in civil and uncivil ways) under certain circumstances; see Candice Delmas, *A Duty to Resist: When Disobedience Should Be Uncivil* (Oxford: Oxford University Press, 2018), as well as her chapter in this volume.

30. Rawls, *A Theory of Justice*, 372–74.

31. For an early argument that the defects of Western democracies can serve to justify disobedience on specifically democratic grounds, see Peter Singer, *Democracy and Disobedience* (Oxford: Clarendon, 1973), 105–32.

32. See, e.g., Francis Dupuis-Déri, "Global Protesters versus Global Elites: Are Direct Action and Deliberative Politics Compatible? *New Political Science* 29, no. 2 (2007): 167–86; Daniel Markovits, "Democratic Disobedience," *Yale Law Journal* 114 (2005), 1897–952; April Carter, *Direct Action and Democracy Today* (Cambridge: Polity, 2005).

33. Hannah Arendt, "Civil Disobedience," in *Crises of the Republic* (New York: Harcourt Brace & Co., 1972): 49–102, esp. 74–75.

34. See Markovits, "Democratic Disobedience"; also, the classic account in Carole Pateman, *Participation and Democratic Theory* (Cambridge: Cambridge University Press, 1970).

35. Ronald Dworkin, *Freedom's Law* (Cambridge, Mass.: Harvard University Press, 1996), 32.

36. See Ronald Dworkin, *A Matter of Principle* (Cambridge, Mass.: Harvard University Press, 1985), chapter 4; and Alexander Kaufman's chapter in this volume.

37. See also Andreas Kalyvas, "Popular Sovereignty, Democracy, the Constituent Power," *Constellations* 12, no. 2 (2005): 223–44; Wolin, "The Liberal/Democratic Divide."

38. Daniel Markovits, "Democratic Disobedience," *Yale Law Journal* 114 (2005), 1897–952. On the radical disobedience of the Occupy movement, see Bernard Harcourt, "Political Disobedience," *Critical Inquiry* 39, no. 1 (2012): 33–55.

39. Jürgen Habermas, "Civil Disobedience: Litmus Test for the Democratic Constitutional State," *Berkeley Journal of Sociology* 30 (1985): 106.

40. See also Çiğdem Çıdam, "Radical Democracy without Risks? Habermas on Constitutional Patriotism and Civil Disobedience," *New German Critique* 44, no. 2 (2017): 105–32.

41. See Iris Marion Young, "Activist Challenges to Deliberative Democracy," *Political Theory* 29 (2001): 670–90.

42. See Arendt, "Civil Disobedience," 92, 96; Balibar, "Sur la désobéissance civique," *Droit de cité* (Paris: Quadrige/ Presses universitaires de France, 2002), 17–22; Balibar, *Equaliberty*, 165–86, 277–94; Michael Walzer, *Obligations* (Cambridge, Mass.: Harvard University Press, 1970), 3–23.

43. This leads to some overlap between the radical democratic and the deliberative democratic view of civil disobedience; see William Smith, *Civil Disobedience and Deliberative Democracy* (London: Routledge, 2013) and his chapter in this volume.

44. Interestingly, this comes close to the epistemic role Niklas Luhmann attributes to protest: compensating the reflexivity deficits inherent in functionally differentiated modern societies (*Risk: A Sociological Theory* [Berlin: de Gruyter, 1993], 142–43).

45. Habermas ("Civil Disobedience," 112) recognizes that the "suspended" position of civil disobedience "between legitimacy and legality" is anchored in this fundamental "ambiguity" of the democratic state, but his own elaborations on the democratizing potential of civil disobedience remain underdeveloped and constrained by the Rawlsian frame he largely adopts.

46. Arendt, "Civil Disobedience"; Young, "Activist Challenges to Deliberative Democracy."

47. See Celikates, "Rethinking Civil Disobedience as a Practice of Contestation."

48. See, e.g., Keeanga-Yamahtta Taylor, *From #BlackLivesMatter to Black Liberation* (Chicago, Ill.: Haymarket Books, 2016).

49. Ulrich Rödel, Günter Frankenberg, and Helmut Dubiel, *Die demokratische Frage* (Frankfurt: Suhrkamp, 1989), 46.

50. Balibar, "'Rights of Man' and 'Rights of the Citizen,'" 51.

51. See Arendt, "Civil Disobedience." On the relation between the associative and the dissociative dimension of disobedience and exit, exodus, withdrawal as modes of disobedience, see Paolo Virno, *A Grammar of the Multitude* (New York: Semiotext(e), 2004), 69–70; and Jennet Kirkpatrick, *The Virtues of Exit: On Resistance and Quitting Politics* (Chapel Hill, N. C.: The University of North Carolina Press, 2017).

52. See the contribution by Luis Cabrera in this volume, and William E. Scheuerman, "Civil Disobedience in the Shadows of Postnationalization and Privatization," *Journal of International Political Theory* 12, no. 3 (2016): 237–57.

53. See the contribution by Theresa Züger in this volume, and Robin Celikates, "Digitalization: Another Structural Transformation of the Public Sphere?" *Yearbook for Eastern and Western Philosophy* 1 (2016): 39–54.

54. On the participatory dimension of digital disobedience, see Gabriella Coleman, *Hacker, Hoaxer, Whistleblower, Spy: The Many Faces of Anonymous* (London: Verso, 2015); on transnational disobedience, also Celikates, "Constituent Power Beyond Exceptionalism."

55. On organization, see Pineda's contribution in Çıdam et al., "Theorizing the Politics of Protest," and Taylor, *From #BlackLivesMatter to Black Liberation*, 153–90; on institutionalization see Lawrence Hamilton, "Resistance and Radical Democracy: Freedom, Power and Institutions," *History of European Ideas* 44, no. 4 (2018): 477–91; and Christian Volk, "On a Radical Democratic Theory of Political Protest," *Critical Review of International Social and Political Philosophy* (2018), https://doi.org/10 .1080/13698230.2018.1555684.

56. See Hannah Arendt, *On Revolution* (New York: Viking, 1965); Andreas Kalyvas, *Democracy and the Politics of the Extraordinary* (Cambridge: Cambridge University Press, 2008), 187–300.

57. See James Tully, *Public Philosophy in a New Key, vol. II: Imperialism and Civic Freedom* (Cambridge: Cambridge University Press, 2009), 195–221, 243–309; Audra Simpson, *Mohawk Interruptus: Political Life Across the Borders of Settler States* (Durham: Duke University Press, 2014); and Nick Estes and Jaskiran Dhillon, eds., *Standing with Standing Rock: Voices from the #NoDAPL Movement* (Minneapolis, Minn.: University of Minnesota Press, 2019).

6   Realist Disobedience

Andrew Sabl

For the last fifteen years or so, an emerging "realist" school of political theory, questioning not only the conclusions of mainstream moral and political philosophy but also, more fundamentally, the questions it asks, has called for a new approach.[1] Rather than deducing moral principles from posited moral ideals, realists aspire to draw normative recommendations from reflections on actual political events and institutions, and from judgments regarding which institutions and practices do better at addressing recurrent problems. Stressing the ubiquity of moral disagreement and the permanence of political conflict – politics is a contest among adversaries, not a reasonable conversation among friends – realists see politics not as a quest for rational consensus but as a set of technologies for ensuring order and providing public goods in spite of the lack of such consensus. Rather than political morality being an instance of "applied ethics" in which the same moral principles we use in private life can be urged upon political life, politics, realists insist, embodies its own characteristic values.

Although realists respect as political facts the force of moral appeals, that is, appeals to duty and justice, they regard moral motivations as imbricated with nonmoral motivations rather than embodying a unique sort of authority. The longing for justice is a very real sentiment, but simply one among others.[2] *Pace* the widespread tendency to emphasize human beings' capacity to respond to practical reason, realists are skeptical that most people most of the time are capable of being persuaded by rational arguments alone – much less the most philosophically sound arguments. Instead of assuming that people's actions are ruled by moral principles, realists observe that

I would like to thank Joseph Dattilo for research assistance and Enzo Rossi for valuable comments.

their principles are sometimes tacit, confused, and more often flouted than observed when their observance becomes inconvenient. Even those principles that seem coherent are more likely to reflect a rationalization of a complex drive, or the outcome of a past social conflict, than freestanding conclusions from unimpeachable axioms.[3] Finally, realists posit that political change is driven by changes in social power and the forcing of new political interests onto the agenda, not by deliberation on shared normative propositions. A realist approach to civil disobedience will regard it as an *inherently* political enterprise: one which seeks to effect change less by raising philosophical questions than by raising recalcitrant opponents' costs. On this realist view, civil disobedience will not assume purity of motives on the part of either disobedients or those whose actions they hope to influence.

This chapter begins by discussing the basic contours of a distinctive realist approach to civil disobedience. It draws a contrast not only to neo-Kantian liberal, but also to spiritual, democratic, and anarchist approaches. These contrasts should help cement the portrait of realism as an approach to civil disobedience that has its own identity and represents more than a mere modification of so-called ideal theory. The chapter then explores what these differences entail regarding the insights and claims of non-realists. Realists should simply reject some non-realist insights, judge others to be of limited interest or use, and recast yet others so as to address civil disobedience from a specifically political standpoint rather than that of pre-political morality. For their own part, I suggest, realists will find certain questions of their own more pressing and salient than those that typically occupy non-realists. Then I turn to discuss the complex relationship between justice and order, arguing for a stronger connection between them than either realists or non-realists typically admit. The chapter then briefly raises questions of method and suggests how realists might seek to draw insights from empirical research. Far from embodying bloody-minded immoralism or quasi-scientific positivism, the chapter concludes, realism offers both its own distinctive approach to ethics, in which attention to political questions is itself an ethical require-ment, and an account of political value more compelling than that of ideal theorists.

Realist treatments of civil disobedience are currently rare. Two articles by Robert Jubb and Karuna Mantena apparently exhaust the literature, and of these only Mantena sketches a positive, substantive realist account of civil disobedience, arguing for Gandhi's defense of nonviolence as being realist.[4] This chapter is therefore largely prom-issory and exploratory. It aims to map out possible contributions that realists might bring to the civil disobedience debate and to argue for their originality and worth.

REALISM AND CIVIL DISOBEDIENCE

Treatments of realism often begin by criticizing an "ideal" or "high liberal" theory usually associated with figures such as Ronald Dworkin, Robert Nozick, and John Rawls.[5] The context of civil dis-obedience renders this particular way of defining realism less apt than it might be elsewhere. Though figures such as Rawls, Dworkin, and Nozick aim at systematic theories of a perfectly just, equal, and free society on the grounds that only such a theory provides a standpoint for criticizing the status quo, theorists of that stripe who defend *civil disobedience* will presumably do so out of a desire to address real-world instances in which society is *not* perfectly just, equal, or free.[6] To the extent that civil disobedience theorists are "liberal" in the neo-Kantian sense, they will adopt Kantianism's *moralism* and *rational-ism*, and thus its aspirations to further human autonomy, its intense belief in human dignity, and its suspicion of political strategy and the search for competitive advantage. They will typically avoid, however, the *utopianism* whereby ideal theorists seek a constructed and static model of what should be, intended to illuminate the flaws of all that is. To this extent, no defender of civil disobedience is likely to uphold what Judith Shklar criticized as theorists' "normal model" of justice, which portrays injustice as a "surprising abnormality," a "prelude to or a rejection and breakdown of justice" before, or after, a normal state of justice is in effect.[7] To study civil disobedience is to view injustice as common and perhaps ubiquitous.

Moreover, whereas high (rationalist or neo-Kantian) liberalism and its deliberative-democratic cousins are plausibly portrayed as hegemonic in political philosophy as a whole, this is much less true of theoretical debates concerning civil disobedience. Other prominent schools of civil disobedience theory are captured by William Scheuerman's useful categories.[8] "Religious-spiritual" defenses of civil disobedience question the status of secular law and the permanence (or at least the desirability) of legitimate moral disagreement; their model of politics involves moral transformation rather than permanent toleration. Democratic defenses of civil disobedience, often drawing on Habermas's deliberation theory, emphasize not the role of deliberation in setting static moral standards (i.e., "could principle X be endorsed in a free and equal deliberative process") but a vision of deliberation as enabling actual progress and change. They praise disobedience for contributing to a "collective learning process" that aims to make better, though never perfect, a democratic order that is always incomplete and distorted by social power.[9] Finally, theorists sympathetic to anarchism (in either the real-world or philosophical sense) defend disobedience easily and in all domains – often dropping the "civil" proviso – because they doubt that state authority is a good thing and that citizens are generally obliged to obey laws.

Engagement with these positions can draw out realism's positive identity by showing how realism differs not only from ideal theory but from other approaches as well. When it comes to spiritual senses of civil disobedience, realists might salute their religiously motivated skepticism that reasoned arguments suffice for political change. Reinhold Niebuhr's Christian realism, which expressed this skepticism in the language of sin – fallen human beings will stubbornly defend their privileges and resist justice and equality – comes to mind.[10] Nonetheless, realists would likely be wary of claims that spiritual transformation can yield permanent moral progress without unacceptable costs in terms of anti-pluralism. Those who regard themselves as having become spiritually purified are likely to end up regarding some religions, and some outlooks within those religions, as far more politically acceptable than others.[11] Moreover, the spiritual activist may culpably denigrate secular citizens who privilege, as most will, their prosaic interests (for example, a desire for safety and economic advancement, over moral crusades for justice).

When it comes to democratic deliberation, realists doubt both its existence and its necessity. There is little evidence that the cacophonous clash of public arguments somehow adds up to a "public sphere" that sifts out the best arguments, or prevents citizens from sorting themselves into tribes of identity and opinion. Realists will agree that civil disobedience can raise issues and shift agendas but will not find the category of deliberation particularly useful in understanding how this works or ought to work. Finally, regarding anarchists: because we wonder what concrete proposals anarchists would substitute for the police who prevent private violence, the bureaucrats who enforce environmental regulation, and the compulsory taxation that funds schools, trains, and hospitals, realists would admit that state authority and legal obligation are not absolute but would question rather sharply the seriousness of theories who deny their importance altogether.[12]

In short, realism has substance. Far from being some shadowy counterpart of ideal theory, it is the other way around. Ideal theory is just one of many theories that might be called "non-realist" in its inability to take seriously, and apply systematically to a pertinent social question such as civil disobedience, the basic categories of real politics: conflict among political adversaries, authority, power, interest, order, security, and the effective provision of public goods on the scale of a large society.

REALIST TRANSFORMATIONS OF NON-REALIST INSIGHTS

Let me now provisionally suggest how realists might treat non-realists' existing insights and theses. A realist approach would *redescribe* certain non-realist claims so as better to reflect the conditions and constraints of real politics. It would *reject* some of them as reflecting, often dangerously, portrayals of how people who lack actual human motivations might act, or how societies that lack actual political struggles might hope to function. And it would – perhaps most gallingly to non-realists – regard some non-realist insights with *indifference*, as giving plausible answers to questions that do not particularly matter. In turn, realists will regard as essential several sets of questions that non-realist accounts rarely even consider.

Redescription

Some non-realist claims can be adopted wholesale by realists. One is that discrete minorities whose needs and interests are neglected by majoritarian politics typically are most in need of civil disobedience.[13] But a realist approach would insist on recasting other non-realist claims so as to reflect the circumstances and demands of real politics as opposed to those of idealized agents who are free to act as if politics did not exist (or perhaps resembled a philosophy seminar). To take two examples:

1. The claim that civil disobedience is justified to the extent that it furthers moral dialogue, interpreted as an "an argument-based, progress-oriented conversation" constituted by "mutual recognition of each party's rights and duties,"[14] seems from a realist perspective to rest on two dubious claims: first, that political argument is predominantly rational; second, that citizens in a diverse polity can more or less agree on their moral rights and duties. Empirically, it seems clear that civil disobedience thrives when adversarial parties' claims of moral rights and duties are radically incompatible. For example, segregationists neither held nor came to hold the view that African Americans were entitled to the same rights and duties that they themselves had. The idea that civil disobedience preserves the conditions for future cooperation better than many alternative forms of resistance (e.g., violence, or inarticulate forms of lawbreaking such as riot or sabotage) remains compelling. But the cooperation in question involves action, not

belief, and disobedients further it not by stating their willingness to heed their opponents' words but by showing their willingness to spare their opponents' persons.[15]

2. A realist cannot argue for civil disobedience on William Smith's grounds that it disrupts the "deliberative inertia" produced by rigid or biased "discourse," thereby enhancing the "cognitive function of the public sphere in a deliberative democracy."[16] Realists do not believe that the authority of democratic decisions derives from democratic deliberation, that politics serves a cognitive function, or that the public sphere is anything but a myth (and not a salutary one). Most of Smith's concrete arguments in favor of civil disobedience do not require their Habermasian trappings and would be more convincing without them. As he argues, civil disobedience is both necessary and justified when the everyday processes of democracy ignore very substantial – often irreversible – setbacks to fundamental human interests: full stop.[17]

Rejection

Other arguments put forth regarding civil disobedience cannot be redescribed in this way. For instance, realists will tend to dismiss arguments from autonomy as philosophical fairy tales. Real people never live under laws they "give themselves" but are necessarily, universally, and pervasively constrained by both natural scarcity and the need to enlist the cooperation of others. A radical skepticism toward the whole idea of autonomy, though not normally numbered among realism's hallmarks, appears to be one reason that realists who are liberals will be prone to describe the central liberal value as diversity, not autonomy.[18] To take another example: doctrines of disobedience that claim that it is more or less justified according to whether its proponents possess certain internal states, for example, conscientiousness or moral seriousness, bump up against the need to structure institutions and practices that will be robust in the face of political agents' pervasive incentives to falsely profess whatever ideas or intentions let them get away with doing what they want. Though it may seem old-fashioned, it seems reasonable to write laws (and enforce norms) that punish behavior, not states of mind, on the grounds that only the former are observable.

In other words, realists will reject the idealist penchant for thinking one can check the excesses of civil disobedience via "parchment barriers": by stipulating *in a philosophical argument* that disobedience would only be justified, and should only be excused, when agents are motivated by certain kinds of convictions, held deeply and sincerely.[19] Politics assumes a condition in which citizens *deeply and permanently disagree* regarding whose reasons are morally valid and which beliefs are held sincerely. That is why legal authority does not presuppose agreement on such matters. Actual, effective limitations on civil disobedience will entail external sanctions: either the much-maligned requirement that disobedients accept (some) legal punishment[20] or some political check, for example, civil disobedients' knowing that their movement will fail unless fellow citizens come to judge the disobedients less harshly than they judge the authorities who punish them. To be sure, neither "external" solution guarantees what some moral philosophers are seeking: that legal and political outcomes will track moral truth. To this the realist will respond, that (1) nothing can guarantee that anyway; (2) the realist attitude toward legal authority and political victory, precisely because it does not claim to align either authority or victory with morality, casts no moral aspersions on politics' temporary losers. They are not necessarily *wrong*; they have just *lost*.[21]

Indifference

Other commonplace non-realist considerations will strike realists as a matter of indifference, as being beside any identifiably significant political point. *Conscience, pace* the claims of many civil disobedience scholars, is not something to which most ordinary citizens instinctively defer. More precisely, when we do defer to something we call conscience, we typically mean that we approve of, or at least do not deplore, the substance of what the person claiming conscience is for. When we see someone moved to flout laws or social norms by strong, principled, and immovable beliefs whose content we regard as absurd and pernicious, we describe those beliefs not as conscientious but as fanatical, and typically condemn such conduct not less but more harshly than we would common criminality. Hannah Arendt, at least a semi-realist in sharply distinguishing political judgment from private morality, is right to claim that conscience is irrelevant to civil disobedience.[22] Similarly, the question of moral rights, which plays a major role in much legal-philosophical scholarship on civil disobedience, seems politically irrelevant. A philosopher who possessed a perfect theory of moral rights would still be at a loss in the face of the vast majority of citizens who did not recognize that theory (or, probably, any other: humans are not particularly theory-driven creatures) and who rejected its conclusions.

REALIST QUESTIONS

If realists should dismiss certain non-realist questions as irrelevant, pernicious, or badly posed, they will also insist on placing at the center of their inquiry concerns that non-realists often treat only briefly, if at all.

First, realists should demand that a theory of civil disobedience "economize on virtue."[23] That is, they will not recommend institutions or practices that will only work on the assumption that disobedients, or those judging them, have to be self-sacrificing, principled, or public-spirited. Theorists often take a first-person plural attitude toward civil disobedience and one that is quite self-congratulatory, adopting an explicit or implicit premise that those disobedients who are most interesting are morally superior to other citizens, as are theorists for praising them. Realists, while rejecting the economist's reduction of all motivations to self-interest, will tend to put forth as not just tolerable but mandatory a political version of the moral relativism or skepticism that philosophers are trained to mock. That is, whatever may be rationally said in defense of the motivations for breaking general laws, those motivations are likely to seem more admirable inside the disobedients' own heads than to political strangers. Actual practitioners of civil disobedience tend to know this. Not surprisingly, they spend much more time thinking about which defenses of their actions *will persuade others*, as a matter of politics and rhetoric, than about which are most likely to meet some philosophical standard.

Second, realists should insist on exploring civil disobedience in terms of the ethics of power, given that it is a form of *countervailing* power.[24] As noted, civil disobedience is plausibly portrayed as a check against the "social power" of special interests that exert private influence on governments in defiance of political equality.[25] But this means that it will work only to the extent that the disobedients themselves exert enough power to make governments more reluctant to ignore the disobedients than to flout the powerful social interests to which they normally defer. Civil disobedience is a plausible and praiseworthy political method only to the extent that it creates power – and unavoidably, therefore, *also* potentially abuses power. Mantena argues convincingly that Gandhi's theory of nonviolence was largely aimed at mitigating this danger. For Gandhi, one reason to avoid violence was to ensure that agents who turn out to be wrong or misguided only harm themselves. His theory was "realist" partly in being aware of precisely this requirement.[26] Realist accounts of civil disobedience will need to resist the temptation to assume that civil disobedients are always right and that the power of successful civil disobedience does not tend to corrupt.

Third, the realist conviction that politics is driven by power and interest more than abstract principles can motivate attention to the kinds of injustices and abuses that reflect not public inattention to principled claims but powerful actors' ability to flout principles that are already generally recognized. Race and gender discrimination is one example, wage theft another: that no one favors these things in principle says nothing about their actual (high) prevalence. Accounts of civil disobedience need to stress instances in which disobedience draws attention to the neglect of crucial interests, or to abuses of power, even when no serious disagreement on avowed legal or political principles exists.

Finally, realists need to insist on taking seriously both the benefits and the hazards of mixed motives. Skeptical that agents typically, or perhaps ever, act out of pure moral motives (in some versions of realism, also skeptical that it would be good if they did, given the tendency of "pure" motives to license crusades that cause harm), realists will not generally insist on "universalist" stipulations that civil disobedients must be willing to disobey the law in every relevant case if they are to defend their actions in the cases they happen to care about.[27] Since the risks of breaking the law can be sizable, most civil disobedients do so in the service of causes they care about personally. In other words, they act selectively, and in ways that probably could not be defended impartially. To object to this kind of partiality is called, in real politics, "whataboutism," which attacks the alleged hypocrisy of opposing one abuse while neglecting another abuse of equal heinousness.[28] Whataboutism, which is to rhetorical practice as universalism is to theory, is pernicious because violations of universalism are themselves universal. To take universalism seriously would entail discrediting all attempts to redress particular injustices. With apologies to Dr. King, the only way to address justice anywhere is to admit that no one opposes it everywhere.[29]

JUSTICE AND ORDER

Ideal theory, following Rawls, typically gives justice priority over order, with the former conceived as "the first virtue of social institutions." Other approaches to civil disobedience likewise tend to subordinate order to moral or spiritual progress, the vindication of alleged autonomy, or democratic evolution and collective reinvention. Against this tendency, realists often give order pride of place as *the* central value of politics, and one that reveals the independence of politics in that order is a political value having no analogue in private life.[30] Even those formulations of realism that more plausibly privilege not order *qua* order, but instead public goods provision more generally, often explicitly subordinate justice to this wider set of what might be called order-goods. Providing adequate public goods at all, and acknowledging *state authority* as the only reliable way of overcoming collective action problems, is said to be a more fundamental and urgent concern than ensuring a proper distribution of government's burdens and benefits.

However, just as I noted that defenses of civil disobedience tend to depart from mainstream ideal theory in assuming the permanence, or at least the permanent threat, of "non-ideal" departures from justice, realists who study civil disobedience tend to depart from the main emphasis of realist theory in stressing the ways that authority can be eroded or forfeited if states depart too far from justice (or allied values such as equality). For this reason, my claim in a previous essay that "the defense of civil disobedience must probably assume that order and law-abidingness are not important values at all, or at least not usually important compared to justice, liberty, or equality," requires modification.[31] For a realist scholar of disobedience order matters, but it may be imbricated with justice and equality rather than a radical competitor to them. Nor does a respect for order entail attachment to the status quo.

Thus Robert Jubb, while stressing that politics needs authority and criticizing individualistic and radical democratic theories of disobedience for neglecting authority and the need to ensure public goods provision, also criticizes Rawls for a rigid, unrealistic view of authority whereby citizens have no duty to obey the law unless the regime they live under is "nearly just" (as will be rare). Instead, Jubb argues for a context-sensitive duty to obey the law, calibrated by the level of a regime's authority with respect to specific policies. In this vein, he defends anti-poll-tax protests' disobedience to law on the ground that the Thatcher government that implemented the tax had won a distinct minority of the vote while other parties loudly opposed to her revenue plans had won, between them, a large majority.[32] Karuna Mantena, while defending Gandhi as a realist in his moral psychology and his skepticism regarding the force of reason, hardly believes that he had a responsibility to respect the political order. On the contrary, his nonviolence was directed not at reform but at the complete removal of a regime whose very presence was illegitimate.[33] In more recent work I have argued against Russell Hardin's conservative view of political conventions, whereby those disadvantaged under a particular political order – Hardin mentions African Americans in the US – must accept it anyway on pain of courting an anarchy that would leave them much worse off. I portray civil disobedience as a contemporary political technology, improving on earlier alternatives of submission or revolution, that allows for "re-coordination" without courting such risks. Disobedients challenge a deeply unjust allocation of rights and social burdens without threatening the state's basic functions of protecting personal security and providing public goods.[34]

In truth, the separation between order and justice may make more sense in theory than in actual politics. Correspondingly, the realist tendency to deny the central relevance of justice may represent a departure from its program of respecting "real politics." Even a staunchly libertarian public choice theorist such as James Buchanan acknowledged that the wealthy have reason to accept certain forms of redistribution in practice lest the poor threaten to upend the whole system.[35] If there is no livable justice without order, there is also – as a matter of concrete fact, not ideal wishes – no durable order without (at least adequate) justice. The complex relationship between justice (along with other moral values) and order (along with other values associated with collective action under acknowledged authority), and the ways in which civil disobedience might either lessen or exacerbate the tension between these sets of values, is understudied. This represents a crucial set of questions for both realist and non-realist scholars of civil disobedience to explore.

QUESTIONS OF METHOD

Realists may differ even more sharply with non-realists on questions of method than on those of substance. Civil disobedience presents these differences in an unusually sharp form. The elevation of conscience and/or moral truth in much non-realist theory leads to a concern that the motivations for disobedience not be "merely strategic," as though there were something wrong with disobeying the law only when one has reason to think that doing so is likely to make society better rather than worse. The realist will tend to say the opposite. Strategic reasons are the *most* defensible reasons for disobedience. Related to this, realists will not share the philosopher's penchant for thought-experiments chiefly valued for their ability to strip away worldly biases to arrive at pure practical intuitions. Kantian dogma aside, there is no reason to think that there is such a thing as practical reason, independent of socialization, education, and trained judgment. On the contrary, all judgments are biased to some degree; attempts to strip away our worldly experience will more than likely produce distilled and purified prejudices. More sympathetic to empiricism (and, in some versions, to a moderated version of Nietzsche's perspectivism) than to apriorism, the realist will want those opining on civil disobedience to learn as much as possible about history and real-world examples. Wisdom derives from experience, not innocence.

This experience can derive from a variety of sources, from political engagement to avid consumption of reliable journalism to living involuntarily in a situation – for example, in a poor or violent society, or at the bottom social rungs of a wealthy and ordered one – that teaches political and social truth the hard way. It is useful, however, to treat in stylized form four scholarly sources of experience from which realist students of civil disobedience might learn: biography, handbooks, political science, and history.

A *biographic* approach to civil disobedience would highlight the centrality of human agency and the role of both character and intellectual virtues – *phronesis*, if one will – in helping human agents make decisions. Given the theorist's professional deformation of writing as if the only proper names that matter are those of authors, and that historical trends would have unfolded the same way even if no specific human beings had made the choices they did, these correctives are very helpful. This approach's central vice would be to stress circumstances and individual idiosyncrasies to such a degree as to make the inquiry anti-theoretical, unable to teach general lessons.[36] To the extent that realists engaging with biography focus on eras when political institutions were undeveloped (such as fifth-century Athens), or else valorize rare episodes of revolution, civil war, or near-anarchy, this approach might also tend to underplay the role of institutions, to exaggerate the degree to which civil disobedients can and should seek to mold new orders from scratch without regard to institutions that already exist and command some authority. Finally, there is the danger of apotheosizing leaders, as if the Indian independence movement were simply Gandhi or the Burmese democracy movement the sole creation of Aung San Suu Kyi.

The desire to stress agency, choice, and the exploitation of fleeting opportunities while seeking to take institutions seriously and to draw general lessons is fulfilled in another genre: a *handbook* of (nonviolent) strategy. In this regard, Peter Ackerman and Christopher Kruegler's *Strategic Nonviolent Conflict* (1994) would repay close attention. It confirms some realist commonplaces while challenging quite fundamentally some non-realists' assumptions. The authors' research reveals that few cases of nonviolent action, including the most successful cases, involve "philosophies of principled nonviolence": most movements that deploy nonviolence do so because it seems the most effective strategy against adversaries when military options are inferior or unavailable. The authors take as a starting point not rational consensus but political conflict, "an inherently adversarial process involving the direct exchange of sanctions, either violent or nonviolent, with a view to inflicting costs on one's opponents, inducing them to change their behavior."[37] The authors claim, in fact, that moralized studies of nonviolence – those portraying it as "an expression of goodness or heroism" – have hindered the study of nonviolence as a strategy that develops and improves over time and from which principles to guide effective action may be derived.[38]

The normative theorist's engagement with *political science* would shift the focus of attention from choice to the circumstances of choice, asking when it is most likely that civil disobedience can effect change. The political science of civil disobedience, attuned to the social scientist's virtues of choosing representative cases and trying to control for the variables that are not the object of one's study, is exemplified by Erica Chenoweth and Maria J. Stephan's *Why Civil Resistance Works* (2011). Their work teaches a variety of salutary lessons: for example, that civil disobedience sometimes simply fails, and that one central virtue of nonviolence is that it lessens opponents' fear for their lives and makes the disobedients seem proper partners for a negotiated settlement.[39] Most fundamentally, however, the authors argue that nonviolence allows a great *number* and *variety* of people to join a movement, whereas violent insurgencies appeal chiefly to zealous and healthy young men. This breadth both enhances a movement's likely strategic repertoire and bodes well for stable democracy. A nonviolent movement, if it wins and takes power, will yield a regime that commands wide, rather than narrow, support and that is used to settling disputes without killing people.[40] That non-realist scholars of civil disobedience often defend the liberal and democratic credentials of their method without appealing to the central values of liberalism (diversity), democracy (the moral power of numbers), or politics itself (peaceful, consensual order), is telling. Political science is a source of learning, but also of relearning: theorists may draw from it respect for values that ordinary citizens remember better than we do.[41] Finally, the political scientist's inquiry as such tacitly reminds theorists to avoid the cult of lonely dissent that moral philosophers find so tempting. The agents of politics are people *in numbers*; the wisest and noblest leaders can accomplish nothing at all without the support of thousands or millions. And those determined to bring about greater justice cannot afford to ignore the causal preconditions of winning such support.

Finally, an engagement with *history* – at its limit in the form of a formal "discourse" on historical work – is one of the few ways in which theorists and philosophers can discover new categories of moral and political value, or else come to fundamentally change their understanding of old ones.[42] A proper example of how this works would require a full-length discourse (analogous to Machiavelli's discourses on Livy) on a history of civil resistance or nonviolence such as Peter Ackerman and Jack Duvall's *A Force More Powerful* (2000). As a tiny taste, however: the authors argue that Max Weber was wrong to regard physical violence as the ultimate resort in politics, since there are too many examples of rulers commanding fearsome armies nonetheless falling to nonviolent resistance, often because portions of the army refuse to fire, or switch sides.[43] David Hume's claim that all governments rest on opinion, or Gene Sharp's view that nonviolence "attacks the most vulnerable characteristic of all hierarchical institutions and governments: dependence on the governed,"[44] are theoretical commonplaces, but their full implications only become solid in the theorist's mind through engagement with extended accounts of how they play out. Absent such engagements, theorists can, and often do, nod sagely at Hume or Sharp while continuing to write treatises on how the basic question of liberalism, perhaps of politics generally, is how to justify the use of coercion backed by violence. The truth is that state violence will not be possible in the first place, whether justified or not, unless the people tasked with deploying and supporting violence continue to believe the pretentions to authority of the regime that orders it.

One should stress that the goal of all these inquiries is to improve our *normative* insights. Political theorists should not aspire to predict events better than empirical political scientists or to have a better feel for nonviolent strategy than practitioners or those who devote their life to systematizing their lessons. The realist claim, instead, is that only an engagement with real politics illuminates the *values* that inhere in politics and that cannot be derived from experience of private life alone.[45]

CONCLUSION

The realism discussed in this chapter does not resemble the bloody-minded, amoral "realism" that asserts that ethics does not matter. Nor does realism deny that people can be moved by appeals to justice. The main claim instead is that politics in general embodies values that are *different* from, though not always opposed to, those of ordinary life. Questions of strategy, of leadership, of mass persuasion, of coalition management, of agency and responsibility under collective action, of wielding and balancing power, of weighing diverse and possibly incommensurable social interests, of balancing the authority of existing institutions with the need to adapt them to new circumstances, hardly occur in everyday life. But politics, including political ethics, consists of little else. Liberal and democratic theory do not excuse us from trying to understand problems of politics and the values that emerge from success in addressing them. They must, on the contrary, propose liberal and democratic answers to the basic political questions.

A realist account of civil disobedience, whether in liberal democracies or elsewhere, means examining political questions, from a normative perspective, with respect to the specific phenomenon under study. What kinds of civil disobedience are likely, under which circumstances, to be perceived as consistent with widely held values or new social demands (with luck, both)? Which kinds are likely, for that reason or another, to command the wide support that would give them democratic legitimacy? What should we do, or judge, if a particular campaign of disobedience is popular in many quarters but persistently unpopular among a subgroup defined (e.g.) by race, religion, or culture? Given that some kinds of disobedience are easier to communicate, and harder for opponents to lie about on a mass scale, than others, what level and kind of responsibility accrues to those who begin actions that will be predictably *mis*-portrayed to the discredit of a cause? What kinds of people will be most trusted to begin a campaign of disobedience; how can they retain trust; how can a movement survive their resignation, arrest, or fall from grace; and should some people, given these considerations, yield leadership roles to others? How can movements combine confidence in opposition with a lack of arrogance and power-hunger if they achieve success? These sorts of questions, utterly familiar both to practitioners of nonviolent resistance and to empirical students of nonviolent movement politics, have garnered very little attention from normative theorists. In other words: the realist study of civil disobedience has just begun.

NOTES

1. As this chapter is not intended as a detailed summary of realism, much less a contribution to the huge literature on what realist theory is and is not, the text admittedly draws broadly on key texts of the realist revival as a whole, including Bernard Williams, *In the Beginning Was the Deed* (Princeton, NJ: Princeton University Press, 2005); Raymond Geuss, *Outside Ethics* (Princeton, NJ: Princeton University Press, 2005) and *Philosophy and Real Politics* (Princeton, NJ: Princeton University Press, 2008). Classic articles describing the realist school include William A. Galston, "Realism in Political Theory," *European Journal of Political Theory* 9 (2010): 385–411; and Enzo Rossi and Matt Sleat, "Realism in Normative Political Theory," *Philosophy Compass* 9/10 (2014): 689–701. Edited volumes containing a variety of perspectives (many critical) include Jonathan Floyd and Marc Stears, eds., *Political Philosophy versus History?* (Cambridge: Cambridge University Press, 2011); Andrew Sabl and Rahul Sagar, eds., *Realism in Political Theory* (Abingdon, UK: Routledge, 2018); and Matt Sleat, ed., *Politics Recovered* (New York: Columbia University Press, 2018). The text is something of a Wittgensteinian "family resemblance" chart: all realists hold some of the beliefs described, but few or none may hold all of them. One belief I have left out is the strong historicism of some realists, the claim that political principles are quite radically relative to a given time or place. I hold this historicism to be an accident of the Cambridge context in which realism developed and not essential to the kind of realism with which I am concerned.

2. "[N]ever explain the ethical in terms of something special to ethics if you can explain it in terms that apply to the non-ethical as well"

(Bernard Williams, "Replies," in *World, Mind, and Ethics: Essays on the Ethical Philosophy of Bernard Williams*, ed. J.E.J. Altham and Ross Harrison [Cambridge: Cambridge University Press, 1995], 204). Williams rejects the accusation that considering ethical sentiments as similar in kind to others that affect our actions entails lowering or diminishing human dignity, as Kantians maintain. Thinkers such as Thucydides, Diderot, Stendhal, Nietzsche, and Hume, whom he praises as models, are aiming at "not the reduction of the human to the non-human, but the placing of the ethical among human motives" (ibid.).

3. See Geuss, *Philosophy and Real Politics*, 9f.

4. Robert Jubb, "Disaggregating Political Authority: What's Wrong with Rawlsian Civil Disobedience?" *Political Studies* 67, No. 4 (2019): 955–71; Karuna Mantena, "Another Realism: The Politics of Gandhian Nonviolence," *American Political Science Review* 106, No. 2 (May 2012): 455–70. Temi Ogunye, "Global Justice and Transnational Civil Disobedience," *Ethics and Global Politics* 8, No. 1 (2015), https://doi.org /10.3402/egp.v8.27217, is close to realist in the claims it puts forth but denies a larger intention to "challenge the methodological primacy of ideal theorizing" (2).

5. Though some realists of a radical stripe oppose realism to liberalism, I prefer accounts that regard the real–ideal distinction as orthogonal to political ideology. Realists can be liberals (though not the neo-Kantian, justification-obsessed kind of liberal), while idealists such as G.A. Cohen, wholly averse to considering social and political reality when arguing about moral principles, can be radicals.

6. "In general, I see all liberal democracies as necessarily imperfect, given the near-inescapable imbalance of power between majorities and vulnerable minorities, and given the near-inevitability that liberal democracies will engage in some injustices, rights-abuses, and neglect of non-contingent needs" (Kimberley Brownlee, *Conscience and Conviction: The Case for Civil Disobedience* [Oxford: Oxford University Press, 2012], 227; Brownlee's work is exemplary of a careful and well-argued approach to civil disobedience on assumptions wholly different from those of realists). Rawls's (1971) famous treatment of civil disobedience is explicitly one of his rare forays into "non-ideal" theory.

7. Judith Shklar, *The Faces of Injustice* (New Haven, CT: Yale University Press, 1990), 17.

8. William E. Scheuerman, *Civil Disobedience* (Cambridge, UK: Polity Press, 2018).

9. Jürgen Habermas, "Civil Disobedience: Litmus Test for the Democratic Constitutional State," *Berkeley Journal of Sociology* 30 (1985): 104; see similarly, William Smith, *Civil Disobedience and Deliberative Democracy* (Abingdon, UK: Routledge, 2013).

10. Niebuhr's political and moral psychology, which heavily influenced Martin Luther King, Jr., counts as realist only because he stresses, like Augustine, that moral transformation is not to be hoped for in this world. Unlike Augustine, Niebuhr hopes to make society substantially better, through the exertion of democratic power, absent such transformation.

11. The determination of figures such as Gandhi and Martin Luther King to avoid religious bigotry is not a sufficient response: realists would be interested in the *typical* and *demonstrable* effects of spiritually based civil disobedience on the *typical* person who practices it.

12. Alternatively, when some anarchists accept the need for coercive governance but want it to be carried out by a "relevant collective" rather than a specialized state set apart from social forces (see Paul Raekstad, "Realism, Utopianism, and Radical Values," *European Journal of Philosophy* 26, No. 1 [2016]: 145–68, 160), realists of a liberal stripe would tend to regard this as a recipe for a dystopian tyranny in which dissenting individuals and despised minorities would be coerced arbitrarily and without remedy (while enjoying as compensation a much lower standard of living than modern states can offer). It seems odd to label "realist" a position that assumes away cultural diversity, group prejudice, and the need to place limits on arbitrary executive power. It does not matter – indeed makes things worse – that the executive is described as "society, *qua* moral community" (ibid., 155).

13. David Lefkowitz, "On a Moral Right to Civil Disobedience," *Ethics* 117, No. 2 (January 2007): 202–33.

14. Brownlee, *Conscience and Conviction*, 218.

15. See the "forward-looking" defense of civil disobedience in Andrew Sabl, "Looking Forward to Justice: Rawlsian Civil Disobedience and its Non-Rawlsian Lessons," *Journal of Political Philosophy* 9, No. 3: 307–30. There (at 321–22) I suggest that Rawls's doctrine of civil disobedience, unlike the rest of his work, can satisfy "'realist' critics" who regard politics "as a struggle."

16. Smith, *Civil Disobedience and Deliberative Democracy*, chapter 3, 9. Along similar lines, while Daniel Markovits's defense of civil disobedience as "correcting democratic deficits" ("Democratic Disobedience," *Yale Law Journal* 114, No. 8 [June 2005], 1897–952) ably criticizes both the pernicious effects of special interests and opportunities for obstruction in the legislative process, his arguments would be more credible if not dressed up in the mythical language of republicanism, popular autonomy, and collective sovereignty.

17. Smith, *Civil Disobedience and Deliberative Democracy*, 71f.

18. Compare William A. Galston, "Two Concepts of Liberalism," *Ethics* 105, No. 3 (1995), 516–34.

19. For instance, Brownlee by stipulation denies that "bigots, racists, and xenophobes" possess a full moral right to civil disobedience. Her only apparent standard for distinguishing such from those who do have such a right is that the latter are "conscientious" in an objective sense, since they have striven hard to formulate universal principles from which they do not exempt themselves, and are willing to defend themselves to others (*Conscience and Conviction*, 148, and chapter 1). Leaving aside the realist suspicions that no principle is truly universal and few or no actual persons act on principle without hypocrisy, the problem is that no one is a bigot in his or her own mind. The bigots and xenophobes whom Brownlee (admirably) opposes see themselves as upholding deeply held principles involving collective defense and the rule of law. The phrase "parchment barriers" is Madison's, from *The Federalist* (No. 48; many editions).

20. Brownlee's objection that attempts to deter frivolous or unjustified civil disobedience through imprisonment entails treating agents "as brutes" rather than "reasoning moral agents capable of responding to moral reasons" (*Conscience and Conviction*, 210) is insufficient. To present prospective civil disobedients with the prospect of punishment is to invite them to engage in a fully human weighing moral and nonmoral considerations bearing on action, and many disobedients still choose to court prison quite deliberately. It is not as if one proposed to drive people with whips. Realists, again, reject as belied by all human experience the claim that only an alleged faculty of practical reason distinguishes human beings from nonhuman animals.

21. Williams, *In the Beginning*, 13; compare 86.

22. "In the market place [*sic*], the fate of conscience is not much different from the fate of the philosopher's truth: it becomes an opinion, indistinguishable from other opinions. And the strength of an opinion does not depend on conscience, but on the number of those with whom it is associated" (Hannah Arendt, "Civil Disobedience," in *Crises of the Republic* [San Diego, CA: Harcourt Brace & Company, 1972], 68). See also Gisli Vogler and Demetris Tillyris, "Arendt and Political Realism: Toward a Realist Account of Political Judgement," *Critical Review of International Social and Political Philosophy* 19 (2019). https://doi.org/10.1080/13698230.2019.1610843.

23. The idea of "economizing on virtue" is actually quite complex. I recommend the literature review, though not the conclusions, of Geoffrey Brennan and Alan Hamlin, "Economizing on Virtue," *Constitutional Political Economy* 6 (1995): 35–56.

24. To be sure, civil disobedience is not countervailing power in the technical sense put forth by John Kenneth Galbraith in *American Capitalism: The Concept of Countervailing Power* (Abingdon, UK: Routledge, 1993 [1952]).

25. William Smith, "Civil Disobedience and Social Power: Reflections on Habermas," *Contemporary Political Theory* 7 (2008): 72–89.

26. Mantena, "Another Realism."

27. Brownlee, *Conscience and Conviction*, mentions odd, suppositious cases (e.g., the "fair-weather pacifist" who opposes only wars against armies who wear blue [201]) – but in fact a partial, non-universal approach to civil disobedience is by far the *usual* case. For instance, not all those who break the law to protest mistreatment of members of their own race also do so to protest mistreatment of members of every racial and ethnic group, or every disfavored minority for that matter, in their own society and around the world. It seems odd to expect that they would.

28. "Whataboutism," *Wikipedia*, last modified April 26, 2020. https://en.wikipedia.org/wiki/Whataboutism.

29. Realists would have a similar objection to the complaint that civil disobedience is "haphazard," that its victories track which groups have the skill, courage, and numbers to engage in disobedience rather than the level of the injustice they face (Daniel Weinstock, "How Democratic Is Civil Disobedience?" *Criminal Law and Philosophy* 10 [2016]: 715). All

politics is haphazard in this sense. Nor is Weinstock's proposed alternative – judicial review – free, to put it mildly, of haphazardness.

30. Geuss, *Philosophy and Real Politics*, 22–3; Williams, *In the Beginning*, 3.
31. Sabl, "Looking Forward to Justice," 325.
32. Jubb, "Disaggregating Political Authority."
33. Mantena, "Another Realism." To the extent that Gandhi denied altogether the British Raj's authority, his actions may seem to transcend many usual definitions of civil disobedience. But then, as David Lyons has pointed out (in "Moral Judgment, Historical Reality, and Civil Disobedience," *Philosophy and Public Affairs* 27, no. 1 [1998]: 31–49), Thoreau and Martin Luther King, who also denied that the US regime as it stood was essentially legitimate or nearly just, would seem to represent similar cases.
34. Andrew Sabl, "Constitutions as Conventions: A History of Non-Reception," in *Morality, Governance, and Social Institutions*, eds. Thomas Christiano, Ingrid Creppell, and Jack Knight (Cham, Switzerland: Palgrave, 2018), 148–50.
35. James M. Buchanan, *The Limits of Liberty: Between Anarchy and Leviathan* (Chicago, IL: University of Chicago Press, 1975), 79.
36. Geoffrey Hawthorn's *Thucydides on Politics* (Cambridge: Cambridge University Press, 2014) has sometimes been faulted on this score.
37. Peter Ackerman and Christopher Kruegler, *Strategic Nonviolent Conflict* (Westport, CT: Praeger Publishers, 1994): 4 (compare 14 and 87) and 2–3.
38. Ibid., 9.
39. "At the end of the day, most people want to survive and to be on the winning side of a conflict" (Erica Chenoweth and Maria J. Stephan, *Why Civil Resistance Works: The Strategic Logic of Nonviolent Conflict* [New York: Columbia University Press, 2011], 220). This is not to deny that people also want *other* things, including justice (as they see it). On the general point that nonviolent disobedients have empirically made themselves, compared to violent ones, "credible negotiating partners," see 43–4, 47, 60, 202, 204f. See also Kurt Schock's contribution to this volume.
40. Chenoweth and Stephan, *Why Civil Resistance Works*, chapters 2 and 8.
41. "All these are platitudes about politics, and that is just the point: liberal political theory should shape its account of itself more realistically to what is platitudinously politics" (Williams, *In the Beginning*, 13).

42. On this see Andrew Sabl, "Hume's History and Politics," in *The Humean Mind*, eds. Angela M. Coventry and Alexander Sagar (London: Routledge, 2019), 307–11.

43. The common gloss that the Weberian state monopolizes the means of "legitimate force" (or "legitimate coercion") is a euphemism. Weber attributes to the state a *"monopoly of legitimate physical violence [physischer Gewaltsamkeit]* within a particular territory."* Max Weber, "Politics as a Vocation," in *The Vocation Lectures*, trans. Rodney Livingstone, eds. David Owen and Tracy B. Strong (Indianapolis, IN: Hackett Publishing Company, 2004), 33, emphasis in original.

44. Cited in Peter Ackerman and Jack Duvall, *A Force More Powerful: A Century of Nonviolent Conflict* (New York: Palgrave, 2000), 9.

45. See Matt Sleat and Ed Hall, "Ethics, Morality and the Case for Realist Political Theory," in Sagar and Sabl, eds. *Realism in Political Theory*, 10–27.

7   Anarchism: Provincializing Civil Disobedience

James D. Ingram

Civil disobedience presupposes a state, a legitimate authority that governs a territorial community through binding law. Yet it is often noted that two of the three canonical inspirations for civil disobedience, with whom the practice is said to have begun and to whom nearly all discussions refer, did not grant this premise. Far from accepting the legitimacy of the authorities against which they protested, Henry David Thoreau and Mohandas K. Gandhi expressly rejected them, not only in their current but in any imminently achievable form. The literature on civil disobedience tends to deal with this by treating them as precursors rather than models, mustered alongside figures such as Antigone, Socrates, or Jesus into expansive prehistories of the practice. While they may be exemplars of morally motivated, nonviolent resistance to unjust authority, they did not practice civil disobedience, strictly speaking.[1]

In this chapter I propose to use the distance between Thoreau, Gandhi, and the tradition they helped inspire to explore the limits of civil disobedience, in particular by displacing the conception of politics that underlies it and most of Western political theory. Though seldom explicitly thematized, this conception is at once historically specific and highly idealized. Many people do not live under conditions that make it an appropriate guide to thought or action. The anarchist tradition can help here because it throws into question a core assumption of modern politics, namely that political life requires a state with legitimate coercive authority over those subject

This chapter benefitted from discussions with audiences at Oxford College at Emory University, Carleton University, the Conference on Philosophy and Social Science in Prague, and the University of Hamburg. My thanks to Josh Mousie, Umut Ösu, Peter Niesen, and the other participants on these occasions for their comments and suggestions, and to Bill Scheuerman for the opportunity to develop these arguments here.

to it. For anarchists, this authority can and should be replaced by free, noncoercive modes of social coordination. Moreover, beyond a different aim, anarchism entails different ways of doing politics. Even if we dismiss the utopia of a society without coercive authority, these alternative conceptions of politics can allow us to see the rationality and viability of forms of political practice that do not take law and the state as the final arbiters of social life. Thoreau and Gandhi can both be read as anarchists in both senses: not only did they call for a society free of coercive authority, they engaged in forms of politics not directed principally toward the state. And yet, as I will argue, each can be read as offering a model of politics that is both coherent and practicable.

What can we learn from understandings of politics that do not, in Martin Luther King, Jr.'s formulation, express "the very highest respect for law,"[2] address themselves to the higher values of a legal order or a community of citizens, or take law and the state as the ultimate reference points of collective life? Among other things, we can see that civil disobedience is just one mode of oppositional politics, tailored to a limited set of circumstances, out of a wide range of alternatives. My aim here is accordingly not to overthrow dominant conceptions of civil disobedience so much as to *provincialize* them, to borrow Dipesh Chakrabarty's term. By gaining a better appreciation of the limits of civil disobedience, we can consider when we might prefer approaches based on other visions of politics.

CIVIL DISOBEDIENCE AND ANARCHISM

Civil disobedience as we know it is the product of a particular moment of postwar US history. It was tailored to defend certain campaigns of the day, above all the US Civil Rights Movement and opposition to the war in Vietnam, which were under attack from law-and-order critics who regarded all lawbreaking as illegitimate and culpable. Canonically defined by John Rawls in *A Theory of Justice* as a "public, non-violent, conscientious yet political act contrary to law usually done with the aim of bringing about a change in the law or policies of the government,"[3] this conception of civil disobedience aimed to show that unlawful protest, within certain bounds, could expose injustice and recall a liberal-democratic state to its higher values. Such action could hope to persuade fellow citizens and/or public officials, especially judges and legislators, without threatening the rule of law, core constitutional values, or the political order as a whole.

Other defenders of civil disobedience sought to go beyond such liberal accounts by opening it up to a more expansive notion of democratic politics. Hannah Arendt emphasized the political, rather than moral or legal, aspect of disobedience by tying it to the practice of voluntary association, which on her councilist conception represented the germ cell of democratic political power. Howard Zinn connected it to the bottom-up power of popular political movements that for him represented the ceaseless struggle for real democracy.[4] And Étienne Balibar has theorized *civic*, rather than *civil*, disobedience in order to underline active dissent as an elementary act of citizenship, an exercise of the constituent power that precedes and underpins any constituted power.[5] These more democratic conceptions focus on the community of citizens who should be authors as well as subjects of law, even if at the limit, with Zinn or Balibar, they verge on revolt or revolution.

Despite the differences between them, liberal and democratic conceptions have certain things in common. Both seek to reform a bounded polity in line with its own higher principles. The ultimate aim of disobedience for both is binding public legislation. And for both, change is demanded from *within* the polity, addressed by a minority to the rest of the community and/or its agents. Above all, liberal and democratic accounts converge on the idea that such politics ultimately takes aim at the state, where its reforms are to be guaranteed for the community as a whole. In this they are hardly exceptional: most political theory understands its domain in terms of bounded communities, and coercive laws and authorities. This, of course, is precisely what anarchism contests.

As befits an ideology united mainly by its rejection of authority, anarchism is diffuse. For present purposes we can understand it as a family of theories and movements that claim that people can and should live without a state or government, without rulers, hierarchy, domination, or exploitation. While anarchists are often portrayed as destructive, driven to smash the state, some reply that, insofar as the state is defined by its coercive power, theirs is the only position that can consistently reject violence. We might rather define anarchism, then, by its refusal to accept the state or any other authoritative, coercive institution as the ultimate reference of social-political life.

Histories of anarchism tend to proceed through a succession of figures from the last 200 years, but it can be seen as a possibility that goes back to the beginnings of Western political thought. Consider the Persian nobleman Otanes, who speaks for democracy in Herodotus's *Histories*. After his proposal is rejected, Otanes says he wishes "neither to rule nor be ruled." For Jean-Jacques Rousseau, Otanes is a prophet of republicanism; Arendt makes him the source of *isonomia*, or legal equality. As Isaiah Berlin points out, however, Otanes demands "the exact opposite of Aristotle's notion of true civic liberty," ruling and being ruled: not democratic, republican, or legal freedom, but what Berlin calls *negative* liberty.[6] If Berlin sees this as compatible with liberalism and the rule of law, anarchists take seriously Arendt's suggestion that we understand *isonomia* as "no-rule."[7] Alongside the classical alternatives of rule by one (monarchy), a few (aristocracy), or the many (democracy), they insist that we consider the possibility of rule by *none*.[8]

The versions of anarchism I discuss here develop the idea of "no-rule" in different directions. The first is negative and individualist.[9] Going back to William Godwin and Max Stirner, it demands the greatest possible individual liberty and rejects any authority that would curtail it. Even when the individualism of such approaches is relaxed, the emphasis remains on achieving freedom by doing away with coercive power. This, I will suggest, leads to a politics of *withdrawal*. The second version is social and collectivist.

Following Pierre-Joseph Proudhon and Peter Kropotkin, it argues that people can organize themselves freely and cooperatively, but only when freed from coercive institutions that deform social life. Here the accent is on forms of collective life, cooperation, and mutual aid – what I will call a politics of *community*.

These categories are neither exhaustive nor mutually exclusive. They are meant to register the diversity of the anarchist tradition while offering a way to make sense of its different notions of politics. For if politics is not understood in terms of law and the state, how can we recognize it? I suggest that we should expect at least two things of any view of politics: first, that it contain some finality or ideal vision, even if one no more immediately achievable than Plato's Kallipolis, Thomas More's Utopia, or Rawls's just constitutional state; and second, more importantly, that it provide guidance for present action that intervenes in collective life with a view to improving it. In the following I consider the examples of Thoreau and Gandhi to show how anarchistic elements of their thought and practice that contradict the liberal-democratic assumptions underpinning civil disobedience can nevertheless be understood not only as political, but as practical – even, under certain circumstances, as attractive.

THOREAU AND THE POLITICS OF WITHDRAWAL

I begin with the "inventor" of civil disobedience, Henry David Thoreau, even if the term was imposed on his essay by a later editor. "Civil Disobedience" (1849) originated as a lecture entitled "The Rights and Duties of the Individual in relation to Government," published as "Resistance to Civil Government" – both more reflective of Thoreau's concerns than the title under which it became famous. With other American Transcendentalists such as Ralph Waldo Emerson, Thoreau saw morality as deriving from a natural "higher law" accessible to individual conscience, and believed that the individual's highest calling was to live authentically in accordance with it. "The only obligation which I have a right to assume," he proclaims, "is to do at any time what I think right."[10] On this basis, he argues that he is not bound to obey a law he sees as unjust.

The occasion for the essay was a night spent in jail for refusing to pay a poll tax on the grounds that he could not support his state's participation in slavery, war on Mexico, and dispossession and persecution of Native Americans. (He was released the next day after his aunt paid the tax.) While at points Thoreau denies any duty actively to combat these evils ("It is not a man's duty ... to devote himself to the eradication of any, even the most enormous, wrong"), he refuses to finance them with his taxes. Thoreau's essay is not entirely consistent and does not present a fully worked-out political theory. Its power lies in radically questioning not only the citizen's obligation to the state, but the priority claimed by law, the state, and even politics in any conventional sense.

Theorists of civil disobedience, while recognizing Thoreau's importance in inspiring the concept (via Gandhi and King), have generally declined to regard his case as an instance of it. Rawls places Thoreau's action in the distinct category of "conscientious refusal," since it lacks civil disobedience's appeal to the political community.[11] For Arendt, it falls short because it is solitary: by acting alone rather than in concert with others, Thoreau fails to perform the basic act of citizenship that, for her as for other democrats and republicans, makes civil disobedience political.[12]

Anarchism puts in question the conceptions of politics on which these judgments rest. Commentators disagree about whether Thoreau himself was an anarchist. He begins his essay by affirming, "That government is best which governs least," and proclaims: "That government is best which governs not at all"; yet he distances himself from "no-government men" such as William Lloyd Garrison, who rejected political in favor of divine authority.[13] This disavowal has not prevented a long line of anarchists from claiming him, from Kropotkin and Leo Tolstoy to numerous twentieth-century writers, Gandhi among them. My aim here is to show that on an anarchist reading he can nevertheless be said to propose a politics.

Philosophical Anarchism

Thoreau's direct heirs are the group of American theorists associated with "philosophical anarchism." The school began with Robert Paul Wolff's *In Defense of Anarchy* (1970). Wolff argues that the puzzle that underlies the liberal-democratic state, combining individual moral autonomy with legitimate authority, has no solution.[14] If legitimacy rests on the ongoing consent of the governed, there can be no presumptive obligation to obey the law. This claim, echoed in different ways by all philosophical anarchists, may have its original in Thoreau's essay: "The authority of government, ... to be strictly just, ... must have the sanction and consent of the governed. It can have no pure right over my person and property but what I concede to it."[15]

John A. Simmons has adapted Thoreauvian philosophical anarchism for debates on civil disobedience. Simmons defines civil disobedience minimally, as "deliberate, principled, plainly illegal conduct."[16] He thereby claims it for philosophical anarchism by paring off its liberal and democratic elements – any reference to law, the state, or the community. "No state," he writes, "no matter how just it might be, could claim genuine moral authority to impose on its subjects moral obligations of legal obedience."[17] Setting aside whether this thin version of disobedience should be regarded as "civil," can it be understood as *political*?

We may doubt this in the case of the philosophical anarchists to the extent that their project is the strictly negative one of depriving the state of its presumptive legitimacy. Like Thoreau, Wolff and Simmons want to return the burden of moral and political judgment to the individual. If there is no obligation to obey even a nearly just and democratic state, laws need be followed only on a case-by-case basis. With Thoreau, they concede that most of the time we will obey the law simply out of convenience. But by denying any presumed obligation, they call on us to make up our own minds. The result, they hope, will be more critical, discerning citizens, even if they act alone.

Philosophical anarchism does point to a utopian horizon on which no one would be forced to do anything contrary to their will. For Wolff, this would be unanimous direct democracy.[18] Thoreau's ideal is more vague and consistently individualist. "Civil Disobedience" concludes by asking, "Is a democracy, such as we know it, the last improvement possible in government? Is it not possible to take a step further towards recognizing and organizing the rights of man?" Thoreau answers by imagining a state that "comes to recognize the individual as a higher and independent power," one that "would not think it inconsistent with its own repose if a few were to live aloof from it, not meddling with it, nor embraced by it, who fulfilled all the duties of neighbors and fellow-men."[19]

Yet this ideal of a state reconciled with individual sovereignty does not exhaust Thoreau's politics in our second sense, as a guide to present action. For while he often appears indifferent to government ("It is not my business to be petitioning the Governor or the Legislature any more than it is theirs to petition me"), Thoreau asserts a duty to combat evil in which one is implicated: "if [injustice] is of such a nature that it requires you to be the agent of injustice to another, then, I say, break the law. Let your life be a counter friction to stop the machine."[20] While he despairs of winning over his fellow citizens, he suggests that his disobedience, repeated on even a modest scale, could have transformative effect: "A minority is powerless while it conforms to the majority; ... but it is irresistible when it clogs by its whole weight."[21]

Here, I suggest, Thoreau begins to outline a politics. Faced with a state that commits evil yet enjoys the support of its citizens, he withdraws his support. Not only will he not be complicit in its misdeeds; if others join him, they may force it to correct its course. What he proposes is not civil disobedience, but what anarchists term *direct action*: practices by which people, rather than petitioning the state, express their demands by disrupting social or official life.[22] Of course Thoreau also wrote and published prodigiously – surely political acts. Yet his withdrawal of consent, if even minimally generalized, can also be seen as political strategy, consonant both with his immediate goals (abolition, pacifism) and his more distant hope of reducing the state's claims on its citizens.

Destituent Power

Thoreau's modest challenge to state authority can also open onto more ambitious projects. Raffaele Laudani, for instance, seeks to rethink politics from the perspective not of obligation and legitimacy, the usual starting points of Western political thought, but refusal.[23] His alternative canon begins with Étienne de La Boétie, whose *Discourse on Voluntary Servitude* (1548) interrogated the statist order then taking shape in Europe. Instead of inquiring, with Bodin or Hobbes, into the bases of state authority, La Boétie asks why subjects submit to it. Tyranny persists, he asserts, only as long as people accept it. All that is necessary to shatter a tyrant's power is for them to refuse to do so: "resolve to serve no more, and you are at once freed."[24]

Like Simmons, Laudani wants to displace the "civil" version of disobedience – not, however, like Simmons, for the sake of individual dissent, but for more revolutionary purposes. He accordingly emphasizes a radical strain in Thoreau's thinking that came out in his later defense of the insurrectionary abolitionist, John Brown. This strain also appears in "Civil Disobedience." Suggesting that "all men recognize the right of revolution," Thoreau argues that "when a sixth of the population of a nation which has undertaken to be the refuge of liberty are slaves, and a whole country is unjustly overrun and conquered by a foreign army, and subjected to military law, I think that it is not too soon for honest men to rebel and revolutionize."[25] Like La Boétie, Thoreau seems sanguine about the prospects of this venture: "when the subject has refused allegiance ... then the revolution is accomplished."[26]

Such a revolution may appear achievable to La Boétie and Thoreau because it consists not, like more familiar versions, in seizing the state, but in the opposite: in withdrawing from it. Rulers are not to be replaced, but left behind. To mark this distinction, Laudani terms it a politics of *destituent* power. Unlike the constituent power of revolutionary republicanism, destituent power (from the Latin *destituens*, or "abandon")[27] does not aim to construct new institutions, but to escape existing ones. Laudani's paradigmatic example is Black struggle against New World slavery, which gave rise to practices of *marronage*, self-organization outside existing political life – strikingly, Laudani assimilates Thoreau's self-exile to Walden Pond to this tradition – as well as various forms of noncooperation, secession, and desertion.[28] From the English Revolution's Levellers and Diggers to the student movement, Black Power, and radical feminism, Laudani narrates a discontinuous history of practices of refusal that aim to weaken and transform the authorities they challenge while nurturing their own autonomy.

Laudani draws his conception of destituent power from Antonio Negri and the autonomist school of Italian Marxism, even if Negri is better known as a thinker of constituent power. The furthest-reaching theorization of destituent power, however, has come from another Italian thinker: Giorgio Agamben. Agamben won a global audience with *Homo Sacer* (1995), whose portrayal of the state as a violent machine premised on the production of vulnerable "bare life" and a generalized state of exception appeared in English shortly before the 9/11 terrorist attacks, and the US turn to extra-judicial force and a global war on terror. But it was only in the epilogue of the seventh and final volume of the series that grew out of *Homo Sacer*, *The Use of Bodies* (2016), that the programmatic counterpart to his dark vision of politics emerged.

For Agamben, destituent power is the solution to a series of ontological, linguistic, theological, and philosophical puzzles, but in its first and most straightforward articulation it was political. The occasion was a lecture in Athens in 2013, after the Greek state had been exposed as bankrupt and subjected to the tutelage of international authorities while being tasked with managing rising numbers of desperate migrants seeking passage to Europe.[29] Facing a situation where democracy had failed and could promise nothing, where the state was unable to help its citizens and was reduced to its disciplinary functions, the aim, Agamben argued, should not be to capture the state, but to disable it:

> Starting with the French Revolution, the political tradition of
> modernity has conceived of radical changes in the form of
> a revolutionary process that acts as the *pouvoir constituant*, the
> "constituent power", of a new institutional order. I think that we
> have to abandon this paradigm and try to think something as
> a *puissance destituante*, a purely "destituent power", that cannot
> be captured in the spiral of security.[30]

If political inclusion, citizenship, and legality exist only by producing their opposites – exclusion, violence, "bare life" – the remedy is not to take over or reform state power, but to undo it, to render it inoperative.

There are important differences between these models of destituent power. Agamben connects the idea to a messianic overcoming of politics as such, with its fatalities of sovereignty, command and obedience, inclusion and exclusion. Yet we can find intimations of his destituent power in any self-conscious withdrawal from oppressive institutions, from strategies of noncooperation under imperialism or occupation to the separatism of ethical, religious, ecological, and other communities. Laudani distances himself from any messianism and indeed from anarchism, insisting that the politics he promotes is *extra-* rather than anti-institutional.[31] His more modest destituent power need not seek to escape state power altogether, only deprive it of its monopoly while asserting the independence of subordinated groups. It can therefore encompass a wider range of cases, from minorities seeking to renegotiate their relationship with a broader community to what Nancy Fraser has called "subaltern counterpublics,"[32] who withdraw tactically in order to articulate their own values, aims, and strategies.

Such approaches may not always be plausible or effective, and they are assuredly not, *pace* Agamben, a universal remedy, but they are recognizably *political* strategies – real ways of doing politics. Moreover, as I will argue in this chapter's conclusion, in certain circumstances, where active engagement with the state or the majority is blocked or unpromising, they may have much to recommend them. To this extent, they are real alternatives to petitioning the state, whether it is imagined by liberal theorists of civil disobedience as the laws, principles, and officers of a constitutional order, or by republicans or democrats as a body of fellow citizens.

GANDHI AND THE POLITICS OF COMMUNITY

We find a very different challenge to liberal-democratic politics in the theory and practice of Mohandas Gandhi. While Gandhi looms large in histories of civil disobedience, his aims, even in his early South African campaign, were hardly reformist: he was, or at least became, a revolutionary. His example is nevertheless central to the tradition of civil disobedience not only because its strict eschewal of violence provided a model of "civility" that went on to inspire the US Civil Rights Movement and others, but also, one suspects, because of its success. The British, after all, quit India. Theorists of civil disobedience tend to insist on the importance of his model of nonviolent struggle while conceding that it fits their models awkwardly, mostly due to its, from their perspective, exotic ethical-religious foundation.[33]

Civil disobedience's difficulty with Gandhi reflects his challenge to Western political theory as a whole. Gandhi was one of the most original and successful political figures of the twentieth century. No one doubts that his thought and action were closely connected, yet they often seem to be only ambiguously political. Here, as with Thoreau, the anarchist tradition can help reveal the specificity of his challenge to more familiar views.

Gandhi was no more a conventional political theorist than Thoreau, and his voluminous writings and self-consciously experimental method lend themselves to diverse interpretations. Some take advantage of the fact that throughout his career, Gandhi interacted with established institutions and tempered his strategies accordingly in order to minimize his challenge to standard versions of politics. Taking his most radical ideas literally, in contrast, leads others to an opposite interpretation, making him into an otherworldly moralist. My reading lies between these poles, showing how Gandhi's radical alternative to the state order at the same time served a canny and viable politics.

Swaraj as Utopia

Gandhi can be straightforwardly deemed an anarchist on the basis of his consistent opposition not just to the British Raj but to the modern state as such, his reverence for Tolstoy, and his pronouncements that his ideal form of government would be "enlightened anarchy."[34] This emerges from his distinction between two types of *swaraj*, or independence, in *Hind Swaraj* (1909). Radical Indian nationalists, represented by the character of the Reader, aim at political independence, a sovereign Indian state, often rendered as "self-government." Gandhi's mouthpiece, the Editor, counters that such independence cannot cure what ails India, for it would only replace foreign oppressors with indigenous ones. More than their rulers, it is Indians themselves who must change. True swaraj or "self-rule," the Editor contends, is in the first place individual: "Swaraj has to be experienced by each one for himself."[35] Only by mastering oneself can one aspire to true political self-rule, which then radically changes its sense.

Gandhi thus begins with the Thoreauvian imperative of personal integrity, but goes beyond it in two ways. First, his program requires not simply holding fast to one's convictions, but becoming a person capable of "self-rule." This involves a hugely demanding ethical program that for him entailed poverty, chastity, and renouncing worldly concerns, overcoming the materialism and selfishness he saw as the bases of modern politics in its liberal-democratic as well as authoritarian forms. British Parliament was a prostitute,[36] on his famous formulation, because it did the bidding of the interests that animated it: selfish, opportunistic politicians, but also distracted, materialistic citizens. Only when people learn self-restraint and self-sacrifice – true swaraj – can more be expected of politics.

Gandhi also goes beyond Thoreau in demanding a sweeping transformation of society. On this level, *Hind Swaraj*, anticipating its author's career as a whole, offers not only a fierce indictment of modern civilization, but an anti-colonial variant on the then-flourishing current of utopian anarchism, poised between Tolstoy and Kropotkin in the late nineteenth century, and Gustav Landauer and Ernst Bloch in the early twentieth. Like them, Gandhi argues that the state is a creature and perpetuator of violence. Closer to William Morris, he draws his alternative vision from an idealized past. Gandhi's utopia is a subcontinental federation of villages, an alternative to the state that would dissolve sovereignty by pushing it down to small, self-governing communities.[37] These would facilitate personal swaraj, creating a framework in which individuals could rule themselves, while realizing political swaraj by enabling communities to do likewise.

Like many anarchist utopias, Gandhi's village republics are models of interdependence and cooperation seemingly untroubled by politics, but they should not for this reason be seen as a- or anti-political. They are utopias neither simply in the pejorative sense of being illusory nor in the theoretical sense of being abstract ideals to be approximated in practice. Rather, they are utopias in the richer political sense developed by theorists such as Bloch, Miguel Abensour, and Ruth Levitas.[38] Political utopianism is not an escape from politics, but a different way of conducting it. On this conception, utopia does political work in a number of ways. Critically, it points out false necessities and articulates new possibilities. Practically, it is in Bloch's terms "concrete," connecting lived realities to future potentials, much as Gandhi's model ashrams embodied an alternative way of life. And politically, it helps construct a new political subject – for Gandhi, a new India united around its rural poor.[39]

In this way, rather than accept a given situation and work within its constraints, political utopianism seeks to transform the situation by acting proleptically, anticipating a radically different future. As Gary Wilder argues, this sort of utopianism had a special place in anti-colonial struggle, where it expressed a desire to escape the institutions and culture imposed by the colonizer.[40] Contemporaneous objections to Gandhi's village utopia still echo today: that it is backward-looking, ill-suited to the modern world, while its corrections for the ills of caste, untouchability, and patriarchy are insufficient.[41] We need not subscribe to all of his vision, however, to recognize that it *was* a politics – one that had transformative effects.

Satyagraha as Prefiguration

If Gandhi's utopian vision of a federation of village republics stands in the anarchist tradition of Tolstoy and Kropotkin, his practice of politics, captured by his term "satyagraha," or "living in truth," presents a still deeper challenge to conventional politics. Uday Mehta crisply summarizes the assumptions of modern politics Gandhi rejects: its focus on relations between individuals and the state, its subordination of means to ends, its continual recourse to violence, and its will to improve the world from above.[42] Against this, Gandhi insists on a politics of pure principle, refusing the state and violence and adhering fiercely to truth and morality regardless of worldly consequences. From this it may seem that he offers an even more radically individualist rejection of politics than Thoreau. Yet this verdict overlooks the place of this program within his broader practice.

We can understand the politics of Gandhi's ethical model by seeing it in light of a concept that has become prominent in anarchist circles over recent decades: prefiguration. Prefigurative politics consists of enacting in practice the values or relationships we want to generalize, such as nonviolence, equality, radical democracy, and personal responsibility.[43] Beyond the bumper-sticker version often attributed to Gandhi ("Be the change you want to see in the world"), which remains at the personal level, political prefiguration is a program for realizing utopia here and now by building the sought-for society in microcosm within the organization that fights for it.

Prefigurative politics revolves around the problem of means and ends. It responds to the tendency of movements that aim at peace, freedom, and democracy to be degraded by the violent, coercive, and authoritarian means they employ. This is a central theme of *Hind Swaraj*. Against the nationalist Reader, who sees no alternative to using the means of modern politics, including violence, to win Indian home rule, the Editor argues that such means will inevitably corrupt the results they achieve. As he puts it: "there is just the same inviolable connection between the means and the end as there is between the seed and the tree."[44] A violent independence struggle can only produce a violent India, even if one ruled by Indians rather than Englishmen. Only a different way of doing politics can lead to a qualitatively different outcome.

These arguments recall Mikhail Bakunin's against Karl Marx within the First International: taking over the state in the name of emancipation can only lead to new forms of despotism, whereas "liberty can only be created by liberty."[45] To be sure, satyagraha, no less than ahimsa, or strict nonviolence, is far from the libertarian program of Bakunin and most anarchists. It is a program of duties rather than rights, self-restraint rather than emancipation. We should prefer to suffer violence than to inflict it, Gandhi insists, because only then can we be capable of self-rule. On his Stoic program, self-rule must be based on boundless courage – a willingness, even desire, to sacrifice ourselves in order to maintain our fidelity to truth. Only then can we hope to convert our adversaries to a more humane politics, be it by the force of our example or out of exhaustion, as they succumb to our immovable, if "passive," resistance.[46]

Yet this ethical appeal was joined to a series of campaigns that engaged Indians in practices that prefigured self-rule. Take *khadi*, the practice of home-spinning. Though on its face an ethical program of simple living, it was more practically a program to break the imperial monopoly over Indian trade and industry that politicized millions by enabling them to participate in *swadeshi*. In *Hind Swaraj*, Gandhi voices the argument of satyagraha in terms that recall Thoreau and La Boétie: "If you do not concede our demand, we will be no longer your petitioners. You can govern us only so long as we remain the governed; we shall no longer have any dealings with you."[47] In campaigns such as the Non-Cooperation Movement, which saw Indians of all classes withdraw from the Raj, this threat was buttressed by the mass performance of an alternative, outside established institutions.

The movement Gandhi helped to inspire exemplifies the anarchist belief that change can be made not only by addressing the state or seeking to control it, but by circumventing it and cultivating other forms of community. Despite its demanding, apparently unworldly foundations and its utopian aims, this politics can count as "realistic" in the sense that it was based on a clear-sighted appraisal of the nature, contexts, and consequences of political action.[48] In this case, its realism was vouchsafed by its success in recruiting millions of Indians and inspiring numerous later initiatives, even if their results never matched the purity of Gandhi's vision.

DISOBEDIENCE BEYOND LAW AND THE STATE

My aim in pulling on the anarchist threads of Thoreau's and Gandhi's thought and practice has been to show how, although they rejected the founding assumptions of liberal and democratic accounts of civil disobedience, they nonetheless engaged in recognizably *political* practices – ones that had major, in Gandhi's case epochal, effects. The significance of these alternative forms of dissent, disobedience, or resistance derives from civil disobedience's enormous prestige, even hegemony, in contemporary political discourse. When individuals or groups engage in practices of dissent or resistance, politicians, journalists, and theorists often hold them to standards derived from theories of civil disobedience – publicity, respect for the law, etc. – that may not be appropriate to their situations or aims.

Anarchist perspectives can be helpful in relaxing the statism and legalism such standards tacitly assume. Those, like Thoreau, who reject the policies of their states and societies may similarly wish to withdraw – be it, like him, by themselves, or, like the groups championed by Laudani, into semi-autonomous communities. Those, like Gandhi, who deny their state's claim to legitimacy or even the way of life it prescribes as a whole, may wish to pursue forms of self-organization rather than loyal opposition.

We need not look far for examples. Should unpopular whistle-blowers or subjects of illiberal regimes choose legal punishment over internal or external exile?[49] Should rightless migrants or minorities subject to majority persecution try to persuade publics and authorities rather than practice evasion or self-organization? Should indigenous peoples or minority nationalities pursue equal citizenship in an externally imposed state rather than try to wrestle from it what autonomy they can?[50]

In such situations, the anarchist tradition offers a reservoir of alternative visions of politics that can inspire means as well as ends. My point is not that we must abandon civil disobedience but that we should recognize that it assumes a highly particular situation: that of a favorably situated citizen of a "reasonably just" liberal-democratic state. And even within these circumscribed parameters, there may be reason to prefer anarchist tactics. Liberal-democratic states often include oppressive, corrupt, or discriminatory institutions and authorities, tolerated if not supported by higher authorities and wider publics. For those subject to such authorities, with little hope of reforming or removing them, anarchism can offer a toolkit of tactics and remedies.

By framing my discussion of Gandhi with the question of success, however, I may be said to have evaded the respects in which he and Thoreau failed. Even if Indian home rule, like abolition, eventually prevailed, neither was achieved in a way or took a form these authors would have liked. The Civil War that ended slavery produced an imperialist American state vastly more powerful and centralized than the one Thoreau denounced, much as the modern Indian state was erected on the abandoned vision of Gandhi's village republics.[51] This raises a perennial objection to anarchism: that in a world of powerful states and global forces, the anarchist ideal of free, egalitarian cooperation cannot hope to take any but the most fleeting and marginal forms. In any foreseeable future, the alternative to the circumscribed liberal-democratic idealism of civil disobedience is not anarchist self-organization, but state or revolutionary violence – not Thoreau and Gandhi, but Abraham Lincoln and Jawaharlal Nehru.

Yet this may miss anarchism's deeper contribution. Even in its utopian versions, anarchy need not be a total goal; indeed, anarchists tend to be suspicious of claims to totality. Withdrawal from unjust institutions, the evasion or destitution of oppressive state power, and the construction of nonhierarchical forms of association may succeed locally or partially, even if the utopia of life without coercion or domination is never realized. Anarchist strategies can help create freer, more equal forms of association alongside official institutions; they can also help temper or reshape parts or aspects of those institutions. From an anarchist perspective, the measure of a movement's success need not be its ability to elect a government, pass a law, or change a policy. It may more importantly lie in the cultivation of forms of community, cooperation, solidarity, and autonomy that escape the view of official politics.

Civil disobedience, with the theories that underpin it, sustains a view on which politics culminates with law and the state. Against this, anarchism insists that politics goes on elsewhere as well. The history of anarchy, it is said, is written on the blank pages of history, which is filled with states and rulers, wars, and conquests. These blank pages, passed over by much of political theory, are not just where most of life is lived. What goes on there may inflect and even redirect the main story.

NOTES

1. Hugo Adam Bedau, ed. *Civil Disobedience in Focus* (New York: Routledge, 1991), 6.
2. Martin Luther King, Jr., "Letter from Birmingham City Jail," in Bedau, ed., *Civil Disobedience in Focus*, 74.
3. John Rawls, *A Theory of Justice*, revised ed. (Cambridge, MA: Belknap Press of Harvard University Press, 1999), 320.
4. Howard Zinn, *Disobedience and Democracy: Nine Fallacies on Law and Order* (Boston, MA: South End Press, 2002 [1968]).
5. Étienne Balibar, "Sur la désobéissance civique," in *Droit de Cité* (Paris: Quadrige/Presses universitaires de France, 2002).
6. Isaiah Berlin, *Liberty* (New York: Oxford University Press, 2002), 33.
7. Hannah Arendt, *On Revolution* (New York: Penguin, 1990), 30.
8. Francis Dupuis-Déri, "Anarchy in Political Philosophy," *Anarchist Studies* 13, no. 1 (2005): 8–22.
9. Most schemas of anarchism, following Kropotkin's 1905 encyclopedia article, recognize an individualist variant alongside various social or collectivist alternatives. See "Anarchism," in *"The Conquest of Bread" and Other Writings* (Cambridge: Cambridge University Press, 1995), 233–47.
10. Henry David Thoreau, "Civil Disobedience," in Bedau, ed., *Civil Disobedience in Focus*, 28. For a revelatory discussion of Thoreau and his reception, see Chapter 1 in this volume.
11. Rawls, *A Theory of Justice*, chapter 6.
12. Hannah Arendt, *Crises of the Republic* (New York: Houghton Mifflin Harcourt, 1972), 96.
13. Thoreau, "Civil Disobedience," 28–29.
14. Robert Paul Wolff, *In Defense of Anarchism, with a New Preface* (Berkeley, CA: University of California Press, 1998).
15. Thoreau, "Civil Disobedience," 48.
16. A. John Simmons, "Disobedience and Its Objects," *Boston University Law Review* 90 (2010): 1809.
17. Simmons, "Disobedience and Its Objects," 1814.

18. Wolff, *In Defense of Anarchism*, 22ff.

19. Thoreau, "Civil Disobedience," 48.

20. Thoreau, "Civil Disobedience," 36.

21. Thoreau, "Civil Disobedience," 38.

22. E.g. David Graeber, *Direct Action: An Ethnography* (Oakland, CA: AK Press, 2009).

23. Raffaele Laudani, *Disobedience in Western Political Thought: A Genealogy* (New York: Cambridge University Press, 2013).

24. Etienne de La Boétie, *Politics of Obedience: The Discourse of Voluntary Servitude* (Auburn, AL: Ludwig von Mises Institute, 1975), 47. The political indeterminacy of individualist anarchism is reflected in the publisher of this English edition as well as its forward by right-wing libertarian Murray Rothbard.

25. Thoreau, "Civil Disobedience," 31.

26. Thoreau, "Civil Disobedience," 38.

27. Laudani, *Disobedience in Western Political Thought*, 4–5.

28. Laudani, *Disobedience in Western Political Thought*, 5, 93. On the tradition of *marronage* and its political significance, see Neil Roberts, *Freedom as Marronage* (Chicago, IL: University of Chicago Press, 2015).

29. This was before the election of the leftist Syriza government, the Greek referendum to defy EU-imposed austerity, and the government's failure to honor that mandate. None of these developments seem likely to have changed Agamben's diagnosis.

30. Giorgio Agamben, *From the State of Control to a Praxis of Destituent Power* (Anarchist Library, 2013), 6, accessed March 20, 2020, https://roarmag.org/essays/agamben-destituent-power-democracy. For Agamben as for Negri, the difference between *pouvoir* and *puissance*, *potere* and *potenza*, marks that between superordinate, top-down power and immanent, bottom-up power, referring back to Spinoza's distinction between *potestas* and *potentia*.

31. Laudani, *Disobedience in Western Political Thought*, 3–4.

32. Nancy Fraser, "Rethinking the Public Sphere: A Contribution to the Critique of Actually Existing Democracy," *Social Text* 25/26 (1990): 56–80.

33. E.g., Bedau, *Civil Disobedience in Focus*; William E. Scheuerman, *Civil Disobedience* (Cambridge: Polity Press, 2018).

34. See Gopinath Dhawan, *The Political Philosophy of Mahatma Gandhi* (Ahmedabad, India: Navajivan Publishing, 2016).
35. Mohandas K Gandhi, *"Hind Swaraj" and Other Writings (Centenary Edition)*, ed. Anthony Parel (New York: Cambridge University Press, 1997), 73. I follow convention in preferring Gandhi's Gujarati terms to the rough English equivalents he found for them in his own translation.
36. Gandhi, *"Hind Swaraj,"* 30.
37. Karuna Mantena, "On Gandhi's Critique of the State: Sources, Contexts, Conjunctures," *Modern Intellectual History* 9, no. 3 (2012): 535–63.
38. E.g. Ruth Levitas, *Utopia as Method: The Imaginary Reconstitution of Society* (Basingstoke: Palgrave Macmillan, 2013).
39. Anshuman Mondal, "Gandhi, Utopianism and the Construction of Colonial Difference," *Interventions* 3, no. 3 (2001): 419–38.
40. Gary Wilder, "Untimely Vision: Aimé Césaire, Decolonization, Utopia," *Public Culture* 21, no. 1 (2009): 101–40.
41. E.g. Arundhati Roy, *The Doctor and the Saint: Caste, Race, and Annihilation of Caste* (Chicago, IL: Haymarket Books, 2017).
42. Uday S. Mehta, "Gandhi on Democracy, Politics and the Ethics of Everyday Life," *Modern Intellectual History* 7, no. 2 (2010): 362–63.
43. E.g. Paul Raekstad, "Revolutionary Practice and Prefigurative Politics: A Clarification and Defense," *Constellations* 11, no. 1 (2017): 359–72; Uri Gordon, "Prefigurative Politics Between Ethical Practice and Absent Promise," *Political Studies* 66, no. 2 (2018): 521–37.
44. Gandhi, *"Hind Swaraj,"* 81.
45. Mikhail Bakunin, *Statism and Anarchy* (New York: Cambridge University Press, 1990), 179.
46. Akeel Bilgrami, "Gandhi, the Philosopher," *Economic and Political Weekly* 38/39 (2003): 4159–65. For a stronger reading of Gandhi's practice on which self-sacrifice is the point, see Faisal Devji, "The Paradox of Nonviolence," *Public Culture* 23, no. 2 (2011): 269–74.
47. Gandhi, *'Hind Swaraj'*, 85.
48. Karuna Mantena, "Another Realism: The Politics of Gandhian Nonviolence," *American Political Science Review* 106, no. 2 (2012): 455–70.
49. If "living in truth," Vaclav Havel's formula for his program of resisting really existing Communism, translates satyagraha, its mostly solitary practice more closely resembled Thoreau.

50. Simmons cites indigenous peoples' rejection of state claims to "stolen or fraudulently acquired land" as a clear case where there can be no presumption of obedience. Simmons, "Disobedience and Its Objects," 1826.
51. Sandipto Dasgupta, "Gandhi's Failure: Anticolonial Movements and Postcolonial Futures," *Perspectives on Politics* 15, no. 3 (2017): 647–62.

PART II   **Different Elements,
Competing
Interpretations**

8 (In)Civility

Candice Delmas

Commentators from all sides bemoan the loss of civility, seeing it as the glue that keeps divided political societies whole. We have become distrustful and contemptuous of those we don't see eye to eye with.[1] No environment is apparently immune from our "incivility epidemic" (the metaphor of virology is apt, since, researchers found, "catching rudeness is like caching a cold," namely, contagious[2]): social media, college classrooms, bedrooms, family gatherings, workplaces, and politics itself are compromised. Online trolls are not the only ones feeding the incivility beast. Political representatives and authority figures exacerbate the problem. In the United States, Rep. Ted Yoho's vulgar and misogynist comments to Rep. Alexandria Ocasio-Cortez on Capitol Hill, Brett Kavanaugh's angry testimony during his Supreme Court nomination hearing, and, most of all, President Donald Trump's own divisive and inflammatory rhetoric model a kind of unbridled incivility that coarsens politics and degrades public discourse.

Protesters, too, are frequently accused of fanning the flames of incivility. Conservative as well as liberal commentators unfavorably compare Black Lives Matter with Civil Rights activists, contrasting the unfailing commitment to nonviolence and dignified and decorous behavior of the latter with the unchecked anger, lack of discipline, and property destruction of the former. Ironically, this contrast results from historical amnesia: the public widely perceived Civil Rights campaigners as impatient and impertinent "rabble rousers,"

Versions of this chapter were presented at Brown University's "Seeing Beyond the Veil" Conference, Bowling Green State University's "The Ethics of Public Discourse" Conference, the University of Delaware's Philosophy Colloquium Series, and the University of Vermont's Ethics Reading Group. I am grateful to the organizers, participants, and audiences at these events for engaging discussions and useful suggestions.

and authorities charged participants in lunch counters sit-ins and other demonstrations with misdemeanors such as loitering and picketing, and felonies such as "intimidation," "conspiracy," and "fomenting anarchy." Iconic figures such as Martin Luther King, Jr. and Rosa Parks were reviled in their own time, called extremists and traitors.

Continuity aside, Black Lives Matter activists have distanced themselves from their predecessors with the slogan "Not Your Grandparents' Civil Rights Movement." They have embraced their expressions of grief and rage, defended the destruction of public property such as police cars and Confederate monuments, and asked the public to stop condemning looting and start condemning police violence. As the Movement for Black Lives suggests, we may have entered a new era of disobedience. Few recent protests neatly fit the common understanding of *civil* disobedience. Indigenous Land and Water Protectors in the US, the *gilets jaunes* in France, hacktivists launching distributed denial-of-service (DDoS) attacks, and the 2019–2020 pro-democracy activists in Hong Kong, among many others, have been branded as "troublemakers," "vandals," and even "terrorists." The loss of civility in disobedience thus seems to run parallel to the loss of civility in the public discourse.

This begs the questions, What is civility? What does it demand? How does it relate to the civility of civil disobedience? What, if anything, is wrong with uncivil conduct, including disobedient acts that fail to satisfy the marks of civility? I begin this investigation with a brief detour into the dominant conceptions of civility, in order to present the problem posed by disobedience (to wit, it is a dangerous way of disagreeing). I then survey the two dominant solutions to this problem: the standard liberal account focuses on the civility of civil disobedience (narrowly defined) to explain why the latter doesn't necessarily threaten order; other theorists discard the criteria of civility and deny the significance of the problem posed by disobedience. Finally, I put forth a third approach, granting the standard marks of civility yet proposing a turn away from civil disobedience, given the limits of civility in societies like ours, and toward *uncivil* disobedience.

CIVILITY AND THE PROBLEM OF DISOBEDIENCE

In its original meaning, "civility," whose etymology points us to the Latin words for city (*cives*) and citizen (*civis*), designates the status of citizen that is granted (male, property-owning) members of the city-state and excludes women, resident aliens (*metics*), and slaves. This sense of civility seems not to have anything to do with good manners. But in fact, it does: the ancients understood civility to involve both decorum ("politeness" also derives from the Greek word for city, *polis*) and civic-mindedness (*sensus communis*, or "the sense of the community," according to Cicero). By conforming to the social norms of decorum, citizens both cultivate in themselves, and display for their fellow citizens, concern for the public good and community. They demonstrate that they "wish their fellow citizens well" and share their values and sense of justice.[3] Through civility, citizens train themselves in the civic virtue of "ruling and being ruled."[4] Civility, thus understood as the set of dispositions befitting good citizens, does not rule out impassioned political speeches, expressions of anger, and other disruptive political interventions, which may stem from, reflect, and promote *sensus communis*.

A shift occurred in the early modern period as political thinkers began to view civility as a virtue not for friends, but for foes – co-citizens divided by deep (especially religious) disagreements. Thomas Hobbes praised the moral virtues – "justice, gratitude, modesty, equity, mercy, and the rest of the laws of Nature" – "as the means of peaceable, sociable, and comfortable living."[5] Key among those means is civility, which defuses the dangers coiled in the fact of our disagreements by restraining the manner of our disagreements, especially by refraining from ever "declaring hatred or contempt of another."[6] Hobbes further extoled the virtue of "complaisance," which demands "that every man strive to accommodate himself to the rest," and smooth off his rougher edges (per Hobbes's own metaphor) for the sake of peaceable coexistence.[7] In practice, this kind of conversational self-restraint – knowing what to say to whom and when – often counsels "civil silence," according to Teresa Bejan.[8] Because expressing one's disagreement, even civilly, always carries the risk of offending some people and hence threatening our "peaceable, sociable, and comfortable living," the most civil manner of disagreeing is ultimately not to disagree at all.

Whereas Hobbes sought "difference without disagreement," in Bejan's phrase, John Locke's teaching on religious toleration promised "difference and disagreement."[9] Locke found disagreement on religious matters consistent with civil peace – and to be tolerated – so long as people endorsed *concordia*, the Christian ideal of unity in diversity, and shared a commitment to inward charity, sincere esteem, and outward civility. However, Bejan argues that Locke ultimately premised civil peace on an agreement between individuals more "fundamental" than the disagreements that divide them, as he only extended toleration to those committed to mutual respect (*concordia*) and willing to disagree civilly to maintain it. Lockean civility in effect excluded as intolerable those who didn't share these commitments.[10]

The Hobbesian and Lockean solutions to the dangers of disagreement reflect the spectrum of today's philosophical positions. Theorists following John Rawls's footsteps conceive of the duty of civility as constraining the kind of reasons that citizens can offer each other when debating in the public sphere. For Rawls, they should offer reasons that all can accept, thus foreclosing "sectarian," especially religious, reasons.[11] In other words, they must practice a Hobbesian civil silence about their fundamental disagreements, especially those regarding the "comprehensive doctrines" that undergird their theories of justice or rights: only certain kinds of disagreement can take place – and they will, following these constraints, be conducted in relative harmony. Amy Gutmann and Dennis Thompson also conceive of civility as a kind of conversational self-restraint conducive to social harmony, though their understanding of the demands of civility differs from Rawls's. In their view, the civil citizen is open- and fair-minded: because she aspires toward consensus, she offers rationales that minimize the risk of her position being rejected and maximize the potential to reach an agreement; and she refrains from presenting her views as unalterable convictions.[12] Civility, on Clifford Orwin's account, is a virtue specific to liberal democratic societies – "the full-time job of the liberal democrat," as he calls it – and a matter of restraining conduct and speech to display proper respect toward others as bearers of equal rights and dignity.[13]

In short, there are many competing accounts of civility, from self-restraint in public conversation to sincere commitment to mutual respect. Yet we can plausibly view each as articulating different conceptions of the same concept of civility, which designates the kind of conduct and attitude befitting good citizens and conducive to social stability. Whatever the account, civility demands abiding by shared social norms of reciprocity and respect – rules such as greeting etiquette and formalities of language that the society deems essential in the practice of disagreement. For instance, most societies exclude insulting name-calling and shouting down of one's opponent, though British civility permits disruptive heckling of speakers in political arenas.

In addition to demanding conformity to shared social norms, civility presumptively demands law-abidance. Indeed – and this is the crux of the problem – even principled disobedience (i.e., politically or morally motivated lawbreaking) appears inherently uncivil – an impermissible way to disagree with a democratic majority. Agents' refusal to conform to accepted legal rules looks like a refusal to take on the burdens of civil self-restraint that everyone else willingly bears. This is problematic on two grounds. One ground is practical or instrumental: disobedience destabilizes society, by practice and by example. The state requires general compliance with law in order to achieve social stability and adequately preserve individual rights. Individuals' lawbreaking hinders or risks hindering this central function of the state. The other ground is semiotic: disobedience signals disrespect for law's authority. The concern is especially acute in democracies, where the sovereign is the people collectively. Agents who disobey the law, like free riders, betray a kind of arrogance and disregard for others – a misplaced sense of entitlement. On both grounds, disobedience appears as an uncivil force and a potential threat even to the modest aim of securing "peaceable, sociable, and comfortable living." Civil citizens who disagree with the law do not and must not disobey it.

In recognition of these problems, Rawls argued that citizens of liberal democracies "have a natural duty of civility not to invoke the faults of social arrangements as a too ready excuse for not complying with them, nor to exploit inevitable loopholes in the rules to advance our interests."[14] Being natural, the duty of civility binds everyone, regardless of one's voluntary undertakings or special ties. It forbids one from disobeying the law "too readily," even in the face of serious injustice. He insisted: "The duty of civility imposes a due acceptance of the defects of institutions and a certain restraint in taking advantage of them."[15] Democratic majorities are bound to sometimes make erroneous decisions in good faith; and in order not to threaten stability and to maintain citizens' mutual trust, "there is normally a duty . . . to comply with unjust laws provided that they do not exceed certain bounds of injustice."[16]

The moral duty to obey the law is thus presumptively entailed by the duty of civility, at least in near-just societies, where injustices are not so severe that they threaten the whole system's legitimacy.[17] Just as civil citizens exercise self-restraint in disagreements by not bringing up certain reasons or by refraining from hateful speech, according to Rawls and Jeremy Waldron, respectively, they restrict their conduct by obeying the law. The point is not just to *be* civil, but also to *show* civility, and the ways of showing the latter are given to us in the form of predetermined social scripts – law-abidance being chief among these. Of course, law-abidance is not sufficient for civility. One may obey the law without abiding civil norms of respect and reciprocity, by being a rude neighbor and a hostile colleague, by cutting lines, etc. And one may also obey the law uncivilly: Jessica Bulman-Pozen and David Pozen conceive of "uncivil obedience" as hyperbolic, literalistic, or otherwise unanticipated adherence to a legal system's formal rules.[18] Their examples include motorcyclists strictly adhering to the speed limit in order to protest it and the creation of a political action committee by the television host Stephen Colbert in order to ridicule Federal Election Commission rules. But in general, law-abidance is necessary for and conducive to social stability – and it plausibly counts as one of civility's established social scripts.

Philosophers have taken one of two roads in response to the problem of disobedience – its apparent incivility and incompatibility with the democratic order. The first, most traveled road, consists of showing that disobedience is not necessarily incompatible with the demands of civility, and can in fact abide by them, despite its otherwise antidemocratic nature. The standard Rawlsian, liberal conception of civil disobedience as a principled, public, nonviolent breach of law in pursuit of reform and undertaken by agents who demonstrate their respect for the law by submitting to legal sanctions epitomizes this argumentative line. It further condemns uncivil disobedience, indeed any act of principled disobedience that fails to satisfy the accepted marks of civility (the "civil disobedience playbook"), as unjustifiable in a near-just society.

More recently, other philosophers have taken a different road, which involves denying that disobedience poses the problem I just described. In this vein, radical democratic theorist Robin Celikates debunks the notion that disobedience is presumptively impermissible and reconceptualizes civil disobedience to include any intentionally unlawful and principled collective act of protest designed to articulate political claims and undertaken through nonmilitary means.[19] While the point of the first, standard liberal account is (or was) to make room for civil disobedience in a law-and-order context that saw civil disobedience as indistinct from criminal or revolutionary disobedience and categorically impermissible, the point of the second, inclusive approach has generally been to make room for even more disobedient activities. For radical democrats such as Celikates, the point is also to contest the liberal presumptions that turn civil disobedience into a problematic practice in need of justification and, in so doing, to empower activists on the ground.

These different approaches ultimately further different lines of inquiry: the standard liberal account squarely takes up the question of what makes a disobedient act civil (as do some liberal proponents of the inclusive approach), whereas the radical democratic account is concerned with the stifling and exclusionary effects of civility and the ways in which a broader conception of civil disobedience could advance emancipatory goals (making it an "ameliorative" project, in Sally Haslanger's terminology).[20]

In what follows, I propose to carve a third way. I am sympathetic to radical democrats' concern with the exclusionary effects of civility, but I think that the site of the ameliorative action is elsewhere: rather than broadening the concept of civil disobedience to include what is commonly seen as its opposites, it is more useful to conceptualize and justify the resort to incivility in disobedience. So, contra the inclusive approach, I give reasons to grant (while paring down) the standard answer to the question of what makes a disobedient act civil, using it then as foil to inquire into what makes a disobedient act *uncivil*. And contra the standard account, I argue that acts of uncivil disobedience may sometimes be justified, even in liberal democratic societies, and especially where the conditions that must be met for civility to become a morally binding norm are not met.

SOLUTION I: THE CIVIL DISOBEDIENCE PLAYBOOK

In response to the instrumental and semiotic objections to disobedience, theorists and practitioners show that a special kind of lawbreaking – *civil* disobedience – neither destabilizes society nor betrays arrogance. First, they draw a bright line between civil and criminal disobedience, contrasting civil disobedients' seriousness, selflessness, nonviolence, and acceptance of legal sanctions, with criminals' covert and self-interested lawbreaking, their use of force and evasion of punishment. Second, they distinguish civil disobedients from militant revolutionaries. Revolutionary actors, like civil disobedients, are moved by moral and political principles to break the law and often seek to address the community. However, revolutionaries share with criminals their willingness to use violence and their evasion of punishment. Third, theorists insist that civil disobedients, unlike criminals and revolutionaries, recognize civility's demands and aspiration toward social concord even as they break the law. Civil disobedients are supposed to accept, while revolutionary agents reject and criminals don't care about, the legal system's legitimacy and the moral duty to obey the law.[21]

The idea is that agents can display mutual respect for their fellow citizens while breaking the law so long as they follow what I call the "civil disobedience playbook" – a model supposedly embodied in some of the iconic Civil Rights campaigns such as the "whites-only" lunch counter sit-ins in the Deep South of the US. The civil disobedience playbook comports four central criteria: publicity, nonviolence, non-evasion, and decorum.

The *publicity* of civil disobedience refers to its openness and nature as an address to the community. The civilly disobedient act must be undertaken in the open (e.g., on the steps of a government building); and it must present itself as a speech act, a communicative address to the community: it is something for others to see and listen to. Civil disobedience's publicity mirrors civility's civic-mindedness and central role in the public sphere. Some theorists take it further by requiring disobedient agents appeal to widely shared principles of justice (thereby modeling civility's constraints on the kinds of reasons that may be brought in the public sphere), though critics have pointed out that limiting the grounds of civil disobedients' appeals thusly is necessary neither for identifying nor for justifying civil disobedience.[22]

The requirement of *nonviolence* prohibits the use or threat of violence, injury to others, and damage to property. Rawls asserts that the communicativeness of civil disobedience – its nature as a speech act – entails nonviolence. Rawls seems to misidentify the nature of the link here: violence doesn't necessarily obscure communication, and may indeed be central to the actors' message.[23] But nonviolence does appear intricately linked to civility's demand of mutual respect, which translates into a prohibition on harming others and an imperative to treat others as interlocutors, to recognize and respect their dignity.[24]

Non-evasion entails that the agent of disobedience must accept the legal consequences of her action and not dodge law enforcement (arrest) or sanctions (prosecution and punishment).[25] Disobedients' willingness to submit to legal sanctions is supposed to reveal their commitment to act within the limits of "fidelity to law" – a crucial function of civility. Their willingness to take on the costs associated with disobedience shows their sincerity and seriousness, and reflects civility's demand to exercise self-restraint. Publicity, nonviolence, and non-evasion together model the self-restraint, civic-mindedness, and mutual reciprocity that are central to the virtue of civility.

Theorists have all but neglected the fourth and final mark of civility, *decorum*. Yet it was central to the ancient sense of civility, through which citizens were understood to reflect their concern for the public good. And it permeates society's judgment of disobedient protests today – so much so that principled acts of disobedience that are public, nonviolent, and non-evasive might be denied the label "civil" if they otherwise appear offensive or disrespectful in some ways. Two radical feminist activists' disobedient protests come to mind: Pussy Riot's "Punk Prayer" in Moscow's Cathedral of Christ the Savior, and Femen's counter-protests to Christian anti-gay demonstrations in Europe (their bare chests proclaiming "Fuck the Church," "Fuck Your Morals," or "In Gay We Trust!"). Pussy Riot members were charged with blasphemy and hooliganism; Femen activists with indecent exposure and disturbing the peace. Opponents don't merely deny that these protests were justified – they outright refuse to categorize them as civilly disobedient. This shows, I think, that decorum is an important mark of civility, supposed to reflect agents' commitment to treat their audience with respect.

To be sure, decorum is a flawed mark of civility, one that is often wielded by powerful groups in order to keep the oppressed in their place. Thus many of the Civil Rights-era campaigns which are now seen as textbook civil disobedience were seen at the time as uncivil and troublesome.[26] It is indeed important to understand civility-as-decorum and the accusations of incivility it brings within the economy of power in which it is tactically deployed, and not to accept it at face value as an objective description of the world. Nevertheless, decorum does matter to understand the civility of civil disobedience, as practitioners have stressed, too.

Gandhi and Martin Luther King, Jr., highlighted the self-discipline, love, and respect necessarily displayed by their disobedience. Gandhi described civil disobedience as "gentle, truthful, humble, knowing, willful yet loving, never criminal and hateful."[27] King likewise contrasted the loving disobedience of his followers with segregationists' hateful defiance of the law. These moral qualities go well beyond decorum (for Gandhi, they make up the core of nonviolence in fact), yet designate it as a bare minimum of civil disobedience (which may be viewed distinctly from nonviolence). Just as political civility demands we continuously engage with others and never shut dialog, so decorum in civil disobedience demands behaving in a dignified, courteous manner and treating one's audience respectfully, as interlocutors who could change their mind.

These four marks of civility articulate what have become the socially accepted norms of civil disobedience. They carve out a space for illegal yet civil protest. Civil disobedience thus understood avoids the instrumental and semiotic problems identified earlier. Though I won't detail their arguments here, liberal philosophers further showed that, instead of destabilizing society, civil disobedients can display heightened concern for the rule of law; and that, through their self-restraint and self-sacrifice, they communicate that they are neither disobeying lightly nor putting themselves above the will of the democratic majority.

However, some theorists and activists have criticized the civil disobedience playbook for imposing excessively demanding standards of conduct on protesters and deterring dissent.[28] These critics have instead relaxed or abandoned the four criteria of civility, blazing an alternate route in the process.

SOLUTION 2: BROADENING CIVIL DISOBEDIENCE

Dissatisfied with the standard account, theorists have put forth "inclusive" approaches that relax the demands of civility and broaden the concept of civil disobedience to encompass all sorts of principled lawbreaking. Kimberley Brownlee's is one such account. For Brownlee, civil disobedience "must include a deliberate breach of law taken on the basis of steadfast personal commitment in order to communicate our condemnation of a law or policy to a relevantly placed audience."[29] What sets civil disobedience apart from other kinds of lawbreaking – what makes it civil – are its constrained, communicative, and non-evasive properties, which mark the agent's efforts to engage an intended public in dialog or at least her willingness to explain herself if called upon (which is how Brownlee defines "non-evasiveness" – not as submission to legal sanctions). Civil disobedience thus understood need not be public, nonviolent, non-evasive, or respectful; but it must be communicative. Brownlee conceives of the suffragist militant tactics as civil disobedience and she has argued that Edward Snowden's unlawful, stealthy acquisition and leaks of classified information about the US government's surveillance programs were civilly disobedient on her account but not on the Rawlsian account adopted (and somewhat amended) by William Scheuerman.[30]

Brownlee is concerned first and foremost with individual conscience – not social stability or democratic respect. She denies that disobedience poses the instrumental and semiotic problems identified earlier. In fact, the problems are reverse: it is society that imposes significant burdens on individual conscience, sometimes compelling people to disobey its demands to privilege their deeply held moral convictions. Brownlee defends a moral right to civil disobedience, which entitles us to freely disobey the law on the basis of our conscientious convictions, even in "a reasonably good society . . . founded on morally legitimate principles and values" because the value of conscience outweighs these principles and values.[31]

Celikates's account also exemplifies an inclusive approach to civil disobedience, though his differs from Brownlee's. Celikates, who spearheads the radical democratic approach, has been a stern critique of the civil disobedience playbook. He challenges and rejects as too narrow and problematic, the criteria of publicity, nonviolence, nonevasion, and even conscientiousness.[32] He understands civil disobedience instead as:

> a principled collective act of protest that involves breaking the law and aims at politicizing or changing laws, policies, or institutions in ways that can be seen as civil – as opposed to organized and conducted in a militarized way and aiming at the destruction of the "enemy."[33]

This broad conception imposes no requirement on the agent's attitude toward the system, her target, or the principles she appeals to. The civilly disobedient act need not be done publicly, nonviolently, or non-evasively. It can shock and offend. Celikates discards the demands of civility because of their ideological conservative underpinnings and conceives of the civility of civil disobedience nonnormatively, simply as marking non-state agents engaged in nonmilitary tactics. On this definition, guerrilla paramilitary movements are engaged in uncivil resistance. But, as with Brownlee, all sorts of violent and evasive acts may still be properly labeled "civil."

Both Celikates's and Brownlee's inclusive conceptions maintain the standard insight that civil disobedience is essentially a communicative act aimed at political change but leave much else up for grabs, relaxing or discarding the four norms of civility. What makes a disobedient act civil, on their view, does nothing to defuse the charges of destabilization and signaling of democratic contempt. The result is a concept of civil disobedience that includes covert, violent, evasive, and offensive acts of disobedience and thereby stretches civility beyond recognition, encompassing in it some features previously deemed to be mutually exclusive. For instance, Celikates dubs Anonymous civilly disobedient despite the fact that the group members conceal their identity, use coerced botnets to launch DDoS attacks, and admit being motivated by a zeal for pranks – thus exhibiting features that are usually seen as "other" to, or even "opposites" of, civil disobedience.[34] Lumping violence, coercion, covertness (anonymity), evasion, and offensiveness together with their opposites is not very useful, insofar as acts of principled disobedience that satisfy the standard norms of civility, and those that don't, exemplify distinct phenomena.

Indeed, inclusive accounts miss the point of many disobedient actions, which is to *refuse* to follow the civil disobedience playbook. Emmeline Pankhurst defended suffragists' use of "militant methods" (including heckling, window-smashing, sabotage, arson, and hunger strikes) and characterized herself as a "soldier" in a "civil war" waged against the state. Ukrainian-French radical feminist collective Femen brands its disobedience as radical and provocative, not civil, by calling its tactics – which include "sex attacks, sex diversions and sex sabotage" – *sextremism*.[35] Cultural critic Mark Dery conceives of "culture jammers" – such as billboard bandits, hacktivists, and media hoaxers – as "artistic terrorists" and "communication guerrilla" fighters.[36] In short, agents may see themselves, and seek to be perceived, as radical and provocative rather than civil.

Inclusive accounts do not equip us to think these departures from the template of civil disobedience, since they erase the distinctiveness of uncivil acts by insisting on their civility (or denying the relevance of the category altogether).

IN DEFENSE OF UNCIVIL DISOBEDIENCE

The civil disobedience playbook has successfully defined the socially accepted norms, which disobedients need to abide by. What makes a disobedient act civil are its publicity, nonviolence, non-evasion, and decorum; and displaying civility by meeting these criteria is usually seen as conveying something like endorsement of the system's overall legitimacy, whether or not agents actually hold and wish to convey such commitment.[37] This means that civility requires abiding by law *or* disobeying it civilly; and that to disobey civilly one must follow the script set out in the civil disobedience playbook.[38] Nevertheless, it doesn't follow from this account of civility in disobedience that any disobedient action that fails to conform to the civil disobedience playbook cannot be justified in "near-just" societies (which are often more unjust than near-just but better than existing alternatives). Incivility in disobedience can sometimes be justified, too. We need to make conceptual and normative room for uncivil disobedience.

By "uncivil disobedience," I mean a principled breach of law in response to perceived wrongs (injustice or wrongdoing), in pursuit of any of a variety of goals (e.g., aid, harm prevention, education, retaliation, expression of discontent, status quo, reform, system overhaul), and that fails to satisfy the basic norms of civility by being either: covert, evasive, violent, *or* offensive. Uncivil disobedience is not a distinct kind or single neat category, but a cluster concept, for whose application we might treat displays of any one of the four features – covertness, evasion, violence, and offensiveness – as sufficient. Certain types of uncivil disobedience can sometimes be justified on the basis of instrumental and non-instrumental reasons.

Violating the marks of civility may be necessary for certain worthwhile ends. For instance, covertness and evasion may be key to rescuing or assisting people in need. Rebecca Solnit praises the "hundreds of boat-owners" who eluded the authorities and defied their orders to get into New Orleans the day after the levees broke in 2005, in order to rescue "people – single moms, toddlers, grandfathers – stranded in attics, on roofs, in flooded housing projects, hospitals, and school buildings."[39] And doctors all over the world have covertly and evasively provided contraception and abortion to women where these services are illegal. Civil – public and non-evasive – disobedience couldn't achieve these goals.

Nonviolence may also hinder the realization of critical goals, including self-defense and defense of others. When the state unjustly fails to protect some minorities from violence in the hands of others, members of these minorities are justified in resorting to force in order to protect themselves and other potential victims from such violence. In response to the lack of police support for victims of domestic violence, women from India's district of Uttar Pradesh founded the Gulabi (aka. Pink Sari) Gang in 2006. This vigilante gang patrols neighborhoods, using violence against abusive husbands and even corrupt police. Political advocacy and civil disobedience are crucial to social movements; but the Gulabi Gang's uncivil threats of violence are essential to their mission of collective self-defense against state-condoned violence.

Lastly, disobedient agents may deliberately resort to breaches of decorum in order to draw attention to their action and cause. Champions of civil disobedience argue that transgressing the law through civil disobedience offers a spectacular way of dramatizing one's protest and is likely to garner media and public attention. But the argument applies a fortiori to uncivil disobedience today, if it is true that decades of civil disobedience have desensitized us somewhat to its power. When members of ACT UP (the AIDS Coalition to Unleash Power) or Pussy Riot stormed churches, they offended decency, were called "hooligans," and magnetized the spotlight.

Much uncivil disobedience is impermissible and wrongful, because it violates people's fundamental interests and/or is undertaken in pursuit of objectionable ends. Hence, the instrumental reasons for uncivil disobedience identified above do not coalesce into a blanket defense of uncivil disobedience. Context, ends, and means must be taken into account to draw the line between, say, the vigilantism of the Gulabi Gang and that of the Minuteman Project, whose members patrol the border with Mexico in pursuit of unauthorized migrants. The point is to show that publicity, nonviolence, non-evasion, and decorum can significantly hinder the realization of some worthy goals of resistance (including mutual aid, bodily autonomy, and self-defense); that circumstances sometimes call for acts of uncivil disobedience; and that the latter neither destabilize society nor signal democratic contempt.

There can also be non-instrumental reasons to disobey uncivilly. To the extent that following the civil disobedience playbook is a way to signal fidelity to law, flouting it can express disrespect toward the legal system. When this disrespect is well grounded, that is, based on facts about the system's unjust and unfair treatment of some members, agents have reasons to express it. Elizabeth Cady Stanton, an American militant suffragist, justified her refusal to submit to the legal system in these terms:

> The insult of being tried by men – judges, jurors, lawyers, all men –
> for violating the laws and constitutions of men, made for the
> subjugation of my sex; to be forever publicly impaled by party,
> press, and pulpit, so far transcends a petty verdict of butchers, cab-
> drivers, and plough-boys, in a given case, that my continuous wrath
> against the whole dynasty of tyrants has not left one stagnant drop
> of blood in my veins to rouse for any single act of insult.[40]

Stanton voices an intense and well-grounded distrust toward the state and its rules. Why ought she (morally) submit to legal sanctions meted out by a state that treats her and her peers as inferior human beings, unfit for self-rule? Why should she take, or act as if she took, this system as morally authoritative and politically legitimate? Civil, non-evasive disobedience would have expressed a kind of respect she had no reason to exhibit. Indeed, she had good reason to evade and reject the state's prosecution and punishment of her disobedience – and the state's authority in general – even if her violation of civility led some portions of the public to deem her "unladylike" and "unworthy" of the political franchise. Civil disobedience may well be a superior method to achieve moral suasion of the community; but moral suasion is not the only legitimate goal of resistance. Expressing distrust, anger, and outrage is an important one, too, especially for the sake of fellow oppressed people.

Uncivil disobedience may be defended not only as an expression of fitting reactive attitudes, but also, depending on the form it takes, as a way to affirm dignity (one's own or others') in the face of laws and practices that deny it, as well as a form of solidarity with the oppressed. For instance, prisoners and detained asylum seekers have launched hunger strikes, rioted, and attempted escapes, against their prisons' unsanitary conditions and medical neglect during the COVID-19 pandemic.[41] These acts of uncivil disobedience signify institutional denials of prisoners' and migrants' dignity, all the while serving to assert and reclaim that dignity. Importantly, incarcerated individuals organized and planned these hunger strikes, riots, and escapes. They defied the institution's rules to act together, show their solidarity, and reassure each other of their worth.

Deliberately offensive acts of disobedience, by definition, intend to offend, and are thus naturally well suited to express disrespect and defiance, to provoke and jolt. Black Lives Matter protests all over the world have featured anti-police chants which are frequently condemned as obscene, virulent, and antagonizing, yet purport to convey the urgent imperative to end lethal police. This kind of incivility stands in direct opposition to the lofty demands of the virtue of civility in the public discourse. Uncivil disobedients do not seek consensus or compromise among democratic equals; they deliberately flout civility in order to denounce democratic equality and civic friendship as mere pretenses and highlight the reality of oppression. As Juliet Hooker argued about the 2015 Black Lives Matter protests, it is unfair to ask black people to enact "appropriate," "civil" democratic politics "when other citizens and state institutions betray a lack of care and concern for black suffering, which in turn makes it impossible for those wrongs to be redressed."[42]

We may identify something like an "uncivil disobedience play-book" in recent uprisings in Hong Kong and the US. In Hong Kong, protesters insist they learned their lesson from the failure of the last pro-democracy protests, the 2014 "Occupy Central" or "Umbrella Movement," which emulated the liberal, Rawlsian conception of civil disobedience.[43] The movement includes a flank of front-line activists who use defensive force against police violence. They set up roadblocks to slow down police vehicles, throw rocks and Molotov cocktails, and neutralize tear gas canisters to protect the crowds of protesters. They act covertly, concealing their hair and faces with hard hats, goggles, and gas masks; and evade law enforcement efforts. Hong Kong residents secretly provide food, equipment, rides home, medical aid, and funds to activists. Protesters' messages – in chants, placards, Lennon walls, and graffiti – feature offensive language and express crude anti-police and anti-Chinese sentiment.

While most of the Black Lives Matter protests have been peaceful, some included stone-throwing, vandalism, and looting. Black Lives Matter activists have defended their expressions of grief and rage, and denounced the focus on property destruction as evincing disregard for black lives and unjustly sanctioning brutal police repression. Some participants say they borrowed tactics from Hong Kong, including wearing goggles, helmets, and homemade shields to protect themselves and other protesters from militarized law enforcement, using leaf blowers against tear gas, and carrying milk and antacids as remedies for the effects of pepper spray. Guerrilla artists have painted murals on the plywood of boarded-up storefronts. They have defaced tainted commemorations connected to historical racial injustice.[44] After protesters toppled a bronze statue of Edward Colston, a seventeenth-century trader of enslaved persons, in Bristol, England, a team of guerrilla artists replaced it with a black resin sculpture by Marc Quinn of a black Bristol resident with her fist raised defiantly into the air.[45]

Interestingly, these recent uprisings in Hong Kong and the US appear to refute the received wisdom that nonviolence and civility are essential to the success of social movements, because they lower the barrier to mass participation and increase support. Erica Chenoweth and Maria Stephan found that only nonviolent movements achieved mass participation and that 3.5 percent or more of the population actively participating guaranteed a movement's success by producing security forces' defection.[46] The overwhelming majority of people in Hong Kong supports the movement and a staggering 45 percent of the population is estimated to have participated in the protests. Yet police brutally repressed the protests and China imposed in June 2020 a draconian national security "anti-sedition" law, which has been used to arrest dozens of protesters and disqualify a dozen pro-democracy legislative candidates. Meanwhile, polls found widespread support for the recent Black Lives Matter protests in the US (but not in 2015). By June 2020, 68 percent of respondents said the protesters were "completely right" or "somewhat right."[47] An estimated 6–10 percent of the US population participated in protests, making it perhaps the largest movement in US history.[48] Both the pro-democracy movement in Hong Kong and Black Lives Matter thus show that incivility is no barrier to mass participation.

Examining the limits of civility strengthens the case for incivility in speech and action. Scott Aikin and Robert Talisse have argued that civility is a "reciprocal public virtue."[49] As such, it establishes a standard of conduct that applies to groups, and which individuals are required to abide by, *as long as others generally do so as well*: "Where the norm corresponding to a reciprocal public virtue is generally violated within a group, the virtue itself is rendered inactive, as it establishes a standard of behavior *only under the conditions where the norm is collectively embraced*." In these cases, group members are not bound to abide by the collective standard of conduct. Aikin and Talisse observe that in the United States, not only citizens, but also "those who are wielding the institutional power of the government" generally disregard the norms of civility in their democratic engagements, so that others are not required to manifest the virtue of civility. This suggests that civilians' incivility may in fact be presumptively permissible.

Of course champions of civility insist that the *point* of civility is to extend a metaphorical hand – to be willing to engage in dialog – with everyone, regardless of how revolting we find their view and how uncivil we view their mode of expression. The point of civility just is *not* to close the dialogic community, not to exclude anyone as beyond the pale. From this perspective, civility does not have the limits Aikin and Talisse delineate. However, the virtue's moral force as an imperative of conduct is clearly diminished by people's and officials' failure to conform to it. And if anyone remains significantly bound by it, it is surely those in power or otherwise in social positions of privilege rather than those who are socially marginalized, for the actions of the former directly influence the nature of the public sphere. It is all the more important for them to model the kind of behavior that should be the norm in democratic engagements. Those in power and positions of privilege should thus enforce the norm of civility among themselves, while refraining from condemning incivility on the part of members of disadvantaged groups.

It is furthermore plausible to contend that the state has a role to play in upholding the conditions necessary for civility to flourish in the public sphere. The Unite the Right rally that took place in Charlottesville in August 2017 is a case in point.[50] Numerous armed white supremacist militia groups were present at the rally, far outpacing the police presence. Two things matter here: first, open carry of firearms is legal under Virginia law (and doesn't require a permit), making rallies and their counterprotests inherently dangerous. That is, calls for civility appear misplaced and problematic when disagreeing parties are allowed to come to the debate armed. To put it more general terms, civility requires a solid basis of safety and mutual respect before it can be expected of everyone. One journalist set to cover the rally fully expected violence: "Given what had happened in the previous months – three people stabbed at a Klan rally in Anaheim, seven people stabbed at a neo-Nazi event in Sacramento, street fighting that stretched on for hours in Berkeley – I feared it might be a bloody scene in Charlottesville."[51] Second, the police ought to have planned accordingly and provided protection for the counterprotesters. The Police Department's "lack of intervention was obvious to everyone present," investigators would later note in an exhaustive 200-page report commissioned by the city of Charlottesville, adding: "It also seems likely that the insufficient police response on Friday night emboldened people who intended to engage in similar acts of violence on Saturday."[52] The Police Department's failure to ensure protesters' safety was culpably wrong in seeming to condone white supremacist violence and incivility.

It also prompted and justified counterprotesters' own incivility. Cornel West gave a sermon at St. Paul's Church in Charlottesville on that day. West later described the white nationalist demonstrators laying siege to the church, the police pulling back, and the 300–350 anti-fascists who defended them – "saved our lives, actually."[53] Given that antifa activists provided security when the police would not, their use of force in defense of others was justified. By the end of the day, dozens were injured and one killed when a white nationalist drove his car in a crowd of counterprotesters. Trump and others condemned the violence "on both sides" and many rejected antifa as "no better than the fascists." Yet equating all acts of violence without distinguishing their source and aims is morally dubious.

Days before the rally, the Federal Bureau of Investigation (FBI) had warned about threats of homegrown racial violence – not by white supremacists, but by "Black Identity Extremists." The FBI merged this new, made-up category and several other classifications in July 2019 under the umbrella term of "racially motivated violent extremism."[54] A number of government officials, including police representatives and mayors, have continued to (incorrectly) refer to Black Lives Matter as a "terrorist organization" in the latest wave of protests following the killings of Ahmaud Arbery, Breonna Taylor, and George Floyd.[55] As of this writing, in August 2020, Trump's Justice Department is targeting Black Lives Matter protesters as domestic terrorists and subjecting them to violent repression instead of protecting them.

The upshot is that the state must uphold the conditions necessary for norms of civility to flourish. When it fails to, it is inappropriate to insist that subordinated groups protest and resist civilly. Not because civility is not a good idea – indeed activists may well aspire to it – but simply because they are not given the resources to make it a default mode of conduct. These resources are to be found both in society's background laws and in authorities' responses to social movements' activities.

CONCLUDING REMARKS

There are reasons to doubt civility's function as the glue that keeps divided societies whole. While civility can promote social stability, its demands are all-too-often used to deter dissent and resistance, and so it tends to further alienate already-marginalized groups as they try to speak out against the status quo. The point of civility is to show mutual respect and achieve concord. Many philosophers have argued that civil disobedience doesn't undermine these goals. But I also showed that uncivil disobedience may sometimes be necessary to promote important goals, and may also serve both to signal extant failures of respect and concord and to highlight the deceptions of civility in structurally unjust societies. Where the state fails to provide the conditions necessary for civility to flourish, then, incivility may be the answer, not the problem.

NOTES

1. Robert Talisse shows this is due to political saturation and belief polarization, which have sharpened and widened extant political divisions. See Robert B. Talisse, *Overdoing Democracy: Why We Must Put Politics in Its Place* (New York: Oxford University Press, 2019).

2. Trevor Foulk, Andrew Woolum, and Amir Erez, "Catching Rudeness Is Like Catching a Cold: The Contagion Effects of Low-Intensity Negative Behaviors," *Journal of Applied Psychology* 101, no. 1 (2016): 50–67.

3. Aristotle, *Nicomachean Ethics*, Book IX.

4. Aristotle, *Politics*, 1252a30.

5. Thomas Hobbes, *Leviathan*, chap. XV (Eighth Law of Nature).

6. Hobbes, *Leviathan*, chap. XV (Eighth Law of Nature).

7. Hobbes, *Leviathan*, chap. XV (Fifth Law of Nature).

8. Teresa Bejan, *Mere Civility: Disagreement and the Limits of Toleration* (Cambridge, Mass.: Harvard University Press, 2017), 11–12. On Hobbes's view, the sovereign can and must realize the virtue of civil silence at the societal level, by disciplining and censoring citizens' speech.

9. Bejan, *Mere Civility*, 97.

10. Bejan, *Mere Civility*, chapter 4.

11. John Rawls, *Political Liberalism* (New York: Columbia University Press, 1996), 129.

12. Amy Gutmann and Dennis Thompson, "Moral Conflict and Political Consensus," in *Liberalism and the Good*, eds. R. Bruce Douglass, et al. (New York: Routledge, 1990), 125–47.

13. Clifford Orwin, "Civility," *The American Scholar* 60, no. 4 (Autumn 1991): 553–64.

14. John Rawls, *A Theory of Justice*, revised ed. (Cambridge, Mass.: Belknap Press of Harvard University Press, 1999), 312.

15. Rawls, *Theory*, 312.

16. Rawls, *Theory*, 312.

17. It is thus plausible to distinguish two different grounds of the moral duty to obey the law: the natural duty of justice and the duty of civility. The duty of civility only yields a presumptive duty to obey the law, while the natural duty of justice establishes a pro tanto (i.e., ordinarily conclusive) duty to obey. On the latter, see Rawls, *Theory*, 293–312.

18. Jessica Bulman-Pozen and David Pozen, "Uncivil Obedience," *Columbia Law Review* 115 (2015): 809–72. For a critique of the category of "uncivil obedience," see Daniel Markovits, "Civility, Rule-Following, and the Authority of Law," *Columbia Law Review* 116 (2016): 32–43.

19. See, most recently, Robin Celikates, "Constituent Power Beyond Exceptionalism: Irregular Migration, Disobedience, and (Re-)

Constitution," *Journal of International Political Theory* 15, no. 1 (2019): 67–81. See also Chapter 5 in this volume.

20. Sally Haslanger distinguishes three approaches to questions about "What is x?" In the first, "conceptual" approach, we investigate our ordinary concept of x using traditional a priori methods. In the second, "descriptive" or "naturalistic" approach, we investigate x's extension, i.e., what people refer to when they use x. In the third, "ameliorative" or "analytic" approach, we inquire into the purpose of having x and see if we can put the concept of x to good use in a liberatory project. Sally Haslanger, *Resisting Reality: Social Construction and Social Critique* (Oxford: Oxford University Press, 2012), chapter 13.

21. See Hugo A. Bedau, "On Civil Disobedience," *The Journal of Philosophy* 58, no. 21 (1961): 653–65; Carl Cohen, *Civil Disobedience: Conscience, Tactics, and the Law* (New York: Columbia University Press, 1971); Rawls, *Theory*.

22. See, e.g., Peter Singer, *Democracy and Disobedience* (Oxford: Clarendon Press, 1973); Kent Greenawalt, *Conflicts of Law and Morality* (Oxford: Oxford University Press, 1987); Robert E. Goodin, "Civil Disobedience and Nuclear Protest," *Political Studies* 35, no. 3 (1987): 461–46.

23. Kimberley Brownlee, *Conscience and Conviction: The Case for Civil Disobedience* (Oxford: Oxford University Press, 2012), 21–22.

24. Todd May, *Nonviolent Resistance: A Philosophical Introduction* (Cambridge: Polity Press, 2015).

25. Elsewhere I identify four attitudes that fall under the label "non-evasion": (1) willing submission to arrest and prosecution, (2) guilty plea in court, (3) no appeal to criminal defenses, and (4) no complaint for the punishment received. Candice Delmas, "Civil Disobedience, Injustice, and Punishment," in *The Palgrave Handbook of Applied Ethics and the Criminal Law*, eds. Kimberley Ferzan and Larry Alexander (Basingstoke: Palgrave Macmillan, 2020), chapter 8.

26. See Austin Sarat, "Keeping Civility in Its Place: Dissent, Injustice, and the Lessons of History," in *Law, Society, and Community: Socio-Legal Essays in Honour of Roger Cotterrell*, eds. Richard Nobes and David Schiff (London: Routledge, 2014), 293–308; Erin R. Pineda, "Civil Disobedience and What Else? Making Space for Uncivil Forms of Resistance," *European Journal of Political Theory* (2019), https://doi.org /10.1177/1474885119845063.

27. Mohandas Gandhi, *The Essential Gandhi: An Anthology of His Writings on His Life, Work, and Ideas*, ed. Louis Fischer (New York: Vintage, 2002), 148.

28. For an overview of these critiques, see Candice Delmas, *A Duty to Resist: When Disobedience Should Be Uncivil* (New York: Oxford University Press, 2018), chapter 1.

29. Brownlee, *Conscience and Conviction*, 18.

30. See William E. Scheuerman, "Whistleblowing as Civil Disobedience: The Case of Edward Snowden," *Philosophy and Social Criticism* 40, no. 7 (2014): 609–28; and Kimberley Brownlee, "The Civil Disobedience of Edward Snowden: A Reply to William Scheuerman," *Philosophy and Social Criticism* 42, no. 10 (2016): 965–70. See also Chapter 15 in this volume.

31. Brownlee, *Conscience and Conviction*, 86.

32. Robin Celikates, "Civil Disobedience as Practice of Civic Freedom," in *On Global Citizenship James Tully in Dialogue*, ed. David Owen (Bloomsbury Press, 2014), 207–28; Celikates, "Rethinking Civil Disobedience as a Practice of Contestation – Beyond the Liberal Paradigm," *Constellations* 23, no. 1 (2016): 37–45.

33. Celikates, "Constituent Power," 70.

34. Robin Celikates and Daniel De Zeeuw, "Botnet Politics, Algorithmic Resistance, and Hacking Society," Hacking Habitat, ed. Ine Gevers (Rotterdam: Nai010 Publishers, 2016), 213.

35. See "About Us," *Femen*, accessed May 15, 2018, http://femen.org/about-us.

36. Mark Dery, "Culture Jamming: Hacking, Slashing and Sniping in the Empire of Signs," *Open Magazine Pamphlet Series* (unknown, 1993).

37. Of course, some civil disobedients explicitly challenge the legitimacy of the system they are protesting. Occupy Wall Street and France's *gilets jaunes* come to mind. But it's worth noting that, precisely because participants of the Occupy movement rejected the political system's legitimacy, Bernard Harcourt proposed to conceive of the protests as "political," not "civil" disobedience. Bernard Harcourt, "Political Disobedience," in *Occupy: Three Inquiries in Disobedience*, eds. M. Taussig, B. Harcourt, and W.J.T. Mitchell (Chicago, IL: University of Chicago Press, TRIOS series, 2013), 45–91.

38. This echoes David Lefkowitz's re-conception of political obligation as the moral duty to obey the law or to disobey it civilly (which he premises on an understanding of democratic politics). David Lefkowitz, "On a Moral Right to Civil Disobedience," *Ethics* 117, no. 2 (2007): 202–33.

39. Rebecca Solnit, *Hope in the Dark: Untold Histories, Wild Possibilities*, second edition (Chicago, Ill.: Haymarket Books, 2016), xxiii.

40. Elizabeth Cady Stanton, Letter from Tenafly, June 25, 1873.

41. Zak Cheney-Rice, "Coronavirus Fears Spark Prison Strikes, Protests, and Riots Around the World," *Intelligencer* (2020), https://nymag.com/intelligencer/2020/03/coronavirus-fears-spark-prison-unrest-world wide.html.

42. Juliet Hooker, "Black Lives Matter and the Paradoxes of U.S. Black Politics: From Democratic Sacrifice to Democratic Repair," *Political Theory* 44, no. 4 (2016): 448–69.

43. Benny Yiu-ting Tai, "Civil Disobedience and the Rule of Law," in *Civil Unrest and Governance in Hong Kong: Law and Order from Historical and Cultural Perspectives*, eds. Michael H. K. Ng and John D. Wong (Abingdon; New York, NY: Routledge, 2017), 141–62. See Candice Delmas, "Uncivil Disobedience in Hong Kong," *Boston Review* (January 13, 2020), http://bostonreview.net/global-justice/candice-delmas-uncivil-disobedience-hong-kong.

44. See, e.g., Chong-Ming Lim, "Vandalizing Tainted Commemorations," *Philosophy and Public Affairs* 48, no. 2 (2020): 185–216; Ten-Herng Lai, "Political Vandalism as Counter-Speech: A Defense of Defacing and Destroying Tainted Monuments," *European Journal of Philosophy* (2020), https://doi.org/10.1111/ejop.12573.

45. See, e.g., Tim Elfrink, "Britons toppled an enslaver's statue. A guerrilla artist replaced it with a Black Lives Matter protester," *The Washington Post* (June 15, 2020), www.washingtonpost.com/nation/2020/07/15/col ston-slave-trader-statue-bristol/.

46. See Erica Chenoweth and Maria J. Stephan, *Why Civil Resistance Works: The Strategic Logic of Nonviolent Conflict* (New York: Columbia University Press, 2011).

47. See Peter Hamby, "New Poll Shows Trump's Black Lives Matter Protest Response Could Cost Him 2020," *Vanity Fair* (July 24, 2020): www.vanityfair.com/news/2020/07/polling-trumps-protest-response-could-cost-him-2020.

48. See Larry Buchanan, Quoctrung Bui, and Jugal K. Patel, "Black Lives Matter May Be the Largest Movement in U.S. History," *The New York Times* (July 3, 2020), www.nytimes.com/interactive/2020/07/03/us/geor ge-floyd-protests-crowd-size.html.

49. Scott Aikin and Robert Talisse, "Civility as a Reciprocal Public Virtue," 3 *Quarks Daily*, July 16, 2018, www.3quarksdaily.com/3quarksdaily/201 8/07/civility-as-a-reciprocal-public-virtue.html.

50. I am grateful to Thomas M. Powers for the suggestion.

51. A.C. Thompson, "48 Hours in Charlottesville: Fear, Nausea, and a Sad Lack of Surprise," *ProPublica*, August 7, 2018, www.propublica.org/art icle/48-hours-in-charlottesville.

52. Quoted in Thompson, "48 Hours in Charlottesville."

53. Cornel West and Rev. Traci Blackmon interviewed for *Democracy Now!*, August 14, 2017, www.democracynow.org/2017/8/14/ cornel_west_rev_toni_blackmon_clergy.

54. See Byron Tau, "FBI abandons use of term 'Black Identity Extremism'," *The Wall Street Journal* (July 23, 2019), www.wsj.com/articles/fbi-abandons-use-of-terms-black-identity-extremism-11563921355.

55. See, e.g., Kaelan Deese, "Giuliani says Black Lives Matter is a 'domestic terrorist' group," *The Hill* (August 6, 2020), https://thehill.com/home news/media/510953-giuliani-says-black-lives-matter-is-domestic-terrorist-group.

9 The Ethical Dimension of Civil Disobedience

Maeve Cooke

Civil disobedience is transgressive ethical action performed in a political context. It is transgressive because it involves breaking the law; on occasion, it also involves transgression of prevailing norms and entrenched values. My concern in the following is primarily with civil disobedience in the context of modern democracies, be they liberal democratic, neo-republican, or radical democratic ones. The normativity specific to the modern democratic context, structuring and shaping it in its many variants, is defined by a complex interplay of ethical ideas of freedom, equality, and human interconnectedness. By "ethical" I mean the idea and conduct of a good human life in association with other entities, human and non-human. I hold that an ethically good life calls for a reflective attitude by individual humans toward their particular ideas of the good, in which reflection is guided by a concern for ethical truth.[1] Its concern for a better society as a precondition for a better life makes civil disobedience a mode of ethical action.

Theoretical accounts of civil disobedience generally define it as a principled or conscience-driven form of political protest that involves breaking the law while observing certain norms of civility such as publicity, non-evasiveness, and nonviolence.[2] Insofar as its ethical dimension is discussed at all, it tends to be treated either in terms of an obligation to obey certain moral and/or legal principles or in terms of an appeal to individual conscience. This perspective is not wrong but it is too narrow. In this chapter I propose a broader view of the ethical dimension of civil disobedience. In the account I offer, it consists in a concern for the realization of a good life for humans in their associations with others – a kind of good life that may be obstructed by the established socio-political structures together with the prevailing, deeply rooted, individual, and collective ethical self-understandings. This broader view has the advantage of capaciousness regarding the kinds of ethical reasons motivating acts and campaigns of civil disobedience, allowing for reasons that are not well captured in the language of either duty or conscience. For example, some ecological activists may be motivated not by a sense of obligation or the voice of conscience but by feelings of connectedness with non-human natural entities; or again, subjugated individuals and groups may be driven to engage in civil disobedience, not because they feel commanded to do so by conscience or bound by obligation but because they perceive their condition of subjugation as unbearably detrimental to their exercise of agency. Its main advantage, however, is in relation to radically transformative modes of civil disobedience. As I argue in the third section, radical -fundamental- societal transformation typically calls for radical transformation of individual and collective identities, together with radical reorientation of human behavior and social practices. Since such radical transformation of thinking, behavior, and practices involves a reorientation of the self, I describe it as a kind of "ethical conversion."

I first discuss conscience and principled obligation as motivations for civil disobedience. Then, focusing on radically transformative modes of civil disobedience, I make the case for a broader perspective along the lines sketched above.

CONSCIENCE

In the history of civil disobedience, conscience has frequently been invoked in justification of morally or legally motivated lawbreaking.[3] Mohandas K. Gandhi, in advocating satyagraha or "soul force" rather than passive resistance in his campaign of nonviolent action against colonial rule, famously proclaimed that "there is a higher court than courts of justice and that is the court of conscience. It supersedes all other courts."[4] Martin Luther King, Jr., who like Gandhi has become an icon for the theory and practice of civil disobedience, also connected such action with conscience. He described civil disobedience as nonviolent direct action that presents "our very bodies as a means of laying out our case before the conscience of the local and national community"[5] and called on his fellow religious leaders to commend "young high school and college students, young ministers of the gospel and a host of their elders courageously and nonviolently sitting at lunch counters and willingly going to jail for conscience's sake."[6] John Rawls could be said to build conscience into his influential definition of civil disobedience, when he characterizes it as "a public, non-violent, conscientious yet political act contrary to law usually done with the aim of bringing about a change in the law or policies of the government."[7]

Leaving aside the question of whether we should distinguish conscientious from conscience-driven behavior,[8] we should note some significant differences between Gandhi's and King's understandings of conscience, on the one side, and the liberal understanding implicit in Rawls's definition, on the other.[9] For Gandhi, conscience is an inner voice that grants human individuals access to God conceived of as Truth. When properly recognized, its voice is unquestionably right and universally binding; for such recognition, the strictest bodily and mental discipline is necessary. King shares the main features of this view. For him, as for Gandhi, the dictates of conscience are spiritual obligations that express God's will and are infallible and universally binding; for him, too, a proper understanding of them has certain bodily and mental prerequisites. By contrast, Rawls's account of civil disobedience is agnostic regarding the spiritual or moral quality of appeals to conscience. While his definition acknowledges that civil disobedients frequently appeal to conscience, the putative validity of such appeals as reasons for transgressive action resides in their coherence with general liberal democratic principles, not in their spiritual or moral quality. Not surprisingly, therefore, Rawls pays no attention to possible mental or bodily preconditions for attaining "conscientiousness." Put differently, for Rawls the normative criterion that has to be met by reasons offered by civil disobedients is not truth but conformity with liberal democratic principles. This is spelled out in his normative theory of political liberalism.[10] According to this theory, citizens must refrain from appeals to their "comprehensive doctrines," be they religious, moral, or ideological, in matters relating to the basic structure of society and constitutional essentials. However, Rawls does not preclude reasons based in part on spiritual or moral grounds. He allows for such appeals when they can be expressed in terms sufficiently general to support constitutional values and accord with public reason.[11] He held that this was true for King's appeals to religious doctrines in general, and for conscience in particular.[12]

As we have seen, Gandhi's and King's conceptions of civil disobedience take a different position on conscience, connecting it with divine truth. In the view of many contemporary political theorists, this makes them inappropriate for pluralist societies in which significant numbers of people are not religious believers. They object that appeals to conscience do not speak persuasively to those uncomfortable with the model's spiritual foundations, querying their normative force "in pluralistic societies where the voice of conscience typically speaks in different tongues."[13] They point out, moreover, that there is a danger of moral elitism on the part of those who claim access to divine truth.[14]

The liberal model of civil disobedience avoids these difficulties. However, its agnostic position with regard to the truth claims of conscience leads to a different sort of problem. Critics object that the liberal model threatens to reduce a universalist ethical claim – the claim that something is right or good for *everyone* – to a purely subjective one. In consequence, it implies that those who engage in civil disobedience are motivated primarily by subjective preference as opposed to concerns that they consider valid universally.[15] Challenging this subjectivist interpretation, Kimberley Brownlee argues that acts of civil disobedience issue an appeal to everyone in their capacity as moral agents.[16] She argues that this is not a reason to reject appeals to conscience in explaining and justifying civil disobedience, and makes the case for the importance of conscience-driven civil disobedience, based on a secular rearticulation of the idea of con-science. However, she also refrains from making conscience a *necessary* component of her normative account and allows for justi-fiable acts of civil disobedience that are not conscience-driven. In doing so, she moves productively beyond Hannah Arendt's conception, in which appeals to conscience are strictly excluded.

Arendt voices her deep suspicion of conscience in public affairs. For her, "conscience is unpolitical."[17] She sees even secular concep-tions of conscience as inescapably infected by their religious origins, contributing to their lack of generalizability. This leads her to distin-guish categorically between conscience-based forms of resistance, which she attributes to Socrates and Henry David Thoreau, and civil disobedience, which possesses the universality required by political action as she conceives of it.[18] Brownlee is right to move beyond Arendt's subjectivist understanding of conscience and to accord it an important role in civil disobedience. More generally, she is right to acknowledge the potentially valuable contribution of conscience-based judgments to democratic public life.[19] A further strength is that she allows for a plurality of justifications for civil disobedience, rather than either insisting on conscience-based reasons or eliminating them entirely. I too favor this approach.[20] One reason for doing so has already been mentioned: it acknowledges the putative validity of reasons for civil disobedience that cannot adequately be expressed in the language of conscience (or duty). But openness to reasons that are not based on conscience does not entail agnosticism with regard to their claims to ethical or spiritual truth. The latter is the Rawlsian position, which as we saw, leads easily to a subjectivism that misses the universality of the ethical appeal issued in civil disobedience.

William Scheuerman runs the risk of this kind of Rawlsian short-sightedness. Certainly, he does not seek to eliminate any refer-ence to conscience from normative accounts of civil disobedience. Despite his wariness of appeals to conscience in justification of civil disobedience, he concedes that Arendt "probably goes too far"[21] and accepts that "conscience probably should remain part of the story."[22]

But in this respect his cautious position seems unequivocally Rawlsian. The Rawlsian position, as we have seen, does not preclude reasons based in part on spiritual or moral grounds. As Scheuerman puts it, its aim is not a one-size-fits-all secularism but instead to take moral and religious differences seriously. However, Rawls is concerned with fostering pluralism rather than avoiding subjectivism. In aligning himself with Rawls in this respect, Scheuerman downgrades the ethical component of civil disobedience. He leaves open the question of whether the commands of conscience are purely subjective and makes no effort to rearticulate the concept of conscience in a way that retains the universality of its ethical appeal without presupposing a religious-spiritual conception of truth. Put differently, he cautiously grants limited space to appeals to conscience in order to respect citizen value differences, but gives no indication that he takes seriously their ethically universalist claims. In consequence, his approach to conscience is not conducive to exploring non-elitist ways of thinking about ethical truth and its accessibility to humans; indeed it is hostile to such exploration.[23] Later in this chapter I argue that normative accounts of civil disobedience that highlight its radically transformative potentials cannot do without an appropriately reconfigured, universalist idea of ethical truth. My argument should be troubling for Scheuerman, if not for Rawls, since like Candice Celikates and Candice Delmas he seeks to resuscitate its radically democratic potential.[24] This aim is not well served by his Rawlsian approach to conscience.

PRINCIPLED DISOBEDIENCE

In his discussion of civil disobedience, Rawls says virtually nothing about conscience. For this reason, the inclusion of "conscientiousness" in his definition may be better understood as a sense of duty to obey the constitutional principles of liberal democratic states.[25] Rawls takes the view that citizens have a general obligation to follow the law, even in manifestly imperfect societies. In consequence, politically motivated conscientious lawbreaking demands a special justification.[26] Construed in this way, Rawls's definition of civil disobedience can be read as characterizing a form of *principled* disobedience for which no mention of conscience is necessary. In current debates, even theorists critical of the Rawlsian view tend to favor this characterization. Thus, Celikates distances himself from Rawls, arguing that the Rawlsian model of civil disobedience, which for him is the standard liberal one,[27] leads to an "overly constrained, domesticated and sanitized understanding of this complex political practice."[28] Like a number of contemporary theorists, he sees the standard view as conformist in permitting only corrective action: it holds that civil disobedience is justifiable only when it aims to correct an imbalance between majority and minority groups, especially a majority violation of a minority's core civil and political rights.[29] It thereby disconnects civil disobedience from the possibility of fundamental political and social change – from its potential as an agent for reconstituting the socio-political order.[30] Moving beyond the Rawlsian view, his alternative account seeks to conceptualize civil disobedience as a "genuinely political and democratic practice of contestation."[31] Nonetheless, in a Rawlsian vein, he defines it as an intentionally unlawful and *principled* collective act of protest.[32] Celikates does not say whether he attributes an ethical dimension to the motivating principles; for him this is not a matter of central concern.[33] His objection is to theories that *reduce* the power of civil disobedience to its moral appeal or which *define* it in terms of conscience.[34]

Its principled character is also central in the normative account of "uncivil disobedience" offered by Delmas. Like Celikates she seeks to move beyond the Rawlsian definition and like him is critical of its perceived conformism (like him, too, she takes the Rawlsian view to be the mainstream liberal one).[35] Furthermore, like Celikates her critique of the Rawlsian view appears to be motivated by a concern to resuscitate the radically transformative potential of civil disobedience. This concern is implicit in her remarks on the ideological functions of the standard view of civil disobedience.[36] She offers some trenchant observations on how the contemporary discourse of civil disobedience, exemplified by the official reading of the US Civil Rights Movement of the 1950s and 1960s, functions as a counter-resistance ideology. This has led, in her view regrettably, to a categorical condemnation of violence that obscures state-authored and state-condoned violence; more generally, it has led to ubiquitous demands for civility that conceal and distract from the uncivility of many contemporary political systems: from the harms that they regularly inflict on citizens.[37] Her alternative proposal is for a concept of principled resistance. Unlike Celikates, she explicitly acknowledges the ethical dimension to such resistance, defining principled resistance as resistance that is morally or politically motivated by an urge to respond to perceived injustice, broadly construed.[38] Civil and uncivil disobedience are subcategories of principled resistance. Her main innovation vis-à-vis other critics of the standard liberal account is to expand the repertoire of potentially acceptable modes of principled disobedience beyond civil disobedience to allow for justified acts of *uncivil* disobedience.[39] In the case of both civil and uncivil disobedience, and, indeed principled resistance in general, protest is justified through appeal to political obligations since "the very grounds supporting a duty to obey also impose duties to disobey under conditions of injustice."[40] Echoing Rawls, by political obligation she means the duty to obey the law in legitimate, nearly just states.[41] Confining herself to common accounts of political obligation within the liberal democratic tradition, she discusses four approaches to political obligation that provide grounds for principled obedience to the law and, conversely, for principled disobedience: the natural duty of justice, the principle of fairness, the Samaritan duty, and the duties of political association.[42]

Both Celikates and Delmas explicitly distance themselves from what they see as the conformist tendencies of the standard liberal (for them, essentially Rawlsian) definition of civil disobedience. Both seek to develop alternative accounts in which disobedience – civil or uncivil[43] – has a radically transformative potential. Both characterize disobedience as principled. However, there are two problems with this characterization. First, it is unduly constraining. To be motivated to act by principles is to feel a sense of obligation or duty to act in a certain way. But recall my counterexamples: ecological activists who engage in acts of disobedience are sometimes driven neither by a sense of duty nor the commands of conscience but by feelings of connectedness with nonhuman natural entities; subjugated individuals and groups do not always rise up in protest in principled outrage but may simply experience their condition as unbearably detrimental to their exercise of agency. Second, from the point of view of reviving the radically transformative potential of civil disobedience, it is insufficiently differentiated. It fails to differentiate between a *static* understanding of moral/legal principles, of the kind Rawls appears to hold, and a *dynamic* understanding. Only a dynamic understanding, of the kind held by Jürgen Habermas, fits with the radically transformative versions of civil disobedience favored by Celikates, Delmas, and Scheuerman. Making a distinction between static and dynamic understandings of moral or legal principles enables us to see that civil disobedience in its radically transformative modes may require ethical self-transformation. In addition, it shows the need for a concept of ethical validity (truth) that is transcending of all human interpretative contexts. These further aspects of the ethical dimension of civil disobedience are largely ignored in the existing theoretical literature.

CIVIL DISOBEDIENCE AND ETHICAL SELF-TRANSFORMATION

Many critics, including Celikates, Delmas, and Scheuerman, observe that, in the Rawlsian account, the transformative potential of civil disobedience is limited to reform of laws and policies in order to bring them back into line with established constitutional principles through appeal to a shared sense of justice. In referring to a shared sense of justice, I take Rawls to mean a political culture that ethically sustains the established constitutional principles. I consider this conception static in the sense that it allows for no fundamental challenge through civil disobedience to the established constitutional principles, to which a predetermined validity is attributed. Nor does it allow for fundamental challenge to the prevailing sense of justice, which held to be similarly pre-given and unshakeable. In other words, in the Rawlsian account, citizens who engage in civil disobedience are principled in the sense of feeling bound by duty to disobey the law because of a deep and abiding allegiance to the constitutional principles of their liberal democratic state and the sense of justice motivating this allegiance.

Habermas offers an argument for civil disobedience that shares many features of the Rawlsian position.[44] It shares, in particular, the view that civil disobedience is a public act, usually announced in advance and subject to the control of the police; nonviolent (interpreted by Habermas to mean purely symbolic in character); morally justified (not founded only on private convictions or individual self-interests);[45] and involving the deliberate transgression of specific legal norms without calling into question obedience to the rule of law as a whole.[46] However, his position also diverges from Rawls's in a key respect. For Habermas, the constitutional state as a whole is not a finished product but a "susceptible, precarious undertaking which is constructed for the purpose of establishing or maintaining, renewing or broadening a legitimate legal order under constantly changing circumstances."[47] Civil disobedience belongs to the indispensable necessities of a mature constitutional state: it signals the fact that "the democratic constitutional state with its legitimating constitutional principles reaches beyond their positive legal embodiments."[48] It is necessary, albeit as a last resort, because the mechanisms for self-correction built into many constitutional states prove insufficient on occasion, allowing for grave injustices. One reason for this is that the downtrodden and oppressed, who experience injustice most immediately, seldom have opportunities for influencing parliaments, unions, or parties, have little access to the mass media, and have virtually no political leverage.[49] Civil disobedience is necessary, in addition, because legal-political institutions inevitably have sclerotic tendencies, immunizing themselves against demands for change.

Scheuerman rightly draws attention to this difference between the Rawlsian and Habermasian positions. He notes that despite the Rawlsian packaging, Habermas "fills [the concept of civil disobedience] with richer democratic content," allowing "active citizens to address *any* grave or potentially serious issues and sometimes push for broad change."[50] In terms of the distinction I have proposed, we could say that Habermas has a dynamic understanding of legal-political principles and Rawls a static one. There is a similar difference in their conceptions of the political culture that ethically sustains the established constitutional principles. Whereas Rawls presupposes a pre-given and unshakeable shared sense of justice, rooted in commitment to the ethical values inscribed within the prevailing political culture, Habermas acknowledges, at least tacitly, that, on occasion, civil disobedience calls into question these ethical values. This acknowledgment is implicit in his characterization of the German peace movement of the 1980s. Although in the first instance the protest was against nuclear missiles, Habermas observes that many "no's" were aggregated in the movement: "the 'no' to nuclear weapons with the 'no' to nuclear power, to large-scale technology in general, to chemical pollution of the environment, to bureaucratic health care, 'slum clearance', the death of the forests, discrimination against women, hatred of foreigners, restrictive immigration policies, etc."[51] He draws the conclusion that the protest was a rejection not just of a particular policy or measure but rather of a *life-form*: one based on competition and production, and tailored to the needs of capitalist modernity, programmed for possessive individualism and for values of material security.[52]

However, neither Habermas nor Scheuerman – nor, indeed, Delmas nor Celikates – develop this line of thinking. Doing so allows us to see some important additional aspects of the ethical dimension of civil disobedience. It is noteworthy, to begin with, that the protestors in this case do not appeal, tacitly or explicitly, to a shared sense of justice. They do not deny that there is a widely shared sense of justice; rather, they challenge the ethical values inscribed within the political culture that underpins it. In consequence, they are likely to encounter a widespread ethical indifference to their concerns. Moreover, this indifference is likely to be based on a general inability to perceive what is wrong with these ethical values, and with the life-form they support, with the result that the majority is unmoved by the protests or, at best, perplexed by them. Delmas grapples with this difficulty in her discussion of four approaches to political obligation, but her conclusions are unsatisfactory. For example, in discussing the Samaritan duty to obey the law, she acknowledges the problem of lack of awareness by societally dominant groups of the persistent structural endangerment of some co-citizens such as "ghetto dwellers, Black and Brown people, LGBTQ people, indigenous women, undocumented migrants, and minority believers."[53] She recognizes that this may be the result of lack of basic information, but also that it may manifest "moral blindness" due to ideology and cultural prejudice.[54] In response she argues that people face secondary duties "to seek information, revise one's beliefs based on evidence, show due care in moral deliberation, exercise self-scrutiny, resist self-deception, and develop empathetic understanding."[55] The last, which she considers ultimately most important, is understood as an interactive enterprise involving moral learning and requiring the civic virtue of open-mindedness.[56]

Delmas is right to emphasize the importance of moral learning of this kind. It is questionable, however, whether open-minded engagement with others is sufficient to counter the moral "blindness" of the kind she describes: an inability to comprehend what is ethically wrong that is engendered by the societal system itself and that structures people's very identities. I contend that, in such cases, in order to be able to perceive the forms of injustice and oppression against which the protest is directed, and to understand the demands of the protestors, fundamental shifts in perception are required: there will have to be a significant shift in perception on the part of the majority groups, and corresponding changes in thinking, behavior, and social practices that enable them to see the world in a profoundly different way. In other words, disobedience that demands fundamental societal transformation calls for fundamental individual and collective ethical self-transformation.

Returning to the 1980s German peace movement as described by Habermas, it is evident that a significant number of protestors sought to disrupt the logic of an entire social, cultural, political, and economic system and to reconfigure it in qualitatively new terms. The same could be said for a contemporary movement such as Extinction Rebellion. This movement seeks to reorient anthropocentric modes of thought and behavior by using nonviolent civil disobedience to achieve thorough-going system change. On its website, it states: "Our vision for Extinction Rebellion puts love at the heart of change."[57] Extrapolating, I take this to mean that the movement seeks to establish a social, cultural, political, and economic system that breaks with the instrumentalizing logic of capitalist modernity, replacing the existing system governed by the principle of instrumental rationality with a system governed by the principle of love. To give a third example, the writer and journalist Ta-Nehisi Coates views racism in the USA not as a tumor that can be isolated and removed from the body of America, but rather as a pervasive system both native and essential to that body.[58] There are evident resonances here between Coates and Malcolm X, who took a similar view in the 1950s and 1960s. Malcolm X criticized Martin Luther King and other civil rights activists for what he saw as their evasion of the need for real revolution.[59] By this I take him to mean a complete reorientation of the existing social, cultural, political, and economic system.[60]

It is important to notice the *totalizing* character of the resisted systems: the instrumentalizing logic of capitalist modernity and the dehumanizing racist logic inscribed within the socio-political order of the USA encroach on every aspect of societal life and impact profoundly on the bodies and minds of the subjects who inhabit the societal systems in question. Their totalizing character means that people subject to these logics will tend to see no need for resistance; if they do, they may misdiagnose what needs to be changed or, if they diagnose the problem correctly, they may see no possibility of resistance and change for the better.[61]

The crucial question is: how does one protest against such totalizing systems with a view to transforming them? In Coates's writings the emphasis is on resistance rather than transformation. Indeed, critics have accused him of encouraging the moral hazards of passivity, resignation, and abnegation of personal responsibility.[62] Nonetheless, implicit in his writings are two points relevant for present purposes.[63] First, his writings suggest that struggles to achieve fundamental social, cultural, political, and economic transformation must also seek to restructure and reshape individual human identities in an ethical sense. Second, that this restructuring and reshaping does not happen once and for all but is an ongoing process.[64] The case of Malcolm X helps to illustrate these points. In his coauthored autobiography, Malcolm X provides an account of a process of fundamental ethical self-transformation that started in 1946 with a prison sentence of ten years for burglary and larceny. While in prison he was captivated by the writings of Elijah Muhammad, the spiritual leader of the Nation of Islam, leading to a complete reorientation of his thinking and behavior. Later on, he underwent a second profound self-transformation following a visit to Mecca, which led among other things to a break with Muhammad. In my view, in order to satisfactorily account for Malcolm X's powerful leadership of movements of resistance to US racism in the twelve years between his release from prison and assassination in 1965, we must pay attention to his ethical identity transformations.[65] While concerned above all with transformation of the moral identities of black Americans, Malcolm X came to see the need for moral transformation on the side of white Americans as well. However, he saw little prospect of achieving transformation on this side, holding that the seeds of racism were too deeply rooted in white people collectively.[66]

The importance of ethical self-transformation on both sides, not just on the side of the dominant societal groups but, in addition, on the side of those subjugated by the societal system in which these groups are dominant, is evident in Gandhi's writings. Gandhi understood satyagraha as a process of conversion, a kind of action that is more affective than intellectual and diametrically opposed to coercion or even persuasion or condemnation.[67] He writes: "We do not seek to coerce . . .. We seek to convert [our opponents]."[68] The strict mental and bodily discipline that, as we have seen, is a prerequisite for recognition of the voice of conscience, is also necessary for conversion of one's opponents. As well as ongoing work on the self in the form of disciplinary practices, it also involves a willingness to impose suffering on oneself (for example, by accepting punishment by the state).[69]

Pace Malcolm X's derisory remarks on King's campaign of non-violent direct action, King, too, seems to have recognized the need for ethical self-transformation, most evidently on the side of the subjugated but also on the side of the societally dominant groups. Admittedly – and this is indeed a significant difference between him and Malcolm X – he appears to think that the required revolution in ethical self-understanding on the part of black Americans *has already happened*. He writes:

> [following years of a pernicious "negative peace"] something happened to the Negro. The Negro masses began to re-evaluate themselves. They came to feel that they were somebody. Their religion revealed to them that God loves all of his children, and that the important thing about a man "is not his specificity but his fundamentum," not the texture of his hair or the color of his skin, but the texture and quality of his soul.[70]

King does not explicitly address the question of whether a corresponding reevaluation of self-understandings is necessary for citizens who are part of the societally dominant groups. However, his impressive efforts to forge connections between subjugated black Americans and the white American majority suggest a tacit awareness of this. King recognized that public performances of protest must be mediated by narratives. The narratives establish semantic connections between the conflicting groups, enabling each side to recognize the other as capable in principle of understanding its point of view and, hence, as a potential partner in mutual deliberation and negotiation. King was exceptionally skillful at this.

Jeffrey Alexander draws attention to this talent: King's ability to create a compelling drama by "reweaving cultural contents, stitching together tactics of Gandhian non-violence, Christian narratives of sacrifice and exodus, and the justice rhetorics of American civil society."[71] Alexander describes it as a talent for "civil translation."[72] Civil translation addresses the problem of how to translate experiences from the particular to the general and back again. It involves making use of the semantic codes dominant in the existing civil sphere in order to elaborate a narrative that makes it possible for the majority to identify with the grievances of the pro-testors. Thus, it is an indispensable part of any social movement that seeks to speak to audiences as yet unable to hear its critical message. Civil translation is a creative enterprise in which a story is unfolded that is at once familiar and unfamiliar to those who hear it. The unfamiliarity of the story means that it must be backed up by care-fully staged, dramatic public performances if it is to be accepted by those who as yet do not support the social movement, and if it is to inspire active engagement with its cause. Moving beyond Alexander, if we look more closely at the practice of civil translation, we can see that it is not just a mediating activity. In addition, it has a *disclosive* force. By this I mean that it has the potential to open people's minds to suffering that they had previously not recognized as such. Thus, like Gandhi, King too could be described as engaged in conversion of his opponents.

For Gandhi, as we saw earlier, conversion has an explicitly spiritual aspect, presupposing a reorientation of the self toward an idea of God as Truth that, when properly recognized, speaks in a voice that is unquestionably right and universally binding. As in the case of conscience, Gandhi's connection of conversion with divine truth may make the concept unpalatable to contemporary political theorists concerned to find norms appropriate for pluralist societies. Nonetheless, in my final remarks, I propose that civil disobedience, in its radically transformative modes, cannot do without an inherently context-transcendent idea of ethical truth, albeit one that is simultaneously unavoidably context-dependent.[73]

Consider more closely the critical aspect of the ethical self-transformation that, on occasion, is required for fundamental social, cultural, political, and economic transformation. In some instances, I contended, demands for fundamental societal transformation will not speak to their addressees until they have undergone profound changes in ethical self-understandings (on occasion, these demands will result from profound changes in ethical self-understanding on the part of the protestors themselves). Put differently, in such instances the protestors' demands do not appeal to a shared sense of justice; instead they radically challenge it. In order to make sense of this kind of ethically motivated challenge, we must presuppose the meaningfulness of an alternative idea of justice that is radically different to the prevailing sense. Furthermore, if in a Habermasian vein we think of fundamental societal transformation in dynamic rather than static terms, as a neverending drive to establish societal conditions that are more conducive to an ethically good life for everyone, the alternative idea of justice must itself permanently be open to challenge on grounds of its ethical shortcomings. From this we can see that fundamental societal transformation, when understood as a dynamic, neverending process, presupposes an idea of justice (more generally, an idea of ethical truth or validity) that is universally binding and always transcends its particular interpretations. The same holds for civil disobedience in its radically transformative modes. Thus, resuscitating the radically transformative impetus of civil disobedience requires not the jettisoning of ideas of universal ethical validity, but rather their reconfiguration in a way that avoids the partiality and elitism that critics rightly identify as dangers inherent in Gandhi's and King's "spiritual" conceptions.

I have endeavored to show that the ethical dimension of civil disobedience extends beyond considerations of conscience and duty. Certainly, these have their place in normative accounts of civil disobedience. However, in contexts where disobedience demands fundamental societal transformation, it also calls for fundamental transformation of individual and collective identities in an ethical sense, which means a transformation oriented by an idea of ethical truth that is inherently context-transcending. This casts a different light on the spiritual model of civil disobedience and invites further exploration both of its truth dimension and of the kind of "work on the self" that self-transformation requires.

NOTES

1. This is a formal definition: I leave open the question of which particular ideas of the good are ethically valid. I use the terms "ethical" and "morally" interchangeably in the following. For a sketch of my account of ethically self-determining agency, see Maeve Cooke, "A Pluralist Theory of Politics," in *What Is Pluralism? The Question of Pluralism in Politics*, eds. V. Kaul and I. Salvatore (London: Routledge, 2020).

2. To be sure, how to interpret these norms and, indeed, the very requirement of civility are matters of ongoing dispute. In contemporary political theory, the standard definition of civility is liberal, specifically the version offered by John Rawls. For a succinct account of the liberal reinterpretation of Gandhi's and King's civility requirement, see William Scheuerman, *Civil Disobedience* (Cambridge: Polity Press, 2018), 44–49; cf. Maeve Cooke, "Disobedience in Civil Regeneration. Radical Transformations in the Civil Sphere," in *Breaching the Civil Order: Radicalism and the Civil Sphere*, eds. J. Alexander, T. Stack, and F. Khoshrokovar (Cambridge: Cambridge University Press, 2020), 235–60. Candice Delmas conducts an extended critique of the Rawlsian requirement of civility in her book, *A Duty to Resist. When Disobedience Should Be Uncivil* (Oxford: Oxford University Press, 2018).

3. Lewis Perry, *Civil Disobedience. An American Tradition* (New Haven, CT: Yale University Press, 2013).

4. Mohandas K. Gandhi, *An Autobiography or The Story of My Experiments with Truth* (Ahmedabad: Navajivan Publishing House, trans. 1927, x); Mohandas K. Gandhi, *Quotes of Gandhi* (New Delhi: UBS Publishers, 1995), 34.

5. Martin Luther King, Jr., "A Letter from Birmingham Jail," in *Civil Disobedience in Focus*, ed. H. Bedau (New York: Routledge, 1991), 68–84 (at 70).

6. King, "Letter," 83–84.

7. John Rawls, *A Theory of Justice*, revised ed. (Cambridge, MA: Belknap Press of Harvard University Press, 1999), 320. On Rawls's theory of civil disobedience, see Chapter 3 in this volume. Rawls's definition has been attacked from numerous angles. The bulk of the criticism is directed against its reformist tendency. Rawls makes this tendency explicit when he cautions that civil disobedience is a form of protest appropriate only for "the special case of a nearly just society, one that is well-ordered for the most part but in which some serious violations of justice nevertheless do occur" (ibid., 319). This reformist tendency plays out in his interpretation of the legal, political, and ethical components implicit in his definition of civil disobedience.

8. Kimberley Brownlee, *Conscience and Conviction* (Oxford: Oxford University Press, 2012), 3.

9. Scheuerman, *Civil Disobedience*, 22–27.

10. John Rawls, *Political Liberalism* (Cambridge, MA: Harvard University Press, 1993).

11. Rawls subsequently adopts a more accommodating stance on appeals to comprehensive doctrines, deeming them permissible in public political discussion at any time, provided that in due course proper political reasons – and not reasons given solely by comprehensive doctrines – are presented. John Rawls, "The Idea of Public Reason Revisited," *University of Chicago Law Review* 64, no. 3 (1997): 765–80.

12. Rawls writes that "[r]eligious doctrines clearly underlie King's views and are important in his appeals. Yet they are expressed in general terms: and they fully support constitutional values and accord with public reason." *Political Liberalism*, 250.

13. William Scheuerman, "Recent Theories of Civil Disobedience: An Anti-Legal Turn?" *The Journal of Political Philosophy* 23, no. 4 (2015): 427–49 (here 429), https://doi.org/10.1111/jopp.12055. See also

Robin Celikates, "Democratizing Civil Disobedience," *Philosophy and Social Criticism* 42 no. 10 (2016): 982–94, https://doi.org/10.1177/0191453716638562.

14. Scheuerman raises both objections in Scheuerman, *Civil Disobedience*, 26–31. For a critique of Scheuerman on this point, see my review of his book in *Political Theory* 47, no. 1 (2019): 589–94, https://doi.org/10.1177/0090591719839351.

15. Maeve Cooke, "Civil Obedience and Disobedience," *Philosophy and Social Criticism* 42, no. 10 (2016): 995–1003 (here, 1000), https://doi.org/10.1177/0191453716659521.

16. Brownlee, *Conscience and Conviction*, chapter 2.

17. Hannah Arendt, "Civil Disobedience," in *Crises of the Republic* (New York: Harcourt, Brace, Jovanovich, 1971), 51–101 (at 60). See also Arendt, "Thinking and Moral Considerations," in *Responsibility and Judgment* (New York: Schocken Books, 1971), 159–89.

18. Arendt, "Civil Disobedience," especially, 51–68.

19. Maeve Cooke, "Conscience in Democratic Public Life," in *Religion in Liberal Political Philosophy*, eds. C. Laborde and A. Bardon (Oxford: Oxford University Press, 2017), 295–308.

20. See also Cooke, "Civil Obedience," 1,000.

21. Scheuerman, *Civil Disobedience*, 67.

22. Scheuerman, *Civil Disobedience*, 67.

23. See Cooke, review of Scheuerman, *Civil Disobedience*, 594.

24. This is evident in his discussion of the subtle but crucial differences between Habermas's and Rawls's characterization of civil disobedience. Scheuerman, *Civil Disobedience*, 76–79. On Habermas's ideas about civil disobedience, see also Chapter 4 in this volume.

25. Scheuerman, *Civil Disobedience*, 39–40. The duty to obey the constitutional principles of liberal democratic states is grounded in what Rawls calls the duty of justice; this comprises a moral duty to obey the law of one's just or nearly just state and a duty to repair or replace institutions where they are unjust. See Delmas, *Duty to Resist*, 73.

26. William Scheuerman, "What Edward Snowden Can Teach Theorists of Conscientious Law-Breaking," *Philosophy and Social Criticism* 42, no. 10 (2016): 958–64 (959).

27. Celikates, together with many contemporary critics, sees the Rawlsian view as the standard liberal one (Celikates, "Democratizing," 983).

Scheuerman comments scathingly on this conflation, which he perceives as a lack of attentiveness to the specific features (and strengths) of Rawls's account (*Civil Disobedience*, 141–47).

28. Celikates, "Democratizing," 983.

29. The Rawlsian view's focus on corrective action is the main worry expressed by contemporary theorists of civil disobedience, especially those who seek to show its radically transformative potential. See Scheuerman, *Civil Disobedience*, 57–58.

30. Robin Celikates, "Constituent Power Beyond Exceptionalism: Irregular Migration, Disobedience, and (Re-)Constitution," *Journal of International Political Theory* 15, no. 1 (2019): 67–81, https://doi.org/10.1177/1755088218808311.

31. Celikates, "Democratizing," 983.

32. Celikates, "Democratizing," 985; Celikates, "Constituent Power," 70, 77. On my reading of his position, the ethical dimension of civil disobedience (insofar as he is willing to concede that it has one) is located solely in its principled character.

33. Celikates contrasts civil disobedience with both legal protest and "ordinary" criminal offenses or "unmotivated" rioting on grounds of its principled character but, so far as I can see, nowhere elaborates on what he means by "principled." Robin Celikates, "Rethinking Civil Disobedience as a Practice of Contestation – Beyond the Liberal Paradigm," *Constellations* (2016), https://doi.org/10.1111/1467-8675.12216. See also R. Celikates, "Civil Disobedience," in *The International Encyclopedia of Political Communication*, ed. G. Mazzoleni (Oxford: Blackwell, 2015), 128–32.

34. Celikates, "Democratizing," 983, 984.

35. Delmas refers to "the ordinary conception of civil disobedience associated with John Rawls" (*Duty to Resist*, 23) and "the standard, Rawlsian account" (35). For Delmas's defense of uncivil disobedience, see Chapter 8 in this volume.

36. Delmas, *Duty to Resist*, 29–35.

37. Delmas, *Duty to Resist*, 29–33.

38. Resistance for Delmas is a broad category that includes various forms of protest. Delmas, *Duty to Resist*, 40.

39. Delmas, *Duty to Resist*, 39.

40. Delmas, *Duty to Resist*, 9. I take a similar line in Cooke, "Civil Obedience and Disobedience."

41. Delmas, *Duty to Resist*, 8. However, she also claims to provide "a unified account of political obligation that focuses on duties of resistance under conditions of injustice and applies to all societies, legitimate and illegitimate." Ibid., 10.

42. Delmas, *Duty to Resist*, 9.

43. In my view, Delmas's distinction between civil and uncivil disobedience is unhelpful. It not only distracts from her evident concern for radical societal transformation: it stands in the way of an alternative account of disobedience in which radical societal transformation entails breaking with the logic of the resisted system and reconfiguring it in qualitatively different terms. Delmas's concept of uncivil disobedience simply inverts the standard concept of civil disobedience; as opposed to rearticulating the concept in a way that makes clear its radically transformative potential.

44. Jürgen Habermas, "Civil Disobedience: Litmus Test for the Democratic Constitutional State," *Berkeley Journal of Philosophy* XXX (1985): 95–116.

45. It is noteworthy that Habermas, while writing that "[c]ivil disobedience is grounded in considerations of conscience," regards conscience as "not just a private affair [but as also extending] to those matters which concern all citizens" ("Litmus Test," 107).

46. Habermas, "Litmus Test," 100–01. He also writes that civil disobedience does not "place the existence and fundamental significance of the constitutional order in question" (ibid., 105).

47. Habermas, "Litmus Test," 104.

48. Habermas, "Litmus Test," 106.

49. Habermas, "Litmus Test," 106.

50. Scheuerman, *Civil Disobedience*, 78.

51. Habermas, "Litmus Test," 110.

52. Habermas, "Litmus Test," 110.

53. Delmas, *Duty to Resist*, 150.

54. Delmas, *Duty to Resist*, 151.

55. Delmas, *Duty to Resist*, 152.

56. Delmas, *Duty to Resist*, 213–14.

57. "FAQS," Extinction Rebellion, accessed June 25, 2020, https://rebellion.earth/the-truth/faqs/

58. Ta-Nehisi Coates, *We Were Eight Years in Power. An American Tragedy* (New York: One World, 2017); cf. Cooke, "Disobedience in Civil Regeneration," 247.

59. Malcolm X and A. Haley, *The Autobiography of Malcolm X as Told to Alex Haley* (New York: Random House, 1999).

60. It is debatable whether Malcolm X's judgment of Martin Luther King is correct. Below I suggest that King, too, sought a complete reorientation of thinking and behavior. However, there are certainly differences between Malcolm X and King in their respective views of how such reorientation can and should be effected. See Cooke, "Disobedience in Civil Regeneration," 245–48.

61. Adorno emphasizes this difficulty in his writings on societal change in the 1950s and 1960s. See Maeve Cooke, "Forever Resistant? Adorno and Radical Transformation of Society," in *The Blackwell Companion to Adorno*, eds. Peter Gordon, Espen Hammer, and Max Pensky (Oxford: Blackwell: 2020), 583–600.

62. See Cornell West's critique of Coates in *The Guardian*, December 17, 2017, www.theguardian.com/commentisfree/2017/dec/17/ta-nehisi-coates-neoliberal-black-struggle-cornel-west and Robin Kelley's article in the *Boston Review*, December 22, 2017, http://bostonreview.net/race/ro bin-d-g-kelley-coates-and-west-jackson.

63. See also Ta-Nehisi Coates, *Between the World and Me* (New York: Spiegel and Grau, 2015).

64. Cooke, "Disobedience in Civil Regeneration," 248.

65. Cooke, "Disobedience in Civil Regeneration," 246–49.

66. Malcolm X and Haley, *Autobiography*, 396.

67. Karuna Mantena, "Another Realism: The Politics of Gandhian Non-Violence," *American Political Science Review* 106, no. 2 (2012): 462–63.

68. Gandhi quoted in Mantena, "Another Realism," 458.

69. Niebuhr quoted in Mantena, "Another Realism," 463.

70. Martin Luther King, "The New Negro of the South: Behind the Montgomery Story," 282. http://okra.stanford.edu/transcription/docu ment_images/Vol03Scans/280_June-1956_The%20New%20Negro%20 of%20the%20South.pdf. On King's views more generally, see Chapter 2 in this volume.

71. Jeffrey Alexander, *The Civil Sphere* (Oxford: Oxford University Press: 2006), 295.

72. Alexander, *Civil Sphere*, 213–34.

73. See Cooke, "Disobedience in Civil Regeneration," 250–53.

10 Nonviolence and the Coercive Turn

Alexander Livingston

Contemporary debates on civil disobedience often turn on the question of what's living and what's dead in nonviolence. When protestors smash security cameras to hide their identities, hurl tear gas canisters back at police lines, or block highways to urge action from elected officials, they refuse the demand that disobedience be strictly nonviolent. The diversity of tactics embraced by recent protest movements around the globe raises questions about the continuing adequacy of the very idea of nonviolent civil disobedience for conceptualizing dissent. Some scholars have responded with calls for a more minimalist definition of civil disobedience that better encompasses these confrontational tactics.[1] Others, such as Candice Delmas in her contribution to this volume, argue for abandoning the concept altogether in favor of theorizing this wider terrain as "uncivil" disobedience.[2] Uniting both sides of this debate is the conviction that any conception of disobedience claiming to be both analytically exact and politically useful needs to make more room for the legitimacy of violent tactics. Being civil, in other words, does not require disobedience be strictly *nonviolent*, only *less violent*.

Historian Howard Zinn laid the groundwork for contemporary defenses of less violent civil disobedience when he argued that dissent needs to be disruptive because it takes a "rude shove ... to waken society." Dissent begins with appeals to authority but where these fall on deaf ears protestors may need to turn to "a mild form of violence" to get their claims across. Occupying buildings, breaking windows, or clashing with police are means of awakening the public to injustices demanding redress. At the same time, Zinn acknowledges that a more expansive conception of civil disobedience requires some sort of self-limiting constraints.

Less violent measures should be disciplined, proportional, and "preferably directed against property rather than people." Acts of violence do seize public attention but they also risk spiraling out of control and becoming counterproductive for persuading the public because of how violence "turns people (rightly) away."[3] A less violent conception of civil disobedience therefore has to walk a fine line to balance *confrontation* (disobedience) and *communication* (civility).

This challenge stands at the core of "the coercive turn" in contemporary theories of civil disobedience. The coercive turn names a recent wave of realist challenges to the moralism of classical liberal theories of civil disobedience discussed by Andrew Sabl in Chapter 6. These challenges come from realists who fault liberal theories with displacing *power*: how power works to dominate and oppress; how power is mobilized from below to resist. New realists argue that a nonviolence requirement too strictly constrains disobedience to a purely symbolic expression. Robin Celikates puts this point forcefully: "In order to be politically effective, however, civil disobedience seems to require a moment of real confrontation that goes beyond the purely symbolic and reasonably constrained form of claim-making allowed for by existing political institutions."[4] Yet just as liberal theories embraced the communicative dimension of disobedience to the exclusion of confrontation, the coercive turn risks enacting a similarly one-sided case for its inclusion. Uniting liberal and realist approaches is a common conflation of power with violence. A critical theory of nonviolence, by contrast, refuses this shared premise. "To resort to power one need not be violent, and to speak to conscience one need not be meek," explains Barbara Deming. "The most effective action *both* resorts to power *and* engages conscience."[5] The power of nonviolence is not a spiritual force cleansed of coercion but a different way of wielding coercion to bind communication with confrontation.

Putting coercion first offers a critical vantage point for reconsidering the power of nonviolence displaced by its moralizing codification and elided by its realist critics. To invoke Deming again, the purpose of nonviolence is occupying the tension between communication and confrontation with *poise* rather than *purity*. Moreover, this conceptual elucidation is reciprocal. Approaching contemporary scholarship on nonviolence from the perspective of the coercive turn challenges strategic theories of nonviolent antagonism and invites a reconsideration of the often-overlooked feminist archive of nonviolent agonism where coercively exerting *power over* an adversary is bound to a transformative project of creating the conditions for sharing *power with* them as well.

One contention of this chapter is that a focus on the uses of coercion represents a more promising avenue for research than continuing to debate the permissibility of violence for three reasons. First, the concept of violence is morally overloaded and conceptually overextended. It is too easily used synonymously for power, coercion, or harm. Second, designating something as violent entails an evaluative moral judgment that coercion does not. Third, the distinction between violence and nonviolence is always politically constructed and contested.[6] All of that said, the dichotomy of violence and nonviolence is unavoidable given its centrality to the theory and history of civil disobedience. Putting coercion first is not meant to offer an alternative language of disobedience. It is a provocation to reorient discussions around the vast domain of political action that falls between the reified moral poles of violence and nonviolence.

AGAINST COERCION

Coercion is a causal relationship between two parties where X influences the rational behavior of Y by threatening or harming Y's professed interests. This can involve X's use of direct force to levy costs on Y's beliefs and behavior as well as the indirect threat to do so. Coercion accordingly occupies the gray zone between violence and nonviolence. The use of force, threats, and even physical constraint to interfere with the freedom of others blurs into violence but it is also at the core of most recognized nonviolent tactics of direct action. Liberal portrayals of coercion, by contrast, are black and white. Liberalism derides coercion as a dangerous threat to its core values.[7] When citizens coercively press their claims, they not only threaten the state's legitimate monopoly on violence, they also risk undermining liberal values of equality, toleration, and respect. Extralegal coercion, in other words, is synonymous with violence in the liberal imaginary.

A telling example of this moralized conflation of coercion and violence is the pamphlet that inspired Zinn's defense of less violent civil disobedience, Justice Abe Fortas's *Concerning Dissent and Civil Disobedience*. Fortas's position exemplifies an elite response to the student radicalism of the late 1960s that defends civil disobedience by containing it within restrictive moral boundaries. Peaceable protest and freedom of assembly are constitutionally protected expressions of free speech even where they take symbolic form as in marches or sit-ins. The First Amendment's protection of dissent is not without its limits, however. It offers no protection to protests where "the method of dissent involves aggression." Fortas includes in this category of aggressive methods: loudly demonstrating inside a library, blocking entrances to a public facility, interfering with traffic, destroying property, or any other means of "willful and unnecessary disruption" affecting the pursuits of fellow citizens. The purpose of dissent in a liberal society is "to communicate a point of view," not serve as a pretext for "hooliganism."[8]

The distinction between expressive speech and coercive conduct framing Fortas's purposefully constrained conception of dissent is repeated by liberals defending a more expansive role for civil disobedience in the American political order. One influential example is John Rawls's *A Theory of Justice*. Rawls echoes Fortas when he defines civil disobedience as "a mode of address." Protest in a liberal polity "may warn and admonish" but "it is not itself a threat."[9] Ronald Dworkin conceives of the limits of civil disobedience in similar terms. When protestors stop trying to merely persuade and start actively interfering with the conduct of others, they move from civil disobedience to "civil blackmail."[10] Uniting these otherwise distinct approaches to civil disobedience is liberalism's anxiety with coercion. To coerce is to impose one's values and opinions on another. A minority that coercively imposes its will on a majority puts democratic institutions at risk and runs roughshod over the need for consent. As Rawls puts this point, coercion is illiberal because it constitutes "a final expression of one's case."[11] A liberal conception of civil disobedience must therefore operate within the bound of strictly symbolic action. It is a form of speech meant to inform the public about some grievous wrong, appeal to a shared sense of justice, and persuade elected officials to reform illiberal laws or policies.

The liberal equation of coercive power with violence limits the definition, justification, and function of this account of civil disobedience. Both Fortas and Rawls invoke the US Civil Rights Movement as exemplifying symbolic nonviolence without acknowledging how this example exceeds their narrow definition of civil disobedience. Picketing, marching, sit-ins, and accepting arrest all involved more than simply free expression; they were tactics meant to disrupt the operations of segregated institutions and provoke crises that forced third parties to intervene.[12] Related is their approach to justification. Both Fortas and Rawls appeal to consensus over shared constitutional principles as the final normative bedrock of a liberal polity. This is a secularized version of the "higher law" to which Martin Luther King, Jr. claims fidelity in "Letter from a Birmingham Jail." Yet much activism, both in the 1960s and today, means to put such presumed consensus into question. Activists often aim to transform the hegemonic "common sense" organizing society, or simply to rebuke ruling groups for paying mere lip service to liberal values that do not in fact hold.[13] Lastly, conceptualizing the function of civil disobedience as a strategy of redressing injustices through persuasion alone mystifies relations of power and domination within liberal society. As Rawls frames his account, civil disobedience presumes "a nearly just society, one that is well-ordered for the most part but in which some serious violations of justice nevertheless do occur."[14] To claim that this "nonideal" portrayal is applicable to any actually existing liberal polity is an ideological distortion of the ways intersecting oppressions of racism, patriarchy, and economic inequality operate under the cover of liberal institutions; that is, the very oppressions activists seek to confront with nonviolent direct action.[15] What follows from these moralizing presumptions is a narrowly *defensive* conception of civil disobedience biased toward the preservation of the status quo.

THE COERCIVE TURN

Bringing coercion back in offers a more realistic portrayal of the political world, and thereby a more reliable horizon of action for activists seeking to change it. A realist theory of civil disobedience begins by acknowledging the profound inequalities of power between members and challengers, and the constraints facing the powerless when it comes to changing laws or policy through official channels. Central among these are institutional inertia, structural injustice, and hegemonic discourses masking these constraints.[16] Under the conditions of actually existing liberal democracies, social change requires more than appeal to "the moral reason of the privileged"; it demands mobilizing "the political power of the oppressed."[17] This is civil disobedience as disruption. Social movements and activists launch critical issues before the public and force others to act by causing a breakdown in the terms of social cooperation. Sidney Tarrow outlines three ways this kind of disruption can enable movements to overcome asymmetries of power and influence: collective acts of confrontation signal commitment and forge solidarity among activists; disruption "obstructs the routine activities of opponents, bystanders, or authorities and forces them to attend to protestors' demands"; and it broadens conflict and escalates experiences of crisis.[18] Seen from the perspective of social movement history, what Fortas denounces as illiberal "hooliganism" has often been a central force in the realization of liberal values of freedom and equality.

The coercive turn builds on social movement scholarship to articulate a more expansive vision of civil disobedience as a communicative mode of political action that rejects liberalism's moralizing dichotomy of persuasion and coercion. These theories take three forms, each more expansive in its embrace of coercion: the *deliberative*, *direct action*, and *expressive* defenses of coercion. At one end of the spectrum stands the deliberative defense.[19] Advocates of deliberative coercion reject the liberal argument that acts of disruption such as strikes, blocking entrance to buildings, and property destruction necessarily inhibit democratic process. Rather, they can enhance democracy by bringing urgent issues to public attention and kick-starting democratic deliberation. Daniel Markovits conceptualizes disobedience in these terms as a "counterweight" to the institutional inertia that creates democratic deficits by precluding inclusion of certain topics from the political agenda. Coercive protest "shocks" the political system, disrupts the inertial status quo, and sparks renewed deliberation over past decisions.[20] William Smith similarly argues that limited coercive tactics can play an important role in promoting deliberative democracy when entrenched hegemonic discourses impact the information-gathering and decision-making functions of the public sphere.[21] Central to the deliberative defense is a clear distinction between democracy-enhancing acts of coercion and democracy-threatening acts of violence.

Built into the deliberative defense is a vision of politics continuous with the liberal model it claims to challenge. The purpose of deliberative coercion is initiating discussion, not settling disputes. It is a strategy for leveling the playing field, correcting anti-deliberative biases of existing institutions, and bringing about conditions of robust deliberative argumentation in the public sphere. Markovits echoes Rawls when he argues that coercion loses all democratic legitimacy when it is used to force policy makers to "change course" rather than simply "reconsider" past decisions.[22] More radical voices in the realist turn reject this idealized vision of a deliberative future free from coercion. Activists who risk arrest and police violence seldom aim at simply sparking deliberation; they mean to directly secure substantive outcomes. The purpose of coercion here is not triggering deliberation but exerting direct action. By making the existing conduct of their fellow citizens too costly or too difficult through a sustained campaign of interference, activists force citizens and their representatives to consider alternatives even in the absence of persuasive reasons.[23] Mark Bray offers the logic of antifascist direct action as an instance of this sort of cost-levying. No-platforming speakers and doxing or disclosing the identities of white supremacists to employers and the public, as well as acts of intimidation, can be effective ways of breaking up fascist organizations by raising the costs of membership.[24]

The shift from a process-oriented deliberative defense to an outcome-oriented direct action defense takes civil disobedience beyond the idealized liberal boundaries of a politics free from coercion, and undercuts any clear analytical distinction between coercion and violence. The purpose of direct action is to impose harm, and nonviolent tactics can in some cases create greater and more widespread harm than some targeted acts of violence.[25] The challenge of sustaining a clear boundary between violence and nonviolence leads to a third position in the coercive turn: the expressive defense. Acts of violent resistance against oppression can serve an important expressive function for the oppressed even when they have little hope of promoting good faith deliberation or effectively leveraging disruption to directly secure outcomes. Avia Pasternack illustrates this position in her defense of political rioting. Rioting that involves acts of violence such as looting, arson, or clashes with police should be considered as a "communicative episode." It provides those excluded from conventional channels a venue for expressing their profound disapproval, even if only to shout "fuck the state."[26] Giving voice to anger and fighting back against oppression, even where there is little hope of substantively transforming structures of oppression, can be an important source of dignity and self-respect. And like disruptive protest actions generally, such collective outbursts of rage can also forge bonds of solidarity and lay the groundwork for future, organized political campaigns of resistance.[27]

Hannah Arendt summarizes the basic claim of these three arguments when she writes, "Violence does not promote causes, neither history nor revolution, neither progress nor reaction; but it can serve to dramatize grievances and bring them to public attention." But she continues that relying on violence as a "weapon of reform" often comes at the cost of mobilizing genuine power.[28] Disruptive protests attract media attention but the content of its coverage often focuses on the acts of violence themselves to the exclusion of the grievances and demands protestors mean to convey to the public.[29] Similarly, fine-grained moral distinctions between coercion and violence, or violence against property and violence against persons, do not reliably find public uptake. Recent polls suggest that the American public is seldom willing to draw a clear distinction between the two, although public perception of the boundaries of "peaceful" assembly is variable and has been more and less expansive at different moments in American history.[30] Finally, arguments for violence and coercion often presume the judging public to be passive onlookers who must be "awoken" to injustice. The emancipatory aura of this common metaphor deflects the reality of political conflict. Protest action does not take place before an audience of passive dupes. It is an intervention in a "field of contention": a socially structured set of adversarial relationships between state officials, movement factions, nonstate elites, news media, and bystanders in dynamic interaction.[31] The public, in other words, is always plural. The consequence of violent action in such a complex field is more typically an escalating dynamic of counterviolence than an educative gesture of public enlightenment.

STRATEGIC NONVIOLENCE

A growing body of scholarship on civil resistance discussed by Kurt Schock in Chapter Sixteen echoes Arendt in articulating a critique of violence on the basis of a wider conception of power.[32] Civil resistance names the comparative study of the ways mass protests use nonviolent coercion to compel regimes to concede to their demands. A central finding of this scholarship is that violence is often a liability for movements seeking to wield power to challenge regimes. Violent movements are repressive states' preferred adversaries. States enjoy asymmetric material advantages in armed conflicts with protestors that they can wield to swiftly repress violent challengers without incurring serious reputational costs. Moreover, sustaining violent campaigns is costly. Activists need to maintain high levels of secrecy and centralized organization, and they risk facing brutal sanctions. Nonviolent direct action, by contrast, poses a unique challenge to regimes and offers tactical advantages to movements for attacking the very bases of state power.

Scholars of civil resistance draw a strong distinction between principled and strategic defenses of nonviolence. They do not advocate nonviolence because it is *right* but because it *works*. And how it works is not how its principled defenders often imagine. On the principled account, nonviolence is a mode of *persuasion*. M.K. Gandhi espouses this view with his claim that nonviolence operates through "soul force" rather than "brute force": "The Satyagrahi seeks to convert his opponent by sheer force of character and suffering."[33] On the strategic account, by contrast, nonviolence is the art of *coercion*. Direct action techniques are costly sanctions used to punish or constrain opponents. Nonviolent struggle aims at forcing opponents to act differently by "separating governments from their means of control."[34] Marshaling an impressive collection of empirical data illustrating how mass nonviolent actions have triggered regime changes in countries around the world, civil resistance scholarship argues that waging nonviolent struggle should be considered less as a spiritual practice and more as warfare by other means.

Underpinning strategic theories of nonviolence is a distinctive theory of power. In a three-volume landmark study from 1973, *The Politics of Nonviolent Action*, Gene Sharp argues that equating power with violence has led to an overestimation of violence's ability to compel political outcomes and a profound misunderstanding of the nature of power. The result is a "monolith" theory of power that equates capacity to command with capacity to exercise violence. This is power as a vertical relationship of command and obedience between state and subjects enforced through the former's material capacity to punish and repress. What a century of unarmed movements around the globe illustrates, however, is that power is in fact horizontal and social, not vertical and material. States' repressive capacity is a function not so much of the size of their arsenals nor the brutality of their security forces but the ongoing consent of populations who choose to cooperate with their regimes. "Obedience," Sharp argues, "is the heart of political power."[35] *Political power* rests on *social power*: the cooperation of officials, bureaucrats, and ordinary citizens who consent to pay their taxes, obey the laws, and follow directives. "No complex organization or institution, including the State, can carry out orders if the individuals and unit organizations that compose such an institution do not enable it to do so."[36] The implication of this simple observation is that political power is more fragile than the monolith theory suggests. The ultimate source of social power – voluntary cooperation – resides outside the state's sovereign control. Mass noncooperation has the potential to dramatically transform power relations between challengers and the state by throttling the state's capacity to command. Disobedience and defiance are not merely modes of appeal in a nearly just society; they are means for seizing power back from the state.

The Politics of Nonviolent Action catalogues 198 methods for withholding cooperation and restricting the sources of political power. Strategies of noncooperation aim to seize control of the conflict situation by undermining the state's ability to govern. Sometimes, as in the case of labor strikes, the aim of these tactics is to reach a compromise. But where noncooperation becomes widespread and diffuses to key institutions, movements can alienate the state from the social power it relies upon, weakening it such that they are able to force through changes against the regime's will. This is the mechanism Sharp calls nonviolent coercion. At its limit, nonviolent coercion so effectively and persistently throttles the sources of power that the targeted regime ultimately dissolves. Where noncooperation and refusal to carry out orders spread to key institutions such as the bureaucracy and security forces, a movement has effectively toppled a regime by pulling down the "pillars of support" on which it rests.[37]

The claim that strategic nonviolence represents a viable alternative to violence suggests both a weak and a strong interpretation. On the weak interpretation, it claims that nonviolent techniques are *no less effective* than violent ones. On the strong interpretation, it says that nonviolence is *more effective* than violence. The social theory of power underpins Sharp's endorsement of the strong claim. Resistance "by noncooperation and disobedience . . . would seem to be the most efficient and certain means for controlling power."[38] This claim finds support only where nonviolent resistance is extended over space and time. Individual acts of noncooperation pose little threat to the sources of regime power; only mass noncooperation threatens to create cleavages in the regime and pull out its pillars of support. Successful civil resistance therefore turns on what strategies most effectively mobilize large numbers of defectors from the regime. As Erica Chenoweth and Maria Stephan conclude from their statistical comparison of violent and nonviolent anti-regime campaigns, violent campaigns are less successful at mobilizing large sections of civil society because they raise higher barriers to participation.[39] These include the physical demands of armed struggle, the need for secrecy and covert planning, the demanding commitment and social sacrifices it asks of participants, and the challenge of overcoming moral prohibitions on violence. Nonviolent campaigns face lower barriers to participation along each front: nonviolent resistance is more easily accessed by women, children, and the elderly; its coordination does not require the same level of secrecy and centralized decision-making; its performance does not demand the same level of commitment, discipline, and sacrifice; and, finally, it does not face the same moral barriers. As a result of this participatory advantage, nonviolent struggles grow larger faster, becoming more resilient, more innovative in their tactics, and more dangerous for regimes.

A secondary advantage of nonviolent resistance is its ability to transform repression from a liability into a strength. Sharp calls this feature of nonviolent action political jiu-jitsu. States intensify violent repression as the consensual foundations of their rule begin to crumble. Repression is a sanction meant to enforce obedience by breaking insurgents' will to fight. But when violent repression is applied on a disciplined nonviolent movement, the effects can be made to "rebound" against the regime itself.[40] Just as in jiu-jitsu where a fighter uses his adversary's own momentum to throw him off balance, nonviolent campaigns can use repression to destabilize the state. Critical to this dynamic is the role of third parties along the current boundaries of the conflict. Violent repression against disciplined nonviolent campaigns puts the spotlight back on the state to illuminate its brutality and illegitimacy. Such spectacles of undeserved punishment can move third parties to support resistance movements and promote shifts in power that further erode the legitimacy of the regime. While figures such as Gandhi and King put great stock in this dramatic dimension of civil disobedience, Sharp warns that it is the least of nonviolence's tactical advantages. Shifts in public opinion can be an important tactic in a broader campaign of nonviolent insurgency but this is only ever a partial factor in the seizing and severing of a regime's sources of power.

The strategic turn in nonviolence mirrors the coercive turn in civil disobedience. Both reject strictly persuasion-oriented conceptions of nonviolence as ideological hindrances to generating the power movements need to effect change. And like the coercive turn, strategic theories of nonviolent struggle risk perpetuating the liberal dichotomy between coercion and persuasion to the detriment of their vision of power. This limitation is evident in Sharp's distinction between social and political power. The centralized state apparatus is the privileged source of oppression on Sharp's account and nonviolent campaigns are a form of warfare civil society wages to bring it crashing down. Sharp insists that nonviolent struggle is a democratizing force but he conceives of democracy in minimalist terms. Democratization for Sharp is a process of breaking up centralized power, dispersing power across civil society, and empowering individuals rather than building, renewing, or refounding shared institutions. Political institutions are more often framed as evils to be contained than potential bearers of popular will that can be democratized through struggle from below. It is this latter view of the democracy-enhancing power of disobedience that animates the coercive turn. Civil disobedience names the generative *agonism* between society and the state, not a generalized *antagonism* that reduces politics to war by other means. A critical theory of nonviolence that aims to bridge communication and confrontation needs to conceive of political struggle in terms of the creative power unleashed through the democratic agonism of forces, factions, and institutions.

AGONISTIC NONVIOLENCE

Another way to put this point is to say that Sharp's theory of political nonobedience fails to address the basic paradox of civil disobedience: namely, that dissent can be defiant and conflictual but still restrained and civil in the service of renewing bonds between adversaries in a shared polity. This is not only a conceptual paradox but a lived one that pulls political action in conflicting directions. Disobedience, particularly the disruptive kind championed by the coercive turn, escalates conflict. It deepens animosities, hardens identities, and triggers reactive counterforce. Civility, by contrast, entails respect, keeping identities fluid, and limiting reaction by seeking understanding. These tensions are what makes civil disobedience such a fraught and challenging practice but also account for its generative power. As mentioned earlier, transformative political action depends on more than simply wielding *power over* an opponent, but also creating possibilities for sharing *power with* others. These two faces of power can be mutually reinforcing, as when expanding circles of participation in a movement augment its capacity to disrupt and empower, but they can also pull apart, as when disruptive action hardens divisions and turns off potential allies. The nonviolence which is central to civil disobedience is not a strategy of war without violence but, more significantly, a means of negotiating the burdens of political action represented by these two faces of power.

Some voices in the coercive turn have begun to acknowledge that a realist account of civil disobedience requires more than a fuller conception of power; it also demands a critical account of civility. Étienne Balibar proposes that "strategies of civility" be seen as a force of "antiviolence" containing the violent dynamics of social transformation.[41] Robin Celikates similarly argues that even a less violent conception of civil disobedience requires "new forms of civility" that contain political contestation from succumbing to "a military logic ... aimed at the physical destruction of the (imagined) enemy." These appeals to civility are not calls for nonviolence. Balibar and Celikates both accept the liberal definition of nonviolence as strictly symbolic and warn that it can too easily be weaponized by the state to preserve the status quo. Civility, by contrast, "is quite compatible with a variety of actions often classified as violent by the media and state," whether directed against property, enacted in self-defense, or inflicted upon the self.[42] What "forms" and "strategies" of protest they imagine may serve this antiviolent logic are left unexplained, however.

This skepticism forecloses valuable resources for giving substance to an agonistic conception of nonviolence found in the archive of social movement theory and praxis. Particularly germane to the arguments of the coercive turn is the work of Deming and other feminist theorists of nonviolence. Feminist theories of nonviolence transgress Sharp's principled and strategic dichotomy by maintaining that nonviolence offers a more effective means of struggle than violence precisely because it resists the temptation to compromise morality for the sake of power.[43] "We can put *more* pressure on the antagonist for whom we show human concern," Deming explains.

"It is precisely solicitude for his person *in combination with* a stubborn interference with his actions that can give us a very special degree of control."[44] What distinguishes this approach as feminist is its fourfold critique of traditional "male-defined" theories of nonviolence. The first is a rebuke to the historical marginalization of women's oppression by nonviolent movements and their failure to understand the continuity of military and police violence with domestic and sexual violence. Second is an embrace of anger. Theories of nonviolence that demand repressing anger affirm patriarchal expectations of women's conduct and fail to understand the ways in which loud and confrontational expressions of anger can be empowering in the face of oppression. Third is a rejection of the "alternative machismo" of sacrifice.[45] Elevating sacrifice and suffering to the core of nonviolence fails to acknowledge the ways in which patriarchy systematically disempowers women to sacrifice their well-being for that of others. Self-assertion, not self-sacrifice, is the path to women's empowerment. Finally, some feminist theorists of nonviolence challenge its incompatibility with self-defense. Learning to physically fight back against oppression can be a source of empowerment and survival that pacifists should not treat lightly.

Deming's response to the case of the D.C. Nine illustrates how these divergent commitments sustain the productive tension between confrontation and persuasion. In March 1969, nine protestors entered the offices of Dow Chemical in Washington, D.C., to protest the corporation's production of napalm gas and defoliants deployed by the American military in Vietnam. Protestors smashed windows and furniture, threw documents out the windows into the streets below, and poured fake blood over company files. The combination of symbolic action and cost-levying exemplifies the vision of disobedience espoused by the coercive turn. Deming defends the protest but questions the protestors' own account of the vandalism's emancipatory potential. "If it were just that we had to stop a death-dealing machine in its tracks, this would be relatively simple to accomplish – although we could count on being hurt in the attempt."

Acts of sabotage that momentarily disrupt the operations of the military-industrial complex do not by themselves mobilize the power required to abolish it. Anticipating Chenoweth and Stephan's findings about participatory advantage, she continues: "To build such a new society, very many people are needed. So as we strike at the machinery of death, we have to do so in a way that the general population understands, that encourages more and more people to join us."[46] Direct action is often urgently needed but it offers no alternative to the labor of suasion that builds collective power. To "engage men's minds one has most often to engage their bodies, drawing them into various actions."[47] Confrontation (power *over*) and communication (power *with*) need to be made to work together in a virtuous circle rather than negating one another in a vicious one.

Deming articulates this challenge in terms of learning to seize the adversary with "two hands":

> The more the real issues are dramatized, and the struggle raised above the personal, the more control those in nonviolent rebellion begin to gain over their adversary. For they are able at once and the same time to disrupt everything for him, making it impossible for him to operate within the system as usual, and to temper his response to this, making it impossible for him simply to strike back without thought and with all his strength. They have as it were two hands – the one calming him, making him ask questions; the other makes him move.[48]

The aim of direct action is control. It means to define the terms of conflict, obstruct the adversary's purposes, and compel him to act differently. This is the work of the hand that makes him move. But what does it mean to calm him at the same time? Critics rightly worry that talk of caring for the oppressor demands acquiescent performances of passivity and weakness. It is just this element of nonviolence Deming and other feminists refuse. "Violence makes men 'dizzy,'" Deming writes, "it disturbs the vision, makes them see only their own immediate losses and fear of losses." A hand that calms is one that aims to resist this contraction of vision and expand the adversary's perception of the conflict "in a way that takes into consideration your needs as well as his."[49] Nonviolence aims to interrupt conflict's contractive impulse by dramatizing oppressive structures and the roles actors play within them rather than moralizing the issue by faulting particular persons. Caring is not empathizing or acquiescing; it is sustaining the possibility of a relationship of sharing power to tackle oppression even as it exerts power over an opponent to force the issue.

This way of framing the logic of nonviolence introduces an affective register to the social theory of power, similar to Gandhi's equation of nonviolent action with sacrifice.[50] Mark and Paul Engler draw from both Gandhi and Sharp to argue that successful campaigns of disruptive protest need to sustain this commitment to the self-limiting and expressive force of sacrifice. Acts of sacrifice and accepting punishment can empower empathic responses, dampen negative reactions, and, as political jiu-jitsu, transform repression from a liability into a strength.[51] Feminist theories of nonviolence, by contrast, challenge the idea that sacrifice deserves any special privilege as a tactic of civility. Enduring repression without retaliation can indeed signal protestors' purposes to the public and interrupt the dynamics of escalation that characterize violence, Deming concedes, but this is not the entirety of nonviolent strategy. *Sacrifice* calls the public's attention to the protestor's sincerity; *dramatization* shifts focus away from the self and redirects it toward social structures. Nonviolent action seeks to seize control of the meaning of political conflict away from the adversary by dramatizing its claims through its very *means*.

> But as we give that shock, we must be communicating something else, too – again not merely with words but above all by our actions. We must be saying: don't be afraid of *us*. It is the system we are attacking that you need to fear – that all of us need to fear. For it is reckless with lives. But *we are not*.[52]

The D.C. Nine action illustrates this dramaturgical sensibility. Destroying corporate property with blood is a theatrical action meant to draw the public's attention to the dangers of a military-industrial complex rather than faulting the moral failures of any particular elected official or group of individuals. Dramatizing the issue means more than creating such widespread disruption that it cannot be ignored; it means the tactical work of struggling to shape both *what* and *how* the public perceives disruption. This public, moreover, is plural. Effective dramatization needs to speak differently to multiple audiences at once: to empower allies in the movement, to illustrate the complicity of private actors with state policy to bystanders, to attenuate resentment and fear of elites directly targeted by the action. The result of these different messages is teaching these many publics to see themselves as bound together by a common crisis demanding a cooperative response. *Provocation* and *pedagogy* must be made to work together against the personalizing and moralizing tendencies of political conflict.[53]

A liberal approach to nonviolence maintains that even symbolic property destruction undermines protestors' ability to dramatize issues in this way. Interfering with the rights of others "tends to obscure the civilly disobedient quality of one's act," Rawls warns.[54] Sharp raises similar concerns about acts of sabotage.[55] Deming shares Rawls's concern while challenging his conclusion that coercion is always antithetical to protestors' purposes. The question is not *if* disobedience should be coercive but *how* to coerce without losing control. From the perspective of those on the receiving end of protest action, disruption of their conduct is often experienced as violence. Fear and resentment set a cycle of recrimination in motion that too easily spins out of control. The challenge of using two hands is containing the vertigo protest unleashes. For Sharp, this control involves making its *consequences* rebound on the state through jiu-jitsu. For Deming, it means confronting its *causes* though the disciplined refusal to injure the other person even as one interferes with the performance of their institutional roles. "It is quite possible to frustrate another's action without doing him injury," Deming argues while conceding that perceptions of injury are deeply subjective. Property surely deserves lesser moral consideration than human life, but protestors should not lose sight of the way adversaries view attacks on some forms of private property as no different from attacks on their very person. This means that seizing the other with two hands perpetually risks overstepping the boundaries of nonviolence which no definitive moral rules can settle in advance, even where the aim of direct action is to reorient the ways audiences draw these boundaries. In the absence of any such moral formula, a feminist theory of nonviolence offers a principle of political judgment for protestors: "May they repeat and repeat to themselves the question: Can we by these acts release the minds of more and more people ... so that they will be free to face the truth of our condition, free to join us."[56] Caution is as important a political virtue as courage. This is an ethic of responsibility that makes morality and power two sides of the same coin.

The uprising sparked in the summer of 2020 by the murders of Ahmaud Arbery, Breonna Taylor, and George Floyd brought these debates about whether or not violence "works" to the center of American politics. The unprecedented swell of popular support for the protests seemed to upend the conventional political science wisdom that acts of rioting, looting, and arson by drives reactionary trends in public opinion, despite President Trump's persistent attempts to stoke white backlash. This overwhelming support for the protests reflects a confluence of contextual factors, ranging from the ways the COVID-19 pandemic dramatically exposed racial inequalities in health and vulnerability, to intensifying party polarization coding racial justice as expressive of "blue" commitments, no less than the long-term success of an earlier protest wave to shift the discursive terrain around issues of racial justice.[57] While the long-term responses to these protests cannot yet be predicted, many on the left have concluded from the groundswell of public support on display in the earliest days of the uprising as flames consumed Minneapolis's

3rd police precinct that nonviolence is only ever self-defeating and violence alone can effectively challenge existing regimes of power.

The non/violence dichotomy framing these debates is unhelpful, not least for how it concedes the state's preferred framing of the event and its false equivalence between the murder of human beings and these limited acts of property destruction. How we name violence is to some degree always an ideological speech act. Recasting this debate within the gray zone of coercion, by contrast, offers some much-needed distance from this charged ideological and moralizing terrain. Elements of deliberative, direct action, and expressive uses of coercion were all on display in the summer protest wave. Debating their effectiveness as tactics can become an exercise in vicious abstraction when coercive tactics become decoupled from liberatory strategy, however. Deming's metaphor of seizing the enemy with two hands is meant to underscore that wielding control presumes more than credible threat; it means attending to how the very means of disruption serve a wider strategy of power. Tactics concern the use of forces in particular battles; strategy is the use of battles in a wider campaign.[58] A strategic perspective looks beyond the singular event to consider coercion in terms of process, where power, escalation, and moral vision are all critical factors in making these moments of intensive conflict add up to more than a series of skirmishes.

A central element of realist theories of disobedience is their claim to ground a genuinely *transformative* conception of political action as opposed to the merely *defensive* aims of liberal accounts. One lesson of the feminist archive examined here is that the means embraced for this more radical conception are often incompatible with its end. Militant tactics such as the antifascist street fighting and rioting are poorly equipped to mobilize the kind of collective power required to confront structural injustice over the long term, even though they can sometimes serve as an initial spark for broader campaigns. Where these tactics are at their most successful is where they serve strategy taking aim at limited defensive ends. These include conventional liberal ends of civil disobedience such as enforcing existing legal protections or resisting transgressions of the limits of state power, as well as more militant purposes of disrupting the formation of illiberal militias and fascist groups before they become established. Cost-levying direct action can be a particularly effective way of securing these kinds of defensive ends. The expressive value of violent resistance represents a more complicated case. There is an intrinsic value in expressing anger at oppression where guided by a wider vision of liberation, yet Deming reminds us that we need always interrogate whether or not that anger is in fact only serving as a mask for fear.[59] Moreover, the virtues of courage and self-respect learned in physical combat are the same virtues required for nonviolent political struggle. It is not accidental that Gandhi encouraged Indians to enlist in the First World War as a laboratory for learning the virtues of satyagraha.

I do not say this to make light of threats posed by fascists or the courage demanded of activists risking harm to fight back under a hail of rubber bullets and tear gas, but to underscore both the multiple legitimate purposes civil disobedience might serve, along with the distance separating violence and power. Exerting power *over* can undercut the transformative potential of sharing power *with*. Where conflicts turn on resisting challenges to established norms, rules, or practices – as one might argue that much antifascist direct action or the street battles with federal forces during the summer of 2020 often aimed to do – this trade-off may be reasonable. But where the ends of protest are bolder and aimed at profound institutional transformation, as mobilizations against structural racism and climate change are, violence may become a liability for the power-enhancing virtuous circle of disruption and communication. Simply because the strategy of defensive disobedience is narrower does not make it any less legitimate, particularly where oppressed people fight to survive under a condition of constant threat, trauma, and degradation. These too are demands for care. Reworking Deming's insights in the current conjuncture of global pandemic, racialized state violence, and climate catastrophe means working to develop an agonistic perspective and pragmatic tactics, that can mobilize power while limiting these inevitable trade-offs between transformation and defense. The question posed by the current uprising is therefore poorly formulated as choosing between violence or nonviolence; it remains vertigo or control.

NOTES

1. Kimberley Brownlee, *Conscience and Conviction: The Case for Civil Disobedience* (Oxford: Oxford University Press, 2012); Robin Celikates, "Rethinking Civil Disobedience as a Practice of Contestation – Beyond the Liberal Paradigm," *Constellations: An International Journal of Critical and Democratic Theory* 23, no. 1 (2016): 37–45. See also Robin Celikates's contribution in Chapter Five.
2. Candice Delmas, *A Duty to Resist: When Disobedience Should Be Uncivil* (New York: Oxford University Press, 2018).
3. Howard Zinn, *Democracy and Disagreement: Nine Fallacies on Law and Order* (Cambridge, MA: South End Press, 2002), 21, 46, 48, 49.
4. Robin Celikates "Democratizing Civil Disobedience," *Philosophy and Social Criticism* 42, no. 10 (2016): 986–87.
5. Barbara Deming, "Revolution and Equilibrium," in *We Are All Part of One Another: The Barbara Deming Reader*, ed. Jane Meyerding (Baltimore, OH: New Society Publishers, 1984), 177 (emphasis in original).
6. Judith Butler, *The Force of Nonviolence* (New York: Verso, 2020). To say that defining violence is always a thorny issue is not the same as saying that it is impossible. This chapter presumes a minimalist conception of violence for analytical purposes in order to better appreciate the ubiquity of coercion in politics as well as the many questions it raises for the study of civil disobedience. At the same time, I also mean to show that definition of non/violence is always a question settled by the public, which is why competition over the framing of coercion is such a central element to binding confrontation and communication.
7. Marc Stears, "Liberalism and the Politics of Compulsion," *British Journal of Political Science* 37, no. 3 (2007): 533–53.

8. Abe Fortas, *Concerning Dissent and Civil Disobedience* (New York: World Publishing 1968), 48, 49, 123, 126.

9. John Rawls, *A Theory of Justice*, revised ed. (Cambridge, MA: Belknap Press of Harvard University Press, 1999), 321, 322.

10. Ronald Dworkin, *A Matter of Principle* (Cambridge, MA: Harvard University Press 1985), 112.

11. Rawls, *A Theory of Justice*, 321.

12. Delmas, *A Duty to Resist*, 29–35.

13. Mathew Humphrey and Marc Stears, "Animal Rights Protest and the Challenge to Deliberative Democracy," *Economy and Society* 35, no. 3 (2006): 416–22.

14. Rawls, *A Theory of Justice*, 319.

15. Alexander Livingston, "Power for the Powerless: Martin Luther King Jr's Late Theory of Civil Disobedience," *Journal of Politics* 82, no. 2 (2020): 700–13.

16. Iris Marion Young, "Activist Challenges to Deliberative Democracy," *Political Theory* 29, no. 5 (2001): 670–90.

17. Clarissa Rile Hayward, "Responsibility and Ignorance: On Dismantling Structural Injustice," *Journal of Politics* 79, no. 2 (2017): 407.

18. Sidney G. Tarrow, *Power in Movement: Social Movements and Contentious Politics*, 3rd ed. (Cambridge: Cambridge University Press, 2011), 101.

19. See William Smith's contribution in Chapter Four. to this volume.

20. Daniel Markovits, "Democratic Disobedience," *Yale Law Journal* 114 (2005): 1928, 1935.

21. William Smith, *Civil Disobedience and Deliberative Democracy* (London: Routledge, 2013).

22. Markovits, "Democratic Disobedience," 1942.

23. Humphrey and Stears, "Animal Rights Protest," 405–08.

24. Mark Bray, *Antifa: The Anti-Fascist Handbook* (Brooklyn, NY: Melville House, 2017).

25. Guy Aitchison, "Coercion, Resistance, and the Radical Side of Nonviolence," *Raisons Politique* 1, no. 69 (2018): 45–61.

26. Avia Pasternack, "Political Rioting: A Moral Assessment," *Philosophy and Public Affairs* 46, no. 4 (2019): 391, ibid.

27. Tommie Shelby, *Dark Ghettos: Injustice, Dissent, and Reform* (Cambridge, MA: Belknap Press of Harvard University Press, 2016), 223–27.

28. Hannah Arendt, *Crises of the Republic* (Orlando, FL: Harcourt and Brace, 1972), 176.

29. Zeynep Tufecki, *Twitter and Teargas: The Power and Fragility of Networked Protest* (New Haven, CT: Yale University Press, 2017), 212–13.

30. Tabatha Abu El-Haj, "Defining Peaceably: Policing the Line Between Constitutionally Protected Protest and Unlawful Assembly," *Missouri Law Review* 80, no. 4 (2015): 961–86.

31. Doug McAdam, Sidney Tarrow, and Charles Tilly, *Dynamics of Contention* (New York: Cambridge University Press, 2001).

32. Dustin Ellis Howes, "The Failure of Pacifism and the Success of Nonviolence," *Perspectives on Politics* 11, no. 2 (2013): 435.

33. M.K. Gandhi, *Non-Violent Resistance (Satyagraha)* (Mineaola, NY: Dover Publications, 2001), 188.

34. Peter Ackerman and Jack Duvall, *A Force More Powerful: A Century of Nonviolent Conflict* (New York: Palgrave 2000), 7.

35. Gene Sharp, *The Politics of Nonviolent Action* (Boston, MA: Porter Sargent Publishers, 1973), 1: 9, ibid.

36. Gene Sharp, *Waging Nonviolent Struggle: 20th Century Practice and 21st Century Potential* (Boston, MA: Porters Sargent Publishers, 2005), 32.

37. Sharp, *Waging Nonviolent Struggle*, 35.

38. Sharp, *Politics of Nonviolent Action*, 1–47.

39. Erica Chenoweth and Maria J. Stephan, *Why Civil Resistance Works: The Strategic Logic of Nonviolent Conflict* (New York: Columbia University Press, 2011).

40. Sharp, *Waging Nonviolent Struggle*, 406.

41. Étienne Balibar, *Violence and Civility: On the Limits of Political Philosophy*, tr. G.M. Goshgarian (New York: Columbia University Press 2015), 103.

42. Robin Celikates, "Learning from the Streets: Civil Disobedience in Theory and Practice," in *Global Activism: Art and Conflict in the 21st Century*, ed. Peter Weibel (Cambridge, MA: MIT Press, 2015), 71, 68, 67.

43. Stellan Vinthagen, *A Theory of Nonviolent Action: How Civil Resistance Works* (London: Zed Books, 2015), 48–51.

44. Deming, "Revolution and Equilibrium," 179 (emphasis in original).

45. Feminism and Nonviolence Study Group, *Piecing It Together: Feminism and Nonviolence* (Westward Ho! and London: The Feminist Nonviolence

Study Group in co-operation with the War Resisters' International, 1983),
35, 44.

46. Deming, "On the Necessity to Liberate Minds," *We Are All Part of One Another*, 198, 199.

47. Barbara Deming, *We Cannot Live Without Our Lives* (New York: Grossman Publishers, 1974), 6.

48. Deming, "Revolution and Equilibrium," 178.

49. Deming, "Revolution and Equilibrium," 181, 180.

50. Karuna Mantena, "Another Realism: The Politics of Gandhian Nonviolence," *American Political Science Review* 106, no. 2 (2012): 455–70.

51. Mark Engler and Paul Engler, *This is an Uprising: How Nonviolent Revolt is Shaping the Twenty-First Century* (New York: Nation Books, 2016), 152.

52. Deming, "On the Necessity to Liberate Minds," 201 (emphasis in original).

53. Alexander Livingston, "Tough Love: On the Political Theology of Civil Disobedience," *Perspectives on Politics* 18, no. 3 (2020): 851–66.

54. Rawls, *A Theory of Justice*, 321.

55. Sharp, *Waging Nonviolent Struggle*, 391.

56. Deming, "On the Necessity to Liberate Minds," 202.

57. On polarization and the Democratic Party "issue ownership" of racial justice, see Daniel Q. Gillion, *The Loud Minority: Why Protests Matter in American Democracy* (Princeton, NJ: Princeton University Press, 2020), 50–79; on the discursive accomplishments of the 2015 Black Lives Matter protest wave in preparing the way for the 2020 uprising, see Deva Woodly, "An American Reckoning: The Fire This Time," *Public Seminar* (2020), accessed August 25, 2020, https://publicseminar.org/essays/an-american -reckoning/.

58. Carl von Clausewitz, *On War*, eds. Michael Howard and Peter Paret (Princeton, NJ: Princeton University Press, 1984).

59. Barbara Deming, "On Anger," *We Are All Part of One Another*, 212–13.

11 Punishment and Civil Disobedience

Christopher Bennett and Kimberley Brownlee

This chapter explores whether civil disobedience can be not just morally justifiable, but also legally defensible and, if it can be, how states should respond to it. The key question is whether states act legitimately when they punish civil disobedients and, if they do act legitimately, on what grounds. Philosophers have advanced numerous grounds to justify state punishment in general, including retribution or just deserts, deterrence, incapacitation, communicating society's censure, vindicating victims, and easing political and social tensions. The question is whether any of these grounds can justify states in punishing people who engage in civil disobedience. If states act illegitimately in punishing civil disobedients, which seems likely in many cases, then what distinguishes civil disobedients from other lawbreakers? We discuss various defenses that civil disobedients might make in a court of law to differentiate their conduct from ordinary offenses. We also examine the countervailing idea that civil disobedience should not be incorporated into the legal system in this way, but instead should operate as a direct challenge to the legal order.

The chapter proceeds as follows. We start by outlining the nature of civil disobedience, before then moving to detail some commonly proposed grounds for state punishment and considering whether these grounds suggest that the state has a right to punish in general. Succeeding sections highlight two distinct strategies to justify civil disobedience both morally and legally, preparing the ground for a discussion of how these justifications might be accommodated within the justice system. The first justificatory strategy, which we call the *limits of state authority strategy*, aims to justify civil disobedience on the grounds that the laws broken were ones the state had no right to make. Thus, this strategy concentrates on limits to the state's *de jure* jurisdiction (that is, not the jurisdiction the state claims to have, but the jurisdiction it actually has a moral *right* to claim). The second strategy, which we call the *communicative value of civil disobedience strategy*, seeks to justify civil disobedience as valuable communicative acts within a (liberal democratic) state. This second strategy takes two forms: one that focuses on political participation rights, and one that focuses on freedom of expression, integrity, and the collision of opinions. Having discussed these two rival strategies, we relate them to the grounds for punishment to determine whether the state can legitimately punish civil disobedients whose conduct is relevantly distinct from other kinds of offending. We conclude that punishing civil disobedience is often indefensible on any of the major grounds for punishment; this should alter how police, prosecutors, courts, and the law respond to civil disobedience. From this conclusion, we move to address the question that naturally arises of how the legal system should accommodate civil disobedients in a way that is compatible with rule of law values such as consistency, publicity, and equality before the law.

THE NATURE OF CIVIL DISOBEDIENCE

Civil disobedience is a specific form of conscientious nonconformity with the law. Take a paradigm case by way of illustration. Suppose a law prohibits people of color from sitting in certain bus seats, and a person of color then sits in one of those seats. This would be nonconformity with the law, but not necessarily civil disobedience, since she might be sitting in the prohibited seat by accident or without knowing about the prohibition. Alternatively, she might sit in the seat knowingly but without any clear aim to object to the law. For an act to be civilly disobedient – in the way that Rosa Parks's refusal in 1955 to give up her bus seat in Montgomery, Alabama, was – other things must be true.[1]

First, paradigmatically, a civil disobedient is motivated by a conscientious wish to oppose a law that she believes is unjust, in this case the law that segregates bus seats. The fact that she is so motivated does not mean that the law she opposes actually is unjust or that the law she breaches is the law she opposes. When she breaches the law that she opposes – as she does in the bus segregation case – then she engages in *direct civil disobedience*. When she breaches a law other than the one she opposes – suppose she engages in trespass to protest the bus segregation laws – then she engages in *indirect civil disobedience*.[2] Sometimes we have no option but to use indirect disobedience, because sometimes we cannot breach the laws we oppose (not all laws apply to everyone),[3] and sometimes we cannot breach them effectively, or we cannot do so without undue cost to highlight their perceived injustice.

Second, to be civilly disobedient, a person must aim to *communicate* her opposition through her disobedience to draw other people's attention to the (perceived) deficiencies of the law. John Rawls's account fleshes out this communicative element in a *publicity* condition: to be civilly disobedient, a person must forewarn authorities of her intention to break the law as part of a general fidelity to the surrounding legal system.[4] Interestingly, although Rosa Parks's breach of law was conscientious and nonviolent (which are two other conditions that Rawls endorses) and was what triggered the ultimately successful Montgomery Bus boycott, nevertheless she did not forewarn the bus driver or local authorities of an intent to break the law and, hence, her conduct was not civilly disobedient on a Rawlsian account.[5] Parks did, however, satisfy a more modest communicative standard favored by most other accounts of civil disobedience in that she took ownership of her disobedience and provided reasons afterward to explain it.[6] In her writings, Parks said: "I had been pushed around all my life and felt at this moment that I couldn't take it anymore."[7]

Third, for a person's act to be civilly disobedient, she must behave in a suitably constrained way; her disobedience cannot be so radical that it drowns out the message she aims to communicate. On some accounts, like Rawls's, her disobedience must be nonviolent and not interfere at all with others' civil liberties, or else she obscures the civilly disobedient quality of her conduct.[8] By contrast, other accounts require only that her conduct be visibly more restrained than riotous protests or terrorization, but it may include some violence.[9]

Finally, in keeping with her communicativeness and conscientiousness, a civil disobedient typically does not seek to evade the costs of her disobedience, but instead accepts the risk or the reality of being punished.[10] That said, in cases such as that of Edward Snowden, who revealed the extent to which the US government engages in secretive surveillance of both US citizens and foreigners,[11] seeking to evade punishment may be the only viable option.

With this conception of *civil disobedience* in hand, let us consider the grounds for justified punishment.

GROUNDS FOR PUNISHMENT

The question that drives this chapter is whether the state has the right to punish people who engage in civil disobedience, and, if it does not, how it should treat them.

We can approach these questions by asking first whether, in general, the state has the right to punish. Philosophers of punishment have appealed to a nonexclusive range of goals that might be furthered by punishment including deterring future crime, incapacitating dangerous people, giving wrongdoers their moral deserts, expressing authoritative disapproval on behalf of the public, vindicating victims, and easing political and social tensions.[12] One important question is whether any of these grounds is sufficient reason to do the things that punishment typically does, such as deprive persons of their liberty, employment, and social contacts for extended periods of time, make them pay fines or do community service, and impose other onerous conditions on them.

Another question, relevant to civil disobedience, concerns how state punishment interacts with political obligation. Put simply, if one or more of the grounds for punishment makes it good for a person to be punished, does it follow that some agent – and in particular, or perhaps exclusively, the state – thereby has a right to punish that person? One might argue that, to have the (exclusive) right to punish, the state requires a special form of political authority or right to rule including, though not restricted to, the right to make and enforce laws in the relevant area of conduct.

It is a further question whether the state has *unlimited* authority to make and enforce whatever laws it chooses and, with that, a comprehensive right to punish all infractions of those laws. Such unlimited authority is highly implausible, of course, even though many states seem to assert that they have it; and, arguably, the state would have to enjoy unlimited authority in order for its right to punish to be unaffected by the justifiability of civil disobedience. Before getting to the justification of civil disobedience, let us consider briefly some of the grounds advanced to support lawful punishment, starting with deterrence.

It might be natural to think that, if states are justified in setting up highly expensive criminal justice apparatuses involving legislation, courts, and systems of punishment, then surely these apparatuses must contribute meaningfully to improving citizens' lives. It might also be natural to think that the distinctive contribution that an institution geared toward inflicting punishment should make is to increase citizens' sense of security by giving everyone a strong incentive to live within the law.[13] Hence, what justifies punishment, on this view, is its deterrent effect.

Now, this view can be criticized on several grounds. For one thing, whether institutions of law and order contribute to or undermine our security depends greatly on the part of the political community we are from, the position we have in the socio-economic hierarchy, and the racial characteristics we are perceived as having. For another thing, the effectiveness of punishment as a deterrent is disputable: the evidence that it does deter offending varies across crimes, but overall is notoriously weak. Moreover, the idea of rule by "orders backed by threats" sits poorly with the broadly liberal idea of political society as something based on consensus and social cooperation: Hegel's charge that deterrent punishment is "like raising a stick to a dog" continues to hit home. Nevertheless, deterrence in various forms continues to be an influential idea in punishment theory.[14]

If deterrence were a compelling ground for state punishment, would that give the state the right to punish people? Or would the state need some further special form of political authority to have this right? One might argue that, if deterrence is needed to protect the vulnerable, and if some party is powerful enough to issue credible threats, then that party requires no further authority to have a license to issue those threats and, if need be, to carry them out: having the power to make credible threats is sufficient for the right to act.[15]

Alternatively, if having the power to do good is insufficient to give that party license to act, then we could introduce a further condition that the person who offended must have done something sufficient to forfeit their rights to noninterference.[16] If this further condition is enough to give powerful agents license to act, then we must confront the possibility that not only states have a right to punish, since not only states have such power. For instance, a local gang or vigilante association might have power sufficient, in a given community, to issue credible threats.

This approach to deterrence and political obligation is overly simplistic. For instance, giving many parties unconstrained license to use force and threats of force could escalate easily into a dangerous situation. For that reason, it may be wise to treat the state as having an exclusive right to issue threats and enforce them. So, while the logic of the deterrent position seems to be that anyone who has sufficient power to protect others by issuing and enforcing threats has a license to do so, nevertheless, as John Locke and many others have thought, we have good reasons to cede our rights in this area to the state.[17]

That said, even if the state did have an exclusive right to punish in the name of deterrence, this would not mean that it has an unlimited right to punish as it chooses. Deterrence theory only licenses punishment that serves the purpose of social protection.

Furthermore, even if some policy of punishment would serve social protection, the value of that protection would have to be weighed against the bad consequences that such a policy might produce, such as deterring behavior that is in some respects desirable. This is an important point to highlight in relation to civil disobedience. Although the state might justifiably want to deter some acts of civil disobedience, a (liberal democratic) state arguably should welcome some such acts and not deter them too forcefully. We develop this thought in greater detail below.

A very different approach to punishment is the just deserts or retributive account. This account says that punishment is necessary, not to bring about some desirable future change in individual or social behavior, but to do justice, avenge the wrong, or vindicate the victims. Judging by the satisfying nature of the narrative arc of films and stories in which the "bad guy" eventually gets their comeuppance, we seem to find it deeply fitting when a person who has preyed on others does not get away scot-free, but instead meets a fate that makes them at least confront the nature of their conduct, if not suffer for what they have done. In general, painful feelings of guilt and remorse seem to be inherently fitting and desirable in cases of serious wrongdoing.[18] Proponents of the just deserts or retributive approach take these reactions as evidence of our sensitivity to a moral requirement to ensure that wrongdoers meet a proportionately unpleasant fate through punishment.[19]

This retributive approach can be criticized on several fronts. First, retributive punishment aims at responding to the past, and struggles to explain the value of inflicting punishment irrespective of whether it brings about some tangible future benefit. A second, related thought sees our tendency to inflict such – strictly unnecessary – punishment as a form of cruelty. A third criticism is that, for someone to *deserve* to suffer for wrongdoing, they must have a significant measure of free will and control over who they are and how they act, but this degree of free will is something that we human beings lack.[20]

Despite these criticisms, our attachment to some broadly retributive reactions is deeply rooted. What are the implications of taking retributivism seriously when we consider state authority and political obligation? What, apart from the validity of retributive justice, would have to be true for the state to acquire a right to inflict retributive punishment? As with deterrence theory, one might argue that, if retributive justice is sufficiently important, then anyone who is powerful enough to carry it out thereby has a right to do so, at least on the assumption that wrongdoers have forfeited their rights to noninterference. Considered in itself, then, a simple version of retributivism might be said to license vigilantism in the same way that deterrence would. Nevertheless, given the conflicts that might arise from never-ending disagreements about who did what, whether it was wrong, and what the punishment should be, we seem to have good reason once again to cede our individual rights to do justice to the state,[21] as long as it carries them out reasonably well, as a result of which the state would end up with, albeit by indirect means, an exclusive right to punish.

Again, however, this exclusive right to punish would not be unlimited. The retributive account says that only the guilty can be punished, and thus it does not give the state the right to punish any conduct that is not independently morally wrong. Related to civil disobedience, it would be only if civilly disobedient conduct were morally wrong and unjustifiable that the state would have any right to act retributively in response to it. By contrast, if plenty of civil disobedience is admirable and justifiable, the state would have no general right to punish it. Furthermore, as we saw with the deterrence account, the state has competing priorities: if pursuing retribution causes too much damage elsewhere, this would be grounds to give it up.

In these comments, we have concentrated on two major approaches to punishment. We have done this to introduce the range of questions that pertain to justified punishment, state authority, and civil disobedience. Admittedly, the deterrent and retributive approaches we have considered are simple, and, certainly, the field of theories of punishment contains many subtler variants on them. For instance, the deterrent approach can be rendered more sophisticated by arguing that, if punishment aims to deter, then the deterrence must be achieved through moral communication and understanding rather than brute threats.[22] Also, the retributive approach can be rendered more sophisticated by arguing that punishment is not simply the infliction of suffering but the expression of deserved censure.[23] Furthermore, a range of so-called hybrid theories aim to combine the features of retributive and deterrent approaches in some form; and other theories aim to give priority to the political question of state authority and the limits and scope of politically legitimate state action, rather than to the moral question of the justifiability of protecting the vulnerable or doing justice which might be pursued on a purely individual basis.[24] While we acknowledge these complexities, the above outline is hopefully useful for illustrative purposes. Furthermore, even hybrid theories or specifically political theories cannot avoid making decisions about whether to prioritize punishing in order to bring about behavior change to reduce harm, on the one hand, or doing justice, on the other. With this introduction to the justification of punishment in place, let us now examine the justifiability of civil disobedience.

FIRST STRATEGY: THE LIMITS OF STATE AUTHORITY

One straightforward way to vindicate civil disobedience is to adopt an extreme anarchist position which denies the idea explored above that states have the right to make law, enforce law, and punish people at least some of the time.[25] If states have no such rights, then there is no special difficulty in showing how breaking the law – be it in civil disobedience or otherwise – could be justified. Of course, we might evaluate an act of civil disobedience on other grounds, as dangerous or imprudent, or as courageous, liberating, and progressive. But, its being a breach of law would not be morally relevant if the law has no moral force.

There is also no special difficulty in justifying civil disobedience if we have no general moral obligation to follow the law, even if states normally do have the right to make and enforce the law.[26] (Political philosophers have isolated at least three distinct conceptions of *legitimate political authority*, only one of which characterizes it as the legitimate power to impose obligations on people. The other two specify *legitimate political authority* in terms of justified coercion, on the one hand, and the right to rule, on the other.[27]) If we have no general moral obligation to follow the law, then we can and should judge acts of civil disobedience based on their character and consequences, not their illegality. This could include the consequences that come from the laws against that disobedience having to be enforced. Hence, the question will be more complex if we agree that, although there is no general moral obligation to follow the law, states do normally have the right to make and enforce law, including the laws that disobedients have broken.

Here the question might become whether civil disobedience unduly hampers or prevents the state from discharging its genuine moral responsibilities. Civil disobedience might unduly hamper the state even when the law broken is not justifiable. For instance, suppose that a group of civil disobedients launches a campaign of non-payment against a regressive tax that is broadly legitimate but nonetheless unfairly burdens the worst-off; suppose also that the state relies on this tax to discharge its moral responsibilities to keep schools and hospitals open and maintain roads and public safety, and its ability to do these things is hampered by the successful disobedience campaign. Here important questions about the justifiability of civil disobedience arise even if we reject the idea that its illegality is a troubling feature.

The question of justifying civil disobedience becomes even more complex and intriguing, if we accept both that (liberal democratic) states normally do have the right to make and enforce laws *and* that citizens have a pro tanto moral obligation to follow those laws based on the state's possession of legitimate authority. In other words, civil disobedience seems particularly problematic if the state has a general pro tanto right to be obeyed by those subject to its authority and, since it is a liberal state, it offers members meaningful, legal ways to oppose its laws. For civil disobedience to be justifiable in such regimes, members' reasons to disobey must clearly outweigh their reasons to obey. Debates about the moral justifiability of civil disobedience in such contexts focus on a range of factors including the justness of the disobedients' cause, their reasons for defending that cause, their willingness to exhaust legal options first, their willingness to coordinate with other minority groups, and the likely and actual effects of their disobedience.[28]

We will focus on the first of these justifying factors – the justness of the cause. This factor is the driving consideration behind the first of the two strategies we consider to vindicate civil disobedience in liberal democratic contexts and show that states that have general rights to rule nevertheless often should afford legal protection to civil disobedients rather than treat their acts as ordinary offenses or aggravated offenses made worse by their civilly disobedient character. This first justificatory strategy focuses on *specific* acts of civil disobedience.

The strategy starts by pointing out that, even if a democratic state has a general right to rule and, presumptively, most of its laws are binding as laws it has a right to make, nevertheless a particular law might not be. If a particular law is not binding, then breaking it in order to protest against it could be justified. In other words, even if we have a moral duty to follow the law *in general*, we may have no moral duty to follow a *particular* law. Indeed, we may have a moral duty to depart from it.[29]

First, we may have no duty to follow and indeed a duty *not* to follow a law if, in making that law, the state exceeded its authority. For instance, quoting former Canadian Prime Minister Pierre Trudeau, the state has no business in the bedrooms of the nation, and, therefore, the state would exceed its authority if it passed laws to regulate the private sexual behavior of consenting adults.

Second, we may have no duty to follow and indeed a duty *not* to follow the law if, in making the law, the state operates in an area in which it *does* have jurisdiction, but it enacts a grossly unjust law such as the segregation laws that Rosa Parks challenged. In this case, the state does not exceed its authority, but exercises that authority improperly.

Now, one might think that a liberal democratic state could not overreach its authority or act excessively unjustly for two reasons. One reason is the very fact that the state is liberal and democratic; this means that it cannot enact certain kinds of laws without ceasing to be that kind of state. The other reason is that citizens' duties to follow the law in a liberal democracy are tied not to the merits of any particular law but to the overall legitimacy of the state's authority. The grounds for that authority might be voluntarist or non-voluntarist, but either way, they suffice to give the state general legitimate political authority that rules out the possibility for indefensible overreach.

This line of thought is implausible, as it is overly general. Ronald Dworkin observes that, in cases of civil disobedience, doubtful law is not an exotic or rare occurrence. In the US, he says, the constitutionality of a law is doubtful whenever a significant number of people would be tempted to disobey it on moral grounds: "The constitution makes our conventional political morality relevant to the question of validity; any statute that appears to compromise that morality raises constitutional questions, and if the compromise is serious, the constitutional doubts are serious also."[30] Since, on most theories of political obligation, not every newly enacted bit of legislation gives citizens a moral duty (rather than a merely presumptive legal duty) to follow it, justificatory gaps can arise in states' authority and this gives us a straightforward line of moral justification and (constitutional) legal defensibility for specific acts of civil disobedience. In a word, when a state enacts laws that either exceed its authority or are severely unjust, citizens are permitted to break those laws, and indeed may have a duty to break them, because the state has no right to make or enforce those laws.

Moreover, even if we had a general moral duty to follow all laws, including unjust and overreaching ones, it would not follow that this duty was invariably our *most* pressing moral duty. We have natural duties of justice as well as duties of fairness and beneficence or Samaritanism that can be more pressing.[31] Michael Walzer contrasts our political obligations (our so-called "primary associative obligations"), which are largely involuntary, with our interpersonal obligations within smaller, tight-knit nonconformist groups such as sects, unions, or revolutionary groups (our so-called "secondary associative obligations"), which are largely voluntary, and concludes that the latter obligations are generally more pressing than the former. The same conclusion might be drawn when our duty to obey the law conflicts with our general humanitarian duties, such as in a case in which someone helps a refugee to evade the authorities and remain in the country when she has been deemed to have no legal right to remain. Some theorists maintain that pressing moral duties such as Samaritanism and humanitarian aid should be able to supply civil disobedients with a legal defense of necessity.[32]

In addition to overreaching, a state can sometimes underreach by not enacting legislation it ought to enact. When it underreaches, people might resort to civil disobedience to hold the state to account for not criminalizing behavior it ought to criminalize, such as the improper disposal of environmentally damaging waste. One problem with disobedience that opposes state nonaction is that, since there is no law on the books to break, this disobedience must be *indirect* (i.e. a breach of a law that the dissenter does not oppose, such as a law against trespass or vandalism, to protest a lack of policy, which she does oppose). Indirect disobedience – both in response to state nonaction and more generally – is hard to justify under the *limited state authority strategy* because this strategy concerns not only the justness of the dissenter's cause but her method, that is, her breach of a law that *should not exist*. When she engages in indirect disobedience, she breaches a law over which (by stipulation) the state's authority is in good standing.

Now, when there is no law that she can break directly, or no law that applies to *her*, her indirect disobedience could be defensible as the next best thing. The gross injustice, the inexcusable underreach, the state's misuse of its authority is what moves her and makes her breach of a legitimate law justifiable. This argument, imperfect as it is, cannot be extended to cases of indirect disobedience when she *could* engage in direct disobedience and does not do so because the "best" law to break for her purposes is one she doesn't oppose. The *limited state authority strategy* cannot help her defend her disobedience in that case because she *does have* a duty to follow the law she is breaching and to opt for the more costly option of direct disobedience. Of course, we can appeal to her natural duties of justice, fairness, or Samaritanism to defend her decision to breach *some* law even if it is a legitimate law, and we can say that her *all things considered duty* is a matter of weighing competing considerations, but our reasons for saying so are consequentialist, not principled. To defend her disobedience on grounds of communicative effectiveness, she must look to the *communicative function strategy* that we discuss below, not to the *limited state authority strategy*.

Now, one complication here resides in the specifically voluntary and second-personal character of reasons of obedience; dictates of authority are issued by one person at will and directed at another with the intention of thereby changing the latter's rights and duties. Some thinkers hold that it is characteristic of a legitimate authority that its dictates constitute reasons for obedience that *exclude* – rather than weigh against – other, competing reasons. Joseph Raz gives the example of the authority possessed by an agent appointed as an adjudicator of a dispute.[33] One thing that the adjudicator needs to be able to do is to settle the matter: they need to be able to make a decision that is final to bring the dispute to a close. On the Razian picture, the adjudicator's decision can only foreclose further debate if the adjudicator has the normative effect of replacing and excluding the reasons that motivated the dispute in the first place. For instance, even if we, as one of the disputing parties, continue to think that the adjudicator's decision is unjust, and that the considerations informing our case remain valid, for the adjudicator's decision to be able to settle the matter, those considerations must be denied their practical effect.

Similarly, seemingly, for a state to maintain its supposed character as an *authority*, it must be able to insist that its dictates rule out the kinds of considerations civil disobedients appeal to to legitimate their conduct. Indeed, this is the view that the state commonly adopts toward its own legislation. A state often acts as though, in creating legislation, it has final adjudicative authority to decide on the practical validity of any competing reasons, and that in making its decision it thereby excludes those competing reasons from citizens' deliberations and replaces them with its own dictates. For the state to contemplate the justness of civil disobedience, then, it would have to accept that it is less than fully sovereign, and that there are some reasons that its decisions cannot exclude or replace.[34] In recent times, our general awareness that there are nonnegotiable standards of human rights has started to erode the idea of unlimited state sovereignty. That said, it is noteworthy that states tend to recognize human rights standards only insofar as they have incorporated them into their own domestic legislation.

Of course, as Raz highlights, the fact that the state and the law claim to have this kind of authority does not mean that they actually have it.[35] It is unlikely that imperfect, real-world states and legislators do ensure across the board that, by following their dictates, we better adhere to the reasons that apply to us – including crucially reasons of justice, fairness, and goodness – than we would do if we followed our own judgment in decision-making.

One further problem with the *limited state authority strategy* to vindicate civil disobedience is that its scope is restricted. Some cases of admirable and perhaps socially necessary civil disobedience would be ones that the state has a right to punish. Take for instance the Greenpeace protests on power stations. It might be argued that the state has a right to make and enforce laws that prohibit trespass on and damage to infrastructure essential to the national power supply: the state neither overreaches nor acts unjustly in making such laws. But, the state arguably does act unjustly at a more basic level here in not shifting away from environmentally damaging power sources. For this reason, it seems wrong to punish the Greenpeace protestors in the same way as trespassers who had malicious motives. We return to this line of thought below. For now, let us turn to the second strategy to justify civil disobedience.

SECOND STRATEGY: THE COMMUNICATIVE FUNCTIONS OF CIVIL DISOBEDIENCE

The second strategy to vindicate civil disobedience looks at the importance of protecting civil disobedience as a communicative practice regardless of disobedients' specific causes. This second, *content-independent* strategy, which we might call the *communicative value strategy*, can take one of two forms.

The first form, which we call the *political participation strategy*, focuses on the role that civil disobedience can play to ensure that people can exercise their rights to participate politically even within a liberal democratic society since minorities have comparatively less power to ensure their views are heard before votes are taken and decisions made.[36] Rights to political participation in a liberal democratic society are held regardless of the causes that citizens use the exercise of those rights to further. Therefore, if political participation rights entail that civil disobedience be protected in order to remedy participatory power imbalances, they will protect such disobedience regardless of the causes disobedients support.

The second form of the content-independent strategy, which we call the *protected expression strategy*, highlights an analogy between civil disobedience and ordinary (legal) freedom of expression. The literature on freedom of expression highlights at least two grounds for protecting it. First, allowing the expression of competing views can further social progress by subjecting conventionally accepted ideas, practices, and institutions to scrutiny, with the result that those views can be recognized as (1) unjustified and hence worth rejecting, (2) partially justified but in need of reform, or (3) justified and supported in a more robust and informed manner than through custom and tradition. This is the crucial Millian idea of political society as a shared discursive, argumentative enterprise through which citizens can raise questions about received ways of social and political life, and engage in informed, collective discussion about the continuing worth of those ways of life.[37]

Second, free speech can further not only social but individual progress, specifically the progress of the individual thinker away from being an unreflective receptacle of the tradition into which they were born, and toward a life and opinions of their own: a being who achieves, in John Stuart Mill's terms, genuine individuality or autonomy. Participation in the collision of opinions, Mill thought, is essential for a person to escape the "dead hand" of tradition to call their received views into question and come to their own answers. For this to be possible, people must be able to express their views and raise controversial questions without fear of punishment.

These two grounds, Mill thought, speak in favor of allowing maximal freedom of speech provided that what people say does not unduly harm others. This constraint may be hard to interpret, but for our purposes it is sufficient to illustrate the spirit of the Millian view.

To these Millian grounds we can add another, which is that being allowed to speak freely gives individuals space to express their inner states of mind, the repression of which can be psychologically damaging for them in view of the self-alienation, loss of self-respect, and loss of integrity that flows from constantly having to appear other than they are.[38] This justification for allowing free expression focuses on the psychological costs of such self-repression: given that the laws of the political community set the boundaries in which a person is likely to live out the whole of their life, the state has a responsibility to allow people to live with integrity as long as they do not greatly harm others.

All three of these grounds favor the protection of civil disobedience. First, civil disobedience, like ordinary free speech, can serve the all-necessary, ongoing collision of competing opinions: as Li Wenliang, one of the COVID-19 whistleblowers in Wuhan, China, put it, "a healthy society does not have just one voice." Equally, both ordinary free speech and civil disobedience can use their declarative content or obstructive forms of expression to hold authorities to account and encourage other citizens to engage in deliberative discussion. Dissent and indeed civil disobedience can correct democratic deficits by prodding members to discuss issues that have fallen off the public agenda.[39] Second, civil disobedience can honor the value for an individual in being a reflective, independent-minded being. Third, civil disobedience gives an individual space to retain her identity, well-being, and self-respect in being able to voice, rather than repress, what she deeply believes.

On this third point, civil disobedience, like ordinary free expression, serves to honor something deep and fundamental about who we are as human beings, specifically, that we are expressive beings who can care very deeply about the things we value. Through our communicative expression – including civil disobedience – we can, as Gandhi put it, make our lives our message. We can seek, not only to live by, but *be seen* to live by, the core values that animate us, and to defend our reasons for living in that way when those values face challenges from the powerful.

Of course, ordinary free expression is legal, whereas civil disobedience is, by nature, illegal, but the personal and societal importance of self-expression – living and being seen to live by what we value – should carry some weight regardless of de facto legality or illegality. Constrained lawbreaking that is conscientiously motivated, that is, motivated by a sincere, communicative intention, should be treated differently from lawbreaking motivated by, for instance, personal gain or other desires that conflict with the values underpinning liberal democratic citizenship.

One of the authors of this chapter, Kimberley Brownlee, holds that civil disobedience is, in important respects, more worthy of accommodation than private conscientious objection is because, unlike a mere demand for an exemption from the law, civil disobedience involves standing up and being counted for one's convictions and attempting to engage with fellow citizens in dialogue to further collective debate. In Brownlee's terms, this makes civil disobedience both communicative and non-evasive. She argues that civil disobedients should be able to advance a legal defense based on *demands of conviction* that recognizes the value of our expressive efforts to defend what we believe, including the value of our autonomously coming to form our own views, the psychological costliness of having to act as though we do not have the views we have, and the social benefit of furthering meaningful collective debate. Hence, this excusatory defense could be appealed to by "bigots, xenophobes, and misguided do-gooders" as well as champions of justice.[40]

The analogy with freedom of speech thus shows how legal protection of civil disobedience can be justified even beyond cases of justificatory gaps in political authority, because even conduct that a state has a right to prohibit (and does prohibit) can be necessary and proportionate to furthering important social and individual goals, or be necessary to individual psychological welfare.

Now, neither form of the content-independent strategy (the *political participation strategy* nor the *protected expression strategy*) would give people an unlimited right to engage in civil disobedience. As with other defenses of civil disobedience, it matters whether the illegality and disobedience are necessary in the situation (and, hence, whether viable alternative legal means had been exhausted) and proportionate (in the sense that the extent of the lawbreaking was not disproportionate to the seriousness of the injustice being opposed). When civil disobedience does meet these conditions, however, the state, even if it is within its rights to make and enforce a given law, may have special reasons not to enforce it against people whose communicative lawbreaking is a conscientiously motivated attempt (1) to further a cause they perceive to be just, (2) to exercise their rights to political participation, or (3) to make a legitimate attempt at communicative expression of commitment.

One objection to the *communicative value strategy* holds that this strategy – with its emphasis on the societal and personal benefits of free expression – seems to ask the state and the law to recognize values other than the law as being higher than the law itself, something the law seems constitutionally incapable of doing.

In reply, the law can and often does acknowledge the importance of values other than adherence to the law. Through its willingness sometimes to grant exemptions to private objectors, through its accommodation – however half-hearted – of assertions of necessity[41] or indeed its accommodation of any justificatory defense, it concedes that, sometimes, following the law is not what matters most.

A second objection comes from the opposite direction, and targets both the *limited state authority strategy* and the *communicative value strategy*. Essentially, this objection is that both strategies to vindicate civil disobedience declaw or deradicalize civil disobedience by bringing it within the constitutional and legal framework of a liberal democratic society. Candice Delmas argues that constitutionalizing approaches – such as the two discussed above – deradicalize, domesticate, and individualize civil disobedience[42] when, in fact, civil disobedience and uncivil disobedience are most potent when they sit outside the legal system and potentially bring with them heavy penalties for dissenters. The true disobedient should not want the protection of a legal defense, since that would deny her the political costs that make her a martyr and her cause a headline, so the thought goes.

In reply, giving a constitutionalized analysis of civil disobedience and other resistance practices cannot declaw and domesticate them entirely. Even though civil disobedience is constrained when compared with other, less conscientious protest practices, it remains radical in nature because it is a deliberate, publicly oriented breach of law. And, it has many radical siblings and cousins including rule departures by officials, jury nullification,[43] judicial disobedience (in which a judge deliberately departs from the law; the act may be communicative and sincere, but it is probably also evasive in not being presented as an act of disobedience), government whistleblowing, and the right of resistance (according to German Basic Law: "All Germans shall have the right to resist any person seeking to abolish this constitutional order, if no other remedy is available"), all of which can and often are "constitutionalized" within existing legal systems, but nonetheless remain paradoxical, disorienting, and vaguely threatening to the orders that seek to accommodate them.

Having unpacked the two strategies to vindicate civil disobedience, we now reflect briefly on the nature of, and possible justifications for, lawful punishment of civil disobedience by the state. Let us also situate the notion of *liability to punishment* in relation to the practice of civil disobedience.

PUNISHMENT OF CIVIL DISOBEDIENCE

Above, we identified good grounds to think that one or more of the strategies to vindicate civil disobedience will succeed. That is, either the disobedient will have no duty to obey and possibly all things considered a duty to disobey; or else she can claim protection of her civil disobedience for the same reasons that society protects free speech. Now we can ask whether, in light of such justifications, it is appropriate to punish civil disobedients.

Take for instance, the views that we canvassed previously that punishment is pro tanto justified whenever it is necessary either to deter people from causing relevant harms in future or to carry out retributive justice. Recall that both of these justifications set a necessary condition on the appropriateness of punishment: for the deterrence account, punishment is not appropriate unless it will deter unwanted or dangerous behavior; for the retributive account, it is not appropriate unless deserved for wrongdoing. The first point we can draw from our discussion above is that many cases of civil disobedience will fail to meet these conditions, since they often reveal admirable and non-evasive political commitments and engagements as well as attitudes which are certainly not immoral and which a vibrant democracy would want to encourage. If this is right, then no punishment would be justified.

Might it be argued that there is something undesirable and wrongfully arrogant in the civil disobedient's refusal to accept the authority of established law, and that this calls for punishment? In other words, far from being legally excusable, civil disobedience is inexcusable because its agents improperly arrogate to themselves license to breach laws that others bind themselves to follow. Their civilly disobedient motivations make their offenses worse than ordinary-offense equivalents, because they aim to apply political pressure through improper means that other citizens have not helped themselves to. In doing so, civil disobedients disregard the fragile accomplishment that is a functioning liberal democracy.[44]

In reply, liberal democracies are more robust and nuanced than this objection suggests. Moreover, it is notoriously true that even allegedly democratic law can fail to take into account all relevant voices, or give them proper consideration; in these cases, we should be grateful to those who are prepared to risk their own welfare to point out the flaws. Civil disobedience is not as undemocratic as the charge implies: to overcome democratic deficits or a top-down chilling effect on opinion collisions, we sometimes need to kick-start debate through civil disobedience. Civil disobedients can sometimes be society's advocates.

Now take the *limits of state authority strategy*. Would it, if successful, show that punishing disobedients is unjustified? Recalling our earlier discussion, it seems that the answer would be "no" if we adopt a simple version of the deterrent or retributive views. The reason is that the simple versions of these views do not rest the justifiability of punishment on the possession of legitimate authority. For an agent to be justified in deterring a person from causing great harm, or to be justified in carrying out retributive justice, the person need not have a duty to obey the agent. We saw, however, that these simple views are *too* simple, and that there are Lockean reasons for thinking that, to avoid endless disagreement and conflict, individuals need to cede to the state their rights to use force to deter or to do justice. If this is the case, then the state would possess a form of political authority that individuals lack, and which includes an exclusive right to punish. However, the state's authority extends only as far as its proper jurisdiction, and where it acts beyond its jurisdiction or severely unjustly, it would have no right to punish those who disobey its illegitimate claims.

Let us now look at the *protected speech strategy*. Here we should recall that our theories of punishment already rule out punishment in cases of civil disobedience in which there is nothing undesirable to deter or no wrongdoing. Thus, civil disobedience that is admirable and useful should fall under the protected speech strategy, just as should admirable and useful speech. What remains for consideration are those cases of civil disobedience that meet this basic necessary condition for justified punishment, and which are objectively wrongful and/or socially harmful. While the question of the justifiability of punishment in such instances might call for resolution on a case-by-case basis, it certainly does not follow automatically that their punishment would be justified. As we said in introducing our theories of punishment, both of them provide only defeasible, pro tanto justification for punishing: that is, considerations (perhaps weighty ones) to be taken into account in deliberation, but not necessarily the only or the decisive considerations. Whether punishment of a particular act, or a particular act-type, is justifiable all things considered depends on a range of other factors such as the negative side-effects of punishment, or the available alternatives to punishment. Thus, although it may seem that a content-independent justification for civil disobedience would be incompatible with either the deterrent or the retributive theory, the consequences for individual autonomy of punishing conscientiously motivated lawbreaking might count more strongly than either deterrent or retributive considerations.

We have now reached the conclusion that punishing civil disobedients is often unjustified. If this is so, then how should the state adapt its criminal justice procedures to discriminate between the non-conscientiously motivated lawbreaker (whom, let us assume, the state does have a right to punish) and the genuine civil disobedient (whom it does not)?

Before we address this question directly, let us take note of a challenge that might be raised against the idea of differential treatment for civil disobedients. This challenge does not appeal to the implausible idea that the state cannot recognize values that trump the value of law-abidingness, but rather starts from the importance of the rule of law. A system of law, it might be argued, should have the rule of law virtues of clarity, comprehensibility, predictability, publicity, transparency, equity, and so on, and should restrict as far as possible the discretion granted to officials. The ideal, in other words, is "the rule of law, not men." The importance of this ideal is not only that these virtues allow people to know where they stand in respect of the law. It is also that it ensures that the law lives up to standards of equity and equal treatment, and reduces the scope for bias and abuse by those who hold the power to make the decisions. Therefore, the challenge goes, if civil disobedients are to be handled differently from ordinary lawbreakers, this will have to be done not just through the discretion of enlightened officials, but through the introduction of procedures adequate to discriminate among the relevant cases. The question is by what means the state can recognize and, as it were, *operationalize* the relevant difference between conscientious and non-conscientious lawbreaking, given that in general the state has a duty to take its laws seriously and use them as a basis for its treatment of all citizens. The reason that this is a challenge is that it would be difficult to capture the defining features of civil disobedience in a way that does not require the extensive use of judgment on the part of the officials applying the rule.

Now one response to this rule of law challenge would simply be to accept and defend the role of discretion in legal adjudication. Given the complexity of cases and the accompanying difficulty of comprehensive codification, a system that reduces adjudication to the application of predetermined rules may have to accept many false positives and false negatives, where authoritative judgments of criminal liability fail to track the purposes of criminal justice, whether these be deterrent, retributive, or whatever. In reality, criminal liability is not an all-or-nothing matter, and the criminal justice system *has* to allow for significant discretion being given to officials. For instance, some acts may be prohibited, but the prohibitions not enforced or enforced only selectively. Both police and prosecutors have significant levels of discretion.[45] Police have discretion, especially during peaceful public protests, in how they respond to dissenters, for example whether they corral them, arrest them, charge them, and so on. Similarly, a prosecuting agency charged with deciding whether a prosecution is in the "public interest" has the discretion not to proceed in cases of civil disobedience. Specifically, guidelines for prosecutors may give them powers to decide not to take a prosecution forward if they judge that the defendant was conscientiously motivated, had a just cause (in some sense of that term), and was acting in a necessary and proportionate way to support that cause. Of course, it would be a formidable task to spell out a way of understanding these conditions that could become consistent across cases; but such prosecutors' discretion has been used, for example, in the UK in recent cases of apparent mercy killing of persons with "locked-in" syndrome, and this way of dealing with what might be thought of as a kind of conscientious objection might provide a model for civil disobedience. The way to ensure that, despite such discretion, rule of law values are respected, need not be to tighten up codification but rather to ensure that there are layers of oversight of decision-making and the possibility of appeal by affected parties. Given that this works elsewhere in the criminal justice system, it could also allow prosecutors, judges, and juries the right to reduce or to dismiss charges where they judge that there is sufficient evidence that the case is one of civil disobedience.

Another alternative is that the prohibitions are indeed enforced through prosecution but the court recognizes that a defense (or various defenses) may be available to the defendant, such as an appeal to *necessity* or *demands of conviction*.[46] The use of such defenses might face the rule of law challenge outlined above; but the "oversight and appeal" response we have provided could again be perfectly adequate to see off this challenge.

Furthermore, even were such defenses unavailable, and a conviction ensues from prosecution, another way in which the specific character of civil disobedience could be recognized is if conscientious motivation is acknowledged as a mitigating factor at sentencing, or if the defendant is given a suspended sentence, that is, a sentence that will only be triggered if some further relevant offending occurs. To sum up, then, it is hard to deny that the punishment of genuine civil disobedients is unjustifiable and, furthermore, that there are numerous ways in which criminal justice systems could make the relevant discriminations.

CONCLUSION

In this chapter, we have looked at whether civil disobedients can justifiably be punished. After introducing the nature of civil disobedience and the standard justifications of punishment, we looked at two major strategies for justifying civil disobedience. According to the *limits of state authority* strategy, space opens up for justifiable civil disobedience when the state overreaches, or underreaches, its authority to legislate and enforce legislation. However, the fact of overreach affects the justifiability of punishment only if punishment itself requires legitimate authority: otherwise the justifiability of punishment would depend on the justifiability of taking the civil disobedience as an occasion for deterrence or retribution, for example. Thus, the justifiability of punishing civil disobedients depends, perhaps unsurprisingly, on what the right view of justifying punishment is. According to the *communicative value strategy*, civil disobedience should be protected from punishment for similar reasons to those for protecting free speech: in order to secure rights to political participation; or to further social or individual progress; or to allow people to be honest about who they are and what they believe. Whether and when the *communicative value strategy* could justify disobedients being punished would depend on whether the goals and values furthered by punishment are more important or urgent than the goals achieved by disobedience. Assuming that civil disobedience is sometimes justifiable, this has the consequence that punishment for illegal actions is sometimes unjustifiable. This is, of course, an important but also a potentially troublesome conclusion. A state committed to equality before the law will need some mechanism that can be applied consistently across cases of lawbreaking, and which will be sufficiently discriminating to pick out those cases of civil disobedience that it would be unjustifiable to punish: such a mechanism might involve a formalized process to decide whether or not to prosecute, or a set of recognized and accepted defenses available to disobedients, or standardized processes for mitigation in sentence.

NOTES

1. In Rosa Parks's case, all of the seats in the whites-only area filled up and she refused to give up her seat in the "colored section" to the next white person who boarded the bus. The driver evicted her and contacted the police to arrest her.

2. Hannah Arendt, *Crises of the Republic: Lying in Politics, Civil Disobedience, On Violence, Thoughts on Politics and Revolution* (New York: Harcourt, 1972), 56.

3. Not all people who find a given law or policy indefensible are in a position to breach it directly. When a state decides to go to war, for example, most citizens are not in a position to engage in direct disobedience of an order to fight.

4. John Rawls, *A Theory of Justice* (Cambridge, Mass.: Harvard University Press, 1971), 366. Hugo A. Bedau, "On Civil Disobedience," *Journal of Philosophy*, 58, no. 21 (1961): 653–61.

5. This claim depends on the assumption that Rawls would adhere to his publicity condition in nonideal circumstances such as segregated Alabama.

6. Joseph Raz,*The Authority of Law: Essays on Law and Morality*, 2nd ed. (Oxford: Oxford University Press, 2009), ch. 14; Kimberley Brownlee, *Conscience and Conviction: The Case for Civil Disobedience* (Oxford: Oxford University Press, 2012), ch. 1.

7. Jeanne Theoharis, "How History Got the Rosa Parks Story Wrong," *Washington Post*, December, 2015, www.washingtonpost.com/poste verything/wp/2015/12/01/how-history-got-the-rosa-parks-story-wrong/.

8. Rawls, *Theory of Justice*, 366.

9. Raz, *Authority of Law*, 267; David Lefkowitz, "On a Moral Right to Civil Disobedience," *Ethics*, 117 (2007): 202–33.

10. Rawls, *Theory of Justice*, ch. vi; Lefkowitz, "On a Moral Right to Civil Disobedience," 202–33.

11. William E. Scheuerman, "Taking Snowden Seriously: Civil Disobedience for an Age of Total Surveillance," in *The Snowden Reader*, ed. David P. Fidler (Bloomington, IN: Indiana University Press, 2015), 70–87; "Whistleblowing as Civil Disobedience," *Philosophy and Social Criticism*, 40, no. 7 (2014): 609–28.

12. David Boonin, *The Problem of Punishment* (Cambridge: Cambridge University Press, 2008). Christopher Heath Wellman, *Rights Forfeiture and Punishment* (Oxford: Oxford University Press, 2017); Victor Tadros, *The Ends of Harm* (Oxford: Oxford University Press, 2011); and Christopher Bennett, *The Apology Ritual: A Philosophical Theory of Punishment* (Cambridge: Cambridge University Press, 2008).

13. Jeremy Bentham, *An Introduction to the Principles of Morals and Legislation* (1789), various editions, ch. 13 §1.

14. Tadros, *The Ends of Harm*.

15. Robert Ladenson, "In Defense of a Hobbesian Conception of Law," *Philosophy and Public Affairs*, 9 (1980): 134–59.

16. Wellman, *Rights Forfeiture and Punishment*.

17. John Locke, *Two Treatises of Government, Second Treatise* (1689), various editions, ch. 9.

18. Christopher Bennett, "The Varieties of Retributive Experience," *Philosophical Quarterly*, 52 (2002): 145–63.

19. Michael Moore, *Placing Blame: A Theory of the Criminal Law* (Oxford: Oxford University Press, 2010), ch. 3.

20. G. Strawson, "The Impossibility of Moral Responsibility," *Philosophical Studies*, 74 (1994): 5–24.

21. Locke, *Two Treatises*.

22. Jean Hampton, "The Moral Education Theory of Punishment," *Philosophy and Public Affairs*, 13 (1984): 208–38.

23. R.A. Duff, *Punishment, Communication, and Community* (Oxford: Oxford University Press, 2001); Andrew von Hirsch, *Censure and Sanctions* (Oxford: Oxford University Press, 1993); Bennett, *The Apology Ritual*.

24. Malcolm Thorburn, "Criminal Law as Public Law," in *Philosophical Foundations of Criminal Law*, eds. R.A. Duff and S. Green (Oxford: Oxford University Press, 2011); Alan Brudner, *Punishment and Freedom* (Oxford: Oxford University Press, 2009).

25. Robert Paul Wolff, *In Defense of Anarchism* (New York: Harper and Row, 1970).

26. Thomas Christiano, "Authority," *The Stanford Encyclopedia of Philosophy*, ed. Edward N. Zalta (Spring 2013), https://plato.stanford.edu/archives/spr2013/entries/authority/.

27. For an argument that a further conception is required, see Christopher Bennett, "The Authority of Moral Oversight: On the Legitimacy of Criminal Law," *Legal Theory*, 25 (2019): 153–77.

28. Kent Greenawalt, *Conflicts of Law and Morality* (Oxford: Oxford University Press, 1987); Rawls, *A Theory of Justice*, ch. vi. Some thinkers question whether *civility* is a necessary condition for justified political disobedience, arguing that, under certain conditions, *uncivil disobedience* – disobedience that fails to meet one or more of Rawls's definitional criteria or fails to be civil (i.e. conscientious and suitably constrained) according to other accounts – can nonetheless be justified, even in liberal democratic societies. See Ten Herng-Lai, "Justifying Uncivil Disobedience," in *Oxford Studies in Political Philosophy*, vol. 5, eds. D. Sobel, P. Valentyne, and S. Wall (Oxford: Oxford University Press (2019), 90–116; and Candice Delmas, *A Duty to Resist* (Oxford: Oxford University Press, 2019).

29. Rawls, *A Theory of Justice*, 319ff.

30. Ronald Dworkin, "On Not Prosecuting Civil Disobedience," *New York Review of Books*, June 6, 1968, www.nybooks.com/articles/1968/06/06/on-not-prosecuting-civil-disobedience/.

31. Delmas, *A Duty to Resist*; Michael Walzer, "The Obligation to Disobey," *Ethics*, 77 (1967): 163–75.

32. Brownlee, *Conscience and Conviction*, ch. 6.

33. Joseph Raz, "The Problem of Authority: Revisiting the Service Conception," *Minnesota Law Review*, 90 (2006): 1003–44.

34. Brownlee, *Conscience and Conviction*, ch. 6.

35. Raz, *The Authority of Law*.

36. Lefkowitz, "On a Moral Right to Civil Disobedience."

37. John Stuart Mill, *On Liberty* (1859), various editions.

38. Brownlee, *Conscience and Conviction*, ch. 5.

39. Daniel Markovits, "Democratic Disobedience," *Yale Law Journal*, 114 (2005): 1897–952.

40. Brownlee, *Conscience and Conviction*, 12 and ch. 5.

41. I.H. Dennis, "Necessity as a Defense to Crime," *Criminal Law and Philosophy*, 3 (2009): 30.

42. Candice Delmas, "From Resistance to Dissent and Back: De-Constitutionalizing Civil Disobedience?" in *The Cambridge Handbook of Constitutional Theory*, eds. Jeff King and Richard Bellamy (Cambridge: Cambridge University Press, forthcoming).

43. Thom Brooks, "A Defence of Jury Nullification," *Res Publica*, 10 (2004): 401–23.

44. Daniel Weinstock, "How Democratic Is Civil Disobedience?" *Criminal Law and Philosophy*, 10, no. 4 (2015): 707–20.

45. William Smith, "Policing Civil Disobedience," *Political Studies*, 60, no. 4 (2012): 826–42; William Smith "Civil Disobedience and the Public Sphere," *The Journal of Political Philosophy*, 19, no. 2 (2011): 145–66; and William Smith, *Civil Disobedience and Deliberative Democracy* (New York: Routledge, 2013).

46. Brownlee, *Conscience and Conviction*, chs. 5 and 6.

PART III **Changing Circumstances, Political Consequences**

12 Global Citizenship, Global Civil Disobedience, and Political Vices

Luis Cabrera

Civil disobedience is typically characterized as morally principled, deliberate, and publicly enacted violation of law by individuals, who do not then seek to evade arrest. It is framed as a "civil" way for citizens to challenge possibly unjust laws or policies: one that is in broad fidelity to their domestic rule of law and good citizenship, even when it involves the refusal to obey some specific law.[1] Similarly, a number of commentators have sought to show that some acts which cross state territorial or citizenship boundaries should be understood as trans-state or global civil disobedience. They have focused on deliberate, principled violations of a state's law by non-citizen activists, asylum seekers, and unauthorized migrants, among others.[2]

This chapter details a conceptual framework of global citizenship within which such principled lawbreaking beyond the state can be situated. It also highlights a significant underlying distinction between domestic and suprastate civil disobedience which has received relatively little attention in the recent literature. That is, a range of acts commonly characterized as domestic civil disobedience can be understood as responses to collective political recalcitrance, where political majorities or dominant power holders formally recognize the standing of others to give input as political equals but largely ignore their interests in the laws actually produced and enforced. By contrast, most acts of resistance which cross citizenship boundaries will be more aptly understood as responses to political arrogance. They involve an inappropriate rejection of others' standing to give input or lodge formal challenges.[3] The distinction is significant because it can help to highlight ways in which lawbreaking beyond the state that does not meet the strict requirements of civil disobedience may still be understood as morally principled and possibly justifiable. Emphasis is given here to unauthorized migration as a potentially justifiable form of conscientious evasion.

The chapter is structured as follows: the first section presents conceptions of civil disobedience and discusses political vices of recalcitrance and arrogance as provocations to principled lawbreaking. The next section works to show how it can be conceptually coherent to posit conceptions of citizenship beyond the state as contexts for civil disobedience and related resistance. Some trans-state and global cases are discussed which display some standard features of civil disobedience.[4] Full analysis of such cases, however, helps to highlight how political arrogance is much more frequently in play than recalcitrance. This limits the corrective or constructive potential of principled lawbreaking, puts lawbreakers at much greater risk, and may justify conscientious evasion or other forms of resistance. Overall, it is argued, an emphasis on political vices can give important guidance on identifying forms of trans-state and global lawbreaking that can be seen as principled, possibly justifiable, and deserving of some leniency.

DOMESTIC CITIZENSHIP, POLITICAL VICES, AND PRINCIPLED LAWBREAKING

Civil disobedience is standardly situated within a framework of citizenship theory and practice, especially in democratic societies. It involves challenges to laws or policies which disobedients believe to be unjust, or more specifically that may be inconsistent with the foundational moral principles informing their society's political and legal institutions. The violation could be of the law in question, or it could involve blocking traffic or other disruptive activities aimed at generating attention for the broader challenge. The latter tactics were, for example, widely used in the waves of protests in the United States over police treatment of African Americans, triggered by the death of George Floyd in custody in May 2020.[5] Other standardly cited features include challengers first trying to use ordinary legislative and legal procedures, and openly perpetrating the lawbreaking, with the aim of communicating resistance and persuading co-citizens to also reject the law or policy. Significantly here, civil disobedients are also expected not to try to evade arrest, as a means of demonstrating their general commitment to the rule of law in their society, and as a further means of publicity or communication.[6] An implication of such a requirement is that disobedients have some expectation that they will not be subjected to unduly harsh punishment after arrest, and that they have some claim to leniency from authorities.

Numerous other forms of domestic law breaking can be identified that are motivated by adherence to principle, or can be framed as normatively justifiable, as opposed to more standard criminal acts motivated by anger, for personal gain not tied to basic needs fulfillment, etc. Such principled acts are typically defined in relation to civil disobedience, with emphasis on standard features they lack. For example, lawbreaking motivated by conscientious objection typically lacks an emphasis on publicity or communication, though objectors do not necessarily seek to avoid arrest. By contrast, such avoidance of arrest is central to forms of conscientious evasion, which is often viewed as a flawed form of principled resistance. Robert Goodin, for example, characterizes those unwilling to accept the consequences of their violation as "just ordinary law breakers."[7] Finally, radical protests, including terror attacks, lack the "civil" dimension, in that they seek to force change rather than persuade co-citizens to support it.[8]

Political vices and virtues have received little explicit attention in the recent civil disobedience literature, though they can be understood as central to it and related types of lawbreaking. William Scheuerman, for example, indicates the vice of political recalcitrance when he observes that, in the liberal approach which has been most prominent since roughly the late 1960s, civil disobedience is understood as "a useful corrective to overbearing political majorities that periodically threaten minority rights."[9] Political recalcitrance again entails a recognition of the formal standing of others to offer input in law or policy making, but also a tendency to ignore their interests or rights in the actual laws produced and enforced. As expressed by Mark Button, in his highly instructive, book-length treatment of political vices, political recalcitrance is manifest in "the settled indifference to the morally valid claims of others." It is typically associated with a rigid democratic majoritarianism, in which majority members implicitly claim an absolute mandate to rule in accordance with their own interests or views.[10]

In such cases of political recalcitrance, civil disobedience may be undertaken in part to call attention to the ignored interests or violated rights, and to persuade the majority to address the harms which have ensued – the "corrective" function noted by Scheuerman. The standard expectation is that such a process would take place within the political system as configured, rather than requiring a more fundamental change. There certainly can be cases, however, of endemic and long-term recalcitrance, as in states which see multiple generations living under the rule of a dominant single party, or are otherwise illiberal or quasi-authoritarian democracies. A need for more extensive systemic change incorporating checks on majority power could be indicated.

The vice of political arrogance, by contrast, involves a more comprehensive rejection of others' standing. Where the recalcitrant at least acknowledges the formal standing of others to give input and lodge challenges, and goes through the motions of a fair decision process, the arrogant reject any such input or challenge when they should not. Where political arrogance obtains, the remedy is thus likely to involve more extensive corrective action and constructive institutional change.[11] It may also justifiably be challenged through forms of principled resistance which are less restrictive or demanding on lawbreakers than standard civil disobedience, including conscientious evasion or, as some commentators have suggested, possibly the coercion of others.[12]

Political arrogance may be manifest in formally unequal citizenship, and especially in lesser participation rights for some longstanding minority groups within a society, or de facto such inequality, where all groups are formally included but some minority groups are prevented from actually participating. Unlike in circumstances of political recalcitrance, dominant groups again do not typically go through the motions of allowing equal participation by all in the polity. Thus, the excluded will typically have fewer means available to challenge the denial of even their most basic rights.

In general, the more that vices of recalcitrance and especially arrogance obtain within a system, the less plausible it may be for individuals to address injustices through the ordinary channels of that system. The more severe the injustices – the more they threaten people's most basic interests and rights – the more that some deviations from standard requirements of civil disobedience may be justifiable. Alternately, virtues such as political humility can be understood as central to more defensible practices of political citizenship. Political humility entails not some form of deference or submission to others, but a full recognition of the equal standing of all persons in a set to give input as equals, and to make use of mechanisms for deliberation, publicity, and formal legal or ombuds challenge.[13] It can thus be seen as foundational to practices of *good* citizenship, involving the good-faith consideration of others' input and interests, and a rejection of political recalcitrance. It is presented here as an overarching aim toward which various kinds of principled resistance are or could be oriented.

Overall, an emphasis on political vices should give clearer guidance on justifiable types of resistance than, for example, Rawls's much-discussed stipulation that civil disobedience is appropriate in societies which are "nearly just."[14] It also helps to highlight features not fully captured by Andrew Sabl's sympathetic reinterpretation of the near-justice presumption. For Sabl, a theoretically consistent interpretation of nearly just would include even clearly hierarchical and segregated societies, so long as the in-group observes a moral code among its own members which could be cited in actions by outgroups seeking full inclusion. Such an approach, however, would not fully capture ways in which the type of political arrogance described by Sabl could justify responses beyond strict civil disobedience, especially where formal inclusion is not a near-term prospect. I return to the political vices below, as provocations to trans-state and global civil disobedience, and conscientious evasion.[15]

A FRAMEWORK OF GLOBAL CITIZENSHIP

Many accounts of trans-state and global civil disobedience posit some notion of global citizenship within which the principled lawbreaking is situated.[16] Yet, it remains the case that, with the partial exception of the European Union, and the possible exception of some other regional organizations as they develop, there is no formalized regime of democratic citizenship beyond the state. Critics have thus long challenged the coherence of a conception of global citizenship[17] – and by extension of *global* civil disobedience as a corrective and potentially constructive practice within it.

In response, we can first note a challenge to a corresponding presumption about the robustness or comprehensiveness of domestic citizenship regimes. That is, many of the elements of citizenship within states are acknowledged to be in development, or in need of significant further development, even by theorists who reject global citizenship as incoherent because it is not sufficiently developed. Elements would include an understanding of the nature of the individual agents acting as citizens, of what binds them together in political community; the rights they hold as citizens, and the specific types of duties they should be asked to discharge correlative to those rights. Most essentially here, they include the substance of citizenship and the status and institutions of citizenship. The substance is the overarching good toward which duties are oriented, and which citizenship practice is ultimately to realize. It could be some conception of basic rights, or more demanding ideals of reciprocity, justice, etc. The status of citizenship includes formally equal "trappings" of citizenship such as passports. Institutions seek to back such trappings and the social guarantees they imply, as well as to promote the substance of citizenship more broadly.

The need to advance the development of specific elements of citizenship has in fact been a staple of domestic citizenship theory. Some accounts, for example, focus on a reciprocity-based substance of citizenship to be promoted among domestic co-citizens.[18] *Developing* reciprocity and mutual recognition among citizens is presented as the ultimate aim of domestic citizenship, and action that those aiming to be good citizens will take.[19] Similarly, domestic political institutions capable of actually backing citizen status and rights/entitlements may be significantly underdeveloped. For example, the Fragile States Index initiative reports that, of 178 states assessed, 70 fall into a "warning" or "alert" category for institutional stability, meaning that their capacity to actually back the entitlements and substance of citizenship is often severely limited.[20] The Rule of Law Index[21] finds protections for fundamental rights, basic order and security highly uncertain in scores of states, and other longstanding surveys find democratic indicators similarly under pressure and in fact declining in recent years.[22]

Even in some affluent states, the actual backing of citizen rights/entitlements can be highly precarious, with large gaps in social welfare guarantees. In the United States, one of the richest states per capita, more than 550,000 persons are estimated to be homeless.[23] Such figures pose a challenge to disanalogy claims by global citizenship critics such as Brett Bowden. He asserts that being a global citizen is tantamount to being a stateless person, while "Being a citizen of any given state is about having a legally constituted authority charged with looking out for and guaranteeing the welfare of you and your fellow citizens."[24] In many states, the ability or willingness to back a range of such guarantees is lacking. In this and the other ways noted, the sharp disanalogy drawn between domestic citizenship and other forms is weakened.

What then of actual developmental regimes of suprastate citizenship? These are most evident at the regional level, where again the

European Union has formalized regional citizenship and free movement among more than two dozen nation states. It provides an important partial exemplar or laboratory for exploring the potential for and challenges to suprastate citizenship development. So do regional organizations such as South America's Mercosur, which has formalized some free movement and considered a formal citizenship statute,[25] as well as other regional projects which have sought to advance more basic worker mobility. None can serve as some ideal type for regional citizenship, given the persistent democratic deficits and lack of social welfare emphases in the EU system, and halting progress toward participatory regional governance elsewhere. The EU in particular, however, provides a framework in which regional citizenship has been formalized, and where some meaningful acts of trans-state/regional civil disobedience can be identified, on which more below.[26]

How, then, might we identify elements of citizenship in development at the global level, or which could be advanced there? One way is to adopt a developmental conceptual framework in which persons act *like* global citizens, or enact some elements and practices of global citizenship, when they:

1. reach across international boundaries, or internal boundaries of differential citizenship;
2. help protect the fundamental rights that would be secured under a more just system of global institutions: one which gave due equal consideration to the interests of all persons; and
3. (in an institutionally oriented vein) support the development of such a system.[27]

Such a framework posits a rights-based substance of citizenship. It is informed by, though not strictly limited to,[28] the "global normative charter" of treaties and some related declarations enshrining rights and an underlying principle of human moral equality. The latter principle, for example, is prominent in the Preamble to the 1945 United Nations Charter, which specifies that the organization was created in part "to reaffirm faith in fundamental human rights, in the dignity and worth of the human person, in the equal rights of men and women and of nations large and small."[29] Such rights are given further shape and substance in the nonbinding 1948 Universal Declaration of Human Rights, and especially in the binding International Covenants on Economic, Social and Cultural Rights (ICESCR) and Civil and Political Rights (ICCPR), ratified by more than 165 and 170 states respectively, as well as in numerous other UN rights treaties.[30]

As in the accounts of domestic citizenship, an account of global citizenship would identify some primary duties to help develop the identified substance of citizenship –individual rights protections – across state boundaries. Examples of those assuming such duties would include Mexican citizens providing shelter and food to unauthorized immigrants from Central America who are struggling to reach the United States. Many such migrants are assaulted and robbed on the journey, or face exhaustion and injury from long treks and/or clinging to the tops of trains, and they are in dire need of assistance.[31] Others would include humanitarian patrollers in the US southwest delivering water, food, and first aid to unauthorized entrants at severe risk on desert crossings, many of whom have been lost or left behind by their smugglers.[32] Such migrants themselves may be framed as "mobile global citizens," crossing territorial and citizenship boundaries to address gaps in economic welfare rights protections for themselves and their families.

Global citizen actors would also include persons seeking to use available global institutions to better secure the rights of their highly vulnerable domestic co-citizens. For example, activists in India's National Campaign on Dalit Human Rights have used United Nations human rights bodies and oversight processes to challenge their own government's efforts against caste discrimination. They have given particular emphasis to the International Convention to Eliminate All Forms of Racial Discrimination, to which India has been a state party for more than fifty years. Their actions, I have argued, are directly salient to criterion (3) of the global citizenship framework above: supporting the development of global institutions which would better back a rights-based substance of global citizenship. That is, they have not only highlighted gaps in rights protections domestically, but also the underdevelopment of global institutions tasked with rights oversight and advancement.[33] They have thus played a potentially institutionally developmental or constructive role, though not one focused on principled lawbreaking.

How, then, might we identify trans-state or global civil disobedients within such a framework of global citizenship? One key factor is that those engaging in civil disobedience beyond the state, or at least acting *like* trans-state and global civil disobedients, can do so by reference to the same foundational moral principles. This may be done explicitly, through specific rights claims, or it may be implicit, through actions broadly consistent with such claims.[34] The next section discusses some salient trans-state and global cases, while also showing how most involve responses to political arrogance rather than recalcitrance. The significance again is that lawbreaking which does not meet the full requirements of civil disobedience, including conscientious evasion, may thus be justifiable in most such cases.

TRANS-STATE, REGIONAL, AND GLOBAL CIVIL DISOBEDIENCE

Trans-state civil disobedience, sometimes called "transnational," can be understood as the principled violation of a state's law or policy by individuals who are not citizens or authorized permanent residents of that state. It may also involve acts targeting a law or policy by the state's own citizens on behalf of outsiders. In either case, the principled claim is at root that the state's law is misaligned with the foundational moral principles of the current global system.

By contrast, acts of *global* civil disobedience would involve claims implicating structural principles of the global system itself, as misaligned with its foundational moral principles. Examples could be public protests by unauthorized migrants communicating claims for inclusion in a state.[35] The target in such cases is not a specific state law or policy. Rather, the lawbreaking represents a more generic violation of the systemic principles of sovereignty affirming each state's right to restrict entry to and independently govern its own territory.

Other prima facie cases of global civil disobedience could include individuals deliberately violating a state's laws – blocking city streets, hanging banners from buildings – to challenge rules developed in and backed by a treaty-based international organization such as the World Trade Organization.[36] Global structural principles also are typically found at the root of such challenges, for example where states' governments exercise privileges of sovereignty to exclude individuals and civil society groups from direct input on such global rules, or greatly restrict the input afforded to citizens' representatives.

In terms of more specific cases, we can note first Greenpeace's Brent Spar campaign as a possible instance of trans-state civil disobedience. The much-chronicled 1995 action involved an international team of activists occupying the Brent Spar floating oil storage facility, in protest of the British government's approval to scuttle it in waters northwest of Scotland. Greenpeace objected that the facility would contaminate the waters with oil, heavy metals, and radioactive waste. The group also objected that Brent Spar was only the first such move, with possibly hundreds of potentially damaging sea disposals like it to come.

The case thus involved foreign nationals targeting a British government policy through violation of the property rights of a firm (Royal Dutch Shell) incorporated in Britain. The force of their claims to *principled* lawbreaking came from underlying claims that the UK policy was misaligned with the foundational moral principles of the global system, specifically with treaty-based security and welfare rights which comprise a broader right to a safe global environment.[37] The activists and their allies communicated their claims to British citizens and globally, and they made themselves vulnerable to arrest, in fact remaining at the site until their apprehension.

The lawbreaking thus features some paradigmatic characteristics of civil disobedience. Yet, it also deviates from a strict interpretation of civil disobedience, in that the non-British activists themselves did not have formal standing to give input on the policy process relating to the decision in question. Nor would they be able to influence as political equals any relevant subsequent decisions – to exhaust legislative and legal remedies in any further cases. And significantly, as nonnationals they would not necessarily receive equal protection with citizens under British law, or have an expectation of leniency in treatment. Thus, their actions cannot be strictly be framed as civil disobedience: acts of corrective citizenship in response to political recalcitrance by the British government.[38] Rather, the provocation would primarily be one of political arrogance, involving an inappropriate rejection of the standing of persons to give input on or lodge challenges to a possibly harmful or unjust law or policy.[39] The distinction again indicates that other forms of principled resistance, including conscientious evasion, might be justifiable in such cases.

Some cases involving the violation of entry laws by asylum seekers would have a better claim to being framed as trans-state civil disobedience enacted in response to trans-state political recalcitrance. That is because the standing of such persons to at least make claims for (or give input on) their own inclusion into another state has been affirmed under the 1951 United Nations Convention Relating to the Status of Refugees, which some 145 states have ratified. In addition, some such cases have featured trans-state civil disobedience by citizens of the receiving state, who have reached across boundaries of citizenship to help the asylum seekers enter without authorization.

A prominent example is the Sanctuary Movement of the 1980s. Then, some US citizens helped Central American asylum seekers enter covertly after the US government had decided on dubious geopolitical grounds that they should be considered "economic migrants" and their asylum claims overwhelmingly rejected.[40] Ultimately hundreds of churches and communities across the United States publicly declared themselves sanctuaries. Those who received sanctuary were requesting an extension in the public eye, and a number of asylum seekers also publicly communicated their claims.[41] Those organizing the sanctuaries and transport to Canada for many asylum seekers communicated their reasons widely to their co-citizens, and all were exposed to arrest alongside asylum seekers. More than a dozen Sanctuary organizers in fact were arrested and prosecuted – actions which the disobedients used to call further attention to their claims, and ultimately to realize some change within US legislative processes.

Such a case thus displays numerous core features of trans-state civil disobedience provoked by trans-state recalcitrance. The United States had formally affirmed under international law the standing of extremely vulnerable persons to make a claim for their own inclusion in the US polity as asylum seekers. At the same time, it had adopted a policy under which the large majority of decisions made did not actually take Central American asylum seekers' input or interests into account. It thus had established a context within which trans-state civil disobedience, more strictly interpreted, could be enacted both by asylum seekers and their US allies.

Some cases have similarly emerged in recent years of trans-state *and* regional civil disobedience by asylum seekers in response to political recalcitrance. For example, some asylum seekers have refused to abide by an EU regional agreement dictating that their claims must be filed in the first EU country they reach. In perhaps the highest profile such case, in 2015 thousands of asylum seekers initially entering Hungary but trying to reach northern Europe were held by authorities at a Budapest train station. Several hundred decided to defy their detention and march some 150 kilometers away to the Austrian border. As Ali Emre Benli details, their actions, which were widely chronicled on television and other media, displayed several standard features of civil disobedience. Those included civility, conscientiousness, publicity or communication, and subjection to possible arrest.[42]

The case also displays features of trans-state civil disobedience, since the marchers were challenging their specific treatment under highly restrictive asylum policies that Hungary had adopted. At the same time, they engaged in prima facie regional civil disobedience by challenging the EU regional policy restricting asylum claims to the first EU country entered. Numerous similar cases have been recorded in recent years, including ones where asylum seekers engaging in disobedience were aided by citizens of EU states.[43]

Such actions by EU citizens, as well as the US citizens acting in the Sanctuary Movement, would most clearly fit the definition of trans-state civil disobedience. They took principled action on behalf of those who did not share their state citizenship to challenge actions by their state which were potentially misaligned with the global normative charter. In the case of asylum seekers themselves, however, the claim to strict civil disobedience is more tenuous. That is because the right of such persons to make a claim for their own inclusion is not inclusion itself. In cases where asylum seekers' claims are almost categorically rejected, and on dubious grounds, the provocation to lawbreaking could be more aptly characterized as political arrogance. It could justify deviations from strict standards of civil disobedience by actors, including possibly the evasion of authorities and unauthorized residence.

Political arrogance is more clearly foregrounded in many cases which display features of *global* civil disobedience. The global variant again involves individual violations of states' laws which represent challenges to more generic framework principles of sovereignty in the current global system. I have argued at length elsewhere that the system is fundamentally oriented to political arrogance.[44] That is, it inappropriately enables states to summarily reject the standing of individuals to lodge rights-based challenges, whether that of their own citizens/population or outsiders. In relation to their own populations, states' leaders effectively cite the prerogatives of sovereignty they possess in their ascribed roles as guarantors of individual rights – the rights at the heart of the global normative charter – in rejecting claims about their flawed actual performance as rights guarantors. Such dynamics were in play when Indian officials rejected the standing of Dalit activists to challenge domestic anti-caste discrimination policies in UN rights bodies, while also rejecting meaningful oversight from those bodies. In relation to outsiders' claims for economic and related rights, including by would-be migrants, governments implicitly cite all states' roles as stewards of their own citizens' rights as reason to reject, while ignoring vast differences in states' ability or willingness to actually serve as rights guarantors.

With such contextual claims in mind, we can consider first some prima facie global civil disobedience actions involving unauthorized migrants. A well-known case is that of the Sans-Papiers movement. It was publicly launched in 1996 with the months-long occupation of a Paris church by some 300 migrants from African countries. Occupiers released a public statement declaring that they would no longer hide in the shadows, and that: "We are people like everyone else …. We demand papers so that we are no longer victims of arbitrary treatment by the authorities, employers and landlords …. We demand papers so that we no longer suffer the humiliation of controls based on our skin, detentions, deportations, the break-up of families, the constant fear."[45]

The occupiers made primary reference to their moral status as human beings in grounding their claims for inclusion and good treatment. Such claims are consistent with the equal moral status foregrounded in the global rights instruments noted above. They offered a generic principled claim for inclusion and the permissibility of their violation of entry law. It was a claim applicable to any state seeking to enforce the territorial rights granted to it in a system of sovereign states. They also perpetrated their violations publicly and with the aim of communicating their stance, while exposing themselves to possible arrest. Again, however, their standing to give input on, or make claims for, their own inclusion is not recognized by states in the current system. If their principled lawbreaking was in fact justifiable, it would be a justified response not to political recalcitrance but broader political arrogance.

The potential significance of such a distinction between the vices can be reinforced through attention to more recent cases. In one extended campaign, more than three million unauthorized migrants and supporters marched through US cities and took part in mass absentee days in 2006–07 to call for their inclusion and a path to citizenship.[46] Prominent at numerous such events were signs declaring "No human being is illegal." Related US protest actions have involved persons brought into the United States as children in families entering without authorization. They have sought in part the passage of "Dream Act" legislation that would regularize their status. The Obama administration suspended deportation of "Dreamers" in 2012 and offered them renewable work permits, but the Trump administration from 2017 sought to reverse those moves.[47]

Each such case displays on its face some standard features of global civil disobedience. Unauthorized residents of states made claims for formal inclusion and domestic civil rights. They did so publicly, communicating to others in their host states, by civil means and exposing themselves to arrest. How, then, does political arrogance figure in such cases? First, it might be argued that it doesn't in the case of the Dreamers: their protest actions clearly represented civil disobedience provoked by political recalcitrance, given that the Obama administration had affirmed at least some formal standing for them as members of the political community. Yet, it is precisely because they did not hold secure such standing that their inclusion proved tenuous and temporary. Dreamers are not able to claim that their exclusion from membership is misaligned with the foundational principles of their domestic society, in the way that other civil disobedients have.

For example, when Martin Luther King, Jr., called for equal civil rights for African Americans, he highlighted some ways in which they were being treated inconsistently with their recognized status *as* American citizens. Such a claim was central to King's "I Have a Dream Speech" of 1963. He noted that the Constitution, along with the Declaration, represented "a promise that all men, yes, black men as well as white men, would be guaranteed the unalienable rights of life, liberty, and the pursuit of happiness."[48] Thus, King justified large-scale civil disobedience in large part as a response to political recalcitrance – though arrogance also would have been in play where persons were prevented by threats of violence or other means from any political participation.

Unauthorized migrants, even those who were brought to a country so young that they have known no other, cannot make their claims for inclusion from the same position as King and his co-activists. Since their status as members of the US polity is highly insecure, they face a chronic risk of expulsion. Thus, when they publicly identify themselves, protest, and make claims for inclusion, they do not engage in resistance strictly provoked by the inappropriate neglect of their interests/rights in a domestic system formally tasked with protecting and promoting them. Rather, they respond to a more comprehensive political arrogance and challenge their lack of formal standing.

The Dreamers' actions, alongside more typical forms of unauthorized immigration, can be seen as an important broader challenge to the political arrogance of the current global system. In that system again, states' sovereign powers, including ones to dismiss individual rights claims without input or challenge, are ultimately grounded in a global imperative to protect individual rights. Entry violations by persons who are trying to address gaps in rights protections for themselves and/or family members would be in broad fidelity to the foundational moral principles of the current system.[49] Their actions can highlight deep tensions between the rights commitments in the global normative charter, including aspirational economic rights, and the segregated and exclusionary institutional structure of the system. The implication is that unauthorized entry can be characterized as a form of principled resistance – conscientious evasion – which is potentially justifiable, given the political context.[50] Rather than being grouped with "ordinary" lawbreaking, it would represent one form of lawbreaking which fulfils a principled or conscientiousness criterion and is one of the means of resistance available to relatively less affluent persons in a global system oriented to political arrogance and stark inequality.

POSSIBLE OBJECTIONS

It might be argued first that such actions fall outside of a framework of principled lawbreaking, because unauthorized entrants do not typically intend to challenge the justifiability of entry laws per se, but simply seek to better their own life opportunities through action that incidentally involves lawbreaking. They are not clearly conscientious evaders. The key factor, however, will not be whether unauthorized entrants intend to call attention to a potentially unjust feature of the global system, but whether their actions are consistent with the foundational moral principles.

Certainly intent can matter in this context, for example in the question of whether those who enter without authorization intend to observe a general fidelity to their receiving state's domestic laws, insofar as those are also in broad fidelity to the foundational moral principles. Smugglers who violate entry laws for the narrow purpose of carrying bales of marijuana to a drop-off point, returning, and doing the same repeatedly,[51] are not so clearly taking action consistent with principled resistance to political arrogance. If, however, unauthorized entry is broadly consistent with the foundational principles, there would be relatively little to distinguish it from lawbreaking motivated more clearly by opposition to entry laws or enforcement regimes – for example by citizens of the receiving state aiding asylum seekers or economic migrants in unauthorized entry.

The concern raised leads to a more general objection, that much principled resistance should itself be viewed as arrogant, in particular where lawbreakers do not make themselves subject to arrest. In evading, they claim inappropriate exemptions for themselves from the input or challenge of others who object to their actions – a hallmark feature of personal arrogance.[52] Again, however, unauthorized entrants do not hold formal standing in the system. They are not able to engage in reciprocity – to receive input or be challenged, nor especially to give input or challenges, as formally recognized equals. They have few means of advancing political humility in a system marked by political arrogance. Thus, their evasion is more clearly justifiable. They can, it should be noted, engage in de facto reciprocity, through seeking to act in ways consistent with the moral equality and rights of others in their host communities, which again can be manifest as broad fidelity to laws consistent with the global principles. This is not construed as some stringent practice of political obligation, but a more general fidelity to a rule of law consistent with moral equality, like that stipulated in conceptions of civil disobedience.

Such responses do not, of course, settle questions around the justifiability of all possible principled suprastate lawbreaking falling outside of strict civil disobedience. Important additional issues must be considered, including proportionality of response to various provocations, permissible means of responding, impact on the rights of other persons, among a range of others.[53] They do, however, indicate some reasons to view a form of lawbreaking perpetrated in the current system by tens of millions of people as principled and possibly justified.

CONCLUSION

This chapter has offered an approach to conceptualizing trans-state and global civil disobedience within a framework of global citizenship. Trans-state such actions have been presented as ones involving nonnationals of a state deliberately violating its laws to challenge a law or policy that may be misaligned with the commitments to human moral equality and individual rights in the UN Charter and numerous global rights treaties. Global civil disobedience entails claims, implicit or explicit, that structural principles of sovereignty themselves are misaligned with the foundational moral principles.

Forms of principled resistance have been distinguished partly by their relation to political vices. Civil disobedience was shown to be most aptly understood as a response to political recalcitrance: the affirmation of individuals' fully equal standing to give political input and lodge challenges, but also a neglect of their interests in decisions actually made. Political arrogance entails a more wholesale rejection of individuals' standing. It was shown that, while many cases of trans-state and global resistance display some standard features of civil disobedience, most are also enacted in circumstances of political arrogance rather than more moderate recalcitrance. In such circumstances, less stringent forms of principled resistance could be justifiable, including conscientious evasion. An implication is that much unauthorized migration may be justifiable as a form of conscientious evasion.

NOTES

1. See William E. Scheuerman, *Civil Disobedience* (Cambridge: Polity Press, 2018), 7; Kimberly Brownlee, *Conscience and Conviction: The Case for Civil Disobedience* (Oxford: Oxford University Press, 2012); Brownlee, "Civil Disobedience," *The Stanford Encyclopedia of Philosophy*, ed. Edward N. Zalta (Fall 2017), https://plato.stanford.edu/archives/fall2017/entries/civil-disobedience/.

2. See Luis Cabrera, *The Practice of Global Citizenship* (Cambridge: Cambridge University Press, 2010), 132–50; Michael Allen, "Civil Disobedience, Transnational," in *Encyclopedia of Global Justice*, vol. 1, ed. Deen K. Chatterjee (Dordrecht: Springer, 2011), 135–37; Allen, *Civil Disobedience in Global Perspective: Decency and Dissent over Borders, Inequities, and Government Secrecy* (Dordrecht: Springer, 2017); Temi Ogunye, "Global Justice and Transnational Civil Disobedience," *Ethics & Global Politics* 8, no. 1 (2015): 1–23; Rikke Wagner, "'Transnational Civil Dis/obedience' in the Danish Family Unification Dispute," *European Political Science Review* 7, no. 1 (2015): 43–62; William Smith, "Civil Disobedience as Transnational Disruption," *Global*

Constitutionalism 6, no. 3 (2017): 477–504; Ali Emre Benli, "March of Refugees: An Act of Civil Disobedience," *Journal of Global Ethics* 14, no. 3 (2018): 315–31; Steve Cooke, "Cosmopolitan Disobedience," *Journal of International Political Theory* (2019): 1–19, https://doi.org/10.1177/1755 088219850196; Frederic Megret, "Migrant Protests as a Form of Civil Disobedience: Which Cosmopolitanism?" in *Migration, Protest Movements and the Politics of Resistance*, eds. Tamara Caraus and Elena Paris (New York: Routledge, 2019), 29–50; see also Simon Caney, "The Right to Resist Global Injustice," in *The Oxford Handbook of Global Justice*, ed. Thom Brooks (Oxford: Oxford University Press, 2020), ch. 25; Gwilym David Blunt, *Global Poverty, Injustice and Resistance* (Cambridge: Cambridge University Press, 2020); and see Javier S. Hidalgo, *Unjust Borders: Individuals and the Ethics of Immigration* (New York: Routledge, 2019).

3. On those and other vices corrosive of democratic politics, see Mark Button, *Political Vices* (Oxford: Oxford University Press, 2016); for an account focused on global dimensions of such vices and corresponding political virtues, see Luis Cabrera, *The Humble Cosmopolitan: Rights, Diversity, and Trans-state Democracy* (New York: Oxford University Press, 2020), esp. chs. 2–4, 6.

4. For discussion of international civil disobedience, involving deliberate violations of international law by states, see Chapter 13 by David Lefkowitz in this volume; also Robert Goodin, "Towards an International Rule of Law: Distinguishing International Law-Breakers from Would-Be Law-Makers," *The Journal of Ethics* 9, nos. 1–2 (2005): 225–46.

5. Audra D.S. Burch, Weiyi Cai, Gabriel Gianordoli, Morrigan McCarthy and Jugal K. Patel, "How Black Lives Matter Reached Every Corner of American," *The New York Times*, June 13, 2020: www.nytimes.com/inte ractive/2020/06/13/us/george-floyd-protests-cities-photos.html.

6. See Brownlee, "Civil Disobedience."

7. Goodin, "Towards an International Rule of Law," 233–34; see Brownlee, *Conscience and Conviction*, 1–2.

8. See Brownlee, "Civil Disobedience," Section 1.3.

9. Scheuerman, *Civil Disobedience*, 6; see Rawls's well-known and often critically engaged treatment: John Rawls, *A Theory of Justice*, revised ed. (Cambridge, Mass.: Belknap Press of Harvard University Press, 1999), 319–43. See also the discussion of Rawls in Chapter 3 of this volume.

10. Button, *Political Vices*, 87; see Cabrera, *The Humble Cosmopolitan*, 38–40.

11. The corrective/constructive distinction is highlighted in Scheuerman's discussion of differences between Rawls's "static" liberal account and Jürgen Habermas's account of civil disobedience as integral to democratic contestation and prospects for more fundamental change: Scheuerman, *Civil Disobedience*, 76–80.

12. See Guy Aitchison, "Domination and Disobedience: Protest, Coercion and the Limits of an Appeal to Justice," *Perspectives on Politics* 16, no. 3 (2018): 666–79.

13. See Cabrera, *The Humble Cosmopolitan*, ch. 2.

14. Rawls, *A Theory of Justice*, 319; see Bernard Boxill, *Blacks and Social Justice* (Lanham, Md.: Rowman and Littlefield, 1992), ch. 10.

15. Andrew Sabl, "Looking Forward to Justice: Rawlsian Civil Disobedience and Its Non-Rawlsian Lessons," *The Journal of Political Philosophy* 9, no. 3 (2001): 307–30, at 310–12. For Sabl's realist views more generally, see Chapter 6 in this volume.

16. See Allen, "Civil Disobedience, Transnational"; Cooke, "Cosmopolitan Disobedience"; Siobhan O'Sullivan, Clare McCausland, and Scott Brenton, "Animal Activists, Civil Disobedience and Global Responses to Transnational Injustice," *Res Publica* 23, no. 3 (2017): 261–80.

17. Hannah Arendt, *Men in Dark Times* (New York: Harcourt Brace Jovanovich, 1968); see Andrew Mason, *Living Together as Equals: Demands of Citizenship* (Oxford: Oxford University Press, 2012), ch. 8. For a more detailed response to this objection, and cognate objections to duties of global justice, see Cabrera, *The Humble Cosmopolitan*, ch. 6.

18. See David Miller, *Citizenship and National Identity* (Cambridge: Polity Press, 2000), 89; Mason, *Living Together*, 36.

19. Mason, *Living Together*, 36.

20. Fund for Peace, "Fragile States Index 2018," *Fund for Peace*, accessed June 27, 2020, https://fragilestatesindex.org/.

21. World Justice Project, "Rule of Law Index 2017–2018," *World Justice Project*, accessed June 27, 2020, https://worldjusticeproject.org/our-work/wjp-rule-law-index/wjp-rule-law-index-2017%E2%80%932018.

22. See, for example, Freedom House, "Democracy in Retreat: Freedom in the World 2019," *Freedom House*, accessed June 27, 2020, https://freedomhouse.org/report/freedom-world/freedom-world-2019.

23. United States Department of Housing and Urban Development, "The 2018 Annual Homeless Assessment Report to Congress," accessed June 27, 2020, www.hudexchange.info/resource/5783/2018-ahar-part-1-pit-estimates-of-homelessness-in-the-us/.

24. Brett Bowden, "The Perils of Global Citizenship," *Citizenship Studies* 7, no. 3 (2003): 349–62, at 359.

25. Diego Acosta, "Global Migration Law and Regional Free Movement: Compliance and Adjudication – The Case of South America," *American Journal of International Law* 111 (2017): 159–64.

26. See, for example, Wagner's discussion of challenges to Danish family unification rules in the context of regional EU citizenship: Wagner, "Transnational Civil Dis/obedience."

27. Cabrera, *Practice*, 73; for an instructive, book-length treatment of the concept, see April Carter, *The Political Theory of Global Citizenship* (Abingdon: Routledge, 2001).

28. A rights-based conception of global citizenship is grounded in the fundamental presumption of human moral equality. Challenges might be raised to specific international treaty rights as inconsistent with such equality, for example, some types of group rights.

29. United Nations, "Charter of the United Nations," accessed June 27, 2020, www.un.org/en/charter-united-nations/.

30. United Nations Office of the High Commissioner for Human Rights, "The Core International Human Rights Instruments and Their Monitoring Bodies," accessed June 27, 2020, www.ohchr.org/en/profes sionalinterest/pages/coreinstruments.aspx.

31. Cabrera, *Practice*, 157–64; see Mark Lusk and Feliza Galindo, "Strength and Adversity: Testimonies of the Migration," *Social Development Issues* 39, no. 1 (2017): 11–28.

32. Cabrera, *Practice*, 107–18; for general discussions of civil society actors, migrants and asylum seekers in a global citizenship context, see Carter, *Political Theory of Global Citizenship*, chs. 5–6.

33. See Cabrera, *The Humble Cosmopolitan*, ch. 6.

34. See Cabrera, *Practice*, 147–49; see also Smith, "Civil Disobedience as Transnational Disruption," 480–86.

35. I discuss various types of unauthorized entry in a framework of global civil disobedience and conscientious evasion in Cabrera, *Practice*, ch. 5; see also Hidalgo, *Unjust Borders*, esp. chs. 5–7.

36. See Allen, "Civil Disobedience, Transnational."

37. Ogunye frames the Brent Spar action as justified by reference to a more general natural duty of justice: "Global Justice and Transnational Civil Disobedience," 16–17.

38. For related discussion of anti-whaling activism, see O'Sullivan, McCausland and Brenton, "Animal Activists."

39. The justification claim here is not strictly an "all affected" one, where those potentially affected by decisions should have input into the decision process. It is not presumed that lawbreakers would have to show likely impact to themselves for their actions to be justifiable. For relevant discussion, see Cooke, "Cosmopolitan Disobedience."

40. James W. Nickel, "Sanctuary, Asylum and Civil Disobedience," *In Defense of the Alien* 9 (1985): 176–87, at 180–81; see also Hidalgo, *Unjust Borders*, 1–3.

41. Nickel, "Sanctuary," 176.

42. Benli, "March of Refugees."

43. Ilker Ataç, Kim Rygiel and Maurice Stierl, "Introduction: The Contentious Politics of Refugee and Migrant Protest and Solidarity Movements: Remaking Citizenship from the Margins," *Citizenship Studies* 20, no. 5 (2016): 527–44.

44. Cabrera, *The Humble Cosmopolitan*, ch. 6.

45. Quoted in Teresa Hayter, *Open Borders: The Case Against Immigration Controls*, 2nd ed. (London: Pluto Press, 2004), 143.

46. Cabrera, *Practice*, 135; see also Megret, "Migrant Protests."

47. See Bill Ong Hing, "Beyond DACA – Defying Employer Sanctions through Civil Disobedience," *U.C. Davis Law Review* 52, no. 1 (2018): 299–342.

48. Martin Luther King, Jr., "I Have a Dream," in James M. Washington (ed.), *A Testament of Hope: The Essential Writings and Speeches of Martin Luther King, Jr.* (New York: Harper Collins), 217–20.

49. For survey responses by Mexican migrants on motivations to enter, see Emily Ryo, "Deciding to Cross: Norms and Economics of Unauthorized Migration," *American Sociological Review* 78, no.4 (2013): 574–603.

50. For a detailed discussion of such claims, though without the emphasis on political vices, see Cabrera, *Practice*, 132–50; see also Hidalgo, *Unjust Borders*.

51. Cabrera, *Practice*, 140.

52. See Alessandra Tanesini, "Calm Down, Dear: Intellectual Arrogance, Silencing and Ignorance," *Aristotelian Society Supplementary* 90, no.1 (2016): 71–92, at 76.

53. For a nuanced framework for analyzing such questions, see Caney, "The Right to Resist Global Injustice"; see also Sabl, "Looking Forward," 315, for bars on acts which could harm possibilities for future peaceful cooperation in a society.

I 3   Civil Disobedience by States?

David Lefkowitz

In this chapter I address three questions regarding civil disobedience by states. First, is state civil disobedience (henceforth, SCD) even possible, or do scholars, officials, activists, and members of the general public commit a category error when they apply the concept of civil disobedience to the actions of states? I argue for the former, while acknowledging that SCD differs in certain fundamental respects from more familiar examples of civil disobedience. Second, assuming SCD is possible, what conditions must it satisfy to be morally justifiable? Here I contend that considerations often thought to be relevant to the justifiability of civil disobedience in a domestic context, such as fidelity to the ideal of the rule of law, may frequently fail to be relevant to the justifiability of SCD. Third, are there any plausible examples of states engaging in (morally justifiable) civil disobedience? Though a number of theorists purport to have identified such cases, I argue that their conclusions rest on either a mistaken conception of civil disobedience or a failure to recognize that the illegal conduct in question does not satisfy all of the conditions necessary for an act to count as an instance of (morally justifiable) SCD. I conclude with two observations regarding theoretical reflection on SCD, and some speculation on why we are unlikely to observe any instances of it in the near future.

THE POSSIBILITY OF STATE CIVIL DISOBEDIENCE

Can states perform acts of civil disobedience? To answer this question, we must first characterize the concept of civil disobedience and

For their many helpful comments on this chapter, not all of which I was able to address here, I wish to thank Alejandro Chehtman, Francisco Garcia-Gibson, Nahuel Maisley, Julio Montero, Philip Pettit, Jose Luis Marti, and the other participants in the Conference on Global Democracy and Global Constitutionalism at the University of Buenos Aires Law School.

articulate precisely what we mean when we talk of states engaging in it. Any attempt to do so is bound to be contested.[1] Nevertheless, the analysis of the concept of civil disobedience that I offer here is both widely shared and has many elements in common with rival conceptions. As for how we should understand the idea of a state engaging in civil disobedience, I maintain that the characterization set out below accurately reflects the views of nearly all of the theorists who have written on this topic. Whether we ought to conceive of it in these terms is not a question I will attempt to address here.

As I conceive of it, civil disobedience consists in principled disobedience to law undertaken for the purpose of publicly contesting the justice of a law or policy.[2] The policy civil disobedients seek to contest may be public, one carried out by government officials, or private (e.g. one carried out by employees of a firm or members of a club). The illegality of civil disobedience distinguishes it from legal means for publicly communicating principled objections to law or policy, such as legally sanctioned rallies, strikes or lawsuits challenging the constitutionality of a particular law. Illegal conduct performed for the purpose of providing a test case to challenge the genuine legality of what at least some officials treat as law is an example of the latter, not civil disobedience.

Unlike ordinary lawbreakers, civil disobedients act conscientiously or from a moral motive; specifically, the judgment that the injustice of some law or policy warrants their violating the law in order to call attention to that fact, and to instigate or further legal efforts to reform that law or policy in ways that reduce or eliminate this injustice. These goals distinguish civil disobedience from three other types of principled disobedience to law. A person who acts contrary to the law purely to mitigate or prevent an injustice the law sanctions engages in conscientious resistance. A person who conscientiously objects to a law or policy asserts that she ought to be exempt from it because she believes that law or policy requires her to act immorally. Finally, whereas civil disobedience has as its aim correcting certain injustices in an existing legal order or a subset of the policies pursued by public or private actors, morally motivated revolution has as its goal the elimination (and, in many cases, replacement) of a legal order, a public actor such as the current government or a private actor such as firms engaged in extracting oil. Oftentimes the same actor may engage in several of these forms of principled disobedience to law. For example, those who conscientiously object to a law may also engage in acts of civil disobedience that aim at the law's reform. Nevertheless, the different ends at which civil disobedience, conscientious resistance, conscientious objection, and morally motivated revolution aim mark distinctions that are both analytically and morally important.

The essentially communicative nature of civil disobedience places several constraints on the form it may take. First, it requires that violations of the law be committed publicly, or at least that they be publicized. Second, civil disobedients must make a good faith effort to effectively communicate to their target audience why they are breaking the law. At a minimum, this includes identifying the law or public policy they believe to be unjust and explaining why they believe that to be the case.[3] Third, civil disobedience must be non-coercive. Arguably, this condition better captures the relevant constraint than does the rival claim that to count as civil disobedience an act must be nonviolent. Limited violence against public property, as in the case of toppling a statue honoring a past political or military leader, need not be coercive. Conversely, passive illegal occupations (e.g. sit-ins) may be coercive even though they are nonviolent, namely if they make it exceedingly costly for those targeted by such acts of civil disobedience to refrain from making the changes in law or policy the civil disobedients demand. The key point is that civil disobedience is a form of *moral* address. The constitutive point of the practice is to engage with others as moral agents, creatures capable of recognizing moral reasons to think that certain laws or policies are unjust and responding to moral arguments for their reform. Coercion addresses agents as *prudential* actors; specifically, it provides the threat of some harm or evil as a reason to perform or not perform a particular act. Civil disobedience often imposes costs on others, of course; indeed, that is a primary reason why it can serve as an effective tool of political and moral communication. Nevertheless, would-be civil disobedients must make a good faith attempt to ensure that the magnitude and duration of the costs they impose on others fall short of what could reasonably be described as coercive.[4]

Some theorists maintain that a willingness to accept punishment for one's illegal conduct is a necessary condition for engaging in civil disobedience. It demonstrates the civil disobedient's commitment to the rule of law even in the face of her violation of a particular legal norm, and so distinguishes her from an ordinary lawbreaker. Yet if this argument is correct, then it is impossible for subjects of a government that exhibits inadequate fidelity to the rule of law to engage in civil disobedience. Do we really want to say that it was conceptually impossible for citizens of Zimbabwe under the Mugabe government to engage in civil disobedience? Is the same now true for Venezuelans ruled by the Maduro government? Better, I suggest, to treat a willingness to accept punishment as relevant to the *moral justifiability* of particular acts of civil disobedience committed within political communities whose officials and subjects generally exhibit fidelity to the ideal of the rule of law.

Given the foregoing characterization of civil disobedience, what would it be for a state to engage it? I contend that most theorists who have written on the topic would answer as follows: SCD consists of disobedience to supranational law (i.e. international or regional law) on the part of state officials who purport to be acting on behalf of the state and its citizens that satisfies the criteria for civil disobedience listed above. For example, state officials who disobey an international legal norm with the immediate aim of publicly contesting the justice of that or some other international law, or a policy pursued or authorized by members of the society of states, and the longer-term goal of instigating or advancing efforts to reform that law or policy via legal means, engage in SCD. So defined, SCD does not encompass any conduct by state officials that concerns the justice or legitimacy of *domestic* law or policy. It also differs from what we might term state conscientious objection, in which officials assert only that their political community is morally entitled to an exemption from an otherwise binding international legal norm while making no effort to initiate or further efforts to reform that law.

We are now prepared to take up the question with which we began this section: is SCD a genuine possibility, or is talk of such conduct conceptually confused? To begin, we should note two respects in which SCD differs categorically from familiar examples that come to mind when we think of civil disobedience. First, while ordinary civil disobedience is undertaken by the governed, SCD is performed by those who govern. Only legal officials can engage in SCD, and their disobedience consists of a refusal to exercise some of the powers attached to their offices in a manner necessary to make good on one or another of their state's supranational legal obligations. Second, a civil disobedient ordinarily acts in her own name, even if for the sake of others. That is, her conduct reflects her own judgment that the law or policy she protests is unjust, and that she is morally justified all things considered in engaging in civil disobedience in order to challenge it. In contrast, because individuals engage in SCD in their capacity as public officials, they act in the name of all the state's citizens. Some citizens may disagree with the official's decision to engage in SCD, either because they do not believe that the international law at issue is unjust or because they do not think SCD is morally justifiable all things considered in this particular case. Nevertheless, these dissenters are held responsible for their state's illegal conduct: it is attributed to them qua citizens of that state, and they will likely bear some share of the costs that follow if their state's noncompliance with international law leads to punitive or compensatory action being taken against it.

As William Scheuerman rightly emphasizes, talk of SCD brings with it a substantial risk of downplaying these critical differences between it and ordinary civil disobedience.[5] Nevertheless, I maintain that they do not entail that SCD is a fundamentally different type of principled disobedience to law, or what is the same, that talk of SCD constitutes a category mistake. Rather, the significance of the aforementioned respects in which SCD differs from ordinary civil disobedience lie in the additional justificatory burdens they impose. An example may serve to illustrate the point.

Given that SCD involves a public official acting on behalf of members of a specific political community, only those officials who possess legitimate domestic authority have a moral right to engage in it. Suppose that only officials in liberal-democratic states meet this condition. If so, then only officials in these states have a *moral* right to civilly disobey international law. However, officials of other states can still engage in SCD if, purporting to act on behalf of their state and its citizens, they refuse to make good on one or more of its international legal obligations for the purpose of contesting the justice of an international legal norm, regime, or policy. Unlike in the case of officials in a liberal-democratic state, these officials can be properly criticized for their conduct on the grounds that they have no moral right to speak for those they rule, or to make them liable to the consequences that may follow from those officials' disobedience to international law. Of course, in some cases a person can be morally justified all things considered in performing an act she has no right to perform. It is possible, therefore, that in certain circumstances even officials who lack a legitimate claim to domestic authority may be morally permitted to engage in SCD.

The publicity conditions pose no obstacle to the possibility of SCD. Like ordinary civil disobedients, state officials can make a good faith effort to ensure that their violation of international law effectively communicates to other participants in the international legal order their reasons for thinking that some international norm or policy is deeply unjust and so warrants immediate reform. To do so, however, state officials must explicitly characterize their conduct as an instance of noncompliance with international law. If they argue instead that international law permits the conduct in question, then they are not engaged in civil disobedience. Their conduct constitutes a challenge to what they maintain is a mistaken understanding of what the law already is, not an attempt to instigate or further efforts to change an (allegedly) unjust law or policy by communicating reasons why it ought to be reformed. This is so even if other participants in the international legal order reject the state's claim that it is complying with the law and act accordingly, for example by withholding certain benefits of cooperation to which the state in question would otherwise be entitled. It may be that international law's constitutional deficiencies cause disputes regarding the legality of conduct by its participants to remain unresolved more frequently than is true in a moderately well-functioning rule of law state. But this fact (if it is one) does not preclude distinguishing conceptually between attempts to engage in civil disobedience and attempts to challenge the perception that the law prohibits certain conduct.

In my view, the necessarily noncoercive nature of civil disobedience poses the most serious challenge to the possibility of SCD. Indeed, if civil disobedience must not only be noncoercive but also nonviolent, and if we follow Weber in treating a monopoly on the legitimate use of force as a defining feature of the state, then it may be paradoxical to describe any conduct by state agents in their official capacity as an example of civil disobedience.[6] Gerald Neubauer offers one response to this Weberian objection to SCD, asserting that we should replace the nonviolence condition with a legitimate coercion condition.[7] Specifically, as long as the use of force by state officials is subject to the rule of law, the fact that their conduct either involves or depends implicitly on the use of violence does not disqualify it as an example of civil disobedience. Alas, Neubauer offers no argument for this substitution, which in any case confronts serious challenges. Even if state officials conform to *domestic* law governing the use of force, their failure to make good on the state's international legal obligations still appears to conflict with fidelity to the ideal of an *international* rule of law. Moreover, insofar as many states' domestic legal orders require state officials to uphold applicable international law, any deliberate refusal to do so would seem to exhibit a lack of fidelity to the domestic rule of law. In response, some might argue that state officials can exhibit fidelity to both the international and domestic rule of law by being willing to accept the legal consequences of having acted illegally. Even if this is true, however, it speaks to the moral justifiability of decisions by state officials to violate international law, rather than the question of whether their conduct can even qualify as an example of civil disobedience.

A different strategy for addressing the Weberian objection turns on the distinction between acts and omissions. Suppose that state officials with a morally justifiable claim to act on behalf of their state and its citizens refuse to take the steps necessary to give domestic effect to an international legal norm, for the purpose of publicly challenging the justice or legitimacy of that norm. Perhaps the legislature chooses not to pass the domestic legislation needed to implement the state's international legal obligation, or domestic judges refuse to apply an international legal norm to cases they acknowledge as falling under it, or if they do then members of the executive elect not to enforce those decisions. In the first two and arguably the third of these examples, the state behaves nonviolently; its officials either refuse to authorize the use of violence or they refuse to exercise whatever violence is authorized, in order to enforce certain obligations international law imposes on the state.

As we observed earlier, however, the key question is not whether civil disobedients engage in violence but whether their illegal conduct is coercive. Therefore, we need to consider whether state officials' refusal to give domestic effect to applicable international law necessarily constitutes coercion. Such a conclusion does not obviously follow from a Weberian conception of the state as necessarily claiming a monopoly on the legitimate use of force within its territory. Moreover, it does not seem particularly far-fetched to imagine a state violating one of its international legal obligations for the purpose of publicly challenging its justice or legitimacy without thereby imposing burdens on others weighty enough to make its illegal conduct coercive. For example, a signatory to the

Single Convention on Narcotic Drugs might legalize the recreational use of marijuana for the purpose of publicly advocating for changes to that treaty in ways it believes will make it more just, without imposing excessive or even any costs on other signatories.[8] More controversially, consider a state that permits the domestic manufacture of a medical drug in violation of the TRIPS agreement, and does so partly for the purpose of publicly challenging the justice or legitimacy of that agreement. As long as the costs this action imposes on both the bearer of the legal right under that agreement (i.e. the patent-holder) and those legally empowered to alter the law (i.e. states party to the WTO) are not too high, it will not count as coercive. A 10 percent reduction in the patent-holder's profits, and an accompanying small loss in tax revenue for the state where the patent-holder is legally domiciled, might satisfy this condition.

Though it differs in analytically and morally important ways from ordinary civil disobedience, I conclude that states can engage in civil disobedience to supranational law. In the next section I examine the conditions they must satisfy to be morally justified in doing so.

CONDITIONS FOR MORALLY JUSTIFIABLE STATE CIVIL DISOBEDIENCE

One place to begin an investigation of the moral justifiability of SCD is with an assessment of a supranational legal order's legitimacy. For instance, does international law in general, or specific international legal norms and regimes in particular, enjoy a morally justified claim to authority over states to which correlates a moral duty on their part to obey it? If so, then either the moral reasons that favor civilly disobeying international law must be weighty enough to override the moral presumption in favor of compliance with the law this duty provides, or it must be the case that the duty does not exclude civil disobedience, conditional perhaps on it satisfying certain conditions. Alas, most theorists writing on SCD say surprisingly little about international law's legitimate authority or states' correlative duty to obey international law.[9] Yet if states have no moral duty to obey international law simply because it is the law, then by itself the illegal nature of their conduct provides them with no moral reason to refrain from it.

Perhaps these theorists assume that states must have a moral duty to obey international law because they have consented to be bound by it, either explicitly in the case of treaties or implicitly in the case of customary international legal norms. There are good reasons to reject this assumption, however. Genuine consent must be voluntary, yet the agreement of militarily and economically weak states to abide by the terms of various international treaties may frequently fail to qualify as such. Moreover, many governments currently lack the moral standing necessary to acquire international legal obligations on behalf of their state and its citizens.[10] There are other considerations besides consent that may serve to ground states' moral duty to obey international law. However, at most they offer only a piecemeal moral justification for international law's legitimate authority, both in terms of which international legal norms are legitimate and which states have a duty to obey them. The upshot is that one weighty moral consideration that may be relevant to the moral justifiability of ordinary civil disobedience within certain domestic legal orders may frequently be irrelevant to the moral justifiability of SCD.[11]

Many theorists argue that to be morally justifiable, civil disobedients must exhibit fidelity to the ideal of the rule of law. But how can actors who deliberately violate the law satisfy this condition? As we noted earlier, one common answer is that civil disobedients must be willing to accept some punishment or penalty for their illegal conduct. By doing so, civil disobedients provide evidence that they are motivated by a concern for justice or the common good and not (merely) personal advantage. They also eschew any claim to be above the law, morally free to act as they think right regardless of what the political community has determined justice permits, requires, or forbids. Relatedly, in their willingness to accept some punishment or penalty for violating the law, civil disobedients publicly affirm the standing of those legally empowered to alter or preserve the law to do so. This condition on the moral justifiability of an act of civil disobedience follows from its nature as a form of moral address. Civil disobedience is not an alternative to the lawful reform of existing law or policy, nor is it simply an example of hard bargaining. Rather, it serves as a mechanism for communicating to other members of the relevant political community the moral necessity of reform to some law or policy, and generally serves as a complement to legal efforts to achieve that end. In her willingness to accept the legal consequences of her conduct, the civil disobedient transforms what would otherwise constitute disrespect for the right of other members of the political community to a (perhaps equal) say in settling the terms on which they will associate into a respectful challenge to how some members of the community have chosen to exercise that right.[12]

Even if committed for principled reasons, deliberate disobedience to law by officials generally poses a graver threat to the rule of law than does ordinary civil disobedience, conscientious objection, or conscientious resistance. This is so for two reasons. First, officials are more often in a position to put themselves above the law, that is to successfully avoid being held legally accountable for their conduct. Second, to the extent others suspect or know of it, officials' disregard for the law is more likely to erode their commitment to the ideal of the rule of law than is disobedience to the law by ordinary legal subjects. Thus, all else equal SCD will be more difficult to morally justify than will ordinary civil disobedience. Yet officials may be able to mitigate the corrosive impact their illegal conduct has on others' respect for the rule of law by offering a moral justification for it, especially if that justification rests on widely shared moral principles and a broad consensus about their implications given certain facts. Doing so may even serve to strengthen community members' commitment to the rule of law, especially if compliance with the law in the case at hand would foster an image of officials as rule-worshippers lacking any genuine concern for justice. Moreover, even if those who perform acts of SCD resist *international* legal efforts to hold them or their state accountable for their illegal conduct, they may still cooperate with *domestic* efforts to do so. For instance, executive officials might acknowledge the right of domestic courts to hold them accountable under domestic law. And at least in moderately well-functioning democracies elections provide a mechanism for holding some officials accountable for their extra-legal actions, albeit one that is less tightly connected to respect for the rule of law than is a trial or administrative hearing concerned solely with an official's illegal conduct.[13]

Of course, the failure to exhibit fidelity to the ideal of the rule of law matters little in societies where that ideal goes largely unrealized. There are some reasons to suspect this is true of the international legal order. These include the challenge the fragmentation of international law poses to government through law; various respects in which power differentials between states undermine their formal equality before the law; and most importantly, the impact that a dearth of international courts exercising compulsory jurisdiction and a general reliance on self-help to enforce international legal rights and obligations has on the supremacy of law. Indeed, a plausible case can be made that international legal rules and institutions simply serve to enhance instrumentally rational choice by utility maximizing agents; that is, to facilitate mutually beneficial interactions among states, each of which seeks to maximize its national interest given its relative power. If this description is accurate, then the international legal order is an example of rule *by* law, not the rule *of* law, and there is nothing morally problematic about disobedience to law per se in such a political order.[14]

Some theorists deny that the moral justifiability of SCD depends on state officials' willingness to accept the legal consequences of their refusal to make good on one or more of their state's international legal obligations. Instead, they argue that a state must pair its illegal conduct with concrete efforts to reform the aspect of the international legal order to which it morally objects, and that these reforms must be publicly defended by appeal to "globally shared principles of justice" or "global public reason."[15] Depending on the details of the changes it attempts to bring about, and how it does so, this might suffice to demonstrate that the state's illegal conduct is not simply an attempt to procure some private advantage. It is less clear whether it can convey a willingness to defer to the political community's determination of what justice requires, permits, or forbids, as set out in its law. Moreover, it may be unfair to internationally weak and/or developing states to make the moral justifiability of SCD conditional on the pursuit of concrete reforms to the international legal order.[16]

SCD may still be morally impermissible even if its illegality raises no red flags. For instance, some theorists maintain that civil disobedience may only be employed to contest laws or policies that systematically violate human rights, or perhaps only a subset of such rights. Many also contend that to be morally justifiable civil disobedience must be a last resort, undertaken only after actors have exhausted the legal means for challenging an (allegedly) unjust law or policy. Finally, the permissibility of civil disobedience may also depend on the likelihood that it will successfully contribute to reforms, or at least to a serious consideration of the disobedients' moral complaint by those she attempts to address. I maintain that each of these conditions can be subsumed under a general requirement of proportionality. Civil disobedience almost always imposes moral costs on others. The greater these costs, the greater the injustice the civil disobedient aims to address must be in order to warrant their imposition. All else equal, this may well entail that it will be easier to justify acts of civil disobedience undertaken to contest laws or policies violating human rights than those that constitute or cause other sorts of injustice. However, it does not categorically prohibit civil disobedience in the latter cases. Similarly, as the moral costs that an act of civil disobedience will impose on others rise, so too does the weight that attaches to the requirements of last resort and likelihood of success.

I can see no reason to believe that an act of SCD could never satisfy this proportionality condition. Moreover, even if states do have a moral duty to obey international (or regional) law, it seems implausible to claim that this duty will always defeat or exclude the moral reasons states may have to engage in civil disobedience. The same is true for the moral duty to uphold the rule of law (where it exists). If so, then we ought to conclude that under the right conditions state officials acting on behalf of their state and its citizens can be morally justified in civilly disobeying supranational law.

EXAMPLES OF (MORALLY JUSTIFIABLE) SCD?

Suppose that SCD is both possible and can be morally justifiable. Are there any examples of state conduct that satisfy both of these conditions? Though several theorists answer in the affirmative, I contend that the cases they offer to support this conclusion fail to do so.

Allen Buchanan and Robert Goodin both argue that unilateral humanitarian intervention can constitute an act of SCD (or at least an act closely analogous to civil disobedience) if the states that conduct it do so partly for the purposes of instigating reforms to existing international law governing the resort to war.[17] NATO's 1998 humanitarian intervention in Kosovo provides the main impetus for these arguments. International law prohibits states from waging war against other states except in self-defense or when authorized by the UN Security Council to restore or maintain international peace and security. Since NATO's intervention in Kosovo met neither of these conditions, it was illegal. Yet it also modeled or at least pointed toward a new legal standard for permissible resort to war, in addition to the two described above, namely when undertaken by a coalition of human rights respecting and minimally democratic states in response to an ongoing or imminent campaign of crimes against humanity or genocide. Thus, NATO's illegal intervention served, or at least could be characterized as serving, as an attempt to instigate a reform to the international legal order that would make it more just.

To be morally justifiable, any attempt at the illegal reform of international law must aim at the creation of new rules that apply universally and are defensible (and defended) on principled grounds. Moreover, the states that perform them must be willing to be held accountable for their illegal conduct by the other members of the international legal order. NATO's intervention in Kosovo clearly fell short in the latter respect, and perhaps also the former, so even if it did constitute an example of SCD it was not morally justifiable. But the description of NATO's conduct as an act of civil disobedience is also highly suspect. The NATO states that participated in it made no real effort to defend their actions as an attempt to reform international law, or to instigate a public debate about whether to do so. Descriptions of NATO's intervention as illegal but legitimate suggest instead that it was (and is) seen as a morally defensible violation of a morally defensible law.[18] If we are looking for a domestic analogy the apt one may be morally motivated jury nullification. Even morally optimal legal norms will sometimes be over- and/or underinclusive, and so officials may sometimes be morally justified in refusing to hold actors accountable for violating them. This need not imply that the law in question ought to be reformed.

There are also conceptual reasons to doubt that NATO's intervention counts as an example of SCD. We noted earlier that civil disobedience encompasses only attempts to communicate to members and officials of the relevant community the moral need for reforms to law or policy, while actual changes are to be brought about by legal means. This entails that if particular violations of international law are also legislative contributions to the emergence of a customary norm of international law that deems the conduct in question legally permissible, then they cannot be examples of civil disobedience. Likewise, if coercion plays a role in the acquiescence of other states to the emerging norm of customary international law an illegal reformer champions, then "civil disobedience" does not provide an apt description of the latter's conduct.

Antonio Franceschet offers as an example of SCD Uruguay's decision to legalize the sale of cannabis for recreational purposes, in contravention of its legal obligation under the 1961 Single Convention on Narcotic Drugs.[19] Sean Fleming does likewise for Canada's decision to pursue a similar domestic legal reform.[20] There is some evidence to support this claim; for example, the Uruguayan Bill legalizing marijuana "calls on the international community to consider marijuana legalization."[21] Yet if Franceschet accurately describes the Uruguayan government's intentions, the changes it has made to domestic law governing the use of cannabis look more like an example of conscientious objection than civil disobedience. Uruguay, he writes, "wants the space to choose a policy that suits its interests ... [and] is asking to be 'left alone' and to be allowed to try something on its own."[22] He adds that "withdrawing from the obligations of a particular set of international institutions may be a legitimate form of self-protection."[23] The idea of being protected from a choice between fidelity to one's moral principles and paying the price attached to breaking the law provides the very core of the concepts of freedom of conscience and of conscientious objection as they figure in many legal orders.[24] Alternatively, Uruguay's and Canada's violations of the 1961 Single Convention may be best described as acts of conscientious resistance to (perceived) injustice. This conclusion follows from Franceschet's suggestion that in legalizing cannabis Uruguay exercised destituent power.[25] As I understand it, actors exercise destituent power when they attempt to nullify norms, and so the practices they constitute, by deliberately refusing to use those norms to hold themselves and others accountable. If it becomes sufficiently widespread this refusal leads to the demise of the norm in question. If this is what Uruguay and Canada are up to, however, then they are engaged in illegal reform of international law, not civil disobedience.

Neubauer argues that Argentina's unilateral declaration of a moratorium on debt repayments in 2001 and its attempt to impose a 70 percent reduction in value on outstanding bonds held by private creditors in 2005 qualify as SCD.[26] In both cases Argentina's leaders offered as a public justification for their refusal to make good on the state's international legal obligations the devastating effects that continued debt repayment would have on the lives of millions of ordinary Argentinians. Argentina's contribution to an effort by several Latin American countries to create the Bank of the South, which Neubauer maintains would morally improve on the IMF and the World Bank, provides evidence that in acting illegally it was not simply seeking to advance its own national interest. Finally, because its Congress passed a law forbidding renegotiation of the reduced repayment it offered to private bondholders, as well as repayment to any bondholders who did not accept that offer, Argentina's conduct did not involve any extralegal use of force.

There are several grounds on which to challenge Neubauer's description of Argentina's conduct as an example of SCD. One is the fact that it attempted to defend its 2001 default ("moratorium on debt repayment") as legally permissible on grounds of necessity.[27] Genuine civil disobedience, I suggested earlier in this chapter, requires that agents successfully act on an intention to violate the law. Consider, too, that the concrete attempt at reform to the international order that Neubauer offers as evidence of Argentina's principled motive addresses only the (alleged) injustices perpetrated by the IMF and World Bank. Yet Argentina's 2005 attempt to impose new repayment terms on bondholders targeted private actors, not these public international institutions. Given Neubauer's account of justifiable SCD, Argentina should have pursued concrete reforms to international law governing *private creditors' claims on states* in order to avoid being justifiably accused of simply engaging in hard bargaining. Finally, the dramatic reduction in the amount to be repaid and the "take it or leave it" nature of Argentina's offer to private bondholders suggests that its conduct may well have been coercive, or at least an attempt to coercively renegotiate the terms of its outstanding debt. If so, this would disqualify it as an act of civil disobedience. Crucially, that conclusion neither equates to nor does it entail the conclusion that Argentina's illegal actions were morally unjustifiable. Perhaps they constituted a morally permissible act of resistance to an exploitative global economic order enshrined in international law. But if so then it is in these terms, not those of civil disobedience, that we should defend it.

CONCLUSION

Though I have defended its possibility, I am unaware of any compelling examples of SCD, let alone morally justifiable ones. Of course, the legal and political developments that provide the background and impetus for theorizing SCD are relatively recent, so perhaps we will begin to see examples of it in the next decade or two. On the other hand, states may generally prefer to offer legal justifications for their ostensible failures to comply with international law. The indeterminacy that still characterizes many international legal norms, the fragmented nature of the international legal order, and the supremacy of domestic constitutional law over international law all provide means by which to do so. Insofar as this strategy will generally be less costly than engaging in SCD, and no less likely to be successful, we should expect it to be the one on which states rely.

If we turn our attention from practice back to theory, two observations warrant emphasis. The first is that civil disobedience is not synonymous with morally permissible illegal conduct. The quality of both our theoretical inquiries and our moral deliberation will improve if we pay careful attention to the different types of principled disobedience in which agents may engage. Second, at least in liberal political theory (and practice) discussion of civil disobedience often presumes some sort of moral reason to conform to the law, either because it enjoys legitimate authority or out of respect for the ideal of the rule of law. We should be cautious about extending these presumptions to the international legal order. If international law frequently lacks legitimate authority and exhibits little fidelity to the ideal of the rule of law, there may be little need to invoke the concept of civil disobedience to morally justify illegal conduct.

NOTES

1. So, too, are the criteria for selecting among rival conceptions of civil disobedience (and, perhaps, of SCD). In my view, analytical utility is by far the most important criterion, followed only distantly by consistency with the use of the phrase "civil disobedience" in particular contexts.
2. For further discussion of many of the claims advanced in this and the following section, see David Lefkowitz, "Civil Disobedience," in *Encyclopedia of Applied Ethics*, 2nd ed., ed. Ruth Chadwick (San Diego, Calif.: Elsevier, 2012), 453–58. Useful analyses of civil disobedience can also be found in many of the other chapters in this volume.
3. Note that civil disobedients can satisfy these two conditions without making their identities known.
4. In contrast to the argument presented in the text, which appeals to the specific nature of civil disobedience to justify noncoercion, pacifism requires that civil disobedience be nonviolent simply because it requires that agents forbear from violence in all their actions. It is unclear whether pacifism excludes coercion.
5. William Scheuerman, "Can Political Institutions Commit Civil Disobedience?" *Review of Politics* 82, no. 2 (2020): 1–23.
6. See Scheuerman, "Political Institutions," 15–16.
7. Gerald Neubauer, "State Civil Disobedience: Morally Justified Violations of International Law Considered as Civil Disobedience," *TranState Working Papers*, no. 86, University of Bremen Collaborative Research Center 597, Transformations of the State (2009): 10.
8. This hypothetical has certain parallels with Uruguay's and Canada's recent decisions to legalize the use and sale of cannabis, but also some crucial differences, as I argue later in this chapter.
9. One notable exception is Matthias Kumm, "The Moral Point of Constitutional Pluralism: Defining the Domain of Legitimate Institutional Civil Disobedience and Conscientious Objection," in *The Philosophical Foundations of European Union Law*, eds. Julie Dickson and Pavlos Eleftheriadis (Oxford: Oxford University Press, 2012), 216–46.

10. This observation is simply the obverse of the point made in the previous section, namely that many state officials lack a moral right to engage in civil disobedience in their political community's name.

11. For a critical survey of international law's claim to legitimate authority, see David Lefkowitz, "The Legitimacy of International Law," in *Global Political Theory*, eds. David Held and Pietro Maffettone (Malden, Mass.: Polity Press, 2016), 101–14.

12. Note that civil disobedients may also have strategic reasons to accept some punishment or penalty for their illegal conduct, in addition to those that follow from fidelity to the ideal of the rule of law. For example, their arguments may garner more serious consideration if they do so.

13. For broadly similar arguments, see Jonathan White, "Principled Disobedience in the EU," *Constellations* 24, no. 4 (December 2017): 643–46.

14. For discussion of skepticism regarding the existence of an international rule of law, see David Lefkowitz, *Philosophy and International Law: A Critical Introduction* (Cambridge University Press, 2020), chapter 4.

15. Neubauer, *State Civil Disobedience;* Danny Michelsen, "State Civil Disobedience: A Republican Perspective," *Journal of International Political Theory* 14, no. 3 (2018): 333, 336; Nancy Kokaz, "Theorizing International Fairness," *Metaphilosophy* 36, nos. 1–2 (2005): 80.

16. Antonio Franceschet, "Theorizing State Civil Disobedience in International Politics," *Journal of International Political Theory* 11, no. 2 (2015): 241–46.

17. Allen Buchanan, "From Nuremberg to Kosovo: The Morality of Illegal International Legal Reform," *Ethics* 111, no. 4 (2001): 673–705; Robert Goodin, "Toward an International Rule of Law: Distinguishing International Law-Breakers from Would-Be Law-Makers," *The Journal of Ethics* 9, no. 1–2 (2005): 225–46. See also Nathan Miller, "International Civil Disobedience: Unauthorized Intervention and the Conscience of the International Community," *Maryland Law Review* 74, no. 2 (2015): 314–75.

18. Morally defensible in decidedly nonideal conditions, which should not be confused with perfectly or even approximately just.

19. Franceschet, "Theorizing State Civil Disobedience," 246–51.

20. Sean Fleming, "A Political Theory of Treaty Repudiation," *Journal of Political Philosophy* 28, no. 1 (2020): 20.

21. Franceschet, "Theorizing State Civil Disobedience," 246.
22. Franceschet, "Theorizing State Civil Disobedience," 250. Insofar as the relevant interests concern harm reduction and perhaps respect for individual autonomy, Uruguay's reasons for legalizing cannabis count as principled.
23. Franceschet, "Theorizing State Civil Disobedience," 251.
24. "Unlike civil disobedience, conscientious objection is not directed towards legal reform. The claim is merely to be left alone with regard to an obligation whose appropriateness for others is not put into question" (Kumm, "The Moral Point," 237).
25. Kumm, "The Moral Point," 250.
26. Neubauer, "State Civil Disobedience," 11–16. See also Michelsen, "State Civil Disobedience," 338–39.
27. For discussion, see Stephan W. Schill, "German Constitutional Court Rules on Necessity in Argentine Bondholder Case," *ASIL Insights* 11, no. 20 (July 31, 2007), www.asil.org/insights/volume/11/issue/20/german-constitutional-court-rules-necessity-argentine-bondholder-case.

14 Coding Resistance: Digital Strategies of Civil Disobedience

Theresa Züger

The transformative effects of digitalization have not left civil disobedience untouched. On the contrary, civil disobedience today is increasingly interlinked with digital technologies, though individual examples exhibit different degrees of dependency on technology and are constituted by varying types of interactions between humans and machines. Digital actions have become integrated into daily life; it may soon seem unnecessary or even counterintuitive to label them *digital* at all. For some members of society, the *digital* becomes an increasingly empty signifier, as human activity in general becomes dependent on technology in unconscious and invisible ways. Despite the ubiquity of computing and human-machine entanglement, political and public discourses linger uneasily between embracing and resisting digitalization. The *digital* still functions as a placeholder that signifies a less familiar, valid, or even less *real* type of action.

Nevertheless, the Internet has changed "almost every aspect of politics, and its presence in politics is ubiquitous."[1] Digital forms of activism and protest have been at the forefront of these changes and have played a vital role in the digital rights movement as a whole.[2] The rise of the World Wide Web in the early 1990s was interpreted as a hopeful event that would democratize the world, in general, and offer new possibilities for civil disobedience, in particular.[3] A culture of enthusiastic experimentalism allowed political interventions from civil society to flourish and evolve as *tactical media*,[4] *intercreative activism*,[5] *connective action*,[6] or *cloud protesting*.[7] Digital forms of civil disobedience soon garnered increased interest, in part because they seem "fundamentally different from more established offline forms of protest."[8]

This chapter focuses on digital strategies of civil disobedience. It aims to discuss their characteristics as forms of democratic political action and also reflect on the political theory discourse provoked by them. Aside from the use of digital technology as a means of organizing, documenting, and communicating about civil disobedience, the history of the Internet provides evidence of new strategies of civil disobedience that depend in their core on digital technology and infrastructure. This chapter investigates such cases in order to understand both their potential and limits in respect to democratic principles.

ELECTRONIC CIVIL DISOBEDIENCE: FROM VISION TO ACTION

"Appealing to the concept of 'civil disobedience' has been a common trope since the beginnings of Internet activism."[9] The most developed early use of this conceptual trope probably first appeared in "Electronic Civil Disobedience and Other Unpopular Ideas," a 1996 statement by the Critical Arts Ensemble, a Florida-based artist collective. The group announced the electronic turn of civil disobedience, envisioning it as a reinvention of civil disobedience that might successfully address hegemonic power manifesting itself on the Internet. Critical Arts Ensemble criticized more conventional left-wing activism on the grounds that it remained blindly and nostalgically enthralled to old-school anti-capitalist political practices.[10] Their visionary approach, they claimed, was better suited to addressing the power structures of late capitalism in the well-guarded realm of "cyberspace." Yet, their vision wasn't completely detached from older activist strategies for civil disobedience: "the strategy and tactics of ECD should not be a mystery to any activist. They are the same as traditional CD."[11] The main commonality they identified was nonviolence, which, in their understanding, allowed for financial damage but implied refraining from harming specific individuals. An even more compelling parallel they established was the translation of well-known physical practices of civil disobedience (e.g., trespassing, physical blockades) into *informational* blockades, an imagined technological counterpart, the technicalities of which were still to be spelled out.

As Graham Meikle has pointed out, there were also some discontinuities. In Critical Arts Ensemble's vision of online civil disobedience, mass participation was deemphasized in favor of cell-based organizations, consisting of small groups of four to ten activists working in a decentralized and clandestine fashion.[12] Electronic civil disobedience's main subjects or agents was the hacker: "Whether you know it or not, if you are a hacker you are a revolutionary."[13] Nevertheless, they acknowledged that their model of electronic civil disobedience had yet to be realized. Most existing hackers, they conceded, were immature coders still tragically unaware of their political significance and latent capacities as a political *avant-garde*.

About the same time, the *StratoNet* Italian activist group in Florence initiated a 1995 protest that arguably anticipated precisely what Critical Arts Ensemble had in mind. They organized a so-called *Netstrike* in which worldwide participants flooded the French government's public website with requests (by simply visiting and reloading) with the aim of overloading the server and forcing it to shut down. This early example of a *distributed denial of service* (DDoS) action caused the website to break down: it received too many simultaneous requests from distributed sources and thus denied service because of the overload. StratoNet described its endeavors as a "networked version of a peaceful sit-in,"[14] targeting French President Jacques Chirac's authorization of nuclear tests.[15]

In 1997, parts of the Critical Arts Ensemble decided to form a new arts and activist collective, the Electronic Disturbance Theater (EDT). The new group declared its solidarity with the Zapatista Movement in Mexico and initiated recurring DDoS actions against websites they understood as "symbols of Mexican neoliberalism."[16] EDT also developed a tool, *Floodnet*, which automated DDoS actions via a Javascript program that performed automated reloads of the website, thus slowing access to the targeted server and making a denial of service more likely than human reloads. In 1999 the EDT made *Floodnet* downloadable as part of an emerging phase of experimental political activity conceived as electronic civil disobedience, interpreted to include DDoS protests directed at mail servers, e.g., *mail bombings*, and *web defacements* that entailed invasive techniques to alter website content.[17]

Increasingly, all of these acts came to be subsumed under the term *hacktivism*, which according to some commentators entailed "a positive, empowering departure from the weaknesses of hacking.... [I]n contrast to hacking it has very definite views as to what constitutes social goodness and badness."[18] Both commonalities and differences between self-described hackers and hacktivists can still be identified today. More importantly, differences between hackers and hacktivists, on one side, and cybercriminals, on the other, are manifest in various ideas about hacker ethics.[19] Many of these implicitly envision hacking (and hacktivism) as morally conscious political practices, and thus – in political terms – as something different from cybercrime, even if both conflict with the law.

Unlike some imitators, the EDT published its members' identities when undertaking protests and also warned others of potential personal consequences. They did so despite the fact that their *Floodnet* protests were not strictly illegal; they usually transpired in cyberlaw's gray zones. DDoSes only later became illegal, and they remain so today in most legal jurisdictions. "I remember the time when the Electronic Frontier Foundation contacted us and said that our actions are actually going to change cyber-laws and probably reduce cyber civil liberties. I certainly did not realize this long-term possibility [that DDoSes would be made illegal] back then," one member revealingly commented in a 2015 interview.[20]

EARLY THEORETICAL REFLECTIONS

Though not all protests taking place in this legal gray area initially qualified as civil disobedience, they nonetheless provoked a lively theoretical debate. Andrew Calabrese (and also Brian Huschle,[21] Mark Manion, and Abby Goodrum[22]) relied on a liberal understanding of civil disobedience to analyze them. In Calabrese's analysis, digital actions of protest failed to live up to the political standards of recognized historical exemplars of civil disobedience.[23] In his critique, Calabrese argued that the digital strategies in question were too disruptive and potentially damaging, and therefore not merely symbolic in character, something he viewed as essential to civil disobedience. Drawing on John Rawls, he criticized emerging digital acts that claimed to stand in the tradition of civil disobedience on the grounds that they vaguely rejected the entire political system and failed to focus properly on a specific law or political issue.[24] Finally, he argued that digital activists did not risk punishment equivalent to those faced by non-digital protesters (for example, in a physical sit-in). For Calabrese, the physical risk of "encountering imprisonment, physical harm, and even death"[25] was nonetheless crucial to civil disobedience, properly conceived.

Calabrese's claim that civil disobedience carried out digitally was less likely to be harshly punished has repeatedly been proven wrong. In fact, those engaging in digital civil disobedience have often been even more harshly persecuted than those pursuing more conventional types of civil disobedience.[26] The relationship between the actual threats posed by digital acts of civil disobedience and the punitive reactions following them has been strikingly asymmetrical. The idea that DDoS actions like the ones enacted by the EDT were invasive and damaging has regularly been contradicted by their artistic staging: the "transparent public spectacle" they have helped to create suggests they in fact have often merely *simulated* a severe and critical intervention, rather than actually causing damage.[27] Contradicting Calabrese's views, their acts have in reality been mainly symbolic.

As Matthias Klang has pointed out, the arguments Calabrese put forward potentially evince a "lack of understanding of technology or even technophobia."[28] Indeed, Calabrese's key argument can be reduced to circling around one, if not *the*, cardinal principle of a mainstream liberal theory on civil disobedience: the necessity of accepting punishment, which in reality turns out to be highly contested in the more general discourse around civil disobedience.[29] Like other approaches that adopt a liberal understanding when evaluating hacktivism, Calabrese's considerations seem to be "unfairly stacked against hacktivists."[30] Klang has pointed out that digital strategies of civil disobedience (e.g., DDoS, web defacements, even hacking) can in fact generally qualify as civil disobedience. In his view, the only remaining challenge to their framing as civil disobedience is the "a-national nature of information technology."[31] Klang argued that a more inclusive definition of civil disobedience that included new digital technologies meant acknowledging that it could take transnational forms directed against a broader variety of actors (e.g., multinational corporations). By doing so, we simply acknowledge that the nation-state has become less relevant as a political point of reference when it comes to many of the issues being addressed by civil disobedients. This shift results from the ongoing transformation of politics in the age of globalization and digitization. The fact that political subjects now interpret their transnational protests as civil disobedience can be interpreted as one way by which they are adapting to major shifts in global political dynamics and power relations.

EXPERIMENTS IN DIGITAL CIVIL DISOBEDIENCE AND POLITICAL DISCOURSE

As the Internet came to pervade all aspects of society during the 2010s, digital activism entered into a broader experimental phase, with even more variegated approaches to civilly disobedient action, very different outcomes, and varying degrees of public attention. Notably, this decade saw the emergence of web-native strategies that left behind the idea of turning established, physical practices into digital versions. Instead, activists turned to digital strategies that were unimaginable without the power of code and the evolving architecture of the Internet. Mass data storage, strong encryption, and the sheer velocity of digital communication encouraged new forms of politically motivated digital action and civil disobedience. From the perspective of democratic theory, this development reinvented political action in promising but also controversial ways.

Following James Tully's idea of public philosophy, I view the practices of civil disobedience as just as relevant a part of the discourse of civil disobedience as philosophical arguments. As Tully argues, the dialogical relation between theory and practice allows a "reciprocal elucidation and mutual benefit between public philosophy and public affairs."[32] In a similar vein, hackers, hacktivists, and other digital activists are reinventing civil disobedience as they put it into practice. However, that does not mean that every claim made by them about civil disobedience necessarily stands up to critical analysis from the standpoint of democratic theory, or that it will necessarily gain approval within public discourse.

The best way to describe this emerging universe of digital political experimentalism is offered by the idea of *"do-ocracy,"* a common denominator across different activist networks. Do-ocracy means "rule by sheer doing: individuals propose actions, others join in (or not)."[33] Under the rule of do-ocracy, courses of action that meet with rough consensus or seem morally sound or even obligatory find their way into political reality. This has sometimes occurred in a well-planned way attuned to the existing discourse of civil disobedience, while at other times it has arisen chaotically, as Gabriella Coleman has aptly described in her research on Anonymous.[34] On many occasions, the actors and their digital strategies seem to have been motivated by a sense of humor, enthusiasm, and perhaps even the "revolutionary spirit" Hannah Arendt has described in her analysis of civil disobedience.[35] William Scheuerman has raised the concern that with the rise of digital tactics and this do-ocratic approach, "civil disobedience starts to mean almost anything and thus perhaps: nothing sufficiently precise or specific."[36] What he rightly points to is the fact that with the normalization of digital activism an increasing number of digital protests have been labeled civil disobedience that nonetheless fail to meet some important standard criteria. Anonymous, for instance, has pursued many controversial DDoS actions in the name of civil disobedience. Even if one were to recognize some cases as legitimate examples of civil disobedience (e.g., the protest against the Lufthansa website by activists fighting against deportation,[37] or *Operation Payback*[38]), this doesn't allow for a general characterization of every DDoS as civil disobedience: many cases do not meet the requisite political standards, or they may represent a criminal tactic to silence or even harm others by eliminating their presence from the Internet.[39]

How then can we make sense of civil disobedience as a political practice undergoing transformation in those cases where digital strategies are at its heart? In the following, I will address this question by looking for general patterns where digital means are deployed and the digital is the realm of action.

ON SYMBOLIC AND INFRASTRUCTURAL POLITICS IN DIGITAL CIVIL DISOBEDIENCE

Generally speaking, civil disobedience was reinvented in digital strategies within two reciprocally related realms of politics, the symbolic and the infrastructural, which are really two sides of the same coin. I now examine each of them.

When engaging in symbolic politics, civil disobedients utilize communicative means as effectively as possible to stage some disobedient act in the public eye. Forms of symbolic civil disobedience that depend on information technology can be quite effective. Politics depends on public representation in the media. This type of disobedience enters the political battleground in a world of signs and meaning by offering information, and, more importantly, by offering alternative interpretations of it.[40] These protests seek to evade the state's or private sector's control and contradict their narratives[41] or powerful conventions. Symbolic acts to be discussed here are no less in conflict with the law than infrastructural protests. Consistent with the "information society" they inhabit, disobedients are "doing things with words,"[42] by expressing illegal opinions, for example, engaging in political criticism of repressive states, posting illegal content (e.g., infringing copyright law), or spreading narratives that conflict with the law.

One example of such a symbolic political action is provided by Gopalan Nair, a lawyer living in the United States, who openly criticized the legal system of his country of heritage, Singapore, on a blog called *Singapore Dissident*. As a result, Nair was arrested and imprisoned for several months in 2008.[43] There are numerous similar cases of public statements we can interpret as symbolic digitally-based civil disobedience from countries such as Egypt, Iran, or Syria.

Other good examples of civil disobedience as a form of symbolic politics are recent interventions by artistic and political collectives such as the Yes-Men, the Center for Political Beauty, or the Peng! Collective.[44] Their digital campaigns enact what we might call a hyperreal narrative: they create simulated parodies of events, or an alternative political narrative that only prove critical when closely examined.[45] In 2014, Peng! Collective infringed Google's trademark to create a website called www.google-nest.org, which appeared to advertise new Google products such as Google Bee, a private drone which allegedly could be used for private surveillance purposes. All products on the website were, of course, fictional and their presentation resulted in threats of prosecution against the Peng! Collective.

The Internet now provides a rich culture of audiovisual formats for political speech and action. Reacting to the fact that as "the semiotic field grows increasingly complex, so does the need for critical attention,"[46] political video remixes have emerged. They may conflict with the law because of copyright infringements. One example is the work of the British mashup-duo Cassetteboy, who published a video parody showing a montage of a speech by British Prime Minister David Cameron. Attracting millions of views on YouTube, it left its producers in fear of prosecution for copyright infringement.[47] At first glance, the group's copyright infringement (now no longer illegal due to 2014 legislative changes) appears as a shallow political act and might easily be mistaken for an insincere creative stunt. Only at closer examination does its critical edge become evident. Some have gone so far as to argue that such video remixes should be viewed as "digital arguments,"[48] a sincere political practice having a rich provenance in the history of politically inspired filmmaking and montage. As entertaining as this type of civil disobedience might prove, it vividly illustrates the centrality of the public battle over the prevailing prerogatives of interpreting and controlling political narratives.

THE ENTANGLEMENT BETWEEN SYMBOLIC AND INFRASTRUCTURAL POLITICS

Two examples of civil disobedience that demonstrate the productive entanglement between the symbolic and infrastructural are *International Arms Trafficker* and whistleblowing along the lines practiced by Edward Snowden.

International Arms Trafficker was a website created in 1996 enabling civil disobedience against the International Traffic in Arms Regulations (ITAR). The protest was part of a major controversy concerning the civilian use of strong cryptography. ITAR had rendered the export of cryptographic code punishable. The activists, whose members referred to themselves as Cypherpunks, protested the law by actively disobeying the new export restrictions. A form on the website allowed anyone to send a piece of crypto-code via email to a server located on Anguilla; in legal terms, this meant in fact illegally exporting the code across national US borders. The activists described what they were doing openly as civil disobedience, in the process referring to Mahatma Gandhi and Martin Luther King, Jr. Additionally, the website supplied arguments opposing ITAR legislation, arguing that online privacy and freedom of expression would be harmed without legal access to strong encryption. Participants on the website could choose to stay anonymous or, alternately, publish their names on a public list; they could even send a signed letter to the US president. Within six months, around 1500 people participated publicly by providing their names, emails, hostnames, and IP addresses.

A successful example of symbolic politics, these so-called "crypto-wars" relied on communicating opposition to ITAR by drawing attention to its supposedly unjust contours. Transmission of code to Anguilla was also symbolic insofar as it exemplified harmless, though now illegal, encryption practices. At the same time, the protest was infrastructural since the digital infrastructure (the crypto script, a receiving server, a website) was essential to an act of collective civil disobedience. This combination of the symbolic and infrastructural may have been one ingredient in its political success: the export of encryption via online traffic was subsequently legalized. Despite differences globally in legislation and ongoing controversies within individual nation-states, access to strong encryption is now widely available for those engaging in digital communication.

Strong encryption is also the reason, as Snowden has correctly noted, his whistleblowing about NSA mass surveillance (viewed by many as a case of legitimate civil disobedience),[49] was possible in the first place. This case illustrates how whistleblowing can effectively intervene in public narratives: Snowden transformed the public's understanding of mass surveillance. By doing so, he laid the groundwork for an alternative narrative about state surveillance, security, and privacy. The download, storage, and transmission of data Snowden made public were also deeply dependent on a secure digital infrastructure. His actions provide an excellent example of how infrastructural politics can become a vital part of civil disobedience in the age of digital media.

THE INTERNET AS INFRASTRUCTURE AND A BASIS FOR CIVIL DISOBEDIENCE

Civil disobedience that focuses on the infrastructure of informational technology entails a different approach from symbolic digital civil disobedience. To better understand infrastructural digital disobedience, we need to understand the term infrastructure, in general, and digital infrastructure, in particular. As Jeanette Hofmann points out, infrastructures cannot be reduced to their technical materiality or functional character.[50] Their meaning is only fully revealed when seen as an amalgam of political governance, societal conventions, and connections to other infrastructures. Infrastructures, on this view, are omnipresent and inherently political; their use and manifestation are constantly negotiated and contested.

This, of course, also applies to digital infrastructure. Within the first decade of the twenty-first century, the Internet's dominance as a general purpose network[51] was fully tested, as it gained traction and took on global importance, albeit unevenly within societies and across the globe. Nonetheless, it became a widely used infrastructure, an economically increasingly relevant marketplace, which, despite being a highly surveilled and controlled architecture, transformed the dynamics of political power and the public sphere.[52] Companies such as Google and Facebook relied on this infrastructure and disrupted established economic paths;[53] they have shifted – and are still shifting – the global dynamics of politics and power in an unforeseen way. Those particularly savvy in terms of controlling and developing information technology recognize that the Internet was – and still is – the result of highly contingent factors. The architecture of hardware and cables, protocols of data transport, and an application layer consisting of software scripts and algorithms are not the results of natural force. The Internet is human-made. Its creation was contested and deeply political at every stage; it could have turned out very differently. Indeed, the Internet's future is still quite open.[54]

A view of Internet governance as in principle multi-layered and multi-stakeholder remains an important reference point. It helps explain the different varieties of civil disobedience that have developed in the context of the digital infrastructure.

Civil disobedience that interferes with the digital infrastructure by exploiting it has emerged (e.g., DDoSes, web defacements, hacks). Even more interesting are cases of infrastructural disobedience that represent *constructive* disobedience in a double sense. They are constructive in a first sense proposed by Leslie Green: the disobedient action constitutes a claim to active political participation in a context where participation otherwise is denied.[55] In a second sense, IT-infrastructure-focused strategies of civil disobedience can be viewed quite literally as constructive insofar as they invent and construct software, a platform, or service that did not previously exist. In these cases, civil disobedience differs clearly from more well-established practices that tend to rely on denied access or disruption. Constructive digital disobedience instead adds something to the world: it does not block or destroy, but instead builds and offers something new, allowing for new types of political action while in conflict with the law. It represents resistance as an elaborated form of direct action in hands-on coding of civilly disobedient infrastructures. It also exemplifies the ways in which the Internet offers novel possibilities for action, with its emerging power structures both offering room for new strategies and providing a basis for civil disobedience.

Two Examples of Infrastructural Digital Civil Disobedience

Prominent cases of the infrastructural approach to digital civil disobedience are offered by Phil Zimmerman's Pretty Good Privacy (PGP) software and the late Aaron Swartz.

In 1991 Zimmermann, a software developer from New Jersey, created and presumably published PGP software on the Internet. PGP used encryption technology based on the public key method to allow regular civilians use of military grade encryption to keep emails private. Zimmerman was accused of exporting encryption (which, as noted, had been made illegal by ITAR) by sharing PGP on the Internet. He then faced court proceedings, in which he almost lost his home, lasting over three years. Zimmerman clearly stated that PGP was, as a principled political action, a tribute to "preserving democracy."[56] The trial ended inconclusively, since Zimmermann was never found guilty of personally spreading PGP. In what may have been an attempt to circumvent draconic legal penalties, Zimmermann opted not to frame his actions as civil disobedience, even though they seem consistent with it.

With the release of PGP, Zimmermann let the genie of strong encryption out of the bottle for civil society, and, at least in most states, it could never again be contained. Even today, PGP remains the basis for most applications that use encryption, and most email traffic is encrypted by default, even though the use of personal email (content) encryption has declined (not even Zimmerman apparently encrypts his emails anymore).

Last but not least, Swartz's case provides an example of how powerful – and politically threatening to the powerful – the infrastructural approach to civil disobedience in the age of digital media has become. In 2011, Swartz was indicted under the American Computer Fraud and Abuse Act for infringing the terms of use of JSTOR, a nonprofit online archive for research articles, as well as the Massachusetts Institute of Technology's (MIT's) terms of conditions. What he had done was to code and secretly deploy a script on a computer in MIT's basement to download 4.8 million research articles (amounting to 80 percent of articles JSTOR provides) with a guest account.[57] This little piece of digital infrastructure allowed Swartz to practice the type of civil disobedience he called for in his *Open Access Guerilla Manifesto*.[58] A leading figure of the Open Access movement, Swartz called for copyright reform and for solidarity among academics to make the privatization of knowledge, in paywall-protected journals, "a thing of the past."[59]

Swartz's sharp and charismatic ability to combine symbolic politics (i.e., his manifesto) and infrastructural acts of political resistance made his protest (potentially) so successful – and thus a real threat to the powerful. Following his indictment, Swartz returned all the downloaded documents and never actually published any of them. The party (allegedly) at harm, JSTOR, decided to withdraw legal complaint and instead voluntarily publish most of the articles to which Swartz had gained access. However, the FBI refused to abandon its efforts to prosecute him. As Lawrence Lessig has accurately commented, "[t]he more they knew about Aaron the more vicious they became .... [T]hey became more intent to fight to make this an example .... You don't need to believe that Aaron was right, to see that what the government did here was wrong."[60] After months of surveillance and pressure from the FBI, Swartz committed suicide in 2013.

(RE)DEFINING CIVIL DISOBEDIENCE FOR THE DIGITAL AGE

In my view, all the examples I have given fit a suitably expansive, forward-looking view of civil disobedience. Such a view takes into account the actions and self-interpretations of real-life political subjects. Building on ideas about civil disobedience from Arendt as well as Robin Celikates,[61] I view civil disobedience as an intentional and principle-based motivated act of protest in conflict with the law, having an intersubjectively shared democratic intention and providing an entry point for democratic political deliberation. The purpose of civil disobedience is to change policies or governance in a way that fosters radical democratization. The focal issue at hand might transcend national laws or borders and instead involve transnational struggles targeting transnational institutions or corporations.

More precise definitions of civil disobedience are problematic, though we still need some common reference points for there to be a shared discourse. Rather than limiting the definition of civil disobedience too restrictively, I propose that civil disobedience's criteria should highlight those features that facilitate political deliberation. For instance, civil disobedience does not necessarily have to be public, despite the claims of Rawls and others. By this I mean that it does not have to be announced in advance or necessarily aim at creating a media spectacle. Nor should it remain clandestine: it needs to facilitate communication with fellow citizens. Anonymity in this setting often inhibits communication, since it prevents trust and reciprocity. However, in those situations where the only way to engage in civil disobedience and generate political deliberation is anonymously, there should be room for it.

Probably the most heated question in debates about civil disobedience concerns strict nonviolence. Though I agree that acts of civil disobedience cannot incorporate any kind of brutality, the term "violence" is problematic since it is too kaleidoscopic and ill-defined.[62] I agree with Andrew Sabl that a better compass is offered by raising the question of whether an act of civil disobedience aims to further cooperation within civil society.[63] To be sure, civil disobedients should carefully consider the consequences of harmful action and weigh the risk of losing the public's good will if they are to avoid being accused of destructiveness.

This position does not ignore the contestability of viewing digital disobedience as a form of civil disobedience. Candice Delmas[64] follows Scheuerman in identifying a danger of "forcing genuinely creative types of digital illegality into a conceptual and normative straitjacket that they should not be forced to wear."[65] Yet the alternative they propose leaves digital disobedients out in the cold and without a (political) jacket they may need to wear. The fact that many digitally disobedient actors "refuse to follow the standard script of civil disobedience"[66] stems from politically creative actions that potentially reinvent civil disobedience.

Following Arendt's view of civil disobedience as a political category that should be separated from how its individual examples are justified in particular cases,[67] we might view some cases of digital political action as a legitimate type of civil disobedience yet unjustified because of harmful or non-inclusive tactics employed. As Arendt argues, civil disobedience is generally legitimate as a realization of political freedom and a reminder of democracy's core aspirations. Etienne Balibar rightly states that "she pushes the idea of a politics of human rights so far as to make dissidence – in the specifically modern form of 'civic disobedience' – the touchstone of the foundation reciprocity of rights."[68] And these rights are not reserved for any specific type of political actor, nor to a specific type of strategy.

It is important to recognize that civil disobedience, by definition, is never bound to or defined by specific strategic actions that conflict with the law. Even though political rituals and conventions are in practice important for recognizing civil disobedience, these can be changed and are always politically negotiable. As Celikates and Denial De Zeeuw argue, it is "only in its push forward, almost beyond itself, to the point of becoming something else altogether, that civil disobedience maintains its full importance."[69] The fact that digital strategies are unfamiliar to conventional discourses about civil disobedience hardly provides a priori reasons for excluding them. Doing so would ignore the fact that civil disobedience is not only a philosophical category but also a consequential term widely employed in political practice. Always closely associated with this term is a political claim for attention and deliberation that generally is denied to other types of activism. Claims to civil disobedience rightfully deserve a second look from the legal system and other political actors.

Against Delmas, who claims that both liberal and radical-democratic philosophical approaches to digital disobedience fail to make the case for it as civil disobedience, my approach here suggests the possibility of a third path that takes the real-life dynamics of political practice seriously. Let me highlight the point that it is always necessary to analyze every specific case of digital civil disobedience, meaning that neither a specific practice (e.g., DDoS) nor a specific group (e.g., Anonymous) nor individual agent (such as Julian Assange) can, in general terms, deploy the term civil disobedience as a justification. Yet, a general rejection of digital actors or practices as civil disobedience falls short as well.

REMAINING CHALLENGES

Despite my view that digital forms of civil disobedience are forms of political practice that deserve to be recognized as such, I recognize that some new challenges have arisen.

First, the constructive power of creating or interfering with IT infrastructure is unevenly and not very democratically distributed in most societies.[70] Those with the requisite expertise often view themselves as part of a digital *avant-garde*,[71] and it is not uncommon for them to embody a technocratic worldview. As David Golumbia notes, these technocratic tendencies come at a high price for democracy:

> (C)oders [claim that] the political world is theirs to do with what they want, and the rest of us should stay out of it: the political world is broken, they appear to think (rightly, at least in part), and the solution to that, they think (wrongly, at least for the most part), is for programmers to take political matters into their own hands.[72]

As exaggerated as this accusation might be, Golumbia rightly points to a real problem, namely that some strategies of digital civil disobedience lack adequate entry points for democratic deliberation. So digitally based civil disobedience in these contexts might presuppose privileges that provide special access and knowledge, and perhaps even undergird the moral determination to act. This poses problems for a more fully democratic society. One important task would be to overcome this troublesome state of affairs by broadening possibilities for political participation by technological means, allowing activists and citizens to practice collective self-determination via a digitally-based community, rather than simply experience the superficial "togetherness" of digital nomads. To make digital disobedience a truly democratic endeavor, digital disobedients need to include others in their strategies. They need to be ready to enter into a pluralistic dialogue with stakeholders having different skillsets and perspectives, and they need to engage in dialogue with broader publics.

As long as infrastructural strategies of civil disobedience (e.g., Zimmerman's or Swartz's) struggle to gain widespread public acknowledgment in part because they presuppose specialized knowledge and expertise, they are probably doomed to remain misunderstood; those engaging in them will also continue to face harsh legal penalties. With so many citizens only in possession of a limited ability to understand the technical realities of digital civil disobedience, activists who opt for such strategies face political disadvantages compared to those pursuing better established strategies.

The ritualization of specific types of political action affects what gets recognized as "proper" civil disobedience. Although sit-ins, for example, might entail direct physical confrontation, they are ritualized performances now widely recognized in the public eye as potentially legitimate types of civil disobedience. However, political rituals are predicated on power inequalities that are defended not only for cultural reasons but for the purpose of privileging some types of political participation over others. They set the rules about who is allowed to speak in the political realm, and by means of which methods and types of arguments they can do so. Significantly, digital civil disobedience is not yet ritualized. In some scenarios, this might prove advantageous – for example, when its creativity and novelty generate media attention. Nonetheless, an excessive reliance on media attention and a "politics of the spectacle" also weakens its democratic credentials: the public can easily argue that the protest in question is nothing more than an apolitical cry for attention. For civil disobedience to become established in digital forms, activists need to develop strategies that better communicate what they do, and why they choose certain methods. And citizens will need to be allowed to educate themselves about digital society's infrastructural realities and the political struggles they generate.

CONCLUSIONS

Any claim to political relevance by a new form of political action risks being accused of a lack of legitimacy. The same arguments now being made against digital disobedients have been made against earlier activist groups that engaged in civil disobedience. As David Lyons argues, this pattern has often resulted in discrimination against underprivileged groups.[73] My intention here is not to imply that the actors using digital strategies of civil disobedience are generally underprivileged. In fact, the opposite is usually the case. It is no coincidence that the cases described mostly involved white males with privileged access to education and technology. Nonetheless, their digital acts are still often perceived as lacking validity. The more knowledgeable societies become in navigating, codeveloping, and questioning the symbolic and infrastructural bases of the digital world, the higher the chances are that digital civil disobedience will be recognized as potentially legitimate, and that it will increasingly take the form of mass-based protest. However, the same contingency we see at work in the history of the Internet applies to digital civil disobedience: there is no script that can tell us in advance how this novel field of resistance is going to develop.

NOTES

1. Engin Isin and Evelyn Ruppert, *Being Digital Citizens* (London: Rowman & Littlefield, 2015), 3.
2. Isin and Ruppert, *Being Digital Citizens*, 161.
3. Graham Meikle, "Intercreativity: Mapping Online Activism," in *International Handbook of Internet Research*, eds. Lisbeth Klastrup, Matthew Allen, and Jeremy Hunsinger (New York: Springer, 2010), 363–77; Stefan Münker and Alexander Roesler (eds.), *Mythos Internet* (Berlin: Suhrkamp, 1997).
4. Geert Lovink, "The ABC of Tactical Media," nettime, May 16, 1997, www.nettime.org/Lists-Archives/nettime-l-9705/msg00096.html.
5. Meikle, "Intercreativity."
6. W. Lance Bennett and Alexandra Segerberg, "The Logic of Connective Action: Digital Media and the Personalization of Contentious Politics," *Information, Communication & Society* 15, no. 5 (2012): 739–68.
7. Stefania Milan, "WikiLeaks, Anonymous, and the Exercise of Individuality: Protesting in the Cloud," in *Beyond WikiLeaks: Implications for the Future of Communications, Journalism and Society*, eds. Arne Hintz, Patrick McCurdy and Benedetta Brevini (Basingstoke: Palgrave Macmillan, 2013), 191–208.
8. Robin Celikates, "Civil Disobedience," in *The International Encyclopedia of Political Communication*, ed. Gianpietro Mazzoleni (Hoboken, N.J.: Wiley-Blackwell), 5.

9. Isin and Ruppert, *Digital Citizens*, 160.

10. Critical Arts Ensemble, "Electronic Civil Disobedience and Other Unpopular Ideas," 1996, accessed September 24, 2019, http://critical-art.net/electronic-civil-disobedience-1996/, 10.

11. Critical Arts Ensemble, "Electronic Civil Disobedience," 18.

12. Graham Meikle, "Electronic Civil Disobedience and Symbolic Power," in *Cyber Conflict and Global Politics*, ed. Karatzogianni Athina (New York: Routledge, 2009), 179; Meikle, "Intercreativity," 367.

13. Critical Arts Ensemble, "Electronic Civil Disobedience and Other Unpopular Ideas," 15.

14. Stefania Milan, *Social Movements and Their Technologies: Wiring Social Change* (Basingstoke: Palgrave Macmillan, 2013), 47.

15. Stefania Milan, *When Politics and Technology Speak the Same Language* (Toronto: Citizen Lab, Munk School of Global Affairs, University of Toronto, 2012), accessed March 30, 2020, https://cyberdialogue.ca/wp-content/uploads/2012/2012papers/CyberDialogue2012_Milan.pdf, 4.

16. Ricardo Dominguez, "Digital Zapatismo," thing.net, 1998, accessed November 14, 2013, www.thing.net/~rdom/ecd/DigZap.html.

17. See Mathias Klang, "Civil Disobedience Online," *Journal of Information, Communication & Ethics in Society* 2, no. 2 (2004), 76.

18. Paul A. Taylor, "From Hackers to Hacktivists: Speed Bumps on the Global Superhighway?" *New Media & Society* 7, no. 5 (2005): 627, 634.

19. Steven Levy, *Hackers: Heroes of the Computer Revolution* (Garden City, N.Y.: Anchor Press/Doubleday, 1984).

20. Leonie Tanczer, "Hacking the Label: Hacktivism, Race, and Gender," *Ada: A Journal of Gender, New Media, and Technology* 6 (2015): accessed March 30, 2020, https://adanewmedia.org/2015/01/issue6-tanczer/.

21. Brian J. Huschle, "Cyber Disobedience," *International Journal of Applied Philosophy* 16, no. 1 (2002): 69–83.

22. Mark Manion and Abby Goodrum, "Terrorism or Civil Disobedience: Toward a Hacktivist Ethic," *ACM SIGCAS Computers and Society* 30, no. 2 (2000): 14–19.

23. Andrew Calabrese, "Virtual Nonviolence? Civil Disobedience and Political Violence in the Information Age," *info* 6, no. 5 (2004): 332.

24. Calabrese, "Virtual Nonviolence?" 329.

25. Calabrese, "Virtual Nonviolence," 329.

26. Giovanni Ziccardi, *Resistance, Liberation Technology and Human Rights in the Digital Age* (New York: Springer, 2013), 29, 75; Maura Conway, "Hackers as Terrorists? Why It Doesn't Compute," *Computer Fraud & Security* 12 (2003): 10–13.

27. Meikle, "Disobedience and Symbolic Power," 180.

28. Klang, "Disobedience Online," 82.

29. Erin R. Pineda, "Civil Disobedience and Punishment: (Mis)Reading Justification and Strategy from SNCC to Snowden," *History of the Present* 5, no. 1 (2015): 1–30. See also Chapter 2 in this volume.

30. Candice Delmas, "Is Hacktivism the New Civil Disobedience?" *Raison politiques* 1, no. 69 (2018): 66.

31. Klang, "Disobedience Online," 82.

32. James Tully, *Public Philosophy in a New Key* (New York: Cambridge University Press, 2008), 28.

33. Quinn Norton, "How Anonymous picks targets, launches attacks, and takes powerful organizations down," *Wired* (June 2012), accessed March 30, 2020, www.wired.com/2012/07/ff_anonymous/.

34. Gabriella Coleman, *Hacker, Hoaxer, Whistleblower, Spy: The Many Faces of Anonymous* (London: Verso Books, 2014).

35. William Smith, "Reclaiming the Revolutionary Spirit: Arendt on Civil Disobedience," *European Journal of Political Theory* 9, no. 2 (2010): 149–66.

36. William E. Scheuerman, "What Edward Snowden Can Teach Theorists of Conscientious Law-Breaking," *Philosophy and Social Criticism* 42, no. 10 (2016): 958–64.

37. Evgeny Morozov, "In Defense of DDoS," *Slate* (December 2010), accessed March 30, 2020, http://www.slate.com/articles/technology/technology/2010/12/in_defense_of_ddos.html.

38. Coleman, *Hacker, Hoaxer, Whistleblower, Spy*, 120ff; Molly Sauter, *The Coming Swarm: DDOS Actions, Hacktivism, and Civil Disobedience on the Internet* (New York / London: Bloomsbury Publishing, 2014), 82ff.

39. Steve Mansfield-Devine, "Hacktivism: Assessing the Damage," *Network Security* 8 (2011): 5–13.

40. Theresa Züger, "*Reload Disobedience. Ziviler Ungehorsam im Zeitalter digitaler Medien.*" Unpublished PhD thesis, Humboldt University of Berlin (2017), 51.

41. Tim Jordan, "Online Direct Action: Hacktivism and Radical Democracy," in *Radical Democracy and the Internet: Interrogating Theory and Practice*, eds. Eugenia Siapera and Lincoln Dahlberg (New York: Palgrave Macmillan, 2007), 73–88.

42. Isin and Rupperts, *Digital Citizens*, 1.

43. Cherian George, "The Internet as a Platform for Civil Disobedience," in *A Companion to New Media Dynamics*, eds. Jean Burgess, Axel Bruns and John Hartley (New York: Wiley-Blackwell, 2013), 385–95.

44. Züger, "Reload Disobedience," 61ff.

45. Jean Baudrillard coined the term "hyperreality" in his simulation theory, as a term to describe the current stage of media reality, in which the simulation or representation of things or actions become indistinguishable from reality.

46. Virginia Kuhn, "The Rhetoric of Remix," *Transformative Works and Cultures* 9 (2012), 2.

47. Casetteboy, "Cassetteboy: Cameron's Conference Rap," 2014, accessed March 30, 2020, YouTube video, 00:01:52, www.youtube.com/watch?v=0YBumQHPAeU&feature=player_embedded.

48. Kuhn, "Rhetoric of Remix," 3.

49. See e.g. William E. Scheuerman, "Whistleblowing as Civil Disobedience: The Case of Edward Snowden," *Philosophy and Social Criticism* 40, no. 7 (2014): 609–28; Kimberley Brownlee, "The Civil Disobedience of Edward Snowden: A Response to Scheuerman," *Philosophy & Social Criticism* 42, no. 10 (2016): 965–70; Theresa Züger, "Digitaler ziviler Ungehorsam. Spurensuche der Dissidenz im digitalen Zeitalter," *Juridikum: Zeitschrift für Kritik – Recht – Gesellschaft* 4 (2014): 472–81. See also Chapter 15 in this volume.

50. Jeanette Hofmann, "Digitale Kommunikationsinfrastrukturen," in *Handbuch Digitalisierung in Staat und Verwaltung*, eds. Tanja Klenk, Frank Nullmeier and Göttrik Wewer (Wiesbaden: VS Verlag für Sozialwissenschaften, forthcoming).

51. David D. Clark, "The Contingent Internet," *Daedalus* 145, no. 1 (2016): 10, accessed March 30, 2020, www.mitpressjournals.org/doi/10.1162/DAED_a_00361.

52. See Yochai Benkler et al., "Social Mobilization and the Networked Public Sphere: Mapping the SOPA-PIPA debate," *Berkman Center Research Publication* No. 2013-16 (2013); Nancy Fraser, *Die Transnationalisierung*

der Öffentlichkeit (Wiesbaden: VS Verlag für Sozialwissenschaften, 2008).

53. Tatiana Bazzichelli, "*Networked Disruption. Rethinking Oppositions in Art, Hacktivism and the Business of Social Networking*" (PhD thesis, Aarhus University: Digital Aesthetics Research Center, 2011).

54. Clark, "Contingent Internet."

55. Leslie Green, "Globalization, Disobedience and the Rule of Law," Institute for International Law and Justice, 2006, accessed September 25, 2019, www.iilj.org/wp-content/uploads/2016/11/Green-Globalization-Civil-Disobedience-and-the-Rule-of-Law-2006.pdf, 6.

56. Philip Zimmermann, "Why I Wrote PGP," Phil Zimmermann on PGP, 1991, accessed March 30, 2020, www.philzimmermann.com/EN/essays/index.html.

57. Nancy Sims, "Library Licensing and Criminal Law: The Aaron Swartz case," *College & Research Libraries News* 72, no. 9 (2011): 535; Declan Butler, "US justice system 'overreach' blamed in suicide of Internet-freedom activist," *Nature News Blog*, 2013, accessed March 30, 2020, http://blogs.nature.com/news/2013/01/us-justice-system-overreach-blamed-in-suicide-of-internet-freedom-activist.html.

58. Aaron Swartz, "Guerilla Open Access Manifesto," *The Internet Archive* (2008), accessed March 30, 2020, https://archive.org/stream/GuerillaOpenAccessManifesto/Goamjuly2008_djvu.txt.

59. Swartz, "Guerrilla Open Access Manifesto."

60. "Transcript: Lawrence Lessig on 'Aaron's Laws – Law and Justice in a Digital Age,'" nakedcapitalism (March 6, 2013), www.nakedcapitalism.com/2013/03/transcript-lawrence-lessig-on-aarons-laws-law-and-justice-in-a-digital-age-section-ii.html.

61. [61]. See Celikates's contribution in this volume.

62. Sybille Krämer, " 'Humane Dimensionen' sprachlicher Gewalt oder: Warum symbolische und körperliche Gewalt wohl zu unterscheiden sind," in *Gewalt in der Sprache. Rhetoriken verletzenden Sprechens*, eds. Sybille Krämer and Elke Koch (Munich: Fink, 2010), 22.

63. Andrew Sabl, "Looking Forward to Justice: Rawlsian Civil Disobedience and its Non-Rawlsian Lessons," *Journal of Political Philosophy* 9, no. 3 (2001): 307–30.

64. Delmas, "Hacktivism."

65. Scheuerman, "Edward Snowden," 310.

66. Delmas, "Hacktivism," 70.

67. Hannah Arendt, *Macht und Gewalt* (Munich: Piper, 1996), 53.

68. Etienne Balibar, *Equaliberty: Political Essays* (Durham: Duke University Press, 2014), 168.

69. Robin Celikates and Daniel De Zeeuw, "Botnet Politics, Algorithmic Resistance and Hacking Society," *Hacking Habitat. Art of Control* (2015): 211.

70. Wendy H. Wong and Peter A. Brown, "E-Bandits in Global Activism: WikiLeaks, Anonymous, and the Politics of No One," *Perspectives on Politics* 11, no. 4 (2013), 1016.

71. Christiane Funken, "Der Hacker," in *Diven, Hacker, Spekulanten: Sozialfiguren der Gegenwart*, eds. Stephan Moebius and Markus Schroer (Frankfurt: Suhrkamp, 2010), 194.

72. David Golumbia, "Tor, Technocracy, Democracy," *Uncomputing* (2015), accessed March 30, 2020, www.uncomputing.org/?p=1647, 162.

73. David Lyons, "Moral Judgment, Historical Reality, and Civil Disobedience," *Philosophy & Public Affairs* 27, no. 1 (1998): 48.

15 Whistleblowing as Civil Disobedience

William E. Scheuerman

From Chelsea Manning and Edward Snowden, to the anonymous intelligence official whose revelations about President Trump's illegal campaign activities in Ukraine helped lead to his impeachment by the House of Representatives, whistleblowers have captivated public attention in the US and elsewhere. Christopher Wylie "blew the whistle" on UK-based Cambridge Analytica, revealing in March 2018 that his former employer had mined Facebook data to manipulate voters. Recent EU-wide attempts to regulate offshore finance have been motivated by the so-called Panama Papers (2015) and Paradise Papers (2017).[1] Candice Delmas may be exaggerating somewhat when claiming that "[i]f the twentieth century was the age of civil disobedience, the twenty-first century is shaping up to be the age of whistleblowing."[2] Yet Delmas is right to highlight whistleblowing's (henceforth, WB) massive global political impact, and the ways in which it increasingly performs functions long standardly associated with civil disobedience (henceforth, CD). Some commentators have gone so far as to dub digitally based WB, along the lines pursued by Manning and Snowden, "the new civil disobedience" better suited than its more familiar types to contemporary social conditions.[3]

It seems like an appropriate political juncture to get a better handle on the nexus between WB and CD. Here I start by revisiting the longstanding view that they constitute related and sometimes overlapping practices, before moving to explore an emerging body of literature that instead draws a sharper line between WB and CD, and envisions them as fundamentally contraposed. Although scholars are

I am grateful to Candice Delmas for astute critical comments on an earlier version.

pursuing this newer path with the promise of achieving greater conceptual clarity, they inadvertently muddy the waters, in part by relying on tendentious empirical as well as theoretical claims. CD and WB remain, in fact, parallel and occasionally fused practices. For conceptual as well as political reasons, we would do well not to create artificial conceptual barriers between them. Although improved whistleblower protections remain a praiseworthy political goal, WB will occasionally entail legal infractions and personal risk-taking that potentially threaten the powerful and privileged. Some intersection between WB and CD, in short, seems likely to endure.

Why does it matter? One consequence of WB's growing prominence is that its practitioners today "are often enshrined in the tradition of civil disobedience," with the two terms frequently used interchangeably in public discourse.[4] WB is associated in the public mind with CD in part because whistleblowers often self-identify as such. They do so because CD possesses a moral and political cachet that alternative terms (e.g., "leaker," "snitch," "traitor") lack. One notable consequence is that state officials (e.g., judges, prosecutors) sometimes treat those viewed as falling under CD's rubric more leniently than other legal offenders. When successfully placing their efforts under the rubric of CD, whistleblowers can claim the mantle of iconic political figures and garner valuable accolades. The intuition that CD and WB sometimes intersect is not only theoretically sound: it also potentially makes a real difference to whistleblowers.

OVERLAPPING TERRITORY

Whistleblowers have repeatedly invoked famous civil disobedients to justify their endeavors. Daniel Ellsberg's autobiographical *Secrets: A Memoir of Vietnam and the Pentagon Papers* vividly recounts the decisive role his readings of Henry David Thoreau, Mahatma Gandhi, and Dr. Martin Luther King played in his decision to leak secret Pentagon documents, while Snowden has regularly channeled King.[5] Tom Mueller's mammoth recent survey of WB reports that major figures in the history of CD represent "recurrent voices" among the whistleblowers with whom Mueller met and whose activities he documents.[6] Mueller documents that many WB practitioners have viewed their acts as analogous to CD and modeled them on lawbreaking by Gandhi, King, and other iconic figures.

Significant differences between the two phenomena nonetheless can be identified. Starting with the conventional view of WB as referring to "disclosures by organization members (former or current) of illegal, immoral or illegitimate practices under the control of their employers, to persons or organizations that may be able to effect action," we can see why WB prospectively encompasses acts that cannot be subsumed under any recognizable or probably coherent view of CD.[7] Specifically, when private or public organizations possess well-functioning internal channels for WB, and those pursuing it are unlikely to face legal penalties or other negative repercussions, WB should not be characterized as "disobedience to the law within the limits of fidelity to the law."[8] WB sometimes lacks CD's *sine qua non*, namely: a politically motivated violation of *some* law, even if one only "indirectly" related to some injustice.

Nonetheless, Ellsberg, Snowden, and countless less prominent whistleblowers are right to see WB as closely related to – and sometimes imbricated with – CD. Given WB's oftentimes precarious and sometimes nonexistent legal protections, those pursuing it regularly run aground of the law and face legal repercussions not dissimilar to those familiar from CD's messy history. It often remains "difficult, in practice, to predict exactly when the law will be used to protect a given whistleblower, or instead to penalize her."[9] Even where WB rests on seemingly firm institutional or legal foundations, its practitioners can face draconian penalties, legal or otherwise (e.g., pariah status at work, unemployment).[10]

The still anonymous US intelligence officer who filed the 2019 internal whistleblowing complaint against President Trump, for example, meticulously followed administrative procedures. Nevertheless, his identity was quickly unveiled by Trump and the President's partisan supporters in a fierce round of tweet-motored outbursts. Although arguably representing *illegal* retaliation against the whistleblower, the President's actions will likely remain unpunished for many political and legal reasons. Of course, the intelligence officer might have opted to file a lawsuit claiming damages against the President, but by all accounts its prospects seemed at best uncertain. His admirers may still hope that he will gain a "future place of honor in the service of his country," but this surely represents meager compensation given the substantial perils he has faced.[11]

To be sure, not all whistleblowers face the wrath of an angry and arguably unhinged US President. Yet many of them still confront grave formal as well as informal sanctions. Without far-reaching reform, there is little reason to expect sudden improvements to whistleblowers' oftentimes precarious institutional and legal status.[12]

Not surprisingly, the substantial scholarly literature on WB draws implicitly and sometimes explicitly on familiar ideas about CD, which can be concisely characterized as *public* and *politically motivated* lawbreaking that exhibits *civility, conscientiousness, nonviolence,* and *legal fidelity,* or what King famously called "respect for law."[13] Because CD is an essentially contested concept, we necessarily encounter starkly competing interpretations of CD and its various components. Like other essentially contested concepts, CD is necessarily "appraisive" or evaluative, internally complex (insofar as it consists of a variety of key traits), and subject to "considerable modification in the light of changing circumstances."[14] Consequently, "there is nothing absurd or contradictory" about the concept taking rival forms.[15]

As I have elsewhere argued, it makes sense to conceive of CD in terms of competing religious-spiritual (think of Gandhi or King), liberal (e.g., John Rawls or Ronald Dworkin), republican or radical democratic (Hannah Arendt or Jürgen Habermas) and sometimes, though somewhat more controversially, anarchist versions (inspired on occasion by Thoreau).[16] However, these rival accounts still rely on a common analytic language that proffers useful parameters for determining which acts can be sensibly placed under CD's complex, multisided ideational rubric. Even if conscientiousness and legal fidelity meant starkly different things to Gandhi and Rawls, for example, their participation in CD's shared conceptual discourse allows us to identify some underlying commonalities. A parallel conceptual claim can be made in reference to WB, which has been similarly defined in competing – yet frequently overlaying – ways.[17] It too constitutes an essentially contested concept whose rival renditions nonetheless possess some underlying family resemblances.

WB clearly mimics CD in its quest to disclose "illegal, immoral or illegitimate practices" in order to effect corrective action.[18] Both activities can also be viewed as forms of dissent that pit individuals or groups against oftentimes powerful institutions and their official representatives; both raise difficult normative questions about how to justify breaches of loyalty – in the case of WB, typically in the context of specific organizations (e.g., a private corporation or government agency); in CD, vis-à-vis an unjust law or political practice. WB's academic defenders often posit that illegal, immoral, or illegitimate practices need to be sufficiently serious for WB to be justified, just as CD's exponents frequently require that protested injustices need to be genuinely egregious for lawbreaking to be legitimate. In both CD and WB scholarship, there is a tendency to privilege acts that are deliberate and well-grounded, with practitioners expected to minimize damage or harm to uninvolved parties. Public-mindedness and some attempt to sway a broader public are widely seen as essential to both, with commentators on CD and WB, revealingly, struggling in parallel ways to grasp when and how some measure of personal anonymity might nonetheless be acceptable.[19]

Similarly, WB and CD tend to be conceived as personally risky activities requiring moral conviction and even personal courage.[20] They both typically involve moral soul-searching and rest on some appeal to individual conscience. Because of their high personal costs and institutionally unsettling ramifications, WB and CD are generally depicted as last resorts justifiable only when more conventional channels for voicing dissent have been exhausted. Even when normatively legitimate, particular acts of either WB or CD may prove pragmatic-ally unsound and counterproductive; both require political judgment and prudence. Finally, some analysts have highlighted WB's impli-citly nonviolent contours, finding parallels between it and nonviolent lawbreaking.[21]

Admittedly, much of the debate about WB pertains to *individ-ual private employees* within *private* organizations (e.g., the corpor-ation), with CD instead interpreted as lawbreaking by *groups* of *citizens* aiming to alter *public* practices and policies – in other words, as taking place in very different institutional settings and involving distinctive social roles. As the examples of Ellsberg and Snowden remind us, however, WB can transpire in state or public organizations and have massive political repercussions, with many whistleblowers endeavoring to "out" public officials and what they view as nefarious state practices. For its part, CD has sometimes targeted "private" institutions and practices, and on certain theoret-ical accounts has been interpreted as legitimately directed at corpor-ations and other ostensibly private organizations.[22] In a social context where the distinction between public and private authority seems increasingly blurred, with states relying heavily on private bodies to undertake even their most basic functions, it may no longer make sense to limit justifiable CD to acts of lawbreaking directed specific-ally at government or state institutions.[23]

WB and CD both rely on some measure of joint or cooperative action. Even the iconic "lonely" whistleblower who regularly appears both in the public imagination and scholarly literature typically depends on a more-or-less extensive social (and sometimes political) networks.[24] Ellsberg and Snowden, for example, famously relied on journalists and media personalities (and many others as well) to "blow the whistle" successfully: without the *Washington Post* or *The Guardian* their messages would never have had the impact they did.

My point so far is relatively straightforward: the boundaries between CD and WB can easily become blurred. Predictably, not just Ellsberg and Snowden but also many academic commentators have correctly acknowledged that when WB involves some politically motivated *legal* breach it may simultaneously constitute CD. As Sissela Bok hypothesized nearly forty years ago (with the example of the ex-CIA agent Philip Agee probably in mind), a "combination of the two [WB and CD] occurs, for instance, when former CIA agents publish books to alert the public about what they regard as unlawful and dangerous practices, and in so doing openly violate ... the oath of secrecy they have sworn."[25] To be sure, in order to fall under the rubric of CD, a whistleblower's actions "must meet certain conditions for that [latter] term to apply," conditions deriving from some plausible interpretation of CD as public and politically motivated lawbreaking, embodying elements of civility, conscientiousness, nonviolence, and legal fidelity.[26] Because CD, as noted, necessarily constitutes a contested concept about which serious disagreements will unavoidably surface, the specific fashion in which WB and CD fuse will vary correspondingly. CD's core elements, as noted, can be interpreted in quite different ways: nonviolence may mean avoiding harm to persons and/or property; publicity can mean requiring that agents are public and/or that their actions rest on some sort of public justification. Any act of WB that claims the status of CD will need to instantiate *some* version of such components. Correspondingly, those that fail to do so *cannot* be plausibly interpreted as CD.[27] Nonetheless, the scope for overlap between WB and CD is likely to remain large and theoretically significant.

Let me preliminarily conclude by briefly illustrating this rather general claim with recourse to Snowden. Identifying overlap between WB and CD does *not* require characterizing either practice in unproductively open-ended or amorphous ways. As we will see in the section to follow, those who minimize or even deny possible overlap, in contrast, tend instead to rely on overly cramped views of both.

Kimberley Brownlee has broken with what she views as inappropriately narrow standard liberal (e.g., Rawlsian) views of CD, redefining it broadly as "*conscientious* communicative breach[es] of the law motivated by steadfast, sincere, and serious, though possibly mistaken, moral commitment."[28] Snowden's 2013 WB revelations about illegal US surveillance, she argues, can be credibly characterized as CD, in part because they were non-evasive, public, intended to provoke debate, and undertaken so as to minimize unnecessary harm.[29] Other theorists have plausibly interpreted Snowden's revelations as CD by appealing to other, even less conventional accounts.[30] Even on stricter interpretations of CD, Snowden's WB can be interpreted as meeting its conditions. Snowden acted *conscientiously*, and, by working with journalists who curated classified government documents to minimize unnecessary harm, also *nonviolently*. He revealed his identity and then publicly justified his acts (*publicity*), and also defended his actions as coherent with his duties as a US citizen (*civility*). Of course, Snowden fled the US and thus far has refused to accept legal penalties. Nonetheless, he has repeatedly stated that he would be willing to return to the US *if* permitted to mount a legal defense apropos his understanding of his acts as CD, something for all practical purposes denied him under the terribly repressive US Espionage Act. In many other ways (e.g., his extensive legal justifications for his actions), he has tried to demonstrate *fidelity to the law*.[31]

In sum, Snowden's claim that he deserves to be treated by state officials as a civil disobedient seems plausible. Whether he will ever get a real chance to make his case in a fair legal hearing remains unlikely, however. Tellingly, US Secretary of State Mike Pompeo declared that the "proper outcome" for any such tribunal "would be that he [Snowden] would be given a death sentence for putting friends of mine, friends of yours, in the military today, at enormous risk," hardly an auspicious starting point for hearings that should be expected to respect basic due process.[32]

Admittedly, Snowden may represent something of an exception among politically motivated government whistleblowers given his decision to come forward publicly: many who engage in government WB are reluctant to do so in light of its potentially disastrous personal consequences. One of the analytic advantages of recognizing CD's status as a contested concept is that doing so reminds us that the publicity condition should not be interpreted in an overly stringent manner. Wherever "institutional societal, and legal circumstance impose unfair burdens on the whistleblower by exacting [extreme] personal and professional costs," it may be unfair to require that she reveal her identity.[33] Then some sort of *public revelation* and *public justification* might suffice for an act of WB to meet CD's publicity demands.

STRICTER BOUNDARIES?

Against this longstanding view of WB and CD as parallel and sometimes intertwined activities, recent writers have tried to draw a sharper line between them. In their view, the "general tendency in the current debate to conceive of whistleblowing as a form of civil disobedience" cannot in fact be coherently defended.[34] Fundamental phenomenological differences between WB and CD, it seems, have far-reaching conceptual and empirical ramifications. Even if WB and CD sometimes evince distant family resemblances, they remain basically discrete creatures.

Theorists in this camp are justifiably worried by the occasionally indiscriminate way in which the terms CD and WB get bandied about. Nonetheless, I fear that their otherwise well-meaning and oftentimes impressive efforts risk generating an unproductive conceptual rigidity as well as a certain disconnect from political reality. In their haste to delineate WB as cleanly as possible from CD, critics of the conventional view risk misrepresenting both phenomena in a manner unlikely to prove useful. By day's end, they paint pictures of CD and WB that probably do justice to neither.

The critics' key analytic pivot usually entails characterizing CD in a narrow and sometimes sectarian fashion in order to highlight WB's distinctive attributes. Rather than recognizing that CD and WB both represent essentially contested concepts capable of multiple, unavoidably rival formulations, writers instead employ the strictest possible – and also arguably least defensible – accounts of CD as a theoretical springboard. By doing so, they can move expeditiously to interpret examples of WB that on alternative – and sometimes perhaps more convincing – readings of CD might be viewed as over-lapping, as instead alien. Circumscribing CD's scope narrowly allows critics to overstate its tensions vis-à-vis WB. The main problem with this strategy is that too much of the analytic work is achieved by a terminological sleight-of-hand: only if we accept the critics' tenden-tious starting point (i.e., a narrow interpretation of CD) do their results hold water.

The least persuasive version of this strategy interprets CD stin-gily as referring to individualistic acts of conscientiousness lawbreak-ing. Emanuele Ceva and Michele Bocchiola argue that unlike CD, WB should *not* be characterized as resting on an individual appeal to moral conscience for the sake of maintaining personal integrity. Consequently, the two practices diverge sharply.[35] Unfortunately, this position obscures a rich tradition of interpreting CD as *both* morally conscientious *and* politically motivated lawbreaking. WB is successfully contrasted to CD, but only because the latter has been misleadingly reduced to a pale copy of what almost universally has been seen as a *political* practice involving collective action and demanding something along the lines of an appeal to what Rawls called common principles of political justice. On Rawls's influential definition, for example, CD represents "conscientious yet political" lawbreaking, justified on the basis of shared principles of justice, and necessarily public, nonviolent, and "within the limits of fidelity to law," thus requiring of disobedients that they typically be ready to accept a legal penalty.[36]

Other critics start from precisely this Rawlsian model.[37] But they do so only in order to contrast his (supposedly) hegemonic view of CD with WB's messy empirical realities, some of which indeed contradict it. Rawls is placed on a theoretical pedestal chiefly in order to knock him down. Why Rawls should be treated as CD's authorita-tive intellectual and political figure, however, remains unclear. His approach has been criticized by many (including contributors to this volume) for its limitations, such as its politically cautious view of CD as suited to a modest reform, but hardly a radical overhaul, of "nearly just" or basically liberal societies.[38] The critics' preoccupation with Rawls does a disservice to historical experience and canonical figures such as Gandhi and King, whose ideas about CD cannot be subsumed under the Rawlsian framework. It also neglects myriad impressive attempts to supersede Rawls, developed partly as a way to proffer more expansive and suitable views of CD.[39] I cannot fully recount that complicated historical and conceptual story here.[40] Yet it bears keeping in mind as we examine recent attempts to draw strict boundaries between CD and WB. How we define and employ the concept of CD will always have far-reaching consequences. Because CD is an essentially contested concept, it irrepressibly generates legitimate disagreements about its precise contours. Nevertheless, we need to avoid rigging the game at the outset by conceptual fiat.

Because Delmas has outlined the most nuanced rendition of this position, her attempt to distinguish CD and WB deserves a close look. Focusing on the legally unauthorized acquisition and disclosure of classified information (as practiced by Manning, Snowden, and others), she zeroes in on a relatively limited subset of WB, that is, precisely those cases involving politically motivated lawbreaking and thus apparently most akin to CD. Why not place unauthorized government WB under the rubric of CD? Unlike CD, such WB represents a form of *political vigilantism*, resting on some "transgression of the boundaries around state secrets, for the purpose of challenging the allocation or use of power."[41] For Delmas, politically minded cases of WB tend to be "uncivil in some ways" and thus cannot pass muster according to notions of *civility* typically associated with CD, as defined by Rawls and other liberal theorists.[42] Despite her general skepticism about the Rawlsian approach, it serves Delmas as a convenient launching pad for her own critical analysis. As she observes, unauthorized government WB is often covert, its practitioners legitimately insist on anonymity and try to evade punishment, and they sometimes put national security at risk.[43] Moreover, their acts do not demand redress from state authorities for injustice, but instead tend irreversibly to undo "the secrecy the state had determined appropriate or necessary."[44] How could such actions possibly be characterized as meeting those conditions usually associated with Rawlsian ideas of CD?

Delmas is right to suggest that some types of WB conflict with influential liberal views of CD; some forms of WB will in fact simply fail to meet their conditions. Yet, by starting with a narrow definition of CD and highlighting cases of incongruent WB, Delmas unfairly downplays the possibility of meaningful overlap. One source of this skepticism is a stringent – and probably misleading – conception of *civility*. Her analysis's Rawlsian target quickly morphs into a straw-person "standard" liberal approach, with CD interpreted as requiring strict publicity, legal non-evasiveness (i.e., the acceptance of legal sanctions), nonviolence, and proper decorum (or "non-offensiveness").[45] Unfortunately, this claim fails to do justice to complex debates not only among many who forcefully reject the Rawlsian approach, but even among those liberals who follow Rawls by breaking with religious-spiritual ideas of CD as a form of divine witness requiring appropriate moral decorum, or what Delmas dubs "a dignified and polite manner" that avoids "causing offense."[46] Gandhi, King, and other spiritually minded advocates have in fact emphasized the centrality of politeness and decorum to CD. However, at least since Rawls most liberals – and countless others – have refused to do so.[47]

Significantly, liberals and others have instead interpreted civility primarily as requiring of politically motivated lawbreakers that they interpret their endeavors as contributions to a *shared political project*. On this view, disobedients should view themselves as agents participating in cooperative or *civic* efforts to realize justice or improve democracy, and thus having some obligation to evince *basic respect* for their peers as political equals.[48] This decidedly political interpretation of civility, to be sure, can take many different forms. But the decisive point for now is that it opens the door to considering some cases of unauthorized government WB potentially as CD. For example, to the extent that Ellsberg, Snowden, and even Manning, though perhaps failing to meet strict Rawlsian conditions for publicity or legal fidelity, still aspired to spur their fellow citizens into political action, they might on this view be plausibly viewed as having engaged in *both* CD *and* WB. Unfortunately, critics' dependence on Rawls as a definitional foil too often impedes a careful consideration of such possibilities.

In fairness, Delmas is right to worry that open-ended ideas about CD risk rendering the concept perilously amorphous: if CD is allowed to mean anything it effectively means nothing, and then it indeed becomes impossible to delineate WB from CD.[49] Recognizing CD's status as an essentially contested concept, however, hardly requires sacrificing conceptual precision. Delmas's understandable terminological anxieties, at any rate, cannot justify her own embrace of a narrow definition that tends to overstate differences between WB and CD.

Delmas is not alone in trying to delineate WB from CD on the basis of a rather rigid Rawlsian launching pad. Nor is she the only contemporary writer who proceeds to make bold – but probably overstated – claims about WB's fundamental phenomenological differences vis-à-vis CD.[50] CD, she argues, necessarily involves a number of actors and participants, whereas WB simply requires a single "lonely" whistleblower. WB can dangerously undermine national security while CD's perils tend to be relatively limited. WB's effects are typically more harmful than CD's.[51] Those engaging in CD usually face minor infractions; whistleblowers instead may face grave consequences for their actions (e.g., prosecution under the US Espionage Act). Last but not least, CD has often been interpreted as suited to "nearly just" or basically liberal societies. In contrast, WB can be well suited to distinctly authoritarian contexts where anonymity and legal evasiveness can be more easily justified.[52]

Even if such contrasts provide a useful shorthand for distinguishing *some* types of WB from CD, they hardly seem sufficiently clear cut. On the one hand (as already noted), the image of the lonely whistleblower is probably more myth than reality: even Ellsberg and Snowden relied on extensive social and political networks to make their revelations publicly accessible. On the other hand, many exemplars from the history of CD began with individual and, yes, occasionally isolated, acts of conscientious defiance.[53] *Sometimes* WB can generate substantial harm and pose threats to national security – a controversial term, by the way, that surely requires systematic interrogation. Yet CD can prove no less politically and socially disruptive: it is hardly accidental that their enemies delighted in describing Gandhi and King as political subversives, traitors, or worse.

Admittedly, in liberal political cultures where CD's political virtues have been widely recognized, politically motivated lawbreakers sometimes only face minor legal penalties. But elsewhere CD is often punished punitively, with protestors facing grave consequences even for minor forms of symbolic lawbreaking. Finally, though Rawls and other liberal theorists viewed CD as well suited to liberal societies, since Gandhi CD has been productively employed as a political tactic against authoritarian states and their leaders.

To be clear: my point is not that WB and CD are equivalent. Nonetheless, the quest to draw strict boundaries between them distorts some messy historical and political realities. It is simply not true, for example, that CD necessarily represents a politically stabilizing and institutionally conservative force, whereas contemporary government WB as practiced by Julian Assange or Manning is an altogether creative, novel activity that poses a radical challenge to the political status quo.[54] Such claims say more about the writer's own political preferences than the complex conceptual and empirical realities at hand.

Other attempts to distinguish WB from CD ultimately prove no more successful. Allison Stanger asserts that WB typically involves an appeal to – while CD challenges – the law, an observation that simply ignores the commonplace view of CD as requiring evidence for what King called the "highest respect for law."[55] Revealingly, Daniele Santoro and Manohar Kumar make precisely the opposite claim, in the process inadvertently suggesting how troublesome such sharp distinctions become on closer examination.[56] They also tell us that unlike CD, WB is typically pursued by those unaffected by the practice being challenged: WB exhibits nonpartisanship by "inject[ing] vital informational resources" into public debate.[57] Yet this conceptual delineation also seems overstated. Both CD and WB can have far-reaching political repercussions and sometimes involve "other-regarding" agents or participants (e.g., upper middle class northern whites who joined southern blacks in the US Civil Rights Movement). Context-dependent considerations also weigh more heavily in determining when WB is justified, they claim, than in similar deliberations about CD.[58] Yet even the most normative-minded philosophers have consistently recognized that political context and prudential considerations matter when evaluating CD.[59]

Following Delmas, Eric Boot posits that government WB not only involves a violation of the law (as in CD) but also "immediately result[s] in the repeal of the contested law" and thus represents a "usurpation of power."[60] Though perhaps accurate in cases of WB involving high-level officials possessing direct access to state power and able effectively to nullify standing law, the contrast works less well with lower-level officials. In the vast majority of cases, WB does not in fact unilaterally revoke or overrule some suspect law or practice. Even if Snowden's dramatic revelations about US surveillance hindered the intelligence apparatus from continuing to conduct "business as usual," for example, he did not "usurp" lawmaking by bringing its most controversial practices to an abrupt standstill. While it is also true that government whistleblowers typically tap privileged "insider" information ordinary citizens lack, it is unclear that such "[p]rivileged information contrasts with civil disobedience" and generates unusual justificatory difficulties.[61] Many civil disobedients have also had "privileged" or at least special knowledge: British colonial subjects in India or African Americans in the segregated US South surely possessed a richer grasp of the terrible political injustices they sought to eliminate than many bystanders or state officials.

Informational asymmetries play a role and generate difficult questions even in familiar cases of CD.

To be sure, much can be learned from recent theoretical attempts to identify WB's distinctive traits. But if we insist on envisioning CD and WB as inhabiting distant and indeed alien worlds, we are likely to lose a clear view of both.

PROTECTING WHISTLEBLOWERS

In this chapter I have insisted on the existence of possible and sometimes significant overlap between WB and CD. Such intersection is hardly surprising: whistleblowers have regularly been inspired by prominent civil disobedients and have modeled their actions accordingly, in part because of CD's substantial moral and political capital. Appeals to CD's imposing practical and intellectual legacy potentially improve whistleblowers' political and legal standing, something many of them clearly appreciate.

Assuredly, even when successfully persuading state officials and publics that their acts constitute CD, whistleblowers may still fail to profit from its moral and political capital. Prosecutors may throw the book at them, or judges sanction them harshly, particularly when their protests seem strikingly dissimilar to the iconic examples of CD state officials rigidly employ as a measuring rod.[62] Despite some real advantages, having one's WB recognized as CD hardly provides secure legal protections.

Why not then push for improved institutional and legal mechanisms making effective and relatively costless WB easily available to all employees, both private and public? After all, if whistleblowers enjoyed better institutional and legal protections, they would no longer ideally have to break the law, let alone worry about legitimizing their lawbreaking by recalling Thoreau, Gandhi, or King. WB might no longer potentially overlay CD because the former would finally be institutionalized and legalized. Whistleblowers could then disclose illegal, immoral, or illegitimate institutional practices without fearing negative repercussions or draconian legal penalties.

There are many sensible reasons to push for better WB protections; the practical and scholarly literatures are filled with powerful calls to do so.[63] In this vein, Ceva and Bocchiola have suggested that by firming up its institutional and legal protections we could finally break with the commonplace – but analytically misleading – image of WB as an individual act of dissent "motivated by *personal* reasons of justice and integrity," rather than "an *organizational practice*, justified as a matter of duty by *public* reasons of justice and accountability."[64] If WB were successfully institutionalized according to sound principles of justice and accountability, they argue, we could cease inaccurately associating it with heroic individuals acting on the basis of conscience. On their view, WB constitutes a moral *duty* owed by members of legitimate organizations to one another having privileged access to information concerning alleged wrongdoing. In any legitimate organization (broadly defined as "entitled [legally or morally] to the power it exercises through the actions of its members"), employees would be expected to report wrongdoing "when facing either some practice within an organization, or the behavior of some of its members, that contradicts the mandate with which power is attributed" to the organization and the specific roles played by individuals within it.[65]

A great deal can be said in favor of this view. Nonetheless, there are still grounds for caution. How many major contemporary institutions (e.g., the state, large corporations) can or should be described as fully or even sufficiently legitimate? Given the *im*perfections of a social and political universe plagued by injustice and inequality, how realistic is it to hope that WB might be seamlessly subsumed under formal institutional and legal channels? WB often targets political and economic elites; it operates in a power field that generally favors such elites.[66] Under present conditions *some* acts of WB, that is, those challenging powerful, entrenched political and social actors, seem destined to remain controversial. Accordingly, whistleblowers will likely continue to pay a high price for their actions, even if that price were no longer sanctioned by law. In an unequal and deeply unjust political and social order, a significant subset of cases of WB will continue to call for courageous, personally risky action. Even when WB has been given a more secure basis and sanctions are "merely" informal, they may remain costly, in part because the powerful and privileged will prefer to keep it that way.

In short, absent a significantly more just and egalitarian social order (and more legitimate institutions), some acts of WB will assuredly generate duress for those pursuing them. For better or worse, whistleblowers – and their defenders – will continue to view their endeavors as conscientious rule violations aimed at checking injustice favoring the powerful and privileged. Even as we continue to fight to improve its legal and institutional protections, we should keep in mind that WB will continue to overlap with CD in ways that Ellsberg, Snowden, and countless others would have recognized.

NOTES

1. The latter examples refer to documents proving massive tax evasion (dating back to the 1970s) by prominent political and economic figures that anonymous whistleblowers brought to the attention of journalists at the German newspaper *Süddeutsche Zeitung*.
2. Candice Delmas, "The Ethics of Government Whistleblowing," *Social Theory and Practice* 41, no. 1 (2015): 77.
3. Danah Boyd, "Whistleblowing Is the New Civil Disobedience," *Medium*, July 18, 2013, https://medium.com/@zephoria/whistleblowing-is-the-new -civil-disobedience-9a53415933a9; Molly Sauter, *The Coming Swarm* (New York: Bloomsbury, 2014). See also Theresa Züger's illuminating chapter in this volume (Chapter 14).
4. Hannah Gurman and Kaeten Mistry, "The Paradox of National Security Whistleblowing: Locating and Framing a History of the Phenomenon," in *Whistleblowing Nation: The History of National Security Disclosures and the Cult of State Secrecy*, eds. Gurman and Mistry (New York: Columbia University Press, 2020), 9.
5. Daniel Ellsberg, *Secrets: A Memoir of Vietnam and the Pentagon Papers* (New York: Penguin, 2002), 212–13; 263–64; Melissa Chan, "Edward

Snowden Invokes Martin Luther King to Defend Whistleblowing," *Time*, May 12, 2016, https://time.com/4327930/edward-snowden-martin-luther-king-whistleblowing/. Ellsberg "blew the whistle" on the US government's secret deliberations about Vietnam, deliberations that revealed a pattern of systematic deceit to the public. Snowden unveiled evidence of its massive (and probably illegal) surveillance.

6. Tom Mueller, *Crisis of Conscience: Whistleblowing in an Age of Fraud* (New York: Riverhead, 2019), 289.

7. Janet P. Near and Marcia P. Miceli, "Whistle-Blowing: Myth and Reality," *Journal of Management* 22, no. 3 (1996): 508. Standard views also distinguish internal from external WB, with the former referring to reports of wrongdoing addressed to internal institutional or organizational channels, and the latter to external channels (e.g., journalists).

8. John Rawls, *A Theory of Justice* (Cambridge, MA: Harvard University Press, 1971), 366.

9. Delmas, "The Ethics of Government Whistleblowing," 83.

10. This is a central theme in C. Fred Alford, *Whistleblowers: Broken Lives and Organizational Power* (Ithaca, NY: Cornell University Press, 2001). On some of the details as they pertain to US government WB, see Gurman and Mistry, "The Paradox of National Security Whistleblowing," 9–44.

11. David Frum, "A Gangster in the White House," *The Atlantic*, December 28, 2019, www.theatlantic.com/ideas/archive/2019/12/donald-trumps-gangster-white-house/604216/.

12. Björn Fasterling, "Whistleblower Protection: A Comparative Law Perspective," in *International Handbook on Whistleblowing Research*, eds. A.J. Brown, David Lewis, Richard Moberly, and Wim Vandekerckhove (Cheltenham, UK: Edward Elgar, 2014), 331–49.

13. Martin Luther King, "Letter from Birmingham City Jail" [1963], in *Civil Disobedience in Focus*, ed. Hugo Bedau (London: Routledge, 1991), 74. On CD and WB, Frederick A. Elliston, "Civil Disobedience and Whistleblowing: A Comparative Appraisal of Two Forms of Dissent," *Journal of Business Ethics* 1, no. 1 (1982): 23–28.

14. W.B. Gallie, "Essentially Contested Concepts," *Proceedings of the Aristotelian Society* 56, no. 1 (1956): 172. See also my discussion in the Introduction to this volume.

15. Gallie, "Essentially Contested Concepts," 172.

16. William E. Scheuerman, *Civil Disobedience* (Cambridge, UK: Polity Press, 2018).

17. For an overview of competing definitions, see Peter B. Jubb, "Whistleblowing: A Restrictive Definition and Interpretation," *Journal of Business Ethics* 21, no. 1 (1999): 77–94.

18. This paragraph draws on a number of sources, including: Sissela Bok, *Secrets: On the Ethics of Concealment and Revelation* (New York: Pantheon, 1982), 210–29; Michael Davis, "Whistleblowing," *Oxford Handbook of Practical Ethics*, ed. Hugh LaFollette (Oxford: Oxford University Press, 2009), www.oxfordhandbooks.com; Richard T. De George, *Business Ethics*, 7th ed. (Upper Saddle River, NJ: Pearson, 2010), 298–318; Jubb, "Whistleblowing: A Restrictive Definition and Interpretation"; John Kleinig, "Loyalty," *The Stanford Encyclopedia of Philosophy*, ed. Edward N. Zalta (Winter 2017), https://plato.stanford.edu/cgi-bin/encyclopedia/archinfo.cgi?entry=loyalty. Also, the many contributions collected in *International Handbook on Whistleblowing Research*, eds. Brown, Lewis, Moberly, and Vandekerckhove.

19. On anonymity in WB, Frederick A. Elliston, "Anonymity and Whistleblowing," *Journal of Business Ethics* 1, no. 3 (1982): 167–77; James Rocha and Edward Song, "Pre-Emptive Anonymous Whistleblowing," *Public Affairs Quarterly* 26, no. 4 (2012): 257–71.

20. Jubb, "A Restrictive Definition and Interpretation," 92.

21. Brian Martin, "Whistleblowing and Nonviolence," *Peace & Change* 24, no. 1 (1999): 15–28.

22. Michael Walzer, *Obligations: Essays on Disobedience, War, and Citizenship* (New York: Simon & Schuster, 1970), 24–45.

23. Scheuerman, *Civil Disobedience*, 101–21.

24. This is an important theme in Kate Kenny, *Whistleblowing: Toward a New Theory* (Cambridge, MA: Harvard University Press, 2019).

25. Bok, *Secrets*, 214. See Philip Agee, *Inside the Company: CIA Diary* (London: Penguin Books, 1975) for a shocking array of CIA moral (and probably criminal) transgressions, particularly in the developing world.

26. Michael Walzer, "Just and Unjust Leaks: When to Spill Secrets," *Foreign Affairs* 97, no. 2 (2018): 57.

27. On the controversial case of Julian Assange and Wikileaks, see Miquel Comas Oliver, "WikiLeaks Under Fire: Is It Electronic Civil Disobedience?" *OXÍMORA Revista Internacional de Ética y Política* 10

(2017) 182–93. On digital disobedience more generally, see Chapter 14 in this volume.

28. Kimberley Brownlee, *Conscience and Conviction: The Case for Civil Disobedience* (Oxford: Oxford University Press, 2012), 23 (emphasis in original).

29. Kimberley Brownlee, "Is Edward Snowden a Civil Disobedient?" *OUPblog*, August 23, 2013, https://blog.oup.com/2013/08/is-edward-snowden-a-civil-disobedient/.

30. Natasha Basu and Bernardo Caycedo, "A Radical Reframing of Civil Disobedience: 'Illegal' Migration and Whistleblowing," in *Global Cultures of Contestation: Mobility, Sustainability, Aesthetics & Connectivity*, eds. Esther Peeren, Robin Celikates, Jeroen de Kloet, and Thomas Poell (London: Palgrave, 2018), 93–111. More generally, David E. Pozen, "Edward Snowden, National Security Whistleblowing, and Civil Disobedience," in *Whistleblowing Nation*, eds. Gurman and Mistry, 327–36.

31. William E. Scheuerman, "Civil Disobedience as Whistleblowing: The Case of Edward Snowden," *Philosophy & Social Criticism* 40, no. 7 (2014) 609–28; Henning Hahn, "The Ethics of Whistleblowing: A Justifiable Act of Global Civil Disobedience or a Misconstruction of the Global Public?" *Yearbook for Eastern and Western Philosophy* 1 (2016): 318–32.

32. Alex Emmons and Naomi LaChance, "Obama Refuses to Pardon Edward Snowden. Trump's New CIA Pick Wants Him Dead," *The Intercept*, November 18, 2016, https://theintercept.com/2016/11/18/obama-refuses-to-pardon-edward-snowden-trumps-new-cia-pick-wants-him-dead/.

33. Daniele Santoro and Manohar Kumar, *Speaking Truth to Power – A Theory of Whistleblowing* (New York: Springer, 2018), 167. Of course, there will be many messy borderline cases.

34. Santoro and Kumar, *Speaking Truth to Power*, 159.

35. Emanuela Ceva and Michele Bocchiola, *Is Whistleblowing a Duty?* (Cambridge, UK: Polity Press, 2019), 49–50. Also, Rahul Sagar, *Secrets and Leaks: The Dilemma of State Secrecy* (Princeton, NJ: Princeton University Press, 2013), 5–7.

36. Rawls, *A Theory of Justice*, 364–66.

37. For example: Candice Delmas, *A Duty to Resist: When Disobedience Should Be Uncivil* (Oxford: Oxford University Press, 2018), 25–46;

Geoffroy De Lagasnerie, *The Art of Revolt: Snowden, Assange, Manning* (Palo Alto, CA: Stanford University Press, 2017); Santoro and Kumar, *Speaking Truth to Power*, 159–69.

38. Scheuerman, *Civil Disobedience*, 52–54.

39. For example, republican and radical democratic defenses of civil disobedience sketched by Arendt, Habermas, Howard Zinn, and others (including Robin Celikates in this volume). Such approaches have usually loosened strict liberal requirements, for example, by claiming that disobedients need not accept legal penalties.

40. See, however, Scheuerman, *Civil Disobedience*, 32–80.

41. Delmas, "Ethics of Government Whistleblowing," 94.

42. Delmas, *A Duty to Resist*, 55. See also her chapter in this volume (Chapter 8).

43. Delmas, *A Duty to Resist*, 55, 98–103.

44. Delmas, *A Duty to Resist*, 55.

45. Delmas, *A Duty to Resist*, 24–35, 42–46.

46. Delmas, *A Duty to Resist*, 43.

47. For some examples, see Scheuerman, *Civil Disobedience*, 44–46.

48. Anthony Laden usefully contrasts ideas of civility as "politeness" to liberal and democratic notions of civility as (political) "responsiveness": Laden, "Two Concepts of Civility," in *A Crisis of Civility: Political Discourse and Its Discontents*, eds. R. Boatright and T. Shaffer (New York: Routledge, 2019), 9–30. On civility's various meanings within the discourse of CD, see Tony Milligan, *Civil Disobedience: Protest, Justification, and the Law* (London: Bloomsbury, 2013).

49. Delmas, *A Duty to Resist*, 35–39.

50. Candice Delmas, "That Lonesome Whistle: Edward Snowden's Actions Can Be Justified, But Not as Civil Disobedience," *Boston Review*, June 14, 2006, https://bostonreview.net/editors-picks-world-us/candice-delmas-lonesome-whistle. The distinctions she makes here have been picked up and endorsed by others (e.g., Eric R. Boot, *The Ethics of Whistleblowing* [New York: Routledge, 2019], 49–51).

51. Boot, *The Ethics of Whistleblowing*, 50. Santoro and Kumar claim in contrast that WB tends to be less disruptive than CD (*Speaking Truth to Power*, 164).

52. Candice Delmas, "Is Hacktivism the New Civil Disobedience?" *Raisons politiques* 69, no. 1 (2018): 63–81.

53. Think, for example, of "individual" acts of CD performed by Thoreau or Gandhi.

54. De Lagasnerie, *The Art of Revolt*. In a related vein, Lida Maxwell (*Insurgent Truth: Chelsea Manning and the Politics of Outsider Truth-Telling* [Oxford: Oxford University Press, 2019]) seeks to contrast what she celebrates as Chelsea Manning's "insurgent truth-telling" in contrast to the staid, socially uncritical practices of both CD and WB. Such arguments downplay CD's possible political radicalism while probably overstating the novelty of the individual figures and protests they instead celebrate.

55. Alison Stanger, *Whistleblowers: Honesty in America from Washington to Trump* (New Haven, CT: Yale University Press, 2019), 4.

56. Santoro and Kumar, *Speaking Truth to Power*, 167–68.

57. Santoro and Kumar, *Speaking Truth to Power*, 165–66.

58. Santoro and Kumar, *Speaking Truth to Power*, 166.

59. Rawls, *A Theory of Justice*, 364, 375–76.

60. Boot, *The Ethics of Whistleblowing*, 50.

61. Santoro and Kumar, *Speaking Truth to Power*, 165.

62. For example, Jeremy Hammond, the Chicago activist who hacked a private intelligence firm with a history of spying on social movements. Though claiming the status of civil disobedient, he was sentenced (in 2013) to ten years in prison by a conservative US federal judge, Loretta Preska, who found the analogy implausible (Scheuerman, *Civil Disobedience*, 122–30).

63. For example, De George, *Business Ethics*, 298–318.

64. Ceva and Bocchiola, *Is Whistleblowing a Duty?* 7–8 (emphasis in original).

65. Ceva and Bocchiola, *Is Whistleblowing a Duty?* 27, 46–47.

66. On WB and power, see Kim Loyens and Jeroen Maesschalck, "Whistleblowing and Power," in *International Handbook on Whistleblowing Research*, ed. Brown, Lewis, Moberly, and Vandekerckhove, 154–73.

16 Consequences of Civil Disobedience

Kurt Schock

Most literature on civil disobedience focuses on defining what it is, philosophical or political justifications for its use, or jurisprudential issues surrounding its use. Much less attention is given to its consequences. After briefly considering methodological challenges in assessing consequences, outcomes, or effects of civil disobedience, I address individual, political, and cultural consequences. Individual consequences of civil disobedience are effects on those who engage in civil disobedience, such as sanctioning by the government or experiencing liberating and empowering emotions. Political consequences are effects of civil disobedience on the political environment, such as initiating public deliberation or debate, mobilizing support for a cause, or tangible change in social practices, law, policy, or government. Cultural consequences include social artifacts, such as literature that provides templates for collective action frames; knowledge, skills, and practical wisdom that are transmitted and incorporated into subsequent enactments of civil disobedience; and shifts in the distribution of beliefs and values in a population concerning social issues. Moreover, civil disobedience may have unintended consequences, including a perception by some segments of a population that civil disobedience leads to a disregard for all laws and authority, whether unjust and illegitimate or just and legitimate, which may be used in attempts to justify authoritarian backlash.

Civil disobedience involves unarmed nonroutine political action in which obedience and submission are withdrawn from authorities, and government laws or orders are intentionally violated for the purpose of contesting an injustice or remaining true to one's conscience. Essential aspects of civil disobedience are its illegality and disruptiveness, which involve moral appeals, aesthetic expressions, or coercive threats. Motivation for civil disobedience may be based on religious beliefs, morality, ideology, or civic duty to contest injustice.[1] Although it is assumed that civil disobedience has consequences, we know surprisingly little about the outcomes or effects of civil disobedience or the causal mechanisms that link civil disobedience to presumed outcomes or effects. To accurately assess the causal impact of civil disobedience on individuals, for example, studies would require a before-after research design and a control group. However, most studies assessing the relation between activism, including civil disobedience, and biographical outcomes rely on retrospective data and lack control groups.[2] It is also difficult to accurately assess the causal impact of civil disobedience on the political or cultural environment, since civil disobedience does not occur in a vacuum; typically, it is implemented as part of a larger campaign or social movement aimed at social change and often overlaps with other forms of contention and dissent. Moreover, there are factors exogenous to campaigns and movements that drive political and cultural change. It is difficult to isolate the specific contributions of civil disobedience or identify its relative contribution to political and cultural change. Moving from the identification of correlations to plausible explanations of impacts to evidence of causal relations is complicated with regard to civil disobedience and other forms of protest and resistance. In order to accurately assess the consequences of civil disobedience, it is necessary to identify causal mechanisms linking civil disobedience with specific outcomes, examine the plausibility of alternative explanations, and defend against spurious relationships.[3] However, little if any research on civil disobedience meets these methodological standards. In this chapter my modest aim is to make preliminary statements about individual, political, and cultural consequences of civil disobedience based on the literature on civil disobedience and the literature on social movement outcomes, and to suggest methodological approaches for future research.

INDIVIDUAL CONSEQUENCES

Individual consequences of civil disobedience may be costly, including arrest, along with violence and humiliation that often accompany arrest and confinement within the criminal "justice" system, followed by criminal prosecution, and if convicted, a criminal record, economic sanctions, and stigmatization from being labeled a deviant.[4] Needless to say, jail sentences and criminal records can have turbulent effects on everyday relationships, such as family relations, education, and employment. Research on social movements has found that activism, especially high-risk activism such as civil disobedience, often has powerful and enduring biographical consequences in the family and work spheres.[5] The most systematic research focuses on consequences of participating in high-risk activism in 1960s progressive social movements in liberal democratic states. For example, for activists involved in the New Left movements of the 1960s, marriage occurred less often than the general population and occurred later in life, divorce was more common, and having children was less likely. Furthermore, 1960s activists often experienced a nontraditional work and life course, and had lower incomes compared to members of the same cohort who did not engage in political protest.

Of course, costly consequences of civil disobedience, such as sanctions meted out by the government, can be interpreted by individuals as a badge of honor and a means of proving the point that social practices, the law, inequalities, or the government are unjust or illegitimate. Moreover, imprisonment may be a transformative experience that radicalizes and deepens one's commitment to challenging injustice, and prison may be a place where a sense of resistance and community are forged.[6] Furthermore, there may be intrinsic beneficial phenomenological, psychological, or emotional effects experienced by civil disobedients irrespective of whether their political goals are achieved. Voicing dissent through civil disobedience rather than repressing what one believes may lead to feelings of integrity and self-respect.[7] For example, a member of a minority group that is a target of discriminatory laws who engages in civil disobedience may experience beneficial intrinsic therapeutic effects, such as feelings of self-affirmation, empowerment, dignity, group solidarity, and the release of negative or repressed feelings.[8] Indeed, Dr. Martin Luther King, Jr. emphasized psychological liberation of African Americans as a consequence of resisting racial oppression.[9] Individuals who are not members of an oppressed group who engage in civil disobedience to challenge discriminatory laws may also experience intrinsic therapeutic consequences, such as empathy or emotional identification with the oppressed or psychological separation from an unjust system.[10] Self-reported intrinsic therapeutic effects of civil disobedience include the "pleasure of resistance" that is derived from openly challenging injustice, which may entail feelings of exhilaration, euphoria, empowerment, and liberation.[11]

Conscientious objection, motivated by the dissenter's beliefs that they are morally compelled to violate the law because it is unjust, has a long tradition by members of various Christian "peace churches" who refuse military service. Conscience-based civil disobedience, however, need not have a religious basis. Henry David Thoreau, for example, argued for civil resistance on the ground of individual conscience and conscience's moral obligation.[12] If civil disobedience is implemented based on religious or moral obligations, or as a matter of conscience, then the immediate individual-level phenomenological, psychological, or emotional effects are self-evident regardless of responses by authorities or extra-individual consequences of the actions.

POLITICAL CONSEQUENCES

Prior to the twentieth century, civil disobedience was often "integrity-based" and enacted individually or on a small scale; that is, individuals or groups engaged in civil disobedience in order to remain true to their conscience, morals, or religious convictions. However, in the twentieth century, civil disobedience was increasingly "justice-based" and large-scale; that is, it was incorporated into mass-based challenges to unjust social practices, laws, policies, or governments.[13] The idea that civil disobedience could be strategically implemented on a mass basis and on a national or transnational scale gained currency in the 1920s and 1930s. Mohandas Gandhi organized mass-based national campaigns of civil disobedience against British exploitation in India, including the Non-Cooperation Movement in the 1920s and the Civil Disobedience Movement in the 1930s, which included the famous Salt March and accompanying direct actions that mobilized millions of people across India. In Europe between the two world wars, Bart de Ligt, a Dutch minister and conscientious objector, maintained that preventing war must go beyond conscientious objection and integrity-based refusals to participate in the military. Inspired by Gandhi, he outlined a systematic plan for civil resistance against militarism and war, and urged anti-war activists across Europe to organize and implement mass-based campaigns of justice-based civil disobedience and strikes.[14]

In the US, there is a long tradition of civil disobedience in movements for peace and justice, including the Abolitionist Movement, the Labor Movement, the Women's Suffrage Movement, the Civil Rights Movement, and Anti-War Movements. It is widely acknowledged that civil disobedience contributed to the attainment of the goals of these movements. As a political instrument, civil disobedience is intended to: (1) draw public attention to a perceived injustice thereby triggering reflectiveness and deliberation, (2) mobilize support for a cause, and (3) change social practices, laws, policies, or government. Thus, political consequences can be assessed in these regards. This is done below with examples from the US Civil Rights, Anti-Vietnam War, and Peace and Solidarity with the People of Central America Movements.

Concerning the US Civil Rights Movement, Rosa Parks's violation of segregation laws by refusing to yield her bus seat to white passengers in Montgomery, Alabama in 1955 and the campaigns of civil disobedience that followed seemingly led to changes in law and public policy. How were acts of civil disobedience related to these changes? First, Rosa Parks's singular act of civil disobedience inspired *supporting civil disobedience actions* such as a bus boycott, in which the African American community in Montgomery openly violated local anti-boycott laws for nearly a year. Second, Rosa Parks's civil disobedience led to the *founding of organizations to facilitate further civil disobedience*, such as the Montgomery Improvement Association, and *mobilized people from the community* into the movement. Third, civil disobedience generated media coverage and *drew public attention* to racial discrimination, segregation, and unconstitutional laws in the American South. As more people became attuned to the issues, were pushed out of their comfort zone, and engaged in reflection, a *shift in public opinion* occurred. Fourth, a contemporaneous legal challenge was initiated by Parks's lawyers that led to *judicial review* by the Supreme Court and its 1956 ruling on the illegality of bus segregation laws. Fifth, *support from outside the community was mobilized*, most notably the leadership of Dr. Martin Luther King, Jr. Recognizing the need for a mass movement to capitalize on the successful civil disobedience actions in Montgomery, King and other activists organized the Southern Christian Leadership Conference, which facilitated the mobilization of people into *additional civil disobedience campaigns*, such as in Albany, Georgia in 1961–1962, Birmingham, Alabama in 1963, and Selma, Alabama in 1965. These campaigns also generated media coverage, impacted public opinion, and raised the awareness of lawmakers. Sixth, the subsequent campaigns led to *legislative action*, such as the passage of the Civil Rights Act of 1964 and the Voting Rights Act of 1965 by the US Congress.[15]

Thus, civil disobedience by Rosa Parks and others triggered processes leading to the striking down of unconstitutional laws and the implementation of new laws through a series of intermediary mechanisms: (1) compelling the public to become cognizant of the injustice of racial oppression and mobilizing public opinion, (2) the formation of organizations to facilitate civil disobedience campaigns,

(3) mobilizing people from the community as well as outside the community, (4) the implementation of additional civil disobedience campaigns (which in turn brought attention to issues, shaped public opinion, and mobilized people), (5) judicial review, and (6) legislative action. As a result of judicial review and legislative action, unconstitutional laws were revoked and new laws were implemented. It is unlikely that overt racism would have been successfully challenged in the absence of civil disobedience.

A second example of political consequences of civil disobedience concerns the Anti-War Movement in the 1960s and early 1970s in opposition to the US military's attempt to suppress the communist national liberation movement in Vietnam. Anti-war groups engaged in peaceful protests in the early 1960s, but as the government escalated its military involvement civil disobedience and direct action were also employed. Increased bombing campaigns against North Vietnam in 1965 were countered by teach-ins on college campuses that educated students about the war and mobilized students into the Anti-War Movement. On April 4, 1967 King spoke out against the war in his seminal "Beyond Vietnam" speech, with many concluding that legal and peaceful means were ineffective in changing US policy and that civil disobedience was necessary.

From 1967 onward more coercive forms of civil disobedience were enacted. In October 1967 nearly 100,000 people attended a rally at the Lincoln Memorial in Washington DC and approximately half of the crowd subsequently marched to the Pentagon for a two-day confrontation that resulted in over 600 arrests and increased national attention on US policies.[16] Tens of thousands of young men burned their draft cards and refused to be inducted into the military, and hundreds of thousands more refused to register for the draft. In 1967, a group called *The Resistance* collected over 1100 draft cards from men who refused induction.[17] Between 1967 and 1972 dozens of draft board raids were carried out, whereby activists broke into government draft board offices and destroyed draft records to disrupt the draft and dramatize their protest against the war. Notable draft board raids included the Baltimore Four in 1967, the Catonsville Nine and Milwaukee Fourteen in 1968, the Silver Spring Three in 1969, and the Camden Twenty-Eight in 1971. The draft board raids along with subsequent trials of the civil disobedients, where elegant defenses of their actions were put forth, received substantial media coverage, thereby shaping the public's opposition to the involvement and conduct of the US military and contributing to the diffusion of the tactic.

Civil disobedience *within* the military also contributed to the withdrawal of the US military from Vietnam. Tens of thousands of military personnel deserted or refused to carry out orders, including refusing orders to engage in combat, which was one of the most effective forms of resistance. Starting in 1968 there was a rapid increase in combat refusals, resulting in at least ten major mutinies and hundreds of minor ones. Over the next few years, thousands of incidents of combat refusal occurred.[18]

Organizations were subsequently formed to provide aid to civil disobedients and encourage further civil disobedience, such as the Vietnam Veterans Against the War and the American Servicemen's Union in 1967, and the Movement for a Democratic Military in 1969. These organizations and others facilitated the rapid expansion and effectiveness of the soldier and veteran movement. Desertions and applications for conscientious objector status rose considerably from 1967 onward.[19]

By 1969 troop levels were being drawn down and in January 1973 the US government ended its direct military involvement in Vietnam with the signing of the Paris Peace Agreement.[20] In addition to ending US military involvement, the Anti-War Movement also contributed to the passage of the Twenty-Sixth Amendment to the US Constitution in 1971 that lowered the voting age to eighteen and contributed to ending the military draft in 1973. How did civil disobedience, by civilian anti-war protestors and draft resisters as well as military personnel, contribute to these changes in policy and law?

It did so through various mechanisms, including: (1) educating the public and *bringing public attention* to the unjust nature and immoral conduct of the military intervention, which *mobilized public opinion*, (2) the *formation of organizations* to facilitate further civil disobedience campaigns and acts of resistance, (3) *mobilizing people* into subsequent acts of civil disobedience through organizational networks and emulation, (4) *influencing legislators* who passed laws that lowered the voting age and ended the military draft, and (5) *limiting the executive branch's options* with regard to prosecuting the military conflict.[21]

A third example of political consequences of civil disobedience concerns opposition of US citizens to their government's Central America foreign policy in the 1980s. In solidarity with Nicaraguans, activists mobilized in opposition to threatened US government military intervention and funding of the Contras, a terrorist organization that opposed the socialist *Frente Sandinista de Liberación Nacional* government that displaced the US-backed right-wing dictator Anastasio Somoza in 1979. In the early 1980s, hundreds of justice- and religious-inspired peace activists traveled to Nicaragua to deter Contra violence, and document and report on the atrocities committed by the Contras. In 1983 Witness for Peace was founded to support these efforts and over the next few years thousands of delegates traveled to Nicaragua. By reporting on the situation in Nicaragua, Witness for Peace and other justice- and faith-based organizations educated the US public and influenced legislators. Coercive acts of civil disobedience within the US such as sit-ins at congressional offices and federal buildings contributed as well. Consequences of the direct actions were the Boland Amendments, a series of acts passed by the US Congress between 1983 and 1985 to limit and then end US government funding of the Contra terrorists.

In 1984 a coalition of peace groups organized the "Pledge of Resistance" campaign whereby people committed to engage in civil disobedience and direct actions if the US military were to invade countries in Central America. By 1986, 300 Pledge groups formed throughout the country and the number of Pledge signers reached 80,000. Activists received training in civil disobedience and nonviolent resistance, and communications networks were established that had the potential to create major social disruption.[22] Pledge activists protested in a variety of ways from 1986–1988, including marches and sit-ins that blocked traffic, occupations of congressional offices, and blockades of trains and trucks carrying munitions to military bases. In 1987 100,000 people marched in Washington DC and afterward 567 were arrested at the CIA headquarters. In 1988 1500 activists protested at the Pentagon with 500 committing civil disobedience, leading to 240 arrests.[23]

The civil disobedience campaigns raised the costs of, and perhaps prevented, direct US military intervention in Central America. However, an unintended consequence of the US Congress's refusal to further fund the Contras was the criminal activity of the Reagan Administration, which engaged in a covert diversion of funds to the Contras. How did civil disobedience and direct action contribute to these changes in policy? It did so through various mechanisms, including: (1) educating the public and *bringing public attention* to human consequences of US foreign policy in Central America, which *shaped public opinion*, (2) *forming organizations* to facilitate further campaigns of civil disobedience and acts of resistance, (3) *mobilizing people* to engage in civil disobedience through organizational networks and emulation, (4) *influencing legislators* who withdrew funding from the Contra terrorists, and (5) *limiting the executive branch's options* with regard to prosecuting a military conflict in Central America.

Collectively, civil disobedience implemented in the three US social movements briefly sketched above – the Civil Rights, Anti-Vietnam War, and Peace and Solidarity Movement with the People of Central America – had a tangible impact on public opinion and government policy. Significantly, all three movements went well beyond conventional protest, and incorporated and disruptive direct action.

By doing so, the movements not only persuaded the public of the justness of their causes, but also coerced authorities by limiting their options. In addition to drawing attention to issues, disruptive and illegal forms of dissent may trigger more widespread mobilization, through emulation or the formation of organizations designed to sustain civil disobedience campaigns. In turn, widespread disruptive and illegal protest can decrease the options that authorities have with regard to enforcing unjust laws, waging wars, or funding terrorist organizations.[24]

Some argue that the impact of social movements and collective action on policy change is mediated by public opinion. That is, political protest is only likely to be related to policy change if public opinion is favorable toward that change.[25] However, civil disobedience is often crucial for bringing attention to issues or raising their profile among the public. In fact, a common purpose of civil disobedience is to communicate a message to the public and shape public opinion as part of the process of initiating social change. The mainstream media tend not to give unpopular views a hearing unless they are advocated through sensationalist means, such as illegal or disruptive protest. Civil disobedience is often dramatic and provides the visuals that the media require, and contributes to a wider dissemination of positions that challenge the interests of the political elite.[26] Moreover, others maintain that social protest, including civil disobedience, can have a direct impact on policy change regardless of public opinion.[27]

Comparative analyses of challenging movements have provided indirect evidence that civil disobedience, as a part of broader campaigns or movements, is related to intended political outcomes. In a study of a sample of fifty-three challenging groups in the US from 1800 to 1945, William A. Gamson found that groups that used disruptive methods of protest, including civil disobedience or unarmed violence, were more likely to attain their objectives than those that did not.[28] Similarly, Frances Fox Piven and Richard A. Cloward argue that disruption contributed to the success of the US Labor Movement in the 1930s and Welfare Rights Movement in the 1960s.[29]

In democracies, civil disobedience may draw attention to, and educate the public about, an issue through persuasion and moral appeal or aesthetic expression, which may contribute to genuine reflection about issues and shifts in public opinion. Civil disobedience may also trigger judicial review or legislative action which culminates in policy change. As discussed above, if widespread, civil disobedience may also coercively limit the policy options available to authorities. By contrast, in non-democracies, there is typically minimal recourse available through institutional channels. In these contexts, the purpose of civil disobedience may not be to persuade government officials to change policies or implement new laws, but rather to mobilize society to withdraw obedience and submission, and topple the existing regime through coercive force. Regime change through mass-based campaigns that include civil disobedience may occur if a challenge is resilient, that is, it is able to weather repression, and it has leverage, that is, it is able to undermine state power through the networks on which it depends for resources and legitimacy.[30]

Drawing on these assumptions, Erica Chenoweth and Maria J. Stephan examined 323 major armed and unarmed resistance campaigns with maximalist objectives such as regime change, liberation from foreign occupation, or separatism, that occurred from 1900 to 2006. Controlling for a number of structural factors such as state strength and level of economic development, they found that unarmed challenges that disrupt through protests, strikes, and civil disobedience – as well as unarmed violence, which they do not explicitly address – are more likely to succeed than are challenges that disrupt and destroy through organized armed resistance.[31] Furthermore, they found that in countries that experienced successful unarmed resistance campaigns, there was a relatively higher level of democracy and lower level of the recurrence of armed conflict in the years following the struggle compared to countries that experienced successful armed struggles. Regime change brought about by armed resistance is more likely to result in a new autocracy while regime change resulting from unarmed resistance is more likely to lead to democracy, since armed resistance campaigns, when successful, tend to result in the centralization of power.[32] Thus, beyond strategic effectiveness, the nature of the resistance may have consequences for the post-transition regime and political culture.

CULTURAL CONSEQUENCES

Cultural consequences of social movements include social artifacts, performances and repertoires, and ideations.[33] Specifically, with regard to civil disobedience, social artifacts includes literature that has sprung from defending and justifying acts of civil disobedience, such as Henry David Thoreau's *Resistance to Civil Government*,[34] Martin Luther King, Jr.'s *Letter from Birmingham Jail*,[35] and Howard Zinn's *The Problem Is Civil Obedience*.[36] Moreover, civil disobedience provides grist from which plays and films about remaining true to one's conscience or contesting injustice while disobeying authority are central themes, such as Sophocles's *Antigone*,[37] *A Man for All Seasons* (a play and subsequent film about Sir Thomas More),[38] and the film *Gandhi*.[39] Documentary films on civil disobedience include *Eyes on the Prize*[40] on the US Civil Rights Movement, and *Sir! No Sir!*[41] on civil disobedience by soldiers during the US government military intervention in Vietnam. Literature, plays, and films provide well-framed arguments for engaging in civil disobedience and contribute to a culture of resistance that may be drawn upon for motivation and inspiration at opportune moments by those challenging unjust authority.

Another cultural consequence is the production of knowledge and organizational skills pertaining to the performances or repertoires of civil disobedience that are documented, systematized, disseminated, and drawn upon in subsequent enactments. Based on their own experiences and the experiences of others, civil disobedients have written training manuals outlining steps to be implemented in planning for and carrying out subsequent acts of civil disobedience and campaigns of direct action, such as *Handbook for Nonviolent Campaigns*,[42] a training manual produced by War Resisters' International, *Beautiful Trouble*,[43] a book and web-based toolbox produced by the Beautiful Trouble collective, and *Path of Resistance: The Practice of Civil Disobedience*, a manual written by a Swedish Plowshares activist.[44] Knowledge and organizational skills are often transmitted through workshops and social movement schools. Social movement schools train and transmit knowledge about oppositional culture and civil disobedience through workshops and facilitate the diffusion of an oppositional culture and civil disobedience across activist networks.[45] More important than the transmission of technical skills is the impartation of practical wisdom and moral development that occurs in workshops and social movement schools.[46]

Civil disobedience may also contribute to changes in ideations, such as cultural beliefs and values. For example, "Question Authority" became a popular cultural meme in the US as a result of the 1960s student and anti-war civil disobedience movements.[47] Moreover, the environmental movement, spearheaded by dramatic acts of direct action and civil disobedience, such as sailing vessels into areas to disrupt nuclear weapons testing and whaling by Greenpeace activists, and tree spiking and disabling logging machinery by Earth First! activists, has contributed to the broad adoption of an ecological sensibility that inspires people to behave in environmentally responsible ways.[48] Nevertheless, systemic sources of environmental degradation, such as capitalist exploitation of nature and dependence on carbon-based energy sources, have yet to be effectively challenged through civil disobedience.

Critics, however, argue that civil disobedience has negative cultural consequences that undermine democracy. Specifically, arguments have been raised that civil disobedience: (1) leads to contempt for the law and lawlessness, (2) promotes selfish interests over societal interests, (3) results in people picking and choosing which laws to obey or disobey, thereby undermining all authority, (4) encourages a general disrespect for the law, and (5) undermines democracy.[49] These arguments are often used to justify a backlash against civil disobedience by authoritarian forces of "law and order."

These claims concerning negative consequences of civil disobedience seem to be off the mark. First, civil disobedients who openly accept punishment demonstrate respect rather than contempt for the law. In such instances civil disobedients, by challenging unjust laws, are attempting to strengthen and improve the system of laws, not subvert them. Second, civil disobedience does not further narrow self-interests; indeed, in efforts to promote societal interests, civil disobedients often damage their private or own interests by experiencing incarceration and stigmatization, which often have negative consequences (see above, individual consequences). Third, if people chose which laws to obey or disobey in a capricious manner, then critics are correct in arguing that legitimate authority is undermined. However, civil disobedients typically disobey laws based on considerable reflection and deliberate choice in order to promote democracy and equality. Indeed, if every law was obeyed by everybody in every situation, then the role of the thoughtful and moral democratic citizen would cease to exist. Fourth, the argument that civil disobedience promotes a general disrespect for the law, which in turn causes riots and other forms of violent protest, is spurious. With regard to the US Civil Rights Movement, for example, racial inequality and systemic oppression were factors underlying both civil disobedience and urban riots; civil disobedience did not cause urban riots. Finally, rather than undermining or subverting the democratic process, civil disobedience preserves and extends rights, restores a balance of power in government, and serves as a corrective to the manipulation of the democratic process.[50] Moreover, civil disobedience and nonviolent direct action have the potential to transform a liberal democracy into a multiracial and economic democracy.[51]

CONCLUSIONS

Activists and scholars assume that civil disobedience has consequences. However, although much has been penned about civil
disobedience, we know surprisingly little about its consequences.
In this chapter, I have drawn on the civil disobedience literature and
the literature on social movement outcomes to provide a brief overview of individual, political, and cultural consequences of civil
disobedience. Much further research is needed to identify and elaborate on the causal processes that link civil disobedience to its
putative outcomes or consequences at the micro- and macro-
levels, both intended and unintended. Given the unfeasibility of
experimental research, scholars must adopt other methodological
approaches for identifying causal effects. Concerning individual
consequences, in-depth interviewing as well as survey research
that compares civil disobedients with non-civil disobedients
would be useful. Concerning cultural consequences, survey
research and content analysis would be useful in tracing the impact
of civil disobedience on ideations, repertoires, and social artifacts
across society and over time. Concerning political consequences,
comparative analyses would be productive. One type of comparison
involves selecting a sample of cases of social movement organizations from the social movement sector in a given time and place,
and then comparing the outcomes of the challenges and relating
these to the presence or absence of the use of civil disobedience.
This approach is approximated in Gamson's *The Strategy of Social
Protest*.[52] A second type of comparison involves examining
a population of campaigns that challenge political authority, in
which some of the campaigns relied on unarmed resistance, including civil disobedience, and others on armed resistance. This
approach was adopted by Chenoweth and Stephan in *Why Civil
Resistance Works*.[53] However, since acts of civil disobedience are
typically part of a stream of contention and are rarely isolated
events, a challenge for scholars is to disaggregate the effects of

civil disobedience from other forms of unarmed resistance, both violent and nonviolent, and in some cases, armed violence that co-occur in highly charged political conflicts.

Broad comparisons must be supplemented with case studies or small-N studies that dig deep to uncover causal mechanisms through causal narratives or process tracing. A mechanistic approach to contentious politics has been elaborated by Doug McAdam, Sidney Tarrow, and Charles Tilly in *Dynamics of Contention*.[54] This approach involves detailed and case-specific yet highly analytical explanations through the identification of mechanisms, that is, events that produce the same immediate effects over a wide range of circumstances, across a broad range of contentious politics. In conclusion, much work needs to be done to accurately identify causal effects of civil disobedience and the causal mechanisms through which the effects occur, and to disaggregate the effects of civil disobedience from the effects of coeval forms of protest and resistance and the impact of broader social and political processes.

NOTES

1. For recent overviews of the literature on civil disobedience, see Kimberley Brownlee, "Civil Disobedience," *The Stanford Encyclopedia of Philosophy*, ed. Edward N. Zalta (Fall 2017), https://plato.stanford.edu/archives/fall2017/entries/civil-disobedience/; and William E. Scheuerman, *Civil Disobedience* (Cambridge: Polity Press, 2018).
2. Florence Passy and Gian-Andrea Monsch, "Biographical Consequences of Activism," in *The Wiley-Blackwell Companion to Social Movements*, eds. David A. Snow, Sarah A. Soule, Hanspeter Kriesi, and Holly J. McCammon, 2nd ed. (London: Wiley-Blackwell, 2019), 499–500.
3. Jennifer Earl, "Methods, Movements, and Outcomes: Methodological Difficulties in the Study of Extra-Movement Outcomes," *Research in Social Movements, Conflicts, and Change* 22 (2000): 3–25.
4. Civil disobedience is a powerful method of protest precisely because it is illegal and potentially results in heavy penalties for the dissenters. Indeed, the consequences of risk of arrest and punishment amplify the communicative power of civil disobedience by impressing upon an audience the

intensity of the civil disobedient's beliefs and the urgency of their cause. See Kimberley Brownlee, *Conscience and Conviction: The Case for Civil Disobedience* (Oxford: Oxford University Press, 2012).

5. See Marco Giugni, "Personal and Biographical Consequences," in *The Blackwell Companion to Social Movements*, eds. David A. Snow, Sarah Soule, and Hanspeter Kriesi (Oxford: Blackwell, 2004), 489–507; Marco Giugni, "Political, Biographical, and Cultural Consequences of Social Movements," *Sociology Compass* 2, no. 5 (September 2008): 1582–600; Doug McAdam, *Freedom Summer* (Oxford: Oxford University Press, 1988); Doug McAdam, "The Biographical Impact of Activism," in *How Social Movements Matter*, eds. Marco Giugni, Doug McAdam, and Charles Tilly (Minneapolis, MN: University of Minnesota Press, 1999), 117–46; Doug McAdam and Jack A. Goldstone, "Contention in Demographic and Life-Course Context," in *Silence and Voice in the Study of Contentious Politics*, eds. Ronald M. Aminzade, Jack A. Goldstone, Doug McAdam, Elisabeth J. Perry, William H. Sewell Jr., Sidney Tarrow, and Charles Tilly (Cambridge: Cambridge University Press, 2001), 195–221; Passy and Monsch, "Biographical Consequences of Activism," 504; Darren E. Sherkrat and T. Jean Blocker, "Explaining the Political and Personal Consequences of Protest," *Social Forces* 75, no. 3 (March 1997): 1049–70; Brenda Wilhelm, "Changes in Cohabitation across Cohorts: The Influence of Political Activism," *Social Forces* 77, no. 1 (September 1998): 289–313.

6. On prison as a space where US Civil Rights activists cultivated solidarity and practiced nonviolence, see Wesley Hogan, *Many Minds, One Heart* (Chapel Hill, NC: University of North Carolina Press, 2007).

7. Brownlee, *Conscience and Conviction*.

8. Kevin H. Smith, "Essay – Therapeutic Civil Disobedience: A Preliminary Exploration," *The University of Memphis Law Review* 31, no. 1 (Fall 2000): 99–134.

9. Martin Luther King, Jr., "The Summer of Our Discontent," in *Why We Can't Wait* (New York: Signet, 1963), 111–12.

10. Smith, "Essay – Therapeutic Civil Disobedience."

11. Jarret S. Lovell, *Crimes of Dissent: Civil Disobedience, Criminal Justice and the Politics of Conscience* (New York: New York University Press, 2009), 20–26. Of course, these feelings may also be experienced by those engaging in armed resistance.

12. Henry David Thoreau, "Resistance to Civil Government," in *Thoreau: Political Writings*, ed. Nancy L. Rosenblum (New York: Cambridge University Press, 1996), 1–22. For Thoreau, the emphasis was on individuals acting in accordance to their conscience rather than organized collective action. (For a discussion, see Chapter 1 in this volume.)

13. Ronald Dworkin distinguishes between integrity-based and justice-based civil disobedience in *A Matter of Principle* (Cambridge, MA: Harvard University Press, 1985), 107–16. (For a discussion, see Chapter 3 in this volume.) See also Hannah Arendt, who differentiates between the individual conscience-based civil disobedience of Thoreau and the collective justice-based civil disobedience of social movements, such as the Indian Independence Movement, US Civil Rights Movement, and US Anti-War Movement in *Crises of the Republic: Lying in Politics, Civil Disobedience, On Violence, Thoughts on Politics and Revolution* (New York: Harcourt Brace & Company, 1972).

14. Bart de Ligt, *The Conquest of Violence: An Essay on War and Revolution* (London: Pluto, 1989).

15. Of course, other civil disobedience campaigns besides these contributed to desegregation and new laws, most notably the sit-in and freedom ride campaigns. Moreover, Rosa Parks's act of civil disobedience was preceded by numerous other refusals to obey unjust segregation laws by African Americans that did not trigger subsequent widespread or sustained mobilizations.

16. Mitchell K. Hall, "The Vietnam Era Antiwar Movement," *OAH Magazine of History* 18 (2004): 14.

17. Hall, "The Vietnam Era Antiwar Movement," 14.

18. Richard Moser, *The New Winter Soldiers: GI and Veteran Dissent During the Vietnam Era* (New Brunswick, NJ: Rutgers University Press, 1996), 45–47.

19. Moser, *The New Winter Soldiers*. See also David Cortright, *Soldiers in Revolt: The American Military Today* (New York: Anchor Press, 1975).

20. Hall, "The Vietnam Era Antiwar Movement."

21. Needless to say, the resilience of the Vietnamese in their armed struggle for national liberation contributed to the US military withdrawal as well.

22. Christian Smith, *Resisting Reagan: The U.S. Central America Peace Movement* (Chicago, IL: University of Chicago Press, 1996), 79–83.

23. Smith, *Resisting Reagan*, 83–85.

24. For a discussion of the persuasive and coercive mechanisms of civil disobedience, see Chapter 10 in this volume.

25. Paul Burstein, "Social Movements and Public Policy," in *How Social Movements Matter*, eds. Giugni, McAdam, and Tilly, 3–21; Paul Burstein and April Linton, "The Impact of Political Parties, Interest Groups, and Social Movement Organizations on Public Policy: Some Evidence and Theoretical Concerns," *Social Forces* 81, no. 2 (December 2002): 380–408; and Marco Giugni, *Social Protest and Policy Change* (Lanham, MD: Rowman and Littlefield Publishers, 2004).

26. Lovell, *Crimes of Dissent*, 182–86.

27. Katrin Uba, "The Contextual Dependence of Movement Outcomes: A Simplified Meta-Analysis," *Mobilization* 14, no. 4 (December 2009): 433–48.

28. William A. Gamson, *The Strategy of Social Protest*, 2nd ed. (Belmont, CA: Wadsworth, 1990).

29. Frances Fox Piven and Richard A. Cloward, *Poor People's Movements: Why They Succeed, How They Fail* (New York: Pantheon, 1977).

30. Kurt Schock, *Unarmed Insurrections: People Power Movements in Nondemocracies* (Minneapolis, MN: University of Minnesota Press, 2005).

31. Erica Chenoweth and Maria J. Stephan, *Why Civil Resistance Works: The Strategic Logic of Nonviolent Conflict* (New York: Columbia University Press, 2011).

32. See also Mauricio Rivera Celistino and Kristian Skrede Gleditsch, "Fresh Carnations or All Thorn, No Rose? Nonviolent Campaigns and Transitions to Autocracies," *Journal of Peace Research* 50, no. 3 (2013): 385–400.

33. Nella van Dyke and Verta Taylor, "The Cultural Outcomes of Social Movements," in *The Wiley-Blackwell Companion to Social Movements*, eds. Snow, Soule, Kriesi, and McCammon, 482–98.

34. Thoreau, "Resistance to Civil Government." Thoreau also provided justifications for violent resistance. (For a discussion, see Chapter 1 in this volume.)

35. King, "Letter from Birmingham Jail," in *Why We Can't Wait*, 76–95.

36. Howard Zinn, "The Problem Is Civil Obedience," in *Voices of a People's History of the United States*, eds. Howard Zinn and Anthony Arnove, 2nd ed. (New York: Seven Stories Press, 2009), 483–88.

37. Sophocles, *Antigone*, trans. Richard Emil Braun (Oxford: Oxford University Press, 1973).

38. Robert Bolt, *A Man for All Seasons*, dir. Fred Zimmerman (London: Columbia Pictures, 1966).

39. John Briley, *Gandhi*, dir. Richard Attenborough (London: Columbia Pictures, 1982).

40. Henry Hampton, *Eyes on the Prize*, dir. Orlando Bagwell, Sheila Curran Bernard, Callie Crossley, James A. DeVinney, Madison D. Lacy, Louis Massiah, Thomas Ott, Samuel D. Pollard, Terry Kay Rockefeller, Jacqueline Shearer, Paul Stekler, and Judith Vecchione (Arlington, VA: PBS, 1987).

41. David Ziegler, *Sir! No Sir!* (Los Angeles, CA: Displaced Films, 2005).

42. War Resisters' International, *Handbook for Nonviolent Campaigns* (London: War Resisters' International, 2014).

43. Andrew Boyd and David Oswald Mitchell, *Beautiful Trouble: A Toolbox for Revolution* (New York: OR Books, 2012).

44. Per Herngren, *Path of Resistance: The Practice of Civil Disobedience*, trans. Margaret Rainey (Philadelphia, PA: New Society Publishers, 1993).

45. Larry W. Isaac, Daniel B. Cornfield, Dennis C. Dickerson, James M. Lawson, Jr., and Jonathan S. Coley, "'Movement Schools' and Dialogical Diffusion of Nonviolent Praxis: Nashville Workshops in Southern Civil Rights Movement," *Research in Social Movements, Conflicts, and Change* 34 (2012): 155–84; and Larry W. Isaac, Anna W. Jacobs, Jaime Kucinskas, and Allison R. McGrath, "Social Movement Schools: Sites for Consciousness Transformation, Training, and Prefigurative Social Development," *Social Movement Studies* (2019): 160–82.

46. Sean Chabot, "Making Sense of Civil Resistance: From Theories and Techniques to Social Movement *Phronesis*," in *Civil Resistance: Comparative Perspectives on Nonviolent Struggle*, ed. Kurt Schock (Minneapolis, MN: University of Minnesota Press, 2015), 227–57.

47. David Farber, *The Sixties Chronicle* (Lincolnwood, IL: Legacy Publishing, 2004), 448.

48. Paul Wapner, "Horizontal Politics: Transnational Environmental Activism and Global Cultural Change," *Global Environmental Politics* 2, no. 2 (May 2002): 37–62.

49. Carl Cohen, *Civil Disobedience: Conscience, Tactics, and the Law* (New York: Columbia University Press, 1971), 131–72.

50. Cohen, *Civil Disobedience*, 131–72; see also Arendt, *Crises of the Republic*; and Howard Zinn, *Disobedience and Democracy: Nine Fallacies on Law and Order* (Cambridge, MA: South End Press, 2002).

51. Judith Butler, *The Force of Nonviolence: The Ethical in the Political* (London: Verso, 2020); and Martin Luther King, Jr. *The Radical King*, ed. C. West (Boston, MA: Beacon Press, 2015).

52. Gamson, *The Strategy of Social Protest*.

53. Chenoweth and Stephan, *Why Civil Resistance Works*.

54. Doug McAdam, Doug, Sidney Tarrow, and Charles Tilly, *Dynamics of Contention* (Cambridge: Cambridge University Press, 2001); see also Charles Tilly and Sidney Tarrow, *Contentious Politics*, 2nd ed. (Oxford: Oxford University Press, 2015).

Index

Printed in the USA
CPSIA information can be obtained
at www.ICGtesting.com
CBHW032024140724
11582CB00001B/9

9 781108 745468